Cultural Competence Compendium

Cultural Competence Compendium

© 1999 by the American Medical Association
Printed in the USA. All rights reserved.

ISBN 1-57947-050-5

Order information

To order additional copies of this book (Product Number OP209199), call toll free 800 621-8335.

Comments or inquiries

Hannah L. Hedrick, PhD
515 N State St
Chicago, IL 60610
312 464-4697
312 464-5830 Fax
E-mail: hannah_hedrick@ama-assn.org
www.ama-assn.org

Foreword

As physicians, our first concern is always our patients, especially the most vulnerable of those who rely on our care. Today's changing and increasingly diverse society, however, makes it clear that virtually every group has its own vulnerabilities and its own special needs. Women, men, children, seniors, African Americans, Hispanics, Asians, whites, people with disabilities, those suffering from chronic conditions or even facing socioeconomic constraints—each has particular concerns, but one common trait: all are our patients. All require our best efforts, our best knowledge, and our best understanding to ensure that the care we provide is the best for each individual, keyed to particular needs.

Unfortunately, for most of us, our traditional training in medical school offers little guidance in how to treat individuals influenced by cultures of different groups with which they identify. For years, for example, we were unaware of the different ways in which women and men with heart attacks present in our offices, and, as a result, many women did not receive life-saving intervention in time. Today, the research is available and is being applied–and more and more, we are treating heart symptoms in women aggressively, and saving lives in the process. In the same way, studies have shown that, all things being equal, Hispanic men receive less pain medication for the same injuries than their white counterparts—even though we still aren't sure whether the reasons for that originate with a patient's culture, physician perception, or some combination of the two.

Getting to the heart of these differences, and learning responsible ways to address them in accord with our ethical values as physicians, is what the AMA's new Cultural Competence Initiative is all about. This volume, the premier edition of the *Cultural Competence Compendium*, is a resource for physicians in identifying issues surrounding different populations—and learning to examine our own issues as well, so that the care we provide is the right care for each and every patient we see and the highest quality of care for every patient as well.

Based on a sound foundation of AMA policy, as well as research, reports, and publications on underserved and underrepresented racial, ethnic, and socioeconomic groups, this *Compendium* is a jumping-off point. In these pages, you will find what we already know about developing what some have called the "Fifth Competence"—the ability to provide culturally competent care to our patients. Included is information about contributions by other general physician associations, state and specialty societies, federal agencies, educational institutions, and other organizations, many of them devoted solely to producing information about cultural competence.

But this volume is only the beginning. By this time next year, you'll be looking at an expanded print edition of the *Compendium*, as well as a searchable Web-based version allowing instant updates, the opportunity for dialogue among contributors, and educational programs that will provide credit toward continuing medical education.

During the year ahead, we will also be convening the first meeting of the AMA's new Cultural Competence Advisory Panel, which will design and carry out specific projects in medical education and clinical care. We'll be looking at the most innovative and effective ways to deliver on the promise of education and training—everything from DirectTV to multimedia tutorials, from videoconferencing to train-the-trainer manuals, as well as face-to-face meetings. What's more, this panel will work with the appropriate accrediting agencies to make sure that competence is recognized as it is achieved.

How do you know whether the care you give is truly culturally competent? Begin by reading the pages of this book, and making use of the information and the resources you find here. And then, begin thinking now about how you can contribute to this vital and exciting effort. We are looking for ways to strengthen awareness of cultural competence across the profession—and for ways to move the profession and the public to action, with results we can measure. We are working within the profession and within the AMA—and by the end of the Year 2000, we will be able to report on the outcomes of staff efforts across the AMA to integrate a cultural competence "track" or other component into their relevant AMA projects, products, and activities. We will also have a progress report on our efforts to raise the level of awareness of our own leaders and staff.

If you will share your ideas and the results of your efforts with us, we will include them in our work as well, including in the next edition of the *Cultural Competence Compendium* and its Web-based companion.

Until then, take full advantage of this volume, the most comprehensive guide on cultural competence ever prepared solely for physicians. And take part in the AMA's leadership on culturally competent care, as we prepare patients and physicians to face the changing needs of medicine's new millennium.

Nancy W. Dickey, MD
President
American Medical Association

Acknowledgments

We gratefully acknowledge the assistance of the individuals and the AMA units or organizations they represent listed below. Many of these individuals serve on the Cultural Competence Initiative Work Group, which has met monthly since early 1998, first to ensure broad input into "Enhancing the Cultural Competence of Physicians" (Council on Medical Education Report 5-A-98) and then to develop strategies to implement the recommendations in that report.

In addition to attending meetings and responding to requests for assistance and information, these individuals have played key roles in infusing the Cultural Competence Initiative throughout the Association, as reflected in the sections in the *Compendium* describing their initiatives, reports, or publications. The following individuals provided editorial assistance throughout the process of identifying and compiling materials:

Susan Anderson, MLS, Professional Standards
    Administration
Jackie Drake, MS, Medical Education
Elizabeth Jacobs, MD, Cook County Hospital
Françoise Kusseling, PhD, Undergraduate Medical
    Education
Patricia Levenberg, PhD, Specialty Society
    Relations
Selby Toporek, Marketing Services

The support of the AMA Board of Trustees, chaired by Randolph D. Smoak, Jr., MD, has been instrumental in drawing national attention to the AMA Cultural Competence Initiative.

AMA Staff

Amy Bishop, Group Practice Liaison
Bruce Blehart, JD, Health Law
Missy Fleming, PhD, Clinical and Public Health
    Practice and Outcomes
Michael Flesher, Resident and Fellow Services
Suzanne Fraker, Product Line Development
Ross Fraser, News and Information
Joe Ann Jackson, Organized Medical Staff Section

Philip R. Kletke, PhD, Health Policy Studies
Phyllis Kopriva, Women and Minority Physicians
Brian McCormick, *American Medical News*
Robert Miller, Marketing
Ben Mindell, *American Medical News*
Michael Murray, Federation Relations
Rebecca Nolind, Clinical and Public Health
    Practice and Outcomes
Rita Palulonis, Foundation and Corporation
    Relations
Becky Rasco, Member Communications
Joseph Rekash, American Medical Accreditation
    Program
Susan Rubin, AMA Alliance
Craig Samuels, AMA Solutions
Michael Scotti Jr., MD, Medical Education
Priscilla Short, MD, Science Research and
    Technology
Reed V. Tuckson, MD, Professional Standards
Marsha Turner, Membership Marketing
Lila Valinoti, Medical Student Services
Linn Weiss, Strategic Communications
Jim Wills, Private Sector Advocacy

Non-AMA Staff

James Alexander, Foundation and Corporate
    Relations
Holly Mulvey, American Academy of Pediatrics
Marla Sutton, American Academy of Family
    Physicians
Jill Stewart, Stewart Communications
Susan Wagner, National Patient Safety Foundation

Other Assistance

Also recognized for their contributions to this product are Enza Messineo and Dorothy Grant of Medical Education Products; Denise Bryson, Florence Steels, and Ronnie Summers of Marketing; editors Christine Di Thomas, Aaron Winslow, MLIS, and Barbara Clark; and the Grillo Group, Chicago, which produced the cover design.

Hannah Hedrick, PhD, Editor
Fred Donini-Lenhoff, Managing Editor

Contents

Introduction

This *Cultural Competence Compendium* is the American Medical Association's most comprehensive response to date to the dramatic changes in the nation's demographics and in health care delivery systems. The *Compendium,* which is available in print and on the Internet, fulfills two of the adopted recommendations from Council on Medical Education Report 5-A-98, "Enhancing the Cultural Competence of Physicians": "continue to inform medical schools and residency program directors about activities and resources related to assisting physicians in providing culturally competent care to patients throughout their life span and encourage them to include the topic of culturally effective health care in their curricula" and "assist physicians in obtaining information about and/or training in culturally competent health care through development of an annotated resource database on the AMA home page."

The *Compendium* consists of an annotated list of resources available from a wide variety of medical professional organizations, national agencies, organizations focusing on cultural competence, educational institutions, and individuals, as well as information about many of the organizations. It is intended to serve as the foundation for the development of initiatives and resources to move the medical profession and the public to create behavioral and institutional changes that will enable physicians to provide individualized care that respects the multiple cultures of their patients. Adopted recommendations from "Enhancing the Cultural Competence of Physicians" also called for formation of an "expert national advisory panel" to guide the development of these initiatives and resources.

Patient-Centered Care Requires Inclusive Definition of "Culture"

Our use of "cultural competence" and "culturally effective health care" reflects an inclusive definition of the word "culture"—*any group of people who share experiences, language, and values that permit them to communicate knowledge not shared by those outside the culture.* Culturally competent physicians are able to provide patient-centered care by adjusting their attitudes and behaviors to account for the impact of emotional, cultural, social, and psychological issues on the main biomedical ailment. The *Compendium* cites resources intended to assist physicians in understanding how their own life experiences and emotional makeup and their "physician culture" affect the care they deliver.

Competence, as defined by Webster's Unabridged Dictionary, 2nd Edition, is a "capacity equal to requirement." Physicians have long been held to requirements in the areas of cognitive knowledge, technical skill, and behavior. Recently, managerial competence has been added to the requirements for medical practice. Given the nation's increasingly diverse patient population, we would propose cultural competence as the "fifth competence" for American physicians. As with the other competencies that delineate the standards for medical practice, cultural competence is necessary to provide good patient care, and it can be acquired through the same tools that provide for physician professional development in other areas. This *Compendium* provides access to some of those tools that will assist the learner in the acquisition of the necessary knowledge, skills, and attitudes.

Cautions Against Generalizing, Stereotyping

Although some social critics hesitate to attribute disease risk factors to racial, ethnic, and other groups because doing so can be stigmatizing, the *Compendium* includes reports of variation in disease risk factors when the authors present them in the context of efforts to reduce disparities. Most of the authors of culture-specific guides listed in the *Compendium* repeatedly remind readers not to use research results or other materials in any way that reflects stereotypical interpretations, that ignores variation within ethnic groups, or that fails to account for individual patient preferences and needs. A typical caution against stereotyping appears in Elaine Geissler's 1994 *A Pocket Guide to Cultural Assessment*: "The reader is strongly cautioned against assuming that people from one country or geographic area . . . hold the same beliefs as those held by their neighbors."

Cultural Competence Initiative

The *Compendium* is intended as a point of departure for fulfilling additional adopted recommendations from the Council on Medical Education report on "Enhancing the Cultural Competence of Physicians," including continued "research into the need for and effectiveness of training in cultural competence, using existing mechanisms such as the annual medical education surveys and focus groups at regularly scheduled meetings." It is also intended to provide support for the adopted recommendation to seek "external funding to develop a 5-year program for promoting cultural competence in and through the education of physicians, including a critical review and comprehensive plan for action," with the goal of restructuring "the continuum of medical education and staff and faculty development programs to deliberately emphasize cultural competence as part of professional practice."

It is hoped that the *Compendium* will provide useful references to designing and carrying out specific projects in medical education and clinical care. Future publications could include the results of examining the most effective means for using Web-based curriculum materials and instruction. The Internet offers the advantages of distance learning, dynamic interactive communication, user-specific feedback, collaborative development of educational materials, and delivery of computer-assisted instruction offering hypertext and branching links, models to manipulate variables and observe the outcomes of processes, and interactive simulations with case-based scenarios.

Future publications may also reflect evaluation of existing multimedia self-instructional programs, video conferencing programs, train-the-trainer manuals and meetings, and audiotapes to identify ways to strengthen the cultural competence content of these modalities.

AMA *Cultural Competence Compendium* Module, Electronic Newsletter

Work has already begun to expand the AMA sections of this *Compendium* as a separate module for distribution in December 1999, including information about the progress of the proposed AMA/ Association of American Medical Colleges Exemplary Practice Replication Grants project. We will provide a report on the progress of efforts across the AMA to integrate a cultural competence component into relevant AMA projects, products, and activities. If these efforts are successful, we will reflect them via an electronic cultural competence newsletter.

Cultural Competence Compendium 2000 and Searchable Web Site

By June 2000, with guidance from the Advisory Panel and an editorial board of recognized experts in cultural competence, a second edition of the print and Web-based _Compendium_ will be available. We will report the outcomes of efforts to work with appropriate accrediting and credentialing agencies to ensure that cultural competence is recognized as it is achieved. We will also describe the efforts of health professions' organizations to assess their level of organizational cultural competence.

Organization of the _Compendium_

AMA resources are identified in _Physician Professional Organizations_ (Section I), with relevant AMA information also featured prominently at the beginning other section. Contact persons have been identified for each AMA area, and readers are invited to direct their content-specific questions to those individuals. Section I also provides information, as available, on policies, publications, educational programs, and relevant activities of other general physician associations, medical specialty groups, and state medical societies.

Many of the resources in _Resources Emphasizing Communication Skills_ (Section II) are designed to obviate potentially adverse outcomes of inadequate physician-patient communications. Some resources include specific techniques for conducting a patient-centered trust-promoting method of inquiry (including health literacy issues). _Curriculum and Training Materials_ (Section III) includes materials spanning the medical education continuum, some of which incorporate assessment tools and evaluation resources. Several recent resources are devoted solely to gauging the effectiveness of efforts to provide culturally effective education and health care. _Virtual Resources_ (Section IX) provides similar types of information about assessment, education, training, and evaluation resources available through Web sites and multimedia resources.

Specific Populations: Needs and Resources (Section IV) is organized to assist readers in identifying cultural groups in which they have the most interest. Resources from other sections are also cited here. The rationale for the categories is explained in the section introduction. Homelessness is included because individuals without a permanent residence are perhaps the most underserved of all groups and because there are relatively few resources to assist physicians in caring for them.

Complementary and Spiritual Practices and Their Impact on Effective Care (Section V) and _Patient Support Materials, Including Self-Help Group Resources_ (Section VII) provide physicians with resources to meet consumers' self-identified needs. As Web-based communications empower consumers to assume responsibility for self-care and to manage their diseases, more care is occurring in the community and home and less in medical centers, health care institutions, and physicians' offices. These resources guide physicians in accessing their patients' cultural connections.

Relevant Materials from Nursing and Other Professional Organizations (Section VI) indicates that nursing and a few other professions have developed more integrated, comprehensive cultural competence programs than many physician associations. Many nursing resources can be used as they are or adapted for other professions. Similarly, physicians may wish to review the "Cultural Diversity Action Agenda" of the American Association for Respiratory Care, which encompasses developing cultural awareness and diversity strategies for its Board of Directors, House of Delegates, and Chartered Affiliates; implementing strategies to promote the commitment to cultural competence; incorporating cultural awareness training in respiratory care programs; and developing and distributing an independent study package on cultural competence.

Representative Cultural Competence Publications (Section VIII) contains general and population-specific references to a wide variety of books, monographs, reports, journals, journal articles, and newsletter and bulletin items. Full-text versions of six AMA reports, seven *American Medical News* articles, and 119 AMA policies with relevance to cultural competence appear in Section X.

A Work in Progress

The *Cultural Competence Compendium* is very much a work in progress, and we welcome comments and information about resources to be considered for future editions.

Hannah L. Hedrick, PhD
Editor

Michael J. Scotti, Jr., MD
Vice President, Medical Education

Section I

Physician Professional Organizations

The information in this section on physician professional organizations was collected from a multitude of sources, including a brief survey of specialty and state societies conducted by the American Medical Association Minority Affairs Consortium in February and March 1999.

Responses to that survey and to communications with other groups revealed that while many medical professional organizations would like to enhance the cultural competence of their member physicians, most of them have not developed their own version of this *Compendium* and do not have a single point of contact for information about issues related to cultural competence, diversity, or decreasing disparities in health.

The AMA entry provides the most comprehensive compilation of contact people, membership and staff units, policies; reports, publications, Web sites, curriculum materials, educational programs, and activities specifically related to patient-centered care, respectful communication, improving the quality of care provided to specific populations, and decreasing disparities in health care. To the extent that it was available through communications, publications, or Web sites, similar information is provided for other professional organizations.

The resources listed with each organization are, in general, not repeated in other sections.

Filling in the Gaps

The 1999 AMA survey of state medical licensing boards included a question about cultural competence activities, and each board that does not respond will be contacted to ensure that we are not missing important resources in the next edition of the *Compendium.*

Some boards have already begun to provide us with information about their cultural competence initiatives. For example, the North Carolina Medical Board has published numerous articles in its *Forum on Diversity Issues*, including "Breaching the Culture and Language Barrier" and "Migrant Health Resource List," and has addressed other issues, such as complementary and spiritual practices, in a variety of forums.

During the second half of 1999, specialty and state societies will be provided with a second opportunity to provide information, and county and local societies will also be asked to submit information.

We welcome any information related to the efforts of physician organizations to enhance the cultural competence of their members and to provide effective care to all patients.

Section Contents

A.   General Physician Associations

B.   Medical Specialty Groups

C.   State Medical Societies

A. General Physician Associations

American Medical Association

Contact

Hannah L. Hedrick, PhD
Medical Education
515 N State St
Chicago, IL 60610
312 464-4697
312 464-5830 Fax
E-mail: hannah_hedrick@ama-assn.org
http://www.ama-assn.org

Selected Published AMA Reports

Council on Ethical and Judicial Affairs

Black-White Disparities in Health Care
JAMA, May 2, 1990; 263(17):2344-6, Review

Caring for the Poor
JAMA, May 19, 1993; 269(19):2533-7

Decisions Near the End-of-Life
JAMA, April 22-29, 1992; 267(16):2229-33

Ethical Considerations in the Allocation of Organs and Other Scarce Medical Resources Among Patients
Arch Intern Med, January 9, 1995; 155(1):29-40
Review

Ethical Issues Involved in the Growing AIDS Crisis
JAMA, March 4, 1988; 259(9):1360-1

Ethical Issues Related to Prenatal Genetic Testing
Arch Fam Med, July 1994; 3(7):633-42

Gender Discrimination in the Medical Profession
Women's Health Issues, Spring 1994; 4(1):1-11

Gender Disparities in Clinical Decision Making
JAMA, July 24-31, 1991; 266(4):559-62

Mandatory Parental Consent to Abortion
JAMA, January 6, 1993;269(1):82-6

Medical Futility in End-of-Life Care
JAMA, March 10, 1999; 281(10):937-41

Physicians and Domestic Violence: Ethical Considerations
JAMA, June 17, 1992;267(23):3190-3

Physician Participation in Capital Punishment
JAMA, July 21, 1993; 270(3):365-8

Trends from the United States with End-of-Life Decisions in the Intensive Care Unit
D Teres
Intensive Care Med, 1993;19(6):316-22, Review

Use of Genetic Testing by Employers
JAMA, October 2, 1991; 266(13):1827-30

Council on Scientific Affairs

Adolescents as Victims of Family Violence
JAMA, October 20, 1993; 1850-6

Alcoholism and Alcohol Abuse Among Women
LN Blum, NH Nielsen, JA Riggs
Journal of Women's Health, September 1998;
7:861-71

Alcoholism in the Elderly
JAMA, March 13, 1996; 275:797-801

Confidential Health Services for Adolescents
JAMA, March 17, 1993; 269:1420-4

Educating Physicians in Home Health Care
JAMA, February 13, 1991;265:769-71

Female Genital Mutilation
JAMA, December 6, 1995; 274:1714-6

Good Care of the Dying Patient
JAMA, February 14, 1996; 275:474-8

Health Care Needs of Gay Men and Lesbians in the United States
JAMA May 1, 1996; 275:1354-9

Health Literacy
JAMA, February 10, 1999; 281:552-7

Hispanic Health in the United States
JAMA, January 1, 1991; 265:248-52

Memories of Childhood Abuse
International Journal of Clinical and Experimental Hypnosis, April 1995; 43:114-7

Physicians and Family Caregivers: a Model for Partnership
JAMA, March 10, 1993;269:1282-4

Violence Against Women
JAMA, June 17, 1992; 267:3184-9

Selected Unpublished AMA Reports

Diversity in Medical Education
Considered at the 1999 Annual Meeting
(Available upon request)

Encouraging Medical Student Education on Alternative Health Care Practices
Council on Medical Education Report 2, I-97

Enhancing the Cultural Competence of Physicians
Council on Medical Education Report 5-A-98

Medical Education and Training in Women's Health
Considered at the 1999 Annual Meeting
(Available upon request)

Nutritional and Dietetic Education for Medical Students
Council on Medical Education Report 3, I-97

Racial and Ethnic Disparities in Health Care
Board of Trustees Report 50-I-95

AMA Efforts to Identify and Incorporate Health Needs of Culturally Diverse Populations into Broader Public Health and Community Objectives
Hannah Hedrick, Michael Scotti, Jr, Bruce Blehart
September 1998

Developed as a presentation summarizing AMA activities related to cultural competence and public health; incorporates much of Racial and Ethnic Disparities in Health Care (BOT Report 50-I-95) and Enhancing the Cultural Competence of Physicians (CME Report 5-A-98)

See Section X for the complete text of selected recent reports and all relevant policies.

AMA Web Sites

Adolescent Health On-Line

http://www.ama-assn.org/adolhlth/adolhlth.htm

AMA Health Insight

http://www.ama-assn.org/consumer.htm

AMA Health Insight – Family Focus – Adolescent Health

http://www.ama-assn.org/insight/h_focus/adl_hlth/teen/teen.htm

AMA KidsHealth

http://www.ama-assn.org/KidsHealth.htm

American Medical News

http://www.ama-assn.orgpublic/journals/amnews/amnews.htm

Ethics: EPEC Resource Guide

http://www.ama-assn.org/ethic/epec/rgbuffer.htm

International Medical Graduate Section – Promoting Diversity in Medicine

http://www.ama-assn.org/ama/pub/category/0,1120,17,FF.html

Issues/Advocacy (Section on Medical Schools)

http://www.ama-assn.org/mem-data/special/mdschool/issues.htm

Minority Physicians Services

http://www.ama-assn.org/mem-data/mimed/mihome.htm

Talking to Patients About Sex: Training Program for Physicians

http://www.ama-assn.org/mem-data/joint/sex001.htm

Women Physicians Services

http://www.ama-assn.org/mem-data/wmmed/wmhome.htm

AMA Membership Units Addressing Cultural Competence

Council on Ethical and Judicial Affairs

515 N State St
Chicago, IL 60610
312 464-5223 or 464-4859
312 464-4613 Fax
E-mail: blaire_osgood@ama-assn.org

In addition to the reports cited above, the Council on Ethical and Judicial Affairs (CEJA) published *Reports on End of Life Care (*1998), a compilation of the following reports issued by CEJA from 1986 to 1987:

- *Do-Not-Resuscitate Orders* (December 1987)

- *Euthanasia* (June 1988)

- *Persistent Vegetative State and the Decision to Withdraw or Withhold Life Support* (June 1989)

- *Guidelines for the Appropriate Use of Do-Not-Resuscitate Orders* (December 1990)

- *Decisions Near the End of Life* (June 1991)

- *Decisions To Forgo Life Sustaining Treatment for Incompetent Patients* (June 1991)

- *Physician-Assisted Suicide* (June 1994)

- *Medical Futility in End-of-Life Care* (December 1996)

- *Optimal Use of Orders-Not-To-Intervene and Advance Directives* (June 1996)

Council on Long-range Planning and Development

515 N State St
Chicago, IL 60610
312 464-4394
312 464-5836 Fax
E-mail: clrpd@ama-assn.org

In January 1999, the Council on Long-range Planning and Development (CLRPD) published *The Environment of Medicine*, which identified changes having an impact on the practice of medicine. The CLRPD described the increasing ethnic diversity of the US population and the way in which that diversity was affecting the types of diseases physicians must be prepared to treat, including the emergence of new infectious diseases and the reemergence of diseases that many US physicians had not encountered.

The report further describes the ways in which physicians will be under pressure from health plans to improve communication with patients in a cost-effective manner. The CLRPD pointed out the necessity of tailoring communications for patients with low literacy skills and of being able to understand and respond to multicultural and multilingual demands.

In accordance with efforts in other areas of the AMA to increase the number of underrepresented minorities in the health professions, the CLRPD cautioned that decreased diversity in the medical student population will eventually have a negative impact on access to services for patients from underserved groups.

Council on Medical Education (CME)

515 N State St
Chicago, IL 60610
312 464-4649
312 464-5830 Fax
E-mail: cme@ama-assn.org

The Cultural Competence Initiative is based on a 1998 Council on Medical Education report, "Enhancing the Cultural Competence of Physicians." The Council, established in 1847, is currently determining its roles and responsibilities in formulating and/or implementing policy and activities related to cultural competence and medical education. The Council's advisory committees for graduate and continuing medical education will continue to consider appropriate roles and activities, including joint activities with the AMA Minority Affairs Consortium.

Council on Scientific Affairs

Barry D. Dickinson, PhD, Secretary
515 N State St
Chicago, IL 60610
312 464-4549
http://www.ama-assn.org/med-sci/csa/csa.htm

The Council on Scientific Affairs (CSA) prepares reports that draw professional and public attention to the scientific aspects of medical practice and biomedical research, thereby enhancing the quality of medical care and promoting the betterment of public health. CSA reports address specific clinical and public health topics as well as broader policy discussions. Of particular interest are 1998 reports on *Race and Ethnicity as Variables in Medical Research* and *Health Literacy*. The CSA has also studied alternative medicine and folk remedies, the health care needs of gay men and lesbians, and violence toward men. The variety of CSA reports related to the *Compendium* is indicated in the list of published reports in Section I and the policies and related reports referenced in Section X. The CSA Web site provides summaries of more than 80 reports produced by the Council from 1994 through 1998. The full text of many of these reports is posted on the site.

International Medical Graduates Section (IMGS)

International Medical Graduates Section and Senior Physicians Services
515 N State St
Chicago, IL 60610
312 464-5624
312 464-5845 Fax
E-mail: img@ama-assn.org

The International Medical Graduates Section works to enhance the participation of graduates of foreign medical schools in organized medicine and to support enhance AMA outreach, communication, and interchange with these graduates.

The Section also addresses discrimination against international medical graduates in the hiring and contracting practices of managed care organizations. The section also assists international medical graduates with problems related to state licensure requirements and residency selection issues. In addition, the section examines workforce issues related to international medical graduates.

Medical Student Section (MSS)

Minority Issues Committee
Medical Student Services
515 N State St
Chicago IL 60610
312 464-4746
312 464-5845 Fax
E-mail: mss@ama-assn.org

The Medical Student Section (MSS) has a distinguished record for addressing various issues related to cultural competence. Activities are currently coordinated through the MSS Minority Issues Committee (MIC), which addresses minority health issues through policy initiatives and community service activities. Organ donor awareness is currently receiving special emphasis.

Policy Initiatives

- *Minority and Disadvantaged Medical Student Recruitment and Retention Programs*

- *Minority Representation in the Medical Profession*

- *Promoting Culturally Competent Health Care*

- *Affirmative Action and the Decrease of Underrepresented Minority Entrants to Medical School*

- *Increasing the Number of Minorities Registered as Potential Marrow Donors*

Community Service Activities

- Minority Community Service Award

- Medical career outreach to minority students

- Minority community health fairs

Organ Donor Awareness

Organ Donor Awareness, selected as the first nationwide community service of the MSS, will publicize cultural barriers in relation to organ and transplant issues. In conjunction with the 1999 AMA House of Delegates meeting, the Section and the AMA Minority Affairs Consortium held a "Live and Then Give" event, "The Many Faces of Organ Donation," to increase organ donations in minority communities. See the organ donation entry in Section IV for more detailed information on the contributions of the MSS to the organ donation initiative.

Minority Affairs Consortium (MAC)

Women and Minority Services
515 N State St
312 464-4392
312 464-5845 Fax
E-mail: mps@ama-assn.org
http://www.ama-assn.org/mem-data/mimed/mihome.htm

The AMA Minority Affairs Consortium (MAC) functions as the AMA conduit for minority concerns, from the grassroots level to the Board of Trustees. It provides a national forum for advocacy on minority health issues and for addressing the professional concerns of minority medical students and physicians. E-mail and the AMA Web site are the primary means through which MAC conducts its member communications and outreach and educational activities.

The nine-member MAC Governing Committee includes formal representation from the National Medical Association, National Hispanic Medical Association, and Association of American Indian Physicians. The primary MAC goal is to build an inter-organizational, grassroots communication network to educate, inform, and advocate for underrepresented medical students and physicians across the nation.

MAC provides a structural framework for physicians committed to addressing minority issues at the national, state, and local levels by developing and supporting efforts to:

- eliminate minority health disparities;

- assist all physicians to become better prepared to deliver culturally effective health care;

- recruit and retain more minority students to promote diversity in the profession;

- increase the membership and leadership participation of minority physicians in organized medicine; and

- advocate on minority health issues at local, state, and national levels.

Membership is free to any interested AMA-member physicians or medical students. Non-AMA members may join on a 1-year introductory basis.

Recent MAC recommendations include urging (1) the AMA Foundation to support programs geared toward increasing diversity, (2) the AMA to explore state medical society/AMA partnerships to increase diversity, and (3) medical schools to weight the likelihood of service to underserved populations as an admission criterion. MAC has recommended that the AMA Advocacy Resource Center be authorized to assist in these efforts.

Organized Medical Staff Section (OMSS)

Joe Ann Jackson
515 N State St
Chicago, IL 60610
312 464-2461
312 464-5845 Fax

The Organized Medical Staff Section (OMSS) has supported and promoted numerous activities related to health care disparities based on racial and ethnic factors. OMSS has also encouraged the AMA and state and local medical societies to cooperate in projects to enhance the cultural competence of physicians.

In 1995 the OMSS surveyed more than 2,000 OMSS members about racial and ethnic disparities in health care. The goal of the survey was to sensitize physicians, collect information on processes to identify and act on disparities in care, and assess willingness to establish such monitoring and action mechanisms.

Only a small percentage of hospitals and other organizations had monitoring mechanisms in place, but more than half would consider monitoring for variations in the delivery and utilization of medical services to racially and ethnically diverse patients. Survey respondents identified specific roles for the AMA and the state and local medical societies in working to address and eliminate care disparities and to assist OMSS members in their efforts to identify and act on disparities in care that could be traced to race, ethnicity, or other cultural factors.

Racial and Ethnic Care Disparities: Identification, Interpretation, and Interventions
http://www.ama-assn.org/mem-data/mimed/recdiii.htm

The 1995 OMSS survey culminated in this 1996 report, which describes the receptivity of physicians and hospitals to information and methods that would help them identify potential care disparities in their own health care systems. The document was designed to identify steps hospital medical staffs and hospital administrators could take to include racial and ethnic analyses in their ongoing quality improvement activities.

The document provides information on calculating six performance measures appropriate to a hospital setting. Each of these indices was listed in one of the major libraries of established performance measures catalogued by the federal government, the Joint Commission for Accreditation of Healthcare Organizations, or a federally funded research team at the Harvard School of Public Health.

Numerators and denominators were provided for six categories:

- Discharge of pneumonia and flu patients

- Postoperative pneumonia rates

- Promptness of treatment initiation for pneumonia

- Rapid readmission

- Medication intervention during acute myocardial infarction

- Rapid readmission postcardiac care

Section on Medical Schools

515 N State St
Chicago, IL 60610
312 464-4690
312 464-5830 Fax
E-mail: sms@ama-assn.org

Established in 1976 to serve as a forum for discussing and disseminating information, the Section on Medical Schools enables academic physicians to participate in AMA policymaking through debate and a vote in the House of Delegates. The Section features speakers on cultural diversity issues and includes information in its publication, the *Section on Medical Schools Report.*

Women Physicians Congress (WPC)

Women and Minority Services
515 N State St
Chicago, IL 60610
312 464-4392
312 464-5845 Fax
E-mail: wps@ama-assn.org

Founded in 1997, the Women Physicians Congress (WPC) serves as a forum for physicians and medical students interested in women in medicine issues. The WPC provides an expanded opportunity for its members to participate directly in the AMA and influence national health policy and advocacy on women's health issues and the professional issues of women physicians.

WPC Goals and Objectives

- Increase the percentage of women physicians in leadership and senior management positions in organized medicine and the profession.

- Provide a forum for mentoring, networking, and communications with women physicians.

- Advance the women's health agenda on medical research, training, and patient outcomes.

- Monitor trends and emerging issues that will affect women in the profession.

- Enhance AMA policy and advocacy on women physician professional issues and eliminate gender bias in medicine.

- Foster cooperation and collaboration between AMA and organizations with mutual concerns.

WPC Member Survey

In 1998, the WPC conducted a mail survey of WPC members to determine their professional interests, priorities, and expectations of the WPC. In addition to increasing the number of women in leadership positions in medicine, other priorities and activities recommended were:

- addressing child care/maternity/sexual harassment issues for women physicians, especially as they affect residents;

- educating on and advocating for women's health issues, including domestic violence, and reproductive issues;

- promoting community services and public health education;

- developing policies to address gender discrimination in medicine;

- addressing issues relevant to women medical students;

- encouraging women to enter medical school;

- providing networking opportunities for women physicians; and

- addressing concerns of all physicians, ie, access, managed care.

Women's Health Advocacy

The WPC often offers programs on women's health issues in conjunction with AMA and other medical association meetings, covering such topics as the latest techniques in breast imaging, awareness of heart disease as the number one killer of women, recent studies on estrogen and heart disease, and the importance of women physicians as healthy role models for their patients.

In addition to the above programs, the WPC participates in the activities of the Society for the Advancement of Women's Health (SAWHR) and other women's health advocacy groups. An SAWHR video on gender-based biology, *Vive La Difference!*, was provided through the WPC to all AMA Medical Student Section chapters and the WPC Liaison Officers.

AMA Staff Units, Projects, and Initiatives

Adolescent Health

Missy Fleming, 312 464-5315
Rebecca Nolind, 312 464-4538

AMA programs in child and adolescent health have been acknowledged as national models of coalition building by such authoritative sources as the Department of Health and Human Services, especially in connection with the *Healthy People 2000* initiative. Adolescent health staff are exploring ways in which the National Coalition on Adolescent Health (a 40-member organization comprising national societies in medicine, psychiatry, related health professions, public health, and education, as well as private foundations and federal agencies) can use its hyperlinks to member Web sites and other communication vehicles to disseminate information about the impact of the AMA Cultural Competence Initiative on adolescent health.

For more detailed descriptions of some of the following publications, see Sections III and IV.

- **Culturally Competent Health Care for Adolescents: A Guide for Primary Care Providers**, 1994

  The guide introduces health care providers to the complex issues involved in working with diverse populations of adolescents and outlines practical strategies for incorporating cultural issues into health care.

- **Partners in Program Planning for Adolescent Health (PIPPAH)**

- **National Coalition on Adolescent Health**

- **Healthy Youth 2000: A Mid-Decade Review**, 1996

- **Guidelines for Adolescent Preventive Services (GAPS)**

- **GAPS Recommendations Monograph, 1997-1998**

- **GAPS Implementation Forms** (Also available in Spanish**)**

- **The Parent Package** (Also available in Spanish)

AMA Adolescent Health On-Line
http://www.ama-assn.org/adolhlth/adolhlth.htm

The Web site for the AMA's Child and Adolescent Health Program is designed to provide information to physicians, health care providers, researchers, parents, and teenagers on important adolescent health issues. Supported through a cooperative agreement from the Health Services and Resources Administration, Maternal and Child Health Bureau's federal Office of Adolescent Health, the Web site is regularly updated with the latest scientific information in the field of adolescent health. It also provides information on GAPS and offers extensive links to other organizations working to improve the health status of young people.

Information about cultural competence resources developed by the Child and Adolescent Health Program are viewable on the Web site. Adolescent Health On-Line will continue to include information for health care providers striving to provide culturally competent health care.

AMA Solutions

Craig Samuels
312 419-5048

AMA Solutions is involved in developing educational programs in diversity training. Enhancing the cultural competence of physicians is congruent with the organization's emphasis on "patient satisfaction."

American Medical Accreditation Program (AMAP)

Joseph Rekash
312 464-4559

The Cultural Competence Work Group has initiated explorations with AMAP staff about the possibility of incorporating a standard related to cultural competence in AMAP.

American Medical News

Brian McCormick
312 464-5411
http://www.ama-assn/org/sci-pubs/amnews.

As a member of the Cultural Competence Work Group, Brian McCormick ensures that members are informed of *AMNews* coverage of cultural competence issues and that *AMNews* reflects newsworthy activities related to the Cultural Competence Initiative. *AMNews* has provided a model for other AMA units by putting articles on cultural awareness on its Web site.

Recent reports in *AMNews* have covered such topics as culturally sensitive end-of-life care, how cancer studies fail minorities, special treatment concerns for gays and lesbians, and the likeliness of Medicaid and managed care plans to introduce standards for cultural competence in patient care. *AMNews* has also examined the important topic of how a physician's own background can affect treatment decisions.

"Culturally Effective Communication," an *AMNews* editorial (see Section X), points out that not all doctors will respond positively to the message about cultural awareness. "To some physicians, this must all seem too politically correct. To others, it may appear divisive, condescending, or simply the road to more bureaucratic meddling in medicine. Physicians may well have concerns about treading what may be a fine line between being culturally sensitive and stereotyping patients on the basis of race or ethnicity."

See Section X for the full text of the following articles:

- *Cancer Studies Fail Minorities*

- *Crossing the Cultural Divide*

- *Culturally Effective Communication*

- *Different Doctors Make Decisions in Different Ways*

- *Managing Diversity*

- *Mistaking Medicine*

- *Pew: Encourage Minority Physicians*

Child Health Initiative

Beth Lipa-Glaysher
312 464-4944

Under the guidance and direction of a steering committee composed of representatives of national organizations with a commitment to, and expertise in, child and adolescent health, this initiative will enhance healthy lifestyles of children and youth and reduce health risk behaviors. The overarching goal of the initiative is to develop a continuum for enhancing infant, child, and adolescent health by identifying culturally consistent strategies for physician, family, and community implementation.

Project activities include identifying the relationship between genetic and environmental factors that influence health behaviors and the resulting health status of infants, children, and adolescents during critical periods of growth and development. The project will also develop, implement, and evaluate recommendations for health promotion strategies that support children and adolescents, families, and communities. Special attention will be paid to health-related sociocultural differences of individuals, families, and communities in order to maximize program impact.

Coding and Technology

Celeste Kirschner
312 464-5932

Current Procedural Terminology, a 200,000-word book contains nearly 8,000 procedure codes, has recently been translated into Spanish.

Consumer Books

Patricia Dragisic
312 464-2536

All AMA consumer books emphasize a working partnership between physicians and patients by showing patients how to take responsibility for their health and well-being. The books also include information specific to various ethnic and racial groups, such as the incidence of particular diseases within different groups and the risk factors for those groups.

For descriptions or summaries of the following books, see Section IV.

AMA Essential Guides
Essential Guides currently cover asthma, depression, hypertension, and menopause.

Complete Guide to Women's Health
Kathleen Cahill Allison, Ramona I. Slupik
New York: Random House, 1996

Complete Guide to Your Children's Health

Encyclopedia of Medicine

Family Medical Guide, Third Edition

Focus on Men's Health

Focus on Women's Health

Domestic Violence

Roger Brown
312 464-5476

The AMA's ongoing national Campaign Against Family Violence has produced numerous resources addressing many of the groups and issues reflected in this *Compendium*. The Campaign includes the 10,000-member National Coalition of Physicians Against Family Violence (created in 1992) and the National Advisory Council on Family Violence (representatives from some 40 state and specialty medical societies and other collaborating members). The Advisory Council has urged the AMA to support (1) a monograph aimed at decreasing abuse in the medical workplace and (2) funding for family violence research by the National Institutes of Health and the Centers for Disease Control and Prevention.

The AMA Campaign Against Family Violence has produced an annotated catalog of videotapes on family violence intended for medical practitioners (1998) and eight diagnostic and treatment guides. *Diagnostic and Treatment Guidelines on Domestic Violence* highlights national hotlines, counseling groups, shelter directories, and publications with materials in English and other languages. This publication also briefly addresses the under-recognized issue of violence within gay and lesbian relationships.

Federation Relations

Michael Murray
312 464-4409

Federation Relations staff reflect Cultural Competence Initiative accomplishments, including the *Compendium*, in their communications with Federation members.

Foundation and Corporate Relations

Rita Palulonis
312 464-4543

James Alexander
312 464-5806

The AMA Foundation advances health care through support of education, research, and service programs at home and abroad. As the philanthropic arm of the AMA, it provides annual grants of more than $2 million, representing donations from the medical family, to medical schools for student assistance and programmatic excellence. The Foundation also supports programs in applied and clinical research and is developing a service program to recognize the community contributions of physicians and their families.

Foundation and Corporate Relations staff have provided advice and encouragement to the Cultural Competence Work Group, including guidance in conceptualizing activities that might be of interest to external funding sources.

Genetics Initiative

Priscilla Short, MD
312 464-4547

For an additional description of this initiative, see Section IV.

The AMA Genetics Initiative spans many cultural competence issues, including discrimination against patients simply because they have genetic disorders. The adverse health effects of this discrimination are intensified if patients also share racial or ethnic characteristics of traditionally underserved groups. The Genetics Initiative is undertaking a broad spectrum of existing and planned activities to address barriers to effective care, including projects in partnership with a national organization for self-help groups, the Alliance of Genetic Support Groups.

Study of Discrimination Against Patients with Genetic Disorders

The AMA recognizes that the findings of the Human Genome Project have already changed the day-to-day practice of medicine. As the genome is mapped, discrimination on the basis of genetic findings may be an unfortunate by-product. AMA staff are using neurofibromatosis (NF) as a model to catalog incidents of discrimination to determine if trends or patterns exist.

Analyze Data on Medical Genetics in the Curricula of US Medical Schools

The AMA is analyzing data on medical genetics curricula compiled from US medical schools, medical students, residents, fellows, and recently graduated physicians. The data will determine:

- What medical schools teach their students/residents/fellows.

- What medical students/residents/fellows appear to be learning.

- Medical geneticists' recommendations for what should be taught.

- Genetics medical education materials available to the practicing physician.

Gene Shop II

A proposed *Gene Shop II* is intended as the AMA's vehicle for accomplishing goals of the Genetics Awareness Campaign (GAC) and for providing useful information to the public and the medical community. An informational kiosk at a public Chicago location will promote ongoing education on the impact of genetics on health and disease. This project is conceived as a collaborative effort. Although the initial educational focus is genetics, the information kiosk may rotate coverage to other AMA programs with cultural competence elements, including domestic violence, adolescent health, and alcohol or tobacco use.

National Institute on Drug Abuse Modular Workshop on Addiction and Genetics

The AMA is initiating conversations with the National Institute on Drug Abuse (NIDA) about facilitating workshops to increase awareness in the medical community of prenatal counseling for risks related to recreational drug and alcohol use and the genetics of addiction.

Alliance of Genetic Support Groups

The AMA is working with the Alliance of Genetic Support Groups to create "standardized genetic patients" to facilitate the education of medical students and resident physicians in interviewing and examining patients with genetic disorders. Tasks include surveying schools on the use of standardized patients and working with the Alliance and the regional genetic networks to match patients with specific curricula.

Web-Based Interactive Module

An on-line continuing medical education module on colorectal cancer screening and the availability of genetic markers for different forms of familial colon cancer is under development, in partnership with the Society of ColoRectal Surgeons. In the interactive module, the physician manages the patient through genetic testing and other traditional interventions with variable outcomes.

GenEthics

A consumer-oriented site on genethics is scheduled for posting on the AMA Health Insight Web site in 1999. The project is a collaboration between the AMA's Institute for Ethics and the Science, Technology, and Public Health Standards group.

Geriatrics

Joanne Schwartzberg, MD
312 464-5355

- **Alcoholism in the Elderly: Diagnosis, Treatment, Prevention,** 1997

- **Guidelines for the Use of Assistive Technology: Evaluation, Referral, Prescription,** 1996

- **Medical Management of the Home Care Patient: Guidelines for Physicians,** 1998

- **Physician's Guide to Diagnosis and Treatment of Dementia,** 1999

Health Literacy Initiative

Joanne Schwartzberg, MD
312 464-5355

Health Literacy
Report of the Council on Scientific Affairs
JAMA, February 10, 1999; 281(6): 552-557

Group Practice Liaison

Amy Bishop
312 464-5172

The Liaison is exploring ways to disseminate information about the Cultural Competence Initiative.

Health Policy Studies

Phil Kletke
312 464-4337

Health Policy Studies coordinates the review of AMA policy related to cultural competence and presents the results to AMA legal and advocacy areas.

Medical Education—Continuing

Dennis K. Wentz, MD
312 464-5531

The first issue of the *Continuing Physician Professional Development Report* (April 1999) included an item on the AMA Cultural Competence Initiative. Recipients were encouraged to share it with continuing medical education advisory committees and with appropriate departments in the medical school to stimulate professional development activities around cultural competence issues.

Online Continuing Medical Education Locator

The CME On-line Locator, a database of more than 2,000 category 1 activities for the AMA Physician's Recognition Award, provides convenient access to multiple data elements about CME activities. In the year 2000, cultural competence topics will be identifiable.

International Continuing Medical Education

The AMA has established a protocol to assist organizations sponsoring international CME conferences that cannot be jointly sponsored by an ACCME-accredited entity. These conferences reflect considerable diversity and frequently include a cultural competence component.

Medical Education—Graduate

Frank Simon, MD
312 464-4395

The Division of Graduate Medical Education provides research findings to support the development of policy and standards. In early 1999, cultural sensitivity was added to the AMA Annual Survey of GME Programs. The May 1999 *Graduate Medical Education Bulletin* described the Cultural Competence Initiative and the *Cultural Competence Compendium.*

Fellowship and Residency Electronic Interactive Database Access (FREIDA) On-line

http://www.ama-assn.org/freida

The interactive menu in FREIDA On-line guides users to current information on nearly 300 variables related to Accreditation Council for Graduate Medical Education (ACGME)-accredited and combined programs. Beginning in 2000, FREIDA On-line will contain information provided by residency programs on their activities to promote cultural competence.

Medical Education Outreach

Barbara Schneidman, MD
312 464-5058

The Office of Medical Education Liaison and Outreach is charged with refining and expanding relationships with external bodies crucial to AMA efforts in developing, assessing, and improving medical education programs and opportunities. The office focuses on formulating and implementing policies and standards that promote quality health care, including cultural competence issues. In addition, this office coordinates the Medical School Visitation Program, in which members of the Board of Trustees and senior staff visit medical schools, another opportunity to present the AMA's Cultural Competence Initiative and related projects.

Medical Education Products

Hannah Hedrick, PhD
312 464-697

Fred Lenhoff
312 464-4635

The Division of Medical Education Products coordinates, records, and reports on implementation of the AMA Cultural Competence Initiative. These responsibilities include editing and desktop publishing the *Cultural Competence Compendium* (June 1999) and making it available through the AMA Web site.

Medical Education Products staff also ensure that all medical education products appropriately reflect the AMA commitment to the initiative. For example, in 1999 a question was added to the survey of licensing jurisdictions requesting information related to cultural competence, which will be reported in the fall 1999 edition of *US Medical Licensure Statistics and Requirements by State*. The Medical Education Group exhibit contains a panel announcing the Cultural Competence Initiative, and the exhibit displays relevant material from throughout the AMA.

Medical Education—Undergraduate

Barbara Barzansky
312 464-4690

Françoise Kusseling
312 464-4694

The Division of Undergraduate Medical Education functions as a major source of information for medical schools, policymakers, the Federation, and the public. During alternate years, this division staffs the Liaison Committee on Medical Education (LCME), which is considering an accreditation standard in the area of cultural competence. The proposed standard reads: "Given the expanding diversity in society, students must demonstrate an understanding of and be able to deal with various belief systems, cultural biases, and other culturally determined factors that influence the manner in which different people experience illness and respond to advice and treatment."

The medical career opportunities program developed in partnership with the Association of American Medical Colleges provides opportunities to encourage diversity in medical education.

Medical Education—Vice President

Michael J. Scotti, Jr, MD
312 464-4804

Jackie Drake
312 464-4389

The Office of the Vice President of the AMA Medical Education Group works to ensure that cultural competence content is added to the processes for collecting, aggregating, and disseminating data on undergraduate, graduate, and continuing medical education (see following chart). Cultural competence topics have been or are being incorporated into all relevant medical education activities.

The Vice President for Medical Education, Michael J. Scotti, Jr, MD, uses these and other information in presentations at national meetings on the importance of developing the "fifth competence," cultural competence. His presentations describe three areas in which associations must manifest professionalism, leadership, capacity, and moral duty:

- *Set standards* (including practice standards and defining how success is measured)

- *Educate members* (including research, meetings, publications, correspondence, coalitions, and advocacy)

- *Educate the public* (including publications, correspondence, coalitions, and advocacy)

Dr. Scotti incorporated a strong segment on cultural competence in the medical education portion of the AMA's Strategic Planning Process.

Jackie Drake provides research support for all phases of the Cultural Competence Initiative, beginning with extensive print and Web-based research for the annotated resource list for the Council on Medical Education report on Enhancing the Cultural Competence of Physicians (5-A-98). She also serves on the editorial board for the print and Web-based *Cultural Competence Compendium*.

AMA Medical Education Surveys, Databases, and Products

*Includes or will include questions on cultural competence

**Includes or will include information or requirements on cultural competence

Surveys

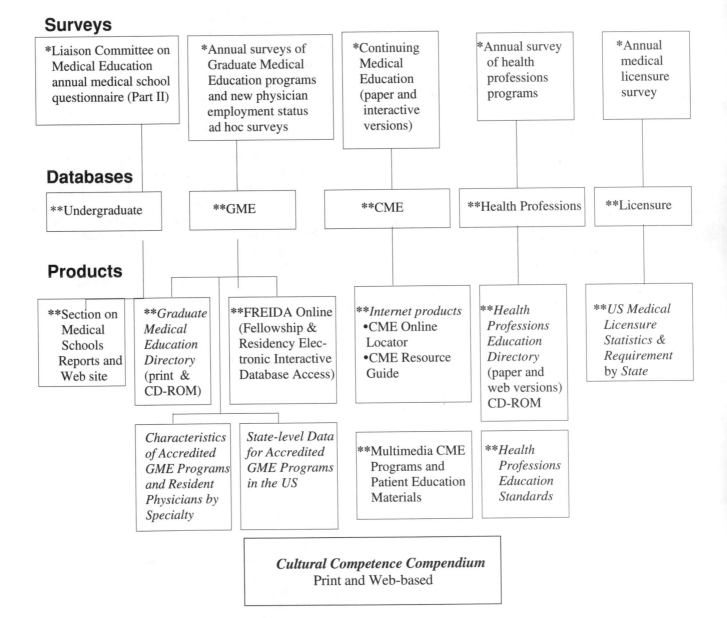

*Liaison Committee on Medical Education annual medical school questionnaire (Part II)	*Annual surveys of Graduate Medical Education programs and new physician employment status ad hoc surveys	*Continuing Medical Education (paper and interactive versions)	*Annual survey of health professions programs	*Annual medical licensure survey

Databases

**Undergraduate	**GME	**CME	**Health Professions	**Licensure

Products

**Section on Medical Schools Reports and Web site	**Graduate Medical Education Directory (print & CD-ROM)	**FREIDA Online (Fellowship & Residency Electronic Interactive Database Access)	**Internet products • CME Online Locator • CME Resource Guide	**Health Professions Education Directory (paper and web versions) CD-ROM	**US Medical Licensure Statistics & Requirement by State

Characteristics of Accredited GME Programs and Resident Physicians by Specialty	State-level Data for Accredited GME Programs in the US	**Multimedia CME Programs and Patient Education Materials	**Health Professions Education Standards

Cultural Competence Compendium
Print and Web-based

Member Communications

Becky Rasco
312 464-5665

Member Communications staff are developing a coordinated communications plan for promoting the Cultural Competence Initiative to members, staff, and external organizations. Represented by Becky Rasco on the Cultural Competence Work Group, communications staff have stimulated member and public interest in the Cultural Competence Initiative and the *Cultural Competence Compendium.*

Membership Marketing

Marsha Turner
312 464-4788

As a member of the Cultural Competence Work Group, Marsha Turner shares information about the Cultural Competence Initiative with Membership Marketing staff so that the Initiative may be appropriately used to retain and recruit members.

Multimedia Education

Mark Evans
312 464-5990

The multimedia area works with software designers and CD-ROM publishers to produce and distribute multimedia interactive CD-ROM-based tutorials, patient simulations, and query-based medical education, some of which are available in Spanish as well as in English.

News and Information

Ross Fraser
312 464-4443

Through his service on the Cultural Competence Work Group, Ross Fraser has become familiar with the extent of related activity across the AMA and in participating external organizations. He uses this information to bring visibility to cultural competence issues in a wide variety of contexts.

Office of International Medicine (OIM)

Dominic Fleming
312 464-5359

The purpose of the AMA OIM, established in 1978 as a focal point for coordinating a wide variety of activities emanating from a long-standing involvement in international medical education and practice, is to position the Association as one of the leaders in international health, provide a global perspective for AMA health policy development, enable the Association to influence international health policy, and have an impact the level and quality of health care worldwide.

Cross-cultural Educational Meetings

The AMA receives numerous requests annually from international organizations and individuals wishing to visit the AMA. As a result, the OIM welcomes approximately 12 international delegations annually, each ranging in size from one to thirty participants. The OIM sponsors cross-cultural educational meetings and symposia at the AMA and also arranges for members of the Association to travel abroad and participate in foreign medical conferences.

World Medical Association (WMA)

As one of the founding members of the WMA, the AMA works in close collaboration with the 70 other members to strengthen the WMA's role as the primary global source of medical ethics and to focus attention on quality of care, professional freedom, and preventive health care.

Cooperative Intervention in Human Rights Violations and Development of Health Care Programs

The OIM cooperates to develop health care programs and to intervene in cases of human rights violations with 14 national or international organizations.

Organ Donation Initiative

Karen Goraleski
312 464-4840
E-mail: karen_goraleski@ama-assn.org

Although organ transplants increased by approximately 600 and tissue transplants increased by 14,000 in 1998, the transplant waiting list also increased, from more than 56,000 registrants in 1997 to more than 64,000 in 1998. Donor trends among whites and Hispanics increased by 6.6% and 7.8%, respectively, while those for African American donors remained relatively unchanged and Asian donors decreased by 8.4%. Concerned about low donor rates in general and within African American populations in particular, the AMA is intensifying activities to implement its organ donation policies.

"Live and Then Give"

"Live and Then Give," an organ donation program modeled after the Texas Medical Association program of the same name, is intended to encourage physicians to become organ donors and to present information to their patients. The December 1998 Interim Meeting included an 11-minute video. The June 1999 Annual Meeting included several organ donation awareness events sponsored by the Medical Student Section and MAC, covering cultural barriers and general awareness of organ and transplant issues and aimed at increasing organ donations in minority communities. Activities included a Minority Issues Forum, a Public Rally for Organ Donation Awareness, and a MAC Consensus Panel/Forum which provided CME credit.

Campaign Manual and Ready-to-Use Materials

Materials supporting "Live and Then Give" are available in formats that give Federation partners the flexibility to develop a campaign unique to their own needs and responsive to the diverse populations they serve. The campaign manual is supplemented by camera-ready artwork, question and answer brochures, two donor cards, and a poster.

Medical Student Section Program Module

800 262-3211, ext 4742
E-mail: mss@ama-assn.org

The AMA Department of Medical Student Services developed the 1999 National Service Project Organ and Tissue Donor Awareness Program Module (February 1999), with assistance from the United Network for Organ Sharing, to encourage Medical Student Section chapters to apply for a policy promotion grant to set up an Organ Donation Awareness National Service Project.

The module includes sections on community and professional education, fact sheets on organ donation and transplantation, understanding the organ procurement process, dispelling fears about organ donation, and religious/spiritual views on donations and transplantation. Specific program activities are suggested, from donor days to appearing on TV and radio programs. The module also includes information about state and regional organ procurement organizations.

Giving Life: Share Your Decision To Be an Organ and Tissue Donor
Mi Young Hwang
(posted on *JAMA Patient Page* AMA Health Insight, http://www.ama-assn.org/public/journals/jama/ppindex9.htm)

A two-page discussion of the need for organ and tissue donation and how to indicate willingness to be a donor that may be reproduced by physicians to share with patients.

Collaborations Sought

The AMA is developing collaborative relationships and projects with the Illinois chapter of the National Medical Association, the Regional Organ Bank of Illinois, and other groups committed to cooperative efforts in the areas of policy development, education, technology, and assessment related to advancing organ availability and transplantation.

See Section IV for a list of national organizations.

Product Line Development

Suzanne Fraker
312 464-5453

Product Line Development and staff from other marketing units supported development and distribution of the *Cultural Competence Compendium* and coordinated efforts to design the cultural competence graphic identifier. Marketing staff will be involved in developing and distributing other products related to the Cultural Competence Initiative. Suzanne Fraker represents marketing units on the Cultural Competence Working Group and coordinates efforts to insert cultural competence components in all relevant AMA publications.

Professional Standards Administration

Susan Anderson
312 464-5961

The Professional Standards Administration area has forwarded references to publications, Web sites, and other resources for the *Compendium*;

located citations for published AMA reports; helped establish appropriate searchable categories for the Web-based resource list; and assisted in determining the cultural competence graphic identifier. Susan Anderson also serves on the editorial board for the print and Web-based *Compendium.*

Private Sector Advocacy

James Wills
312 464-5528

As a member of the Cultural Competence Work Group, James Wills brought the services of the Health Care Advisory Board to assist in identifying resources for the *Cultural Competence Compendium.*

Public Health

Karen Peters
312 464-4636

Cooperative Actions for Health Program

Includes 19 states working on small pilot projects linking medicine and public health; information available on two Web sites involved in the project, one at the AMA and the official site at the University of Texas.

Specialty Society Relations

Patricia Levenberg
312 464-4108

Patricia Levenberg serves as the liaison between the specialty society areas and the Cultural Competence Work Group. She assists Specialty Society Relations staff in incorporating a cultural competence component in their communications, reports, and other activities, as appropriate.

Strategic Communications

Linn Weiss
312 464-5566

Working closely with the Vice President of Medical Education, Strategic Communications staff are championing a coordinated communications plan for promoting the Cultural Competence Initiative and the *Compendium* to members, staff, and external organizations.

Tobacco Control Programs

Tom Houston, MD
312 464-5957

The tobacco control coalitions (SmokeLess States) funded by The Robert Wood Johnson Foundation and administered by AMA are active in recruiting diverse ethnic/racial organizations and individuals as partners in tobacco prevention and control. Particular success has occurred in coalitions in the District of Columbia, Washington state, Oregon, and California.

Traditional Health Law

Bruce Blehart
312 464-4039

Bruce Blehart facilitates communication between the Cultural Competence Work Group and AMA legal areas, including the Office of the General Counsel. He contributes his expertise to the Cultural Competence Initiative on how physicians respond to patients' rights and to employer concerns. He is committed to infusing awareness of the importance of cultural competence throughout the AMA.

Women in Medicine/Minority Physicians

Phyllis Kopriva
312 464-4392

As part of her responsibilities in providing staff services to the Women's Physicians Congress and the Minority Affairs Consortium (see elsewhere in this section), Phyllis Kopriva conducts surveys of state and specialty societies related to those two constituencies and maintains the MAC Web site, for which she produces periodic communications.

Selected AMA Policies Related to Cultural Competence

See Section X or the AMA Policy Compendium for the full text of the following policies. Some policies related to special issues in Section IV are not included below.

B-1.50   *Discrimination*

E-8.11   *Neglect of Patient*

E-8.18   *Informing Families of a Patient's Death*

E-9.035   *Gender Discrimination in the Medical Profession*

E-9.065   *Caring for the Poor*

E-9.12   *Physician-Patient Relationship: Respect for Law and Human Rights*

E-9.121   *Racial Disparities in Health Care*

E-9.122   *Gender Disparities in Health Care*

E-9.131   *HIV-Infected Patients and Physicians*

H-5.989   *Freedom of Communication Between Physicians and Patients*

H-20.966   *AMA HIV Policy Update*

H-20.974   *AIDS Prevention Through Educational Materials Directed at Minority Populations*

H-20.977   *Reducing Transmission of Human Immunodeficiency Virus (HIV)*

H-20.979   *Alternatives to Inpatient Care for Persons with AIDS or ARC*

H-25.993   *Senior Care*

H-25.994   *Increased Liaison, Communication, and Educational Efforts with the Elderly*

H-25.999   *Health Care for Older Patients*

H-30.952   *Alcoholism in the Elderly*

H-55.984   *Screening and Treatment for Breast and Cervical Cancer*

H-55.999   *Symptomatic and Supportive Care for Patients with Cancer*

H-60.974   *Children and Youth with Disabilities*

H-65.990   *Civil Rights Restoration*

H-65.999   *Equal Opportunity*

H-85.966   *Hospice Coverage and Underutilization*

H-85.967   *Good Care of the Dying Patient*

H-85.968   *Patient Self-Determination Act*

H-85.971   *Resource on Death and Dying*

H-85.972   *Compassionate Care of the Terminally Ill*

H-85.979   *Informing Families of a Patient's Death: Guidelines for the Involvement of Medical Students*

H-140.953   *Patient Responsibilities*

H-140.966   *Decisions Near the End of Life*

H-140.970   *Decisions to Forgo Life-Sustaining Treatment for Incompetent Patients*

H-140.975   *Fundamental Elements of the Patient-Physician Relationship*

H-140.977   *Residency Training in Medical-Legal Aspects of End-of-Life Care*

H-140.990   *Ethical Considerations in Health Care*

H-350.980   AMA's Role in Preparing Minority and Disadvantaged Youth for Careers in Medicine and the Health Professions

H-350.981   AMA Support of American Indian Health Career Opportunities

H-350.982   Project 3000 by 2000-Medical Education for Under-Represented Minority Students

H-350.983   Federal Guidelines for Standardization of Race/Ethnicity

H-370.974   Working Toward an Increased Number of Minorities Registered as Potential Bone Marrow Donors

H-370.975   Ethical Issues in the Procurement of Organs Following Cardiac Death

H-370.977   The Inclusion of Advance Directives Concerning Organ Donation in Living Wills

H-370.978   The Use of Minors as Organ and Tissue Sources

H-370.979   Financial Incentives for Organ Procurement—Ethical Aspects of Future Contracts for Cadaveric Donors

H-370.980   Strategies for Cadaveric Organ Procurement—Mandated Choice and Presumed Consent

H-370.982   Ethical Considerations in the Allocation of Organs and Other Scarce Medical Resources Among Patients

H-370.983   Tissue and Organ Donation

H-370.984   Organ Donation Education

H-370.986   Donor Tissues and Organs for Transplantation

H-370.987   Transplant Centers

H-370.994   Sale of Donor Organs for Transplant

H-370.995   Organ Donor Recruitment

H-370.996   Organ Donor Recruitment

H-370.999   Computerized Donor Registry

H-385.963   Physician Review of Accounts Sent for Collection

H-410.995   Participation in the Development of Practice Guidelines by Individuals Experienced in the Care of Minority and Indigent Patients

H-420.962   Perinatal Addiction—Issues in Care and Prevention

H-420.972   Prenatal Services to Prevent Low Birthweight Infants

H-420.978   Access to Prenatal Care

H-420.995   Medical Care for Indigent and Culturally Displaced Obstetrical Patients and Their Newborns

H-430.990   Bonding Programs for Women Prisoners and Their Newborn Children

H-480.964   Alternative Medicine

H-480.967   Alternative Therapies for the Symptoms of Menopause

H-480.973   Unconventional Medical Care in the United States

H-500.992   Tobacco Advertising Directed to Children, Minorities, and Women

H-515.969   Domestic Violence Intervention

H-515.970   Campaign Against Family Violence: Annual Update

H-515.971   Public Health Policy Approach
            for Preventing Violence in America

H-515.972   Violence Toward Men

H-515.975   Alcohol, Drugs, and Family Violence

H-515.976   Mental Health Consequences of
            Interpersonal and Family Violence

H-515.979   Violence as a Public Health Issue

H-515.980   Update on the AMA's National
            Campaign Against Family Violence

H-515.981   Family Violence—Adolescents
            as Victims and Perpetrators

H-515.983   Physicians and Family Violence

H-515.984   Violence Against Women

H-515.985   Identifying Victims of Adult
            Domestic Violence

H-515.986   A Proposed AMA National Campaign
            Against Family Violence

H-515.991   Elder Abuse and Neglect

H-515.992   Abuse of Elderly Persons

H-515.993   Child Sexual Abuse

H-515.994   Child Abuse and Neglect

H-515.997   AMA Diagnostic and Treatment
            Guidelines Concerning Child Abuse
            and Neglect

H-515.998   Violence Against Women

H-525.988   Gender Differences in Medical
            Research

H-525.990   Gender Disparities in Clinical
            Decision Making

H-525.991   Inclusion of Women in Clinical Trials

H-555.982   Participation of Minorities
            in Organized Medicine

American Medical Association Alliance

Sue Rubin
JoAnna M. Johnson
AMA Alliance
515 N State St
Chicago, IL 60610
312 464-4470
http://www.ama-assn.org/alliance

The American Medical Association Alliance (AMA Alliance) is a national grassroots organization of 50,000 physician spouses. As the proactive volunteer voice of the AMA, the Alliance promotes the good health of America and the family of medicine. For more than 75 years, Alliance members have participated in numerous local activities and projects that reflect a commitment to health care for diverse populations. The AMA Alliance strongly supports the AMA efforts to enhance the ability of physicians to provide culturally effective care.

Programs and Activities

SAVE: Stop America's Violence Everywhere

Since its inception in 1995, the SAVE initiative has been implemented at the grassroots level by more than 700 local Alliances. These programs are tailored to the communities they serve, but all assist victims of violence or teach violence prevention. For the 1999-2000 AMA Alliance year, SAVE activities will focus on situations that threaten the health and safety of children daily—violence in our schools.

To help address this growing problem, the AMA Alliance has developed a SAVE Schools from Violence campaign. It encourages Alliances nationwide to adopt a school in their community and provide those students with conflict resolution materials that teach nonviolent behaviors and enhance self-esteem. With the support of the community and the country, the AMA Alliance believes the SAVE program can help break the cycle of violence.

Consumer Education and Resources

Alliance volunteers educate their communities about health-related issues by distributing AMA Alliance publications and resources. Alliance consumer resources include:

Hands Are Not for Hitting Conflict Resolution Activity Book and Place Mat

Teaches preschool through third grade children positive, nonviolent activities and acceptable ways to treat others. "Hands" identifies what children's hands should and should not do.

Monitor the Media

Series of brochures that provide suggestions on ways to supervise a child's television viewing, video game playing, and Internet surfing. Each contains startling statistics and provides a realistic look at what is really coming into your living room through your television and computer.

Shape Up for Life

Series of brochures that address specific health issues and concerns such as child abuse, stress, teen suicide, elder abuse, eating disorders, and drug abuse.

Project Bank: The Encyclopedia of Public Health and Community Projects

Contains more than 500 projects conducted by state and county Alliances nationwide from 1994-1998. Project ideas range from domestic violence posters to teen health fairs, medical marriage seminars to medical textbook collections, and HIV-awareness campaigns to elder care programs.

Physician Spouse Series

Series of pamphlets that addresses the needs of physicians' spouses. Topics include impairment and well-being, marriage, medical family support, working in a spouse's office, and retirement.

Fundraising and Legislation

The AMA Alliance is the primary fund-raiser for medical education and research on behalf of the AMA Foundation. The funds provide financial assistance for medical schools and their students.

The AMA Alliance is also an important ally in AMA legislative advocacy. Alliance members are encouraged to work with their county medical societies on issues of concern on the grassroots level.

American Medical Women's Association

801 N Fairfax St, Ste 400
Alexandria, VA 22314
703 838-0500
703 549-3864 Fax
info@amwa-doc.org
http://www.amwa-doc.org

The 10,000-member American Medical Women's Association (AMWA) functions at local, national, and international levels to advance women in medicine and improve women's health by providing and developing leadership, advocacy, education, expertise, mentoring, and strategic alliances. When AMWA was founded in 1915, women physicians were an underrepresented minority. As of 1996, 21% of all practicing physicians were women.

Policy and Activities

AMWA's policy agenda includes a focus on affirmative action, tobacco control and prevention, reproductive health, and managed care. Some of the women's health issues AMWA has worked to improve include smoking prevention and cessation, osteoporosis, violence against women, heart disease, gender equity, breast cancer, and reproductive health. AMWA has worked to improve gender equity in medical education.

Journal of the American Medical Women's Association

In 1998, the *Journal of the American Medical Women's Association* published a supplement on *Cultural Competence and Women's Health in Medical Education* (Vol 53, No 3).

The articles in the supplement were presented at the National Conference on Cultural Competence and Women's Health: Curricula in Medical Education, sponsored by the Offices of Women's Health and Minority Health of the US Public Health Service. They are available online at http://www.jamwa.org/vol53/toc53_3.html.

Curriculum Enhancement in Medical Education: Teaching Cultural Competence and Women's Health for a Changing Society (editorial)
Elena V. Rios, Clay E. Simpson, Jr.

Required Curricula in Diversity and Cross-Cultural Medicine: The Time Is Now
Melissa Welch

Development and Evaluation of an Instrument to Assess Medical Students' Cultural Attitudes
Lynne S. Robins, Gwen L. Alexander, Fredric M. Wolf, et al

A Cultural Diversity Curriculum: Combining Didactic, Problem-Solving, and Simulated Experiences
BUK Li, Donna A. Caniano, Ronald C. Comer

Primary Care Fellowship in Women's Health
Kathleen M. Thomsen

A Women's Health Curriculum for an Internal Medicine Residency
Janice L. Werbinski, Sandra J. Hoffmann

Women's Health Curriculum at Stanford
JoDean Nicolette, Marc Nelson

American Public Health Association

1015 Fifteenth St NW
Washington, DC 20005-2605
202 789-5600
202 789-5661 Fax
E-mail: comments@apha.org
http://www.apha.org

Founded in 1872, the American Public Health Association (APHA) is the largest organization of public health professionals in the world, representing more than 50,000 members and affiliates from over 50 public health occupations, including researchers, practitioners, administrators, educators, and health workers. APHA publications include *The American Journal of Public Health*, a monthly peer-reviewed journal that frequently addresses diversity issues, including those related to complementary practices and spirituality, and *The Nation's Health*, which reports on legislation and policy issues affecting all public health professionals.

Units Addressing Cultural Competence

Alternative and Complementary Health Practices Special Primary Interest Group (ACHP SPIG)

Founded in 1994, the ACHP SPIG serves as a discussion point for interventions for improving, maintaining, and promoting health and well-being, preventing disease, or treating illness that are not part of a standard North American biomedical regimen of health care or disease prevention. "Standard" refers to practices commonly taught in schools of medicine or health sciences in North America or commonly covered by major insurers.

The ACHP SPIG sponsors multiple sessions at the APHA annual meeting focusing on topics such as cross-cultural communication, integrating and synthesizing alternative and complementary health practices into Western medical practice, attitudes of the medical community, practicing and teaching alternative and complementary health care, and value of outcomes research to assess efficacy, effectiveness, and the cost-effectiveness of alternative medicine.

Other Sections and Interest Groups

Other APHA sections and interest groups, such as those for Chiropractic Health Care, Community Health Planning and Policy Development, Food and Nutrition, International Health, Public Health Nursing, and Social Work, also consider issues related to cultural competence.

Representative Cultural Competence Presentations and Publications

Presentations at APHA annual meetings reflect the full spectrum of populations categorized in this *Compendium*. Topics include:

- Alternative Medicine: Efficacy and Safety

- Cancer in Communities of Color

- Children's Health

- Chiropractic Issues: Scope of Practice, Utilization, and Consumer Attitudes

- Culturally Competent Mental Health Care for the Latino Population

- Culture and Religion in Disease Promotion

- Domestic Violence: Cultural Connections

- Domestic Violence as a Women's Health Issue: National Women's Health Network

- Domestic Violence Interventions in the Health Care Setting

- Expansion of Alternative and Complementary Health Care into Mainstream Medicine

- Genetics and Public Health Interface

- Homelessness: Critical Topics

- The Impacts of Race, Ethnicity, and Gender in Caring for the Elderly

- The Influence of Race on Access to and Use of Prevention, Primary, and Acute Care Services by Older Adults—HCFA's Historically Black Colleges and Universities Health Services Research Initiative

- Minorities and Managed Care

- Minority Investigative Issues

- Nutraceuticals: Definitions, Health Concerns, and Public Policy

- Nutrition for Special Population Groups

- Promoting the Well-Being of Women With Disabilities

- Vulnerable, Underserved, and Invisible Populations

- Where Alternative and Complementary Medicine Meets Public Health Policy

Representative APHA Publications

Contact the APHA for information about its numerous publications related to cultural competence. Two that are closely related to this publication include:

Latino Health in the US: A Growing Challenge
C Molina, M Aguirre-Molina, eds.
American Public Health Association, 1996

Comprehensive volume reflecting the research, knowledge, and expertise of nationally recognized Latino researchers, scholars, educators, and activists. Includes profiles of Latinos in the health care system; life cycle and family health; patterns of chronic disease; occupational health; and alcohol, drug, and mental health issues.

Homelessness in America
APHA Reprint Series #3

Reflects research on the problem of homelessness and specific conditions associated with homelessness, including racial and ethnic factors.

Association of American Indian Physicians

Margaret Knight
1235 Sovereign Row, Ste C-7
Oklahoma City, OK 73108
405 946-7072
405 946-7651 Fax
http://www.aaip.com

Founded in 1971, the Association of American Indian Physicians (AAIP) is an organization of American Indian and Alaska Native physicians who are at least one-eighth American Indian and who are licensed to practice medicine in the United States. Collectively, members have hundreds of years of experience in direct primary care of Indian people in reservation and urban settings and tribal and Indian Health Service (IHS) clinics.

Mission and Activities

The organization's mission is to raise the health status of American Indians and Alaska Natives to a level equal to that of the predominant non-Indian population. It works to:

- Increase the number of American Indian physicians and other health care practitioners.

- Improve the quality of health care delivered to American Indians and Alaska Natives.

- Make recommendations to government and private organizations regarding the health conditions of American Indians and Alaska Natives, and the quality and manner in which health care is delivered to them.

- Support and encourage organizations that work to improve health conditions of Indian people.

- Provide scholarship funds to Indian students preparing to enter a health profession.

- Enter into contracts with government and private agencies to provide direct service consultation regarding the health care of American Indians and Alaska Natives.

- Assign every American Indian and Alaskan Native medical student a preceptor from the membership of AAIP to provide guidance, counseling, and friendship to the student throughout his or her formal medical education and training.

- Preserve Indian culture and foster Native American practices.

- Provide support and guidance to the Association of Native American Medical Students (ANAMS) and facilitate their participation at the AAIP annual meeting.

AAIP Web Site

The AAIP's Web site (http://www.aaip.com) disseminates health information to local American Indian and Alaska Native communities and Indian and non-Indian health professionals. A portion of the site is dedicated to traditional Indian medicine, though which health professionals around the country can obtain information and learn about traditional Indian medicine as well as strategies to help them collaborate with traditional Indian healers.

Annual Meeting Addresses Health and Education Issues

The annual meeting provides a continuing medical education program to educate members on current health issues in the Indian community, provides a social forum for American Indian physicians to network and foster Native American practices, and initiates new members with a sweat lodge ceremony. The meeting also provides an opportunity for medical students to participate in American Indian cultural activities and learn more about traditional Indian medicine clerkships and other available opportunities and experiences in Indian country.

Relevant Minority Population Health Care Issues

The AAIP believes that American Indian physicians need to explore the role of the Indian physician in approaching American Indian health problems, including linking traditional Indian medicine and modern Western medicine. Physicians able to provide such links can advocate for those Indian patients who desire both approaches to health care and for the increasing number of Indian patients who seek a traditional approach to their health care needs.

The AAIP points out that the Indian physician is in a unique position to aid the Indian community, especially concerning the major health problems affecting American Indian communities. Diseases and their consequences of particular concern include:

- diabetes

- heart disease

- alcoholism

- accidents

- cancer

- suicide

- homicide

- depression

- fetal alcohol syndrome

The AAIP encourages Indian physicians trained in Western medicine to translate the implications of modern research data into new treatments and prevention strategies that benefit Indian communities. It also encourages examination of the ways in which traditional Indian cultural practices may augment Western medical strategies to effect more successful treatment outcomes for American Indian and Alaska Native patients.

Association of American Medical Colleges

2450 N St NW
Washington, DC 20037-1126
202 828-0982
202 828-0972 Fax
http://www.aamc.org

Contact

Deborah Danoff, MD
202 828-0400
202 828-1125 Fax
E-mail: ddanoff@aamc.org

The Association of American Medical Colleges (AAMC) is a nonprofit association representing all 125 accredited US medical schools; the 16 accredited Canadian medical schools; some 400 major teaching hospitals, including 56 affiliated health systems and 75 Department of Veterans' Affairs medical centers; and 86 academic and professional societies, representing 88,000 faculty members. The AAMC conducts a broad range of programs and studies on medical education, research, and health services and represents its members before Congress and the Executive Branch in its efforts to improve the nation's health.

Units Addressing Cultural Competence

Division of Medical Education activities that directly relate to cultural competence include the Special Interest Group (SIG) on Cross Cultural Education, established in 1995. The SIG meets at and participates in the AAMC Annual Meeting and participates in programs at regional meetings.

Contact the Division of Community and Minority Programs (202 828-0572 or lmjohnson@aamc.org) for information on its wide range of initiatives and activities intended to increase participation by and services for underrepresented and underserved non-majority populations.

Project 3000 by 2000—Health Professions Partnership Initiative

The AAMC administers the Project 3000 by 2000 Health Professions Partnership Initiative. This project, co-funded by the S. K. Kellogg Foundation, offers funding to generate interest among students of all racial and ethnic groups in entering the health professions and to enhance their academic preparedness as they progress from one educational level to the next. The grants fund partnerships to coordinate the effort between predominantly minority high schools and minority community-based organizations with health professional schools and colleges. For information contact Timothy Ready, PhD, at 202 828-0584 or tpready@aamc.org.

Policies

Cultural competence and cultural awareness are recognized as important issues by the AAMC. The AAMC has had a long-standing commitment to increasing diversity in the medical community.

Publications

Academic Medicine, formerly the *Journal of Medical Education*, a monthly peer-reviewed journal, contains study reports, book reviews, editorials, bibliographies, and papers on national and international developments in academic medicine, all of which have addressed cultural competence issues. *AAMC Reporter/Washington Highlights* report on the Association's studies, major meetings and activities, and relevant federal legislation, regulations and health policy initiatives. The *AAMC Reporter* is a monthly newsletter covering the major nongovernmental issues of importance to academic medicine. *Washington Highlights* is a weekly report summarizing relevant federal, legislative, regulatory, and health policy initiatives. Both newsletters contain items related to diversity concerns.

Programs and Activities

Cultural Competence Needs

In 1997, the Division of Medical Education surveyed all Liaison Committee on Medical Education (LCME)-accredited medical schools and Accreditation Council for Graduate Medical Education (ACGME)-accredited programs in six core areas for information on established programs in cultural competence and on identified program needs. Both undergraduate and graduate medical programs indicated that their greatest need was for resource materials and assessment tools. Partial data from the survey are available in a February 1998 fact sheet titled *Contemporary Issues in Medical Education*.

Resources for Teaching/Evaluation

In response to the needs identified in the AAMC survey, the Division of Medical Education has solicited detailed information from a number of programs. Programs interested in these materials may contact Deborah Danoff for additional details. Materials include program outlines, information on evaluation tools, and resource individuals at a number of schools and programs.

The AAMC is currently cataloguing this information and plans to have a compendium of material available in 1999. For information, contact Deborah Danoff (above) or http://www.aamc.org/meded/edres/cime/start.htm.

Medical School Objectives Reports

Several sections of the AAMC Medical School Objectives Project contain language supportive of promoting cultural competence. *Report 1* encourages medical schools to develop objectives that reflect an understanding of the implications of "evolving societal needs, practice patterns, and scientific developments."

Guidelines for Medical Schools

The following excerpts from *Report 1* reflect the document's sensitivity to cultural issues.

"At all times [physicians] must act with integrity, honesty, respect for patients' privacy, and respect for the dignity of patients as persons. In all of their interactions with patients they must seek to understand the meaning of the patients' stories in the context of the patients' beliefs, and family and cultural values. They must avoid being judgmental when the patients' beliefs and values conflict with their own. They must continue to care for dying patients even when disease-specific therapy is no longer available or desired."

The objectives would require physicians to "be sufficiently knowledgeable about both traditional and nontraditional modes of care to provide intelligent guidance to their patients" and to understand the economic, psychological, occupational, social, and cultural factors that contribute to the development and/or perpetuation of conditions that impair health.

The guidelines state that the medical school must ensure that before graduation a student will have demonstrated, to the satisfaction of the faculty, "the ability to obtain an accurate medical history that covers all essential aspects of the history, including issues related to age, gender, and socioeconomic status."

The objectives also call on medical schools to ensure that graduates have knowledge of the "important non-biological determinants of poor health and of the economic, psychological, social, and cultural factors that contribute to the development and/or continuation of maladies." They would also require of graduates a "commitment to provide care to patients who are unable to pay and to advocate for access to health care for members of traditionally underserved populations."

Report 3 To Focus on Cultural Issues

Report 3, which focuses on communication skills and on integrating spirituality, end-of-life issues, and cultural issues into the practice of medicine, will be published in summer 1999. It will provide specific suggestions for learning objectives, educational methods, and strategies for evaluation. For additional information contact M. Brownell Anderson at 202 828-0562 or mbanderson@aamc.org.

Promoting a Cultural Competence LCME Accreditation Standard

The AAMC Task Force on Cultural Competence (Diversity) as an Accreditation Standard has representatives from the Group on Student Affairs—Minority Affairs Section, Group on Student Affairs, Group on Educational Affairs, Organization of Student Representatives, and Organization of Resident Representatives. The Task Force has been instrumental in developing and supporting a proposed standard on cultural diversity, which is currently under consideration by the LCME (see Section I). The Task Force will also work to develop strategies and models to assist schools in implementing curriculum content on cultural diversity and competence. For additional information, contact the Division of Community and Minority Programs at lmjohnson@aamc.org or 202 828-0562.

Health Services Research Institute

Division of Minority Health, Education, and Prevention
202 828-0579

The Health Services Research Institute, sponsored by the AAMC, with funding from the Agency for Health Care Policy and Research, was established to prepare more medical school faculty to be knowledgeable about cultural competence issues. Since 1991, more than 50 minority medical school faculty members have received fellowships to research issues, such as cultural barriers affecting the patient-doctor relationship and how sociocultural backgrounds, economic factors, and other variables are related to the prevalence of diseases.

Alternative and Complementary Medicine

The AAMC has established a special interest group on alternative and complementary medicine.

For more information, see Section V or contact:

Patricia A. Muehsam, MD
212 946-5700
E-mail: pm2@doc.mssm.edu

Gay and Lesbian Medical Association

459 Fulton St, Ste 107
San Francisco, CA 94102
415 255-4547
415 255-4784 Fax
E-mail: info@glma.org
http://www.glma.org

The Gay and Lesbian Medical Association is an organization of 2,000 lesbian, gay, bisexual, and transgendered (LGBT) physicians, medical students, and their supporters in all 50 states and 12 countries. Founded in 1981, GLMA works to combat homophobia within the medical profession and in society at large; to promote quality health care for LGBT and HIV-positive people; to foster a professional climate in which our diverse members can achieve their full potential; and to support members challenged by discrimination on the basis of sexual orientation

Activities

- Publish the *Journal of the Gay and Lesbian Medical Association*

- Meet with top leadership of the Health Resources and Services Administration (HRSA) to address methods of incorporating LGBT health issues into current and future HRSA projects

- Lead the CDC and HRSA to convene the meetings of major medical associations to look at ways to improve provider sensitivity in treating LGBT patients

- Promote quality research through the *Lesbian Health Fund*

- Campaign to ban discrimination based on sexual orientation within the AMA

- Encouraged publication of the AMA's gay-sensitive report, "Health Care Needs of Gay Men and Lesbians in the US"

- Lead the effort to revise the restrictive CDC guidelines on HIV-positive health care workers

- Spearhead national efforts to unite an array of national youth, LGBT, and health organizations behind the need for the American Psychiatric Association to develop a task force to address specific problems related to the diagnosis of Gender Identity Disorder in Children

- Urge the National Institutes of Health to gather and publish information on lesbians

- Involved with the President's Advisory Council on HIV/AIDS

National Coalition of Hispanic Health and Human Services Organizations

Jane L. Delgado, PhD, Chief Executive Officer
1501 16th St NW
Washington, DC 20036
202 387-5000
202 797-4353 Fax
E-mail: info@cossmho.org
http://www.cossmho.org

The National Coalition of Hispanic Health and Human Services Organizations (COSSMHO) was founded in 1973 as the Coalition of Spanish-Speaking Mental Health Organizations to represent and advocate for the mental health needs of Mexican American, Puerto Rican, Cuban American, Central American, and South American communities in the United States. Membership consists of thousands of front-line health and human service providers and organizations serving Hispanic communities. COSSMHO focuses on the health, mental health, and human services needs of diverse Hispanic communities.

Mission

COSSMHO's mission is to connect communities and create change to improve the health and well-being of Hispanics in the United States and to create strong, healthy Hispanic communities whose contributions are recognized and valued by a society that fosters the health, well-being, and prosperity of all its members. COSSMHO fulfills its mission by working with community-based organizations; universities; federal, state, and local governments; foundations; and corporations.

Priorities, Activities, and Services

Priority areas include many of the categories featured in this *Compendium*:

- Women's health
- Environmental health
- Health system and welfare reform
- HIV/AIDS, cancer, diabetes, and heart disease
- Maternal and child health
- Immunizations
- Adolescent health
- Mental health
- Substance abuse

These priorities are addressed through the following activities and services:

- Consumer education and outreach
- Training programs
- Technical assistance
- Model community-based programs
- Policy development and dissemination
- Research and data analysis
- Advocacy
- Infrastructure support and development
- Development and adaptation of materials

Cultural Competence Training Materials and Curricula

COSSMHO has produced hundreds of resources in support of the activities and services listed above. The products described below represent the kinds of print and training materials that are available to health care professionals.

Delivering Preventive Health Care to Hispanics: A Manual for Providers

This manual is intended to assist health providers in responding more effectively to the growing needs of Hispanics for greater access and utilization of health services. It addresses many of the barriers Hispanics face in obtaining health care, including language gaps between patient and provider, cultural misunderstandings, Hispanics' distrust of the medical system, cost, and institutional policies that are not sensitive to Hispanics' cultural values.

Chapters cover:

- The diversity of Hispanic groups in the United States

- Hispanic health status, risk factors, and patterns of seeking care

- Cultural values and beliefs affecting Hispanics' health

- Cultural and language considerations affecting patient-provider interactions

- techniques for bridging the gaps inherent to direct service and community-wide interventions

Also included are references, resources, and list of Spanish-language publications.

Proyecto Informar: A Training Program for Health Care Providers

The comprehensive cross-cultural training program described in this publication is designed to improve access to health services by preparing health care providers to offer culturally competent health services to Hispanics. The 2-day training allows participants to actively gain knowledge about delivering health services to Hispanics, examine their attitudes towards Hispanics, and have opportunities to practice new behaviors.

The training program's five modules include:

- Understanding Hispanics in the United States

- Understanding the role of culture in health

- Navigating cultural differences

- Navigating language differences

- Developing a culturally competent system of care

National Hispanic Medical Association

Elena Rios, MD, MSPH, President
1700 17th St NW, Ste 405
Washington, DC 20009
202 265-4297
202 234-5468 Fax
E-mail: nhma@earthlink.net
http://home.earthlink.net/~nhma

The National Hispanic Medical Association (NMHA) was formed in 1994 to provide advocacy and support for Hispanic physicians. It also works to improve health care for Hispanics and other underserved populations and to address the health care needs of underprivileged communities. The NHMA represents 26,000 licensed Hispanic physicians (4% of all practicing physicians in the United States), including 1,800 full-time Hispanic medical faculty with MD degrees.

Mission and Goals

To fulfill its mission of improving health care for Hispanics and the underserved, the NHMA has established the following goals:

- Provide support for and guidance to physicians of Hispanic origin in the United States and those physicians serving the Hispanic populations in the United States.

- Provide continuing medical education programs to members.

- Enhance career opportunities for members.

- Promote increased access to quality health care for members of the Hispanic community in the United States and address the health care needs of this community.

- Address cultural reasons why Hispanic populations underutilize existing facilities.

- Promote Hispanic health policy issues in relevant forums.

Projects

- In Texas and Massachusetts, the NHMA Medical Student Mentorship Program pairs Hispanic doctors-in-training with local Hispanic physicians.

- The NHMA annual conference, held in March, offers tracks on such topics as Hispanic families with chronic illnesses and health promotion strategies that target Latinos.

- The NHMA Leadership Fellowship Program offers 20 mid-career Hispanic physicians training in government and public policy.

- The NHMA Residents Leadership Program, which will begin in fall 1999 in California and New York, will work to expose Hispanic resident physicians to the state and federal public service arena.

- The NHMA is collaborating with the Hispanic-Serving Health Professions Schools to increase Hispanic admissions, retention, and faculty.

- The NHMA Cultural Competence Project includes a medical education curriculum survey, speakers' list, and policy reports and programs.

National Medical Association

Lorraine Cole, PhD, Executive Director
1012 10th St NW
Washington, DC 20001
202 347-1895
202 347-0722 Fax
E-mail: nma@nmanet.org
http://www.nmanet.org/

Established in 1895, the National Medical Association (NMA) is a national professional and scientific organization representing the interests of more than 25,000 physicians and their patients.

Mission and Goals

The collective body is committed to

- preventing the diseases, disabilities, and adverse conditions that disproportionately or differently impact African Americans and underserved populations;

- supporting efforts that improve the quality and availability of health care to poor and underserved populations; and

- increasing the representation and contributions of African Americans in medicine.

Programs and Activities

Professional Education

NMA, which is accredited by the Accreditation Council for Continuing Medical Education, offers numerous professional education opportunities annually through workshops, symposia, and conferences conducted on national, state, and local levels, as well as through innovative media such as special journal supplements, teleconferences, the NMA Web site, CD-ROM, and audio- and videotapes.

Research and Scientific Exchange

NMA's Annual Convention and Scientific Exhibition is considered the nation's foremost forum on medical science and African American health. The *Journal of the National Medical Association*, published continuously since 1901, is a leading resource on medical science pertaining to African American medical concerns. The NMA also provides clinical trial education for physicians and patients and facilitates opportunities for NMA members to conduct practice-based research of clinical trials.

NMA News serves as the official house organ for association updates and scholarly information.

Patient Education

NMA works to prevent health problems and to promote healthy lifestyles, particularly among African Americans and other underrepresented and underserved groups. To eliminate racial disparities in health status, NMA conducts a myriad of programs and campaigns promoting public health among African Americans:

- Patient education programs and products on health topics that disproportionately impact African

Americans, such as cancer, cardiovascular disease, HIV/AIDS, asthma, arthritis, and diabetes;

- Public service announcements with culturally relevant messages, appropriately placed in media markets that reach large numbers of African Americans; and

- Outreach efforts to increase vital early detection, disease prevention, and health promotion practices such as immunization, blood pressure screening, cholesterol screening, cardiovascular risk assessment, and smoking cessation.

National Health Policy

Health policy directed to improving the status of health and the quality and availability of health care, particularly among African Americans and disadvantaged people, continues to be a top priority of the NMA. To impact national health policy, the NMA:

- Convenes expert consensus panels and develops policy statements;

- Expresses NMA positions publicly through the media and in press conferences;

- Forms coalitions with other groups around common concerns;

- Educates legislators and other opinion leaders; and

- Generates grassroots support among physicians and health consumers.

Medical Workforce Diversity

NMA works to increase the representation of African Americans and other underrepresented groups in medicine. NMA is committed to increasing the African American physician workforce in the United States to reflect the nation's growing diversity by:

- Providing medical student scholarships,

- Mentoring young medical students and residents,

- Promoting opportunities for research fellowships, and

- Facilitating opportunities for career advancements.

Recognition

NMA recognizes those who have made outstanding achievements pertaining to health, medicine, and the National Medical Association through several annual awards:

- Meritorious Achievement Award
- Local Society of the Year
- Distinguished Service Award
- Practitioner of the Year
- Scroll of Merit

Other General Physician Associations

American Association of Chinese Physicians

Henry Zhou, MD, PhD, President
NYU Medical Center
Department of Anesthesiology
550 First Ave
New York, NY 10016
212 263-5072
212 263-7254 Fax

American Association of Physicians of India

Box 4370
Flint, MI 48504
313 767-4946

American Association of Physicians of Indian Origin

Kalpalatha Guntupalli, MD, President
17 W 300 22nd St, Ste 250
630 530-2277
630 530-2475 Fax
Oak Brook, IL 60181-4490
E-mail: AAPI@aol.com
http://www.aapiusa.org

American Association of Surgeons of Indian Origin

Surendra K. Purohit, MD, President
Highland Park Plaza, #209
Covington, LA 70433
504 892-6811
504 892-8767 Fax

American College of International Physicians

Jamal Eskander, MD, President
370 S Lowe Ave, Ste A-309
Cookeville, TN 38501
877 422-4172

American Lebanese Medical Association

Joe Jabre, MD, President
65 Arlington Rd
Woburn, MA 01801
617 937-3071, Fax 617 937-3081
E-mail: jjabre@bu.edu

American Russian Medical and Dental Society

6221 Wilshire Blvd, #607
Los Angeles, CA 90048
213 933-0711

American Yugoslav Medical Society

Dushan Kosovich, MD, President
524 E 72nd St, #41A
New York, NY 10021
212 371-8420
212 753-1135 Fax
E-mail: dushan@akula.com

Argentinian Medical Society

Louis Palma, MD, President
333 Broadway, Ste 4
Amityville, NY 11701
516 789-5656

Asian-American Medical Society

Vijay Dave, MD, President
8695 Connecticut, Ste D
Merrillville, IN 46410

Asian-American Physician Association of Western New York

Kailash Lall, MD, President
725 Orchard Park Rd
West Seneca, NY 14224
716 675-1001

Association of Haitian Physicians Abroad

Jean Talleyrand, MD, President
234 Conway Ct
South Orange, NJ 07079
201 763-3056

Association of Kerala Medical Graduates

Sovi Joseph, MD, President
15 Fred St
Old Tappan, NJ 07675
718 299-4144
201 664-6885 Fax

Association of Pakistani Physicians

6414 S Cass Ave, Ste L-2
Westmont, IL 60559
630 968-8585
630 968-8677 Fax

Association of Pakistani Physicians of North America

Shabbir H. Safdar, MD, President
6414 S Cass Ave
Westmont, IL 60559
630 968-8606
630 968-8677 Fax
E-mail: appna@appna.org
http://www.appna.org

Association of Philippine Physicians in America

Modesto Rivera, III, MD, Executive Director
806 Solomon's Island Rd
Prince Frederick, MD 20678
410 414-2554
410 535-4983 Fax

Association of Philippine Surgeons in America

2147 Old Greenbriar Rd
Chesapeake, VA 23320
804 424-5485

Bangladesh Medical Association of North America

A. Hafiz, MD, President
1575 Woodward Ave, #105
Bloomfield Hills, MI 48013
313 338-8182
516 484-2889 Fax

California Hispanic-American Medical Association

1020 S Arroyo Pkwy, Ste 200
Pasadena, CA 91066
818 799-5456

Chinese American Medical Society

Raymond Fong, MD
President of the Board of Directors
535 E 86th St, #6H
New York, NY 10028
718 780-1005
E-mail: hw5@columbia.edu
http://www.camsociety.org

Chinese American Physicians' Society

Lawrence M. Ng, MD, Executive Director
345 Ninth St, Ste 204
Oakland, CA 94607-4206
510 895-5539
510 895-5539 Fax
E-mail: society@caps-ca.org
http://www.caps-ca.org

Colegio Medico Cubano Libre

Enrique Huertas, MD, President
Box 141016
Coral Gables, FL 33114-1016
305 446-9902

Colombian Medical Society

Oscar Pelaez, MD, President
944 Park Ave
New York, NY 10028
212 472-2139

Columbia Medical Association

PO Box 857
Northbrook, IL 60065-0857

Confederation of Hispanic American Medical Associations

Adrian Ortega, MD, President
900 Ridge Side Dr
Monterey, CA 91754

Dominican American Medical Society

Manuel Acevedo, MD, President
610 W 145th St
New York, NY 10031
212 234-9100

Hellenic Medical Society

Peter Tsairis, MD, President
523 72nd St, 3rd Floor
New York, NY 10021
888 467-6337

Hudson Valley Indian Physician Practitioners

Jai K. Jalag, MD, President
97 Main St
Fishkill, NY 12524
914 897-3210
914 897-3290 Fax

Hungarian Medical Association of America

John Schuetz, MD
Chair, Membership Committee
2845 Lakeside Dr
Coal City, IL 60416-9508
815 942-6822
E-mail: hmaa@hmaa.org
http://www.hmaa.org

Icelandic Medical Association

Hakon Hakonarson, MD, President
Children's Hospital
34th and Civic Center
Philadelphia, PA 19104
215 590-3469

Illinois-Peruvian American Medical Society

S. Guillermo Philipps, MD, President
1123 N Oak Park Ave
Oak Park, IL 60302
708 386-1322

Interamerican College of Physicians and Surgeons, Inc

Rene F. Rodriguez, MD, President
1712 I St NW, #200
Washington, DC 20006-3702
202 265-4297
E-mail: icps@icps.org
http://www.users.interport.net/~icps

International College of Surgeons— U.S. Section

Raymond Dieter Jr., MD, President
1516 N Lake Shore Dr
Chicago, IL 60610
312 787-6274

Iranian American Medical Association

Masood A. Khatamee, MD, President
877 Park Ave
New York, NY 10021
212 744-5500
212 744-6536 Fax

Islamic Medical Association

4121 S Fairview Ave, Ste 203
Downers Grove, IL 60515-2236
630 852-2122 or 7622
630 852-2151 Fax
E-mail: imana@aol.com
http://www.islam-usa.com/e2

Islamic Medical Association of North America

G. Jeelani Dhar, MD, President
950 75th St
Downers Grove, IL 60516
630 852-2122
630 435-1429 Fax
E-mail: IMANA@aol.com
http://www.imana.org

Italian American Medical Association

1127 Wilshire Blvd
Los Angeles, CA 90017
213 481-0896

Janusz Korczak Medical Society

Zev Kohn, MD, President
140 Cabrini Blvd, #108
New York, NY 10093
212 740-4824

Japanese Medical Society of America

Mitsugu Shimmyo, MD, President
345 E 37th St
New York, NY 10016
212 867-5700

Korean-American Medical Association of the U.S.

Richard S. Rhee, MD, President
1270 Broadway, Ste 205
New York, NY 10001
212 268-4443
212 643-8294 Fax

Medical Association of the US and Mexico

Bev Richter
1221 W Carol Ann Way
Phoenix, AZ 85023

Morgagni Medical Society

Antonia Delli-Pizzi, MD, President
14 E 75th St
New York, NY 10021

National Arab American Medical Association

Elias Tawil, MD, President
1025 E Maple Rd, Ste 210
Birmingham, MI 48009-6483
248 646-3661
248 646-0617 Fax
E-mail: naamausa@aol.com
http://www.naama.com

National Hispanic Medical Association

Elena Rios, MD, MSPH, President
1700 17th St NW, Ste 405
Washington, DC 20009
202 265-4297
202 234-5468 Fax
http://home.earthlink.net/~nhma

National Medical and Dental Association (Polish)

72-41 Grand Ave
Maspleth, NY 11378
607 733-7503

National Taiwan University Medical School Alumni Association

Shyan-Yih Chou, MD, President
225 Bayberry Drive S
Hewlett Harbor, NY 11557

North American Taiwan Medical Association

Chuang-Shiah Kiang, MD, President
7831 Sioux Rd
Orland Park, IL 60462
708 229-5812
708 499-2337 Fax

Peruvian American Medical Society

Edgar Malparatida, MD, President
4488 Tamerland Dr
West Bloomfield, MI 48322
813 785-5677

Philippine Medical Association of America

Eduardo Macalino, MD, President
142 Joralemon
Brooklyn, NY 11201
718 852-8564

Polish-American Medical Society

Marek Gawrysz, MD, President
6318 W Irving Park Rd
Chicago, IL 60634
773 286-1717
773 286-0440 Fax

Rajasthan Medical Alumni Association

N. Hadpawat, MD, President
89 Shore Rd
Manhasset, NY 1030
516 825-5505

Rumanian Medical Society of New York

Napoleon Savescu, MD, President
2126 Broadway
Astoria, NY 11106
718 932-1700

Salvadoran American Medical Society

Arturo E. Aviles, MD, President
9509 S Dixie Hwy, Ste 218
Miami, FL 33156
305 412-9435
800 360-7267 Fax

Semmelweis Scientific Society

Kurt Altman, MD, President
863 Park Ave
New York, NY 10028
212 831-3332

Serbian-American Medical Society

Zeljko Attagic, MD, President
30 N Michigan Ave, Ste 510
Chicago, IL 60602
312 422-1033

Society of Asian-Indian Surgeons of America

Vellore S. Parthivel, MD, President
Department of Surgery
Bronx Lebanon Hospital Center
1650 Selwyn Ave, #4H
Bronx, NY 10457
718 960-1251

Society of Philippine Surgeons in America

Domingo Alvear, MD, President
2600 N Third St
Harrisburg, PA 17110

Spanish-American Medical Society

Franklin A. Caldera, MD, President
420 Lakeville Rd
Lake Success, NY 11042
516 354-0710   516 354-8181 Fax

Thai Physicians Association of America

Sathien Suntrachai, MD, President
1200 N Tustin Ave, Ste 200
Santa Ana, CA 92705-3534
http://www.tpaa.org

Turkish American Physicians Association

Saedettin Sun, MD, President
1350 Lexington Ave
New York, NY 10128
212 697-2813

Ukrainian Medical Association of North America

Wasyl Marchuk, MD, President
2247 W Chicago Ave
Chicago, IL 60622
312 278-6262

Venezuelan American Medical Association

Box 15460
Plantation, FL 33318-5460
E-mail: vama@vama.org
http://www.vama.org

Vietnamese Medical Association

Ngai X. Nguyen, MD, President
398 E Santa Clara St, Ste B
San Jose, CA 95113
408 971-1333

B. Medical Specialty Groups

American Academy of Child and Adolescent Psychiatry

Virginia Q. Anthony
Executive Director
3615 Wisconsin Ave NW
Washington, DC 20016
202 966-7300
202 966-2891 Fax
http://www.aacap.org

Units Addressing Cultural Competence

Contact: Mary Crosby
E-mail: mcrosby@aacap.org

- **Committee on Diversity and Culture**

- **Work Group on Consumer Issues**

Policies

*Principles of Universal Access: Child
and Adolescent Psychiatric Services, August 1992*

Relevant Health Care Issues

The American Academy of Child and Adolescent Psychiatry (AACAP) addresses all areas of mental health care specific to children and adolescents, including those affected by broadly defined cultural considerations. Special populations for AACAP include those from high trauma areas, neighborhoods, and countries.

Minority Medical Students and Physicians

The AACAP supports three $2,500 summer research and clinical fellowships for minority medical students:

- James Comer Minority Research Fellowship for Medical Students

- Jeanne Spurlock Research Fellowship in Drug Abuse and Addiction

- Jeanne Spurlock Clinical Fellowship in Child and Adolescent Psychiatry

Improving Access to Care for Underserved Groups

The AACAP has recently developed a detailed training curriculum for diversity and culture, with a comprehensive annotated reference list and other resources. In addition, the Work Group on Consumer issues translated the Facts for Families series into Spanish.

Publications and Other Resources

Frequently features diversity and culture issues in a special section and in articles in *AACAP News.* Typical titles include:

Your Child: What Every Parent Needs to Know: What's Normal, What's Not, and When to Seek Help

Your Adolescent: What Every Parent Needs to Know: What's Normal, What's Not, and When to Seek Help

See summaries in Section IV.

Other Programs/Activities

A special roundtable on diversity and cultural issues is conducted at annual meetings.

American Academy of Dermatology

Sam Flint, PhD
Executive Director
930 N Meacham Rd
PO Box 4014
Schaumburg, IL 60168-4014
847 330-0230
847 330-0050 Fax
http://www.derm-infonet.com

Unit Addressing Cultural Competence

The Diversity Task Force of the American
Academy of Dermatology (AAD) is charged
with serving as a resource and the conscience of
the Academy on issues facing minority
physicians, medical students, and patients.

Relevant Health Care Issues

Several skin diseases predominantly affect
minorities or affect minorities differently. One of
the AAD's pamphlets focuses on disorders of the
skin, hair, and mucous membranes that affect
African Americans.

Programs and Activities

The Academy has sponsored didactic sessions on
a number of issues relevant to culture.
Educational sessions have discussed the practice
of "coining" in the Asian community. This
practice can leave pronounced red blotches on
the skin, which is sometimes mistaken for
cutaneous signs of domestic violence.

The Academy's President-elect, Darrel Rigel,
MD, has included a working group on diversity
issues as part of the Dermatology in the 21st
Century initiative.

Summer Minority Mentorship Program

The Academy offers a Summer Minority Mentorship
program, open to minority medical students in their
first or second year. The purpose of the program is to
open the door for minority medical students to
consider the specialty as a career choice. Since the
program's inception in 1995, the number of
applicants has grown fourfold. The program is also
very popular with dermatologists, who have found
great satisfaction as volunteer mentors.

Publications and Other Resources

- The Academy publishes public educational pamphlets that are relevant to minority patients and supports didactic programming at its annual and summer meetings on skin disorders that predominantly affect minority patients.

- The Academy is a member of the Association of American Medical Colleges Health Professionals for Diversity.

American Academy of Family Physicians

Robert Graham, MD
Executive Vice President
8880 Ward Pkwy
Kansas City, MO 64114
816 333-9700
816 333-2237 Fax
E-mail: bgraham@aafp.org
http://www.aafp.org

Units Addressing Cultural Competence

- **Committee on Special Constituencies**

- **Commission on Public Health—
  Subcommittee on Inner City/Urban Health**

Policies

Access to Health Care

Complementary Practices

Cross-Cultural Health Care

Family Violence

Female Genital Mutilation

Fragmentation of Health Care

Optimum Health Care

Parity in Mental Health Coverage for Patients

*Rationing of Health Care—Principles to Guide
Allocation of Resources*

Mental Health—Physician Responsibility

Migrant Health Care

Minority Health Care

*Minority Students: Family Physician as Role
Models*

Relevant Minority Population Health Care Issues

- Diabetes

- High Blood Pressure

- Domestic/Family Violence

- Access to Care

Programs and Activities

- Minority Special Interest Groups

- Listserv

- The National Conference of Women, Minority, and New Physicians

Improving Access to Care for Underserved Groups

Committee on Special Constituencies

Publications and Other Resources

American Family Physician

Continuing Medical Education (CME)

The Academy offers CME courses that include ethnic/cultural/minority health, homosexual health, and American Indian health issues, including the following:

- Southwest Association of Hispanic American Physicians

- Spanish Intensive Medical Instruction

- Cultural Diversity Training Workshop

- Primary Care 2000: Minority Health

- Deadly Diseases and Ethnic Communication

- Medical Preparation and Cross-Cultural Care

- Transcultural Health Perspectives

- Cardiovascular Risk in African Americans

- Health Care in China, Japan, and Taiwan

- Women in Medicine

- Indian Health

- Advances in Indian Primary Health Care

- Heart Disease in American Women

- Diabetes in Native Americans

- Domestic Violence

American Academy of Orthopaedic Surgeons

William W. Tipton Jr, MD
Executive Vice President
6300 N River Rd
Rosemont, IL 60018-4262
847 823-7186
847 823-8028 Fax
http://www.aaos.org

Units Addressing Cultural Competence

- Diversity Committee

- Ruth Jackson Society

Policies

The American Academy of Orthopaedic Surgeons
(AAOS) has position statements addressing
disparities and/or access to health care.

Relevant Health Care Issues

- Musculoskeletal health

- Safety

- Rehabilitation

Minority Medical Students and Physicians

- Mentor programs

- Brochures for medical students

- Communications to residency program
  directors encouraging them to support
  diversity

Improving Access to Care for Underserved Groups

- Committee on Volunteerism

- Orthopaedics Overseas Program

Publications and Other Resources

- Articles in *AAOS Magazine*

American Academy of Otolaryngology-Head and Neck Surgery

Michael Maves, MD
Executive Vice President
One Prince St
Alexandria, VA 22314
703 836-4444
703 519-1553 Fax
http://www.entnet.org

Unit Addressing Cultural Competence

The Otolaryngology Section of the National Medical Association, the Harry Barnes Society, is the representative body for minority issues related to otolaryngology-head and neck surgery.

Relevant Health Care Issues

A disproportionate number of cases of head and neck cancer occur within the African American population. Native Americans and native Alaskans have increased incidents of chronic otitis media.

Programs and Activities

The American Academy of Otolaryngology-Head and Neck Surgery (AAO-HNS) and its Foundation presidents have highlighted the need to increase diversity within the AAO-HNS/F.

The AAO-HNS indirectly provides support for diversity issues through its Office of Internal Affairs.

American Academy of Pediatrics

Joe M. Sanders, MD
Executive Director
141 North West Point Blvd
PO Box 927
Elk Grove Village, IL 60007
847 228-5005
847 228-5097 Fax
E-mail: jsanders@aap.org
http://www.aap.org

Unit Addressing Cultural Competence

The American Academy of Pediatrics (AAP) Office of the Executive Director convened a consultants' group in 1997 to address cultural competence issues on an ongoing basis.

Reports

Report of AAP Task Force on Minority Children's Access to Pediatric Care (includes 66 recommendations)

Policies

The AAP Committee on Pediatric Workforce recently published a policy statement, "Culturally Effective Pediatric Health Care: Education and Training Issues." (*Pediatrics*, January 1999)

The statement defines culturally effective health care and describes its importance for pediatrics. It also defines cultural effectiveness, cultural sensitivity, and cultural competence and describes the importance of these concepts for medical school, residency, and continuing medical education. The statement is based on the premise that culturally effective health care is important and that the knowledge and skills necessary for providing culturally effective health care can be taught and acquired through:

- educational courses and other formats developed with the expressed purpose of addressing cultural competence and/or cultural sensitivity

- educational components on cultural competence and/or cultural sensitivity that are incorporated into medical school, residency, and continuing medical education curricula

Other policies include the following:

- Encourage the Indian Health Service to take steps to increase the cultural awareness of physicians who are paying back a service obligation and have little knowledge of Native American children and their families.

- Urge pediatricians, other health care providers, and health policymakers to be educated about and sensitive to the sociocultural background of their patients and to appreciate the impact that cultural norms may exert on health status.

- Provide resources needed to ensure that pediatricians attain cultural competency by addressing pertinent issues in professional publications and manuals and through workshops at professional meetings.

- Work with the Residency Review Committee for Pediatrics and the Association of Pediatric Program Directors to recommend curricular changes in residency training that will involve integration of cultural sensitivity, tailored to local patient populations.

- Work with the Association of American Medical Colleges and other pediatric organizations to promote training in cultural competency and sensitivity to the local patient population.

- Emphasize changes in medical education and training that promote community-based clinical training and experience and training in medico-social problems to the poor, to deliver better health care and contribute more effectively to the solutions of medicosocial problems that severely impact health outcomes.

- Devise an educational program for pediatricians regarding health care in border regions, which include: health care of the children of migrant workers who cross borders, both national and interstate; criteria to establish relations with workers' families; and reliable information on the legal status of international workers' children regarding health care access.

- Emphasize changes in medical education and training that promote community-based clinical training experience.

Other policies, currently in progress, include:

- Enhancing the Diversity of the Pediatric Workforce, from the Committee on Pediatric Workforce

- Race/Ethnicity, Gender, Socioeconoic Status—Research Exploring Their Effects on Child Health, from the Committee on Pediatric Research

Relevant Health Care Issues

The AAP is concerned with all minority population health care issues that relate to child health.

Programs and Activities

Minority Medical Students

Through the Committee on Pediatric Workforce for Minority Group Medical Students, the AAP hosts programs and activities at the national conferences of minority medical student groups. This program has been very successful in involving minority group pediatricians and minority group medical students in AAP activities and in providing students who attend national conferences of minority medical student groups with information on pediatrics as a profession.

Improving Access to Care for Underserved Groups

- **CONACH (Committee on Native American Child Health)**

  CONACH develops and implements projects that promote the health of Native American children, including conducting child health consultation visits and educational seminars with accompanying continuing medical education credit at Indian Health Service locations.

- **CATCH (Community Access to Child Health)**

  CATCH supports pediatricians who work with communities to provide medical homes for children by providing training, networking opportunities, and technical assistance.

- **CATCH Planning Funds Program**

  This program provides funding to pediatricians collaborating at the local level to address barriers to access to health care for children.

- **Healthy Tomorrows Partnership for Children Program**

  The Health Tomorrows Partnership is a collaborative with the federal Maternal and Child Health Bureau (MCHB) that provides financial support and technical assistance to innovative community-based projects, fosters cooperation among public and private community organizations, and involves pediatric health professionals in providing care to underserved children and their families.

American Academy of Physical Medicine and Rehabilitation

Ronald A. Henrichs, CAE
Executive Director
One IBM Plaza, Ste 2500
Chicago, IL 60611-3604
312 464-9700
312 464-0227 Fax
E-mail: aapmr1@aapmr.org
http://www.aapmr.com

Minority Medical Students and Physicians

The American Academy of Physical Medicine and
Rehabilitation sponsors a special interest group for
underrepresented populations.

American College of Surgeons

Paul A. Ebert, MD
Executive Vice President
55 E Erie St
Chicago, IL 60611
312 664-4050
312 440-7014 Fax
E-mail: pebert@facs.org
http://www.facs.org

Unit Addressing Cultural Competence

The American College of Surgeons (ACS) has
formed a committee to identify and mentor
minority students.

Programs and Activities

The ACS offers continuing medical education
programs and scientific studies related to diversity
issues.

Minority Medical Students and Physicians

- Medical Student Educational Programs

- Resident Enrollment Program

American Gastroenterological Association

Robert Greenberg, JD
Executive Vice President
7910 Woodmont Ave, Ste 700
Bethesda, MD 20814
301 654-2055
301 654-5920 Fax
E-mail: robertg@gastro.org

Unit Addressing Cultural Competence

The American Gastroenterological Association
(AGA) has developed a Committee on
Underrepresented Minorities.

Relevant Health Care Issues

- Esophageal cancer

- Colorectal cancer

- Hepatitis C

- Intravenous drug abuse

Minority Medical Students and Physicians

The AGA program of research awards for medical
students and junior faculty includes specific awards
for minority members.

American Pediatric Surgical Association

Keith T. Oldham, MD
Secretary
Box 3815
Duke University Medical Ctr
Durham, NC 27710
919 681-5077
919 681-8353 Fax
E-mail: oldha001@MC.Duke.Edu

Relevant Health Care Issues

The American Pediatric Surgical Association is committed to ensuring access to specialty care for all children, regardless of socioeconomic status.

American Psychiatric Association

Steve Mirin, MD
Medical Director
1400 K St NW
Washington, DC 20005
202 682-6000
202 682-6353 Fax
E-mail: smirin@psych.org
http://www.psych.org

Units Addressing Cultural Competence

The following special American Psychiatric Association (APA) groups address cultural competence issues:

- Council on National Affairs

- American Indians and Alaska natives

- Hispanic psychiatrists

- Committee on Women

- Committee on Gay, Lesbian, and Bisexual Issues

Programs and Activities

Members of the APA's minority and underrepresented component committees have written four of a series of six articles (see Publications, below) on residency education curricula. All published in *Academic Psychiatry,* these articles cover:

- Gender and women's issues

- American Indians and Alaska natives

- Hispanics

- Homosexuality

Similar curricula are also being developed for African-American and Asian patients.

Commissioned by the APA Assembly, these curricula are intended to represent collectively a state-of-the-art description of psychiatric education regarding the needs of individuals from minority and traditionally underrepresented populations within the United States. They may be seen as a companion work to the growing body of clinically oriented volumes on the subject of the interaction of psychiatry, culture, and ethnicity.

Publications

Cultural Considerations in the Classification of Mental Disorders in Children and Adolescents

G Canino, I Canino, W Arroyo
In *DSM-IV Sourcebook, Volume 3*, chapter 42, 873-883; TA Widiger et al, eds.

A Curriculum for Learning About American Indians and Alaska Natives in Psychiatry Residency Training

JW Thompson
Academic Psychiatry, 1996; Vol 20, no 1:5-14

Describes a proposed curriculum for teaching psychiatric residents about the diagnosis and treatment of American Indians and Alaska natives. Presents the historical context, contemporary myths, and rationale for the inclusion of the proposed curriculum materials. Outlines the knowledge, skills, and attitudes needed by residents. The curriculum for the first and second years includes a basic history and description of Indian people, information on myths about the group, and psychiatric epidemiology and psychopathology. The third year includes clinical care and related areas such as service utilization and illness prevention, and the fourth includes a seminar to discuss psychotherapy and other clinical cases. Includes 70 references.

A Curriculum for Learning in Psychiatry Residencies about Homosexuality, Gay Men, and Lesbians

TS Stein
Academic Psychiatry, 1994; Vol 18, no 2:59-70

Recent research has greatly expanded knowledge about homosexuality, gay men, and lesbians.

This article proposes a basic model for integrating a nonpathological perspective into psychiatric residency curricula. Includes 85 references.

A Psychiatry Curriculum Directed to the Care of the Hispanic Patient

ES Garza-Trevino, P Ruiz, K Varegos-Samuel
Academic Psychiatry, 1997; 21:1-10

Describes a model curriculum for psychiatric residency programs that addresses the sociodemographic, epidemiological, psychosocial, cultural, and behavioral characteristics of Hispanics. It emphasizes that faculty who are knowledgeable about and sensitive to Hispanic culture should be available to supervise and teach psychiatric residents and that supervision should focus on cultural formulation, family dynamics, and other factors of importance in clinical psychiatric practice. Includes a 29-item bibliography and 56 references.

A Psychiatric Residency Curriculum About Gender and Women's Issues

A Spielvogel, LJ Dickson, GE Robinson
Academic Psychiatry, 1995; Vol 19, no 4:187-201

Over the last 30 years, major advances have been made in understanding how biological factors and sociocultural influences contribute to gender differences, gender identity formation, and gendered role behavior. This article presents an outline for a curriculum in gender and women's issues, including educational objectives, learning experiences through which residents could meet these objectives, and recommended readings. It discusses potential obstacles and suggests helpful strategies for implementing the proposed curriculum. Includes 96 references and suggested core readings.

American Society of Addiction Medicine

James F. Callahan, DPA
Executive Vice President
4601 N Park Ave, Upper Arcade, Ste 101
Chevy Chase, MD 20815
301 656-3920
301 656-3815 Fax
E-mail: jcal@asam.org
http://www.asam.org

Unit Addressing Cultural Competence

- **Cultural Issues Committee**

Programs and Activities

The American Society of Addiction Medicine
regularly addresses cultural competence issues at
annual medical-scientific conferences.

Improving Access to Care
for Underserved Groups

Patient Placement Criteria

American Society of Anesthesiologists

Glenn W. Johnson
Executive Director
520 Northwest Hwy
Park Ridge, IL 60068-2573
847 825-5586
847 825-1692 Fax
http://www.asahg.org

Policy

The American Society of Anesthesiologists has a policy addressing disparities and/or access to health care.

American Society of Clinical Oncology

John R. Durant, MD
Executive Vice President
225 Reinekers Ln, Ste 650
Alexandria, VA 22314
703 299-1080
703 299-1044 Fax

Policies

The American Society of Clinical Oncology has a
policy statement that is part of a coalition effort.

Relevant Health Care Issues

Scientific studies show an increased incidence of
certain cancers in minority populations.

College of American Pathologists

Lee VanBremen, PhD
Executive Vice President
325 Waukegan Rd
Northfield, IL 60093-2750
847 832-7500
847 832-8151 Fax
http://www.cap.org

Programs and Activities

The College of American Pathologists
encourages involvement in public advocacy and
ethics programs.

Relevant Health Care Issues

- Pap smear initiative targeting Latina,
  Hispanic, and Native American women

- Video news report encouraging organ
  donation within the minority community

Publications

- **America's Women: In Pursuit of Health**

- **Pap Examination: It Can Save Your Life**

- **Latinas at Higher Risk for Cervical Cancer**

Society for Adolescent Medicine

Lawrence Neinstein, MD
President
1916 NW Copper Oaks Circle
Blue Springs, MO 64015
816 224-8010
http://cortex.uchc.edu/~sam

The Society for Adolescent Medicine (SAM) is a multidisciplinary organization committed to improving the health and well-being of young people. The Society's goals are fulfilled through activities that include the development and dissemination of scientific research on adolescent health issues, professional development, and advocacy work at the local, state, and national level.

Organizational Body Addressing Cultural Competence

Special Interest Group for Multicultural/Multi-Ethnic Health Issues

Policies

- Further educate adolescent health coordinators on adolescent sexuality, including about gay and lesbian youth.

- Support programs of education and training on homosexuality and related issues for professionals working with children, youth, and families.

- Develop a more experiential learning approach for adult health providers and parents to enhance their skills for coping with adolescents.

- Health leaders should explore the impact of all discussions that deal with public health problems on special populations of adolescents, especially gay and lesbian youth.

- Services, providers, and delivery sites must consider the cultural, ethnic, and social diversity among adolescents.

- Educate the police about alienated youth and reduce homophobia through education.

- Provide culturally sensitive teaching staff that reflect the ethnic and cultural mix of society and provide appropriate role models.

- The basic educational programs for teachers, physicians, nurses and other health-related occupations should include information on the etiology, demography, and health implications of sexual orientation.

Relevant Minority Population Health Care Issues

The Special Interest Group on Multicultural/Multi-Ethnic Health Issues addresses both the health needs of racially and ethnically diverse groups of adolescents and also looks at issues of diversity in the health care workforce.

Publications

Journal of Adolescent Health

The September and October 1998 issues of the *Journal* were devoted to cultural competence and adolescent health. Journal articles included information on adolescents from a variety of racial and ethnic backgrounds and on lesbian, gay, and bisexual youth.

- **Cultural Diversity and Health Care Delivery, Part I**
  Volume 23, no 3, September 1998

- **Cultural Diversity and Health Care Delivery, Part II**
  Volume 23, no 4, October 1998

C. State Medical Societies

Indiana State Medical Association

Richard R. King, JD
Executive Director
322 Canal Walk, Canal Level
Indianapolis, IN 46202-3252
317 261-2060
317 261-2076 Fax
E-mail: Rking@ismanet.org
http://www.ismanet.org

Policies

Resolution 90-33A – Care—Compassion & Dignity

Massachusetts Medical Society (MMS)

Harry L. Greene II, MD
Executive Vice President
1440 Main St
Waltham, MA 02154
781 893-4610
781 893-9136 Fax
E-mail: hgreene@mms.org
http://www.massmed.org

Unit Addressing Cultural Competence

- **Committee on Ethnic Diversity**

Policies

The Massachusetts Medical Society (MMS) has policy addressing disparities and access to health care. The policy reads, in part, that the Society "will promote a coordinated strategy for increasing access to medical care for minority populations; heightening awareness of cultural practices through education; and creating greater opportunities for minorities and immigrants within the medical profession, including participation in the MMS."

Programs and Activities

- Educational program: "Practice in a Multi-Cultural Society: Are Physicians Culturally Competent?"

- Joint Committee Educational Series, which covered the topics of Ayurvedic medicine, Chinese medicine, and the Brigham & Women's Hospital Medical Student Mission to Central America

- Strategic planning meeting: "Meeting Health Care Needs in Minority Communities"

Minority Medical Students and Physicians

Biomedical Science Careers Project: a cosponsored educational program and mentorship career fair.

Improving Access to Care

- Cosponsors Multi-Cultural Senior Citizen Program

- Participates in numerous free clinics serving ethnic minorities

Publication

Refugees and Immigrants in Massachusetts

Medical Association of Georgia

Paul L. Shanor
Executive Director
1330 W Peachtree St NW, Ste 500
Atlanta, GA 30309
404 881-5031
404 881-5021 Fax
E-mail: PShanor@mag.org
http://www.mag.org

Policies

245.000 Infant Health

245.007 Black-White Infant Mortality GAP Policy

245.004 Infant Mortality Investigation of Deaths

245.003 Infant Mortality Risk Factors

245.002 Maternal and Infant Health Council

245.006 Perinatal Care Delivery Plan

255.000 International Medical Graduates

Relevant Health Care Issues

- Infant mortality

- AIDS

- High blood pressure

- Teenage pregnancy

Medical Society of the District of Columbia

K. Edward Shanbacker
Executive Director
2175 K St NW, Ste 200
Washington, DC 20037-1809
202 466-1800
202 452-1542 Fax
E-mail: shanback@msdc.org
http://www.msdc.org

Units Addressing Cultural Competence

- **Council on Grassroots and Community Activities**

- **Task Force on Family Violence**

Relevant Health Care Issues

The medical society addresses issues of concern to African Americans.

Minority Medical Students

The medical society conduts a Medical Student Spanish Education Program.

Programs and Activities

The Task Force on Family Violence addresses physician understanding of patients' culture in a symposium format on a regular basis.

Publications and Other Resources

The Task Force on Family Violence offers printed resources.

Medical Society of the State of New York

Charles N. Aswad, MD
Executive Vice President
420 Lakeville Rd, PO Box 5404
Lake Success, NY 11042-5404
516 488-6100
516 488-6136 Fax
E-mail: ccaplan@mssny.org
http://www.mssny.org

Unit Addressing Cultural Competence

The medical society has a unit that deals with
cultural competence.

Policies

The medical society has a policy addressing
disparities and/or access to health care.

Improving Access to Care for Underserved Groups

The medical society has programs to improve
access to care for underserved groups.

Publications and Other Resources

The medical society has publications and other
resources related to cultural competence.

Minnesota Medical Association

Contact

Paul S. Sanders, MD
Chief Executive Officer
3433 Broadway St NE, Ste 300
Minneapolis, MN 55413-1760
612 378-1875
612 378-3875 Fax
E-mail: psanders@mnmed.org
http://www.mnmed.org

Unit Addressing Cultural Competence

The Minnesota Medical Association (MMA) has a
committee that deals with minority health issues.

Relevant Health Care Issues

- Infant mortality

- Teen pregnancies

- HIV/AIDS

- TB

- Immunizations

Improving Access to Care for Underserved Groups

The MMA is currently developing a mentoring
program directed specifically at minority students in
junior high schools.

North Carolina Medical Society

Contact: Mike Edwards
Director, Communications
PO Box 27167
222 N Person St
Raleigh, NC 27601
919 833-3836 or 800 722-1350
919 833-2023 Fax
E-mail: medwards@ncmedsoc.org

Unit Addressing Cultural Competence

- Several different units of the North Carolina Medical Association (NCMS) are addressing the issue of cultural competence. Programs that address cultural competence in part are described under "Relevant Health Care Issues."

- The NCMS Executive Council is currently considering whether to insist "whenever practical" that medically trained interpreters be provided for non-English-speaking patients who need medical treatment.

Policies

Facilitating Medical Services for North Carolina's Migrant and Immigrant Populations addresses the needs of the state's fast-growing Hispanic population.

Relevant Health Care Issues

- Creating Healthy and Responsible Teens (CHART)

- Recruitment of physicians by NCMS to serve as volunteer mentors in a program targeting underprivileged and minority youth who are interested in health careers

Improving Access to Care for Underserved Groups

The NCMS Foundation seeks to improve access to care for underserved groups by increasing school-based health centers and bringing physicians and health educators into schools through the CHART program. The Foundation is also developing materials for patients in Spanish and other languages.

The NCMS will offer its members educational programs that discuss the special problems encountered by migrant workers in seeking and receiving appropriate health care.

The NCMS Kate B. Reynolds Community Practitioner Program focuses on providing primary health care to underserved communities through consultation with community and primary practices and assistance in obtaining primary care providers in their area, through repayment of educational loans in exchange for service in underserved communities.

Oklahoma State Medical Association

Brian O. Foy
Executive Director
601 W I-44 Service Rd
Oklahoma City, OK 73118
405 843-9571
405 842-1834 Fax
E-mail: foy@osmaonline.org
http://www.osmaonline.org

Unit Addressing Cultural Competence

The Oklahoma State Medical Association (OSMA)
formed a unit to address cultural competence in
early 1999.

Relevant Health Care Issues

The OSMA is addressing African-American,
Native-American, and Hispanic-American health
care issues.

South Dakota State Medical Association

Robert D. Johnson
Chief Executive Officer
1323 S Minnesota Ave
Sioux Falls, SD 57105
605 336-1965
605 336-0270 Fax
http://www.usd.edu/med/sdsma/

Relevant Health Care Issues

The South Dakota State Medical Association (SDSMA) works to address Native American health care issues, particularly diabetes and alcoholism.

Programs and Activities

Minority Medical Students and Physicians

The SDSMA has a program in which practicing physicians pay dues for all medical students.

Improving Access to Care for Underserved Groups

The medical association has programs for physicians on Native American culture and diversity issues.

Texas Medical Association

Louis J. Goodman, PhD
Executive Vice President/CEO
401 W 15th St
Austin, TX 78701-1680
512 370-1300
512 370-1633 Fax
E-mail: lou_g@texmed.org
http://www.texmed.org

Units Addressing Cultural Competence

- Committee on Physician Distribution and Health-Care Access

- International Medical Graduate (IMG) Section

- Council on Public Health

Policies

The Texas Medical Association (TMA) has policy in support of access to care for all Texans.

Minority Issues

Relevant Health Care Issues

- Large Hispanic population living along the Texas-Mexico border that suffers disproportionately from diabetes and environmentally related health risks, including poor water quality and infectious diseases.

- Large African American and Native American populations.

- Disproportionate incidence rates among Black Texans for diabetes, heart disease, and strokes.

- Many minority Texans are indigent and unable to pay for health services.

- The Texas Medical Association's (TMA) Physician Oncology Education Program offers training materials on cancer control in special populations.

Minority Medical Students and Physicians

- International Medical Graduate Section

- Minority Scholarship Program for medical students with goal to increase the number of minority physicians serving underserved populations.

Improving Access to Care for Underserved Groups

The TMA Council on Public Health oversees matters relating to border health, which affect large numbers of Hispanics.

The TMA is also the originator of "Live and Then Give," an organ donation program adopted by the AMA Medical Student Section and the Minority Affairs Consortium. The program is intended to encourage physicians to become organ donors and to present information to their patients; it is particularly aimed at increasing organ donations in minority communities.

State Medical Society of Wisconsin

John E. Patchett, JD
Executive Vice President
330 E Lakeside St
PO Box 1109
Madison, WI 53701-1109
608 257-6781
608 283-5401 Fax
E-mail: JohnP@smswi.org
http://www.district-1.org/rps.html

Unit Addressing Cultural Competence

International Medical Graduate Section

Relevant Minority Population Health Care Issues

- Underserved areas and populations

- Medicaid reimbursement

- Insurance coverage

- Lead poisoning

Improving Access to Care for Underserved Groups

The medical society has a policy addressing
disparities and/or access to health care and offers
two programs to help improve access to care for
underserved groups: PartnerCare and
WisconsinCare.

Section II

Resources Emphasizing Communication Skills

Because accurate communication is essential for all stages of medical care, from diagnosis to discharge planning and beyond, the importance of respectful communication permeates all strategies to provide culturally effective health care. Physician communication has been examined as a diagnostic and treatment tool for the past 20 years, and improved communication skills have been shown to facilitate quality medical care within the managed care setting and cut the risk of malpractice suits.

Adverse outcomes of inadequate physician-patient communication are exacerbated when patients' backgrounds and expectations differ from those of the physician, providing compelling medical and financial arguments for requiring "cultural competence" of all health care staff. But current medical education and care delivery systems present multiple barriers to the provision of culturally effective care. Moreover, there is now a perceived crisis in the area of physician-patient communication in general, as noted in medical publications (*AMNews*, May 11, 1998) and in the public press (*Chicago Tribune* interview with Nancy Dickey, MD, May 31, 1998). The effects of inadequate communication are readily apparent in such crucial areas as organ donation, with the rate of donors changing very little in spite of increased legislation in recent years.

Poor literacy is one of the areas receiving widespread attention as a barrier to communication and hence to effective care. "The AMA's Environment," a February 1999, report from the AMA Council on Long-Range Planning and Development, points out that, "Poor literacy is a national crisis. One quarter of the adult population, 40 to 44 million Americans, is functionally illiterate. Another 50 million have only marginal literacy skills, meaning almost half our adult population has basic deficiencies in reading, computational skills, or English." The February 10, 1999, issue of the *Journal of the American Medical Association* reports that low health literacy is a major cause of rehospitalization and other unnecessary and expensive complications among the elderly, the group that uses medical services most often; the decline in health literacy occurs regardless of education level.

As indicated in the following pages, efforts are under way to improve physician-patient communication. Physicians and behavioral scientists regularly offer undergraduate, graduate, and continuing physician professional development courses in patient-centered care and the physician-patient relationship that focus on respectful communication. In some medical specialties, especially those with mental health and primary care components, accredited residencies are required to have a specific curriculum in behavioral and psychosocial medicine, and some curricula include specific units of instruction on communicating with special populations. Professional associations and accrediting bodies are beginning to discuss revising accreditation standards to reflect the communication skills needed to care for patients from diverse cultural backgrounds in a variety of health care settings.

The following information is provided to assist physicians in their efforts to break down the multiple barriers to respectful communication and to provide the best possible care to each individual patient.

Section Contents

A. Organizations

- American Medical Association

- Other Organizations

B. Publications

- Books

- Journal Articles and Book Chapters

A. Organizations

American Medical Association

Policies

E-5.05	*Confidentiality*
E-8.18	*Informing Families of a Patient's Death*
E-9.12	*Physician-Patient Relationship: Respect for Law and Human Rights*
H-85.979	*Informing Families of a Patient's Death: Guidelines for the Involvement of Medical Students*
H-160.931	*Health Literacy*
H-140.948	*Medical Futility in End-of-Life Care*
H-140.953	*Patient Responsibilities*
H-140.975	*Fundamental Elements of the Patient-Physician Relationship*
H-140.990	*Ethical Considerations in Health Care*
H-210.986	*Physicians and Family Caregivers – A Model for Partnership*
H-295.950	*Patient Physician Communication*
H-295.975	*Educating Competent and Caring Health Professionals*
H-350.987	*Hispanic Health in the United States*
H-350.996	*Health Care of the American Indian*

Selected Reports

Adolescents as Victims of Family Violence
JAMA, October 20, 1993; 1850-1856

Alcoholism and Alcohol Abuse Among Women
LN Blum, NH Nielsen, JA Riggs
Journal of Women's Health, September 1998;
7:861-871

Alcoholism in the Elderly
JAMA, March 13, 1996; 275:797-801

Confidential Health Services for Adolescents
JAMA, March 17, 1993; 269:1420-1424

Decisions Near the End-of-Life
JAMA, April 22-29, 1992; 267(16):2229-33

Educating Physicians in Home Health Care
JAMA, February 13, 1991; 265:769-771

Encouraging Medical Student Education on Alternative Health Care Practices
Council on Medical Education Report 2, I-97

Enhancing the Cultural Competence of Physicians
Council on Medical Education Report 5-A-98

Gender Discrimination in the Medical Profession
Women's Health Issues, Spring 1994; 4(1):1-11

Gender Disparities in Clinical Decision Making
JAMA, July 24-31, 1991; 266(4):559-62

Good Care of the Dying Patient
JAMA, February 14, 1996; 275:474-478

Health Care Needs of Gay Men and Lesbians in the United States
JAMA May 1, 1996; 275:1354-1359

Health Literacy
JAMA, February 10, 1999; 281:552-557
Council on Scientific Affairs, Ad Hoc Committee on Health Literacy June, 1998

IN CSA Report 1-A-98 the AMA called on medical schools, residency programs, and CME courses to teach doctors to deal more effectively with patients who have poor literacy skills. The AMA also encouraged the US Department of Education to include questions about health and problems communicating with health care workers on its National Adult Literacy Survey of 2002.

The report described the complex array of communications difficulties resulting from inadequate health literacy. Preliminary studies indicate that inadequate health literacy may increase the risk of hospitalization.

Hispanic Health in the United States
JAMA, January 1, 1991; 265:248-252

Medical Education and Training in Women's Health
Considered at the 1999 Annual Meeting
(Available upon request)

Medical Futility in End-of-Life Care
JAMA, March 10, 1999; 281(10):937-41

Physicians and Family Caregivers: a Model for Partnership
JAMA, March 10, 1993; 269:1282-1284

Racial and Ethnic Disparities in Health Care
Board of Trustees Report 50-I-95

Violence Against Women
JAMA, June 17, 1992; 267:3184-3189

Publications

See complete text of AMNews *articles in Section X.*

Culturally Effective Communication
AMNews, Feb 22, 1999

Different Doctors Make Decisions in Different Ways
M Moran
AMNews, Feb 8 1999

Mistaking Medicine
DL Shelton
AMNews, September 21, 1998

Patients' Lack of Literacy May Contribute to Billions of Dollars in Higher Hospital Costs
Charles Marwick
JAMA, 1997; Vol 278, pp 971-972

Physician-Patient Communication Skills for Improving Patient Relations
Christine Hinz
American Medical Association, Anticipated Publication date: Fall 1999

Based on interviews with key medical experts, this book covers:

- Effective medical interviewing

- Differing communication styles of men and women

- Communication strategies with various personality types, including the so-called "difficult" patient

- How doctors can understand their own reactions

- Recognizing the mentally ill patient

- Overcoming cultural barriers

- Breaking bad news to the patient and family

- Understanding family dynamics and other lifestyle situations

- Improving treatment outcomes with good communication and listening skills

- Ethics in communications

Other Organizations

American Academy on Physician and Patient (AAPP)

A 500-member physician organization that collaborates with the Bayer Institute to provide interpersonal training for health care professionals.

AT&T Language Line Services

Building 2
1 Lower Ragsdale Dr
Monterrey, CA 93940
800 752-0093

Offers over-the-phone translator services 7 days a week, 24 hours a day, in 140 languages for a per-minute fee. Subscription/volume rates available.

Bayer Institute for Health Care Communication

400 Morgan Lane
Westhaven, CT 06516
800 800-5907
http://bayerinstitute.com

Offers workshops stressing the importance of interpersonal skills for which physicians can receive continuing medical education credits. Listening is presented as a means of enhancing the accuracy of diagnosis and treatment.

Center for Health Care Strategies (CHCS)

353 Nassau St
Princeton, NJ 08540

CHCS and Pfizer sponsored a national conference (June 3, 1997, Washington, DC) addressing the importance for patients to be functionally literate in order to navigate the health care system. Illiterate patients were found to be at greater risk of misunderstanding their diagnosis, prescriptions, and self-care instructions.

Center for Multicultural Health (CMH)

105 14th Ave, Ste 2C
Seattle, WA 98122
206 461-6910

The CMH program provides interpreters in over 30 languages to increase access to community health center services for individuals with limited English proficiency.

Center for the Study of Adult Literacy

Georgia State University
University Plaza
Atlanta, GA 30303-3083
404 651-2405

The widely used *Short Test of Functional Health Literacy in Adults* was co-developed by Joanne R. Nurss, former director of Georgia State University's Center for the Study of Adult Literacy.

Cross Cultural Health Care Program

1200 12th Ave S
Seattle, WA 98144d
http://www.xculture.org

Has bilingual medical glossaries, guides for interpreters, articles on interpreting, and videos including, *Communicating Effectively Through an Interpreter*.

Health and Literacy Compendium

http://hub1.worlded.org/health/comp/index.html

An annotated bibliography of print and Web-based health materials for limited-literacy adults.

Henry J Kaiser Family Foundation

2400 Sand Hill Road
Menlo, CA 94025
650 854-9400
800 656-4533
http://www.kff.org

Ensuring Linguistic Access in Health Care Settings: Legal Rights and Responsibilities
Publication # 1362

Language Barriers to Health Care
Papers from the Henry J Kaiser Foundation Forum
Journal of Health Care for the Poor and Underserved, Vol. 9 (Suppl), 1998

Topics include:

- The Pervading Role of Language on Health

- Improving Access for Limited English-Speaking Consumers: A Review of Strategies in Health Care Setting

- Legal Protection To Ensure Linguistically Appropriate Health Care

Langua Tutor

30150 Telegraph Rd, Ste 385
Bingham Farms, MI 48025
248 645-6663
translat@languatutor.com
http://www.languatutor.com

Offers telephone and on-site interpreter services and document translation in 25 languages.

Language Interpreter Services and Translations (LIST)

Department of Social and Health Services (DSHS)
Box 45820
Olympia, WA 98504-5820
360 902-8117

In 1991, DSHS initiated an effort to certify medical and social service interpreters and translators; LIST was created to develop and oversee the testing process.

Massachusetts Medical Interpreter Association in conjunction with Education Development Center

750 Washington St
NEMC Box 271
Boston, MA 02111-1845
Education Development Center
800 225-4276

This project developed comprehensive medical interpreter standards of practice based on a content analysis of interpreter skills and work responsibilities. Resource for interpreters around the country, guidelines for assessing the quality and qualifications of interpreters, publications, videos, training.

Meharry Medical College Institute on Health Care for the Poor and Underserved

1005 Dr DB Todd Jr Blvd
Nashville, TN 37208
615 327-6204

The *Journal of Health Care for the Poor and Underserved p*ublished four times a year by the Institute on Health Care for the Poor and Underserved at Meharry Medical College. Papers from the Henry J Kaiser Foundation Forum: Language Barriers to Health were presented in the *Language Barriers to Health Care* issue (Vol 9 Suppl, 1998).

Minnesota Department of Health

717 Delaware St SE
Minneapolis, MN 55440
651 215-5800
http://www.health.state.mn.us

Offers a variety of multilingual videotapes available on loan or for purchase in the following broad categories: general health, women's health, infant and child health, and nutrition. Titles include *Hmong Family Planning; A Visit to the Doctor* and *A Visit to the Hospital* (Cambodian, Hmong, Loatian, Vietnamese and Spanish versions); *A Beautiful Future* (Vietnamese); *Before It's Too Late, Vaccinate* (Spanish); and *Choosing Cambodian Food Wisely.*

National Patient Safety Foundation (NPSF)

515 N State St
Chicago, IL 60610
312 464-4848
312 464-4154
E-mail: npsf@ama-assn.org
http://www.npsf.org

Founded in 1997, the National Patient Safety Foundation (NPSF) is an independent, nonprofit research and education organization dedicated to the measurable improvement of patient safety in

the delivery of health care. Through the NPSF, health care clinicians, institutional providers, health product manufacturers, researchers, legal advisors, patient/consumer advocates, regulators, and policy makers are working together to make health care safer for patients.

The NPSF Communications Program will explore ways to raise awareness of the influence of cultural competence on patient safety. Activities toward this goal will include an article in the NPSF quarterly newsletter, *Focus on Patient Safety*. NPSF staff are also recommending that cultural competence be addressed at NPSF regional forums, which bring together community and health care leaders for candid discussions of patient safety. Local planners of the Wisconsin regional forum, for example, are considering the topic for a breakout session.

In addition to the NPSF quarterly newsletter, *Focus on Patient Safety*, other resources include the *News Brief*, a semimonthly glance at patient safety activities occurring nationwide; the NPSF Clearinghouse, a repository of information on patient safety and related topics; and the NPSF Web site, an online resource for patient safety literature, activities, and related Web sites.

New York University School of Medicine

New York Task Force on Immigration Health
Division of Primary Care
550 First Ave
New York, NY 10016

The Task Force has several publications on interpreting, including:

Access Through Medical Interpreter and Language Services: Research and Recommendations, 1997

An Introduction to Medical Interpretation: A Trainer's Manual, 1997

Pacific Interpreters

1020 SW Taylor, Ste 280
Portland, OR 97205
800 223-8899
503 223-8899
information@pacinterp.com
http://www.pacinterp.com

Offers fee-for-service telephone and
videoconference interpreting as well as document
translation services in more than 100 languages
and translators trained in clinical terminology.
Telephone service available 24 hours a day, seven
days a week. On-site interpreters available in
Pacific Northwest area.

Resources for Cross Cultural Health Care

Julia Puebla Fortier, Director
8915 Sudbury Rd
Silver Spring, MD 20901
301 588-6051
http://www.diversityrx.org

National network of individuals and organizations
in ethnic communities and health care organized to
offer technical assistance and information on
linguistic and cultural competence in health care.
Focuses on medical interpretation program design
and training, policy analysis and development,
research, and community advocacy. Has an
Interpreter Associations section in its DiversityRx
website. (See additional information in Section IV.)

B. Publications

Books

Caring for Patients from Different Cultures: Case Studies from American Hospitals
GA Galanti
University of Pennsylvania Press, 1997

Includes 172 case studies of actual conflicts and misunderstandings. Illustrates how conflicts may result in inferior medical care.

Communicating with Medical Patients
M Stewart, D Roter, eds.
London: Sage, 1989

Culture and the Clinical Encounter: An Intercultural Sensitizer for the Health Professions
RC Gropper
Intercultural Press, 1996

Reviews 44 critical incidents in which cultural differences played a part in the breakdown of health professional/client communication. The incidents include coverage of 23 cultural and ethnic groups. The reader is asked to choose from four possible explanations; answers and discussion are provided in a separate section of the book.

Developing Intercultural Communication Skills
V Ricard
Krieger Publishing Co, 1993

Aims to identify human responses to commonality and diversity; identify and develop intercultural communication and interaction skills in valuing, observing, listening, thinking, speaking, and gesturing; recognize the influence of human values on the interaction process; and use a practical, flexible framework for ongoing learning and personal development in the area of intercultural communication and interaction.

Directing Health Messages Towards African Americans: Attitudes Toward Health Care and the Mass Media
JL Sylvester
Garland Publishing, 1998

Explores diversity and similarities between white and African-American populations, with specific information on how health messages can be effectively communicated to African Americans. Includes chapters on communication theories and crafting an effective health campaign.

Educating Doctors: Crisis in Medical Education, Research and Practice
S Wolf
Transaction Publishers, 1997

Critiques the current status of medical education, with specific emphasis on lack of doctor-patient discussions and proper medical history taking. Has extensive bibliography.

An Examination of the Long-Term Effects of Psychosocial Teaching on the Practice of Medicine [Thesis]
J Lyles
East Lansing, MI: Michigan State University, 1996

An Introduction to Spanish for Health Care Workers
RO Chase, CB Medina de Chase
Yale University Press, 1998

Focuses on vocabulary and grammar, including colloquial terms and slang used by Spanish-speaking patients. Provides informative cultural notes on Hispanic values and customs.

The Medical Interview: Clinical Care, Education, and Research
M Lipkin, S Putman, A Lazare, eds.
New York: Springer-Verlag, 1995

The Medical Interview: A Three Function Approach
SA Cohen-Cole
Mosby-Year Book, 1991

Medicine and the Family: A Feminist Perspective
L Candib
New York: Basic Books Publishers, 1995

The Patient's Story: Integrated Patient-Doctor Interviewing
RC Smith
Boston: Lippincott-Raven, 1996

The Physician's Guide to Better Communication
BF Sharf
Scott, Foresman and Company, 1984

Practical guide for the improvement of communication skills to enhance the physician-patient relationships, as well as relationships with other health care professionals.

Teaching Supplement for the Patient's Story: Integrated Patient-Doctor Interviewing
RC Smith
East Lansing, MI: Michigan State University, 1996

Who Has Seen a Blood Sugar? Reflections on Medical Education
F Davidoff
Philadelphia: American College of Physicians, 1996

Journals, Journal Articles, and Book Chapters

Are Patients of Women Physicians Screened More Aggressively? A Prospective Study of Physician Gender and Screening
MW Kreuter, VJ Strecher, R Harris, SC Kobrin, CS Skinner
J Gen Intern Med, 1995; 10:119-125

Bad News: Delivery, Dialogue, and Dilemmas
TE Quill, P Townsend
Arch Intern Med, 1991; 151:463-468

Becoming a Doctor: Critical-Incident Reports from Third-Year Medical Students
W Branch, RJ Pels, RS Lawrence, R Arky
N Engl J Med, 1993; 329:1130-1132

Calibrating the Physician: Personal Awareness and Effective Patient Care
DH Novack, AL Suchman, W Clark, RM Epstein, E Najberg, C Kaplan
Working Group on Promoting Physician Personal Awareness
American Academy on Physician and Patient
JAMA, 1997; 278:502-509

Describes how each physician needs "insight into how one's life experience and emotional makeup affect one's interactions with patients, families and other professionals." "Support groups, Balint groups, and discussions of meaningful experiences" are recommended for physicians to assess how their various "cultural" manifestations can interfere with delivering patient-centered care.

Includes 141 references covering cultural competence issues relating to the physician-patient relationship and patient-centered care.

Changes in Student's Attitudes Following a Course on Death and Dying: A Controlled Comparison
J Kaye, E Gracely, G Loscalzo
J Cancer Educ, 1994; 9:77-81

Communication Through Interpreters in Health Care: Ethical Dilemmas Arising from Differences in Class, Culture, Language and Power
JM Kaufert, RW Putsch
J Clin Ethics, 1997; 8:71-87

Contributions of the History, Physical Examination, and Laboratory Investigation in Making Medical Diagnoses
MC Peterson, JH Holbrook, D Von Hales, NL Smith, LV Staker
West J Med, 1992; 156:163-165

A Controlled Trial To Improve Care for Seriously Ill Hospitalized Patients: The Study To Understand Prognoses and Preferences for Outcomes and Risks of Treatment (SUPPORT)
SUPPORT Principal Investigators
JAMA, 1995; 274:1591-1598

Cross-Cultural Communication in the Physician's Office
JD Mull
West J Med, 1993; 159:609-613

Cross-Cultural Communication: The Special Case of Interpreters in Health Care
Robert Putsch III
JAMA, 1985; 254:3344-3348

Cultural Diversity Meets End-of-Life Decision-Making

B Jennings
Hospitals and Health Networks, September 20, 1994, p 72

Dealing with Patients from Other Cultures

Robert W Putsch III, Marlie Joyce
In *Clinical Methods,* 3rd edition.
HK Walker, WD Hall, JW Hurst, eds.
Boston: Butterworth - Heinemann, 1990, pp 1050-1065

The Difficult Patient: Prevalence, Psychopathology, and Functional Impairment

SR Hahn, K Kroenke, RL Spitzer, et al
J Gen Intern Med, 1996; 11:1-8

The Efficacy of Intensive Biopsychosocial Teaching Programs for Residents: A Review of the Literature and Guidelines for Teaching

RC Smith, AA Marshall, SA Cohen-Cole
J Gen Intern Med, 1994; 9:390-396

The Effect of Race and Sex on Physicians' Recommendations for Cardiac Catheterization

KA Schulman, JA Berlin, W Harless, et al
N Engl J Med, Feb 25, 1999; 340(8):618-626

The study found that "the race and sex of a patient independently influence how physicians manage chest pain." The authors suggest that this is due to "bias on the part of the physicians [which may] represent overt prejudice on the part of physicians or, more likely, could be the result of subconscious perceptions." The negative outcomes from such perceptions could be reduced as a result of a more culturally competent physician workforce and a medical profession that better reflects a diverse population.

The Effectiveness of Intensive Training for Residents in Interviewing: A Randomized, Controlled Study

RC Smith, JS Lyles, J Mettler, BE Stoffelmayr, LF Van Egeren, AA Marshall, et al
Ann Intern Med, 1998; 128:118-126

The 76 references guide readers to resources that emphasize "patient-centered" interviewing skills.

The Effects of Two Continuing Medical Education Programs on Communication Skills of Practicing Primary Care Physicians

W Levinson, D Roter
J Gen Intern Med, 1993; 8:318-324

Empowerment Techniques: From Doctor-Centered (Balint Approach) to Patient-Centered Discussion Groups

PB Luban
Patient Educ Counseling, 1995; 26:257-263

Ethnicity and Attitudes Towards Patient Autonomy

LJ Blackhall, et al
JAMA, 1995; 274:820-825

Evaluating a Faculty Development Course on Medical Interviewing

GH Gordon, K Rost
In: *The Medical Interview: Clinical Care, Education and Research*
M Lipkin Jr, SM Putnam, A Lazare, eds.
New York: Springer-Verlag NY, 1995:436-447

An Evaluation of Residency Training in Interviewing Skills and the Psychosocial Domain of Medical Practice

DL Roter, KA Cole, DE Kern, LR Barker, M Grayson
J Gen Intern Med, 1990; 5:347-354

Gender in Medicine: The Views of First and Fifth Year Medical Students

D Field, A Lennox
Med Educ, 1996; 30:246-252

Health and Literacy Compendium

http://hub1.worlded.org/health/comp/index.html

An annotated bibliography of print and web-based health materials for use with limited-literacy adults.

The Health Care Experience of Patients with Low Literacy

DW Baker, RM Parker, MV Williams, K Pitkin, NS Parikh, W Coates, M Imara
Arch Fam Med, 1996; 5:329-334

Patients with low literacy harbor a deep sense of shame, which is reinforced by hospital staff who become frustrated or angry when someone cannot complete a form or read instructions. Seeking medical care is intimidating for patients with low literacy because they cannot understand signs and registration forms. Many patients recounted medication errors resulting from their inability to read labels.

Health Literacy Among Medicare Enrollees in a Managed Care Organization

Julie Gazmararian, et al
JAMA, February 10, 1999, Vol 281, No 6, pp 545-551

Researchers at the Prudential Center for Health Care Research (Atlanta), along with physicians from Emory University and Case Western Reserve School of Medicine, used the *Short Test of Functional Health Literacy in Adults* to survey 3,260 Medicare patients enrolled in the Prudential HMO. Results showed that even literate people may have low literacy in a health care setting because there is so much medical jargon. They found that the decline in literacy at advancing age occurs regardless of education. Patients with low health literacy and chronic diseases, such as diabetes, asthma, or hypertension, have less knowledge of their disease and its treatment and fewer correct self-management skills than literate patients. These factors may explain why patients with inadequate functional health literacy are more likely to be hospitalized than those with adequate health literacy. Some patients could not read basic items commonly found in the health care setting, such as prescription bottles and appointment slips.

The Heart of Darkness: The Impact of Perceived Mistakes on Physicians

JF Christensen, W Levinson, PM Dunn
J Gen Med, 1992; 7:424-431

How Do Patients Want Physicians To Handle Mistakes? A Survey of Internal Medicine Patients in an Academic Setting

AB Witman, DM Park, SB Hardin
Arch Intern Med, 1996; 156:2565-2569

The Illness Narratives: Suffering, Healing, and the Human Condition

A Kleinman
New York: Basic Books, 1988

Incorporating Multiculturalism Into a Doctor-Patient Course

AR Gupta, TP Duffy, MC Johnson
Academic Medicine, 1997; 72:428.

The Influence of Gender on Physician Practice Style

KD Bertakis, LC Helms, EJ Callahan, et al
Med Care, 1995; 33:407-416

Informed Consent, Cultural Sensitivity and Respect for Persons

LO Gostin
JAMA, 1995; 274:844-845

Language in Cross-Cultural Care

Robert W Putsch, Marlie Joyce
In *Clinical Methods*, 3rd edition
HK Walker, WD Hall, JW Hurst, eds.
Boston: Butterworth - Heinemann, 1990

The Language of Medical Case Histories
William J. Donnelly
Ann Intern Med, 1997; 127:1045-1048

Case histories are "formative institutions that shape as well as reflect the thought, the talk, and the actions of trainees and their teachers," according to William Donnelly, who urges that the patient's personal situation or perspective be made an integral part of the written record. Donnelly examines seven "language maladies" that recur in writing case histories (and offers useful remedies for them):

1. "Introducing the sick person solely as a biological specimen, . . . [which] paves the way for a case history that describes the patient's sickness primarily, or even exclusively, in terms of disordered biology."

2. "Translating the patient's 'chief complaint' into biomedical language . . . [, which] banishes the voice of the patient from the one place specifically reserved for it even in disease-oriented case histories."

3. "Using rhetorical devices that . . . enhance the credibility of physicians and laboratory data and cast doubt on the reliability of the patient's testimony. In these histories, the patient 'says,' 'reports,' 'states,' 'claims,' or 'denies.'"

4. "Converting the patient's story of illness, his or her human experience of being sick, disabled, or simply worried, into a history of present illness focused solely on the onset and course of biological dysfunction."

5. "Categorizing what the patient says as 'subjective' and what the physician learns from physical examination and laboratory studies as 'objective.' "

6. "Pathologizing the patient's thoughts or feelings (for example, by calling a poor understanding of a medical condition 'denial' or labeling mere sadness 'depression')."

7. "Failing to elicit and record important changes in the patient's perspective,"

especially at the end of life, when "failing to determine the medical goals and preferences of a seriously ill patient in a timely, proactive manner can result in unwanted interventions."

Donnelly believes that "the dubious language practices used in conventional 20th-century medical case histories harm students and practitioners of medicine as well as patients." He advocates an "accurate understanding of the probabilistic, observer-mediated nature of all clinical knowledge" and advises physicians to work with patients "as partners, not adversaries, . . . to attend adequately to patients' suffering."

Managing Personal and Professional Boundaries: How To Make the Physician's Own Issue a Resource in Patient Care
SH McDaniel, TL Campbell, B Seaburn
Fam Syst Med, 1989; 7:1-12

The Medical Interview and Psychosocial Aspects of Medicine: Block Curricula for Residents
PR Williamson, RC Smith, DE Kern, M Lipkin, LR Baker, RB Hoppe, et al
J Gen Intern Med, 1992; 7:235-242

Medical Interviewing and Interpersonal Skills Teaching in US Medical Schools. Progress, Problems, and Promise
DH Novack, G Volk, DA Drossman, M Lipkin
JAMA, 1993; 269:2101-2105

Medical Interviewing: The Crucial Skill That Gets Short Shrift
F Davidoff
In *Who Has Seen a Blood Sugar? Reflections on Medical Education*
Philadelphia: American College of Physicians, 1996, pp 76-80

Medical Records, Medical Education, and Patient Care: The Problem-Oriented Medical Record as a Basic Tool
LL Weed
Cleveland, OH: Press of Case Western Univ, 1969

Methodology in Cross-Cultural Care
RW Putsch and M Joyce
In *Clinical Methods*, 3rd edition
HK Walker, WD Hall, JW Hurst, eds.
Boston: Butterworth-Heinemann, 1990

A Model of Empathic Communication in the Medical Interview
AL SuchmanL, K Markakis, HB Beckman, et al
JAMA, 1997; 277:678-682

The Narrative Road To Empathy
R Charon
In *Empathy and the Practice of Medicine: Beyond Pills and the Scalpel*
New Haven, Conn: Yale University Press, 1993:147-159

One America in the 21st Century: Forging a New Future
The President's Initiative on Race
Advisory Board to the President
September 1998

Complete text available at:
http://www.whitehouse.gov/Initiatives/OneAmerica/cevent.html

Reflects the results of a 15-month effort by seven board members, chaired by John Hope Franklin, to discover the role race plays in civil rights enforcement, education, poverty, employment, housing, stereotyping, the administration of justice, health care, and immigration. The 121-page report contains a section on "Cultural Competency of Providers," which addresses structural inequities and provider discrimination, as well as other causes of racial disparities in health care access.

The recommendations to reduce these disparities include strategies similar to those espoused by the AMA:

- Continue advocating for broad-based expansions in health insurance coverage.

- Continue advocacy of increased health care access for underserved groups.

- Continue pushing for full funding of the race and ethnic health disparities initiative.

- Increase funding for existing programs targeted to underserved and minority populations.

- Enhance financial and regulatory mechanisms to promote culturally competent care.

- Emphasize importance of cultural competence to institutions training health care providers. HHS should strongly encourage medical training institutions and accrediting associations to require that students receive some training in cultural competency.

Patient-Centered Medicine: A Professional Evolution
C Laine, F Davidoff
JAMA, 1996; 275:152-156

Patient-Centered Medicine: Transforming the Clinical Method
M Stewart, JB Brown, WW Weston, IR McWhinney, et al
Thousand Oaks, CA: Sage, 1995

Patient-Centered Clinical Interviewing
JH Levenstein, JB Brown, WW Weston, EC McCracken, I McWhinney
In *Communicating with Medical Patients,* M Stewart, D Roter, eds.
London: Sage, 1989, pp 107-120

Patient Preferences for Communication with Phyicians about End-of-Life Decisions
JC Hofmann, NS Wenger, RB Davis, et al
Ann Intern Med, 1997; 127:1-12

Patients' Lack of Literacy May Contribute to Billions of Dollars in Higher Hospital Costs
Charles Marwick
JAMA, Vol 278, pp 971-972

**Patients' Perspectives on Dying
and on the Care of Dying Patients**
TR McCormick, BJ Conley
West J Med, 1995; 163:236-243

**Physician-Patient Communication.
The Relationship With Malpractice
Claims Among Primary Care Physicians
and Surgeons**
W Levinson, DL Roter, JP Mullooly, VT Dull,
RM Frankel
JAMA, 1997; 277:553-559

**Physicians' Emotional Reactions to
Patients: Recognizing and Managing
Countertransference**
AA Marshall, RC Smith
Am J Gastroenterol, 1995; 90:4-8

**Preventive Care For Women: Does
the Sex of the Physician Matter?**
N Lurie, J Slater, P McGovern, et al
N Engl J Med, 1993; 329:478-482

**Providing Culturally Competent Care:
Is There a Role for Health Promoters?**
JE Poss
Nurs Outlook, 1999; 47:30-36

**Relationship of Functional Health
Literacy to Patients' Knowledge of Their
Chronic Disease: A Study of Patients
with Hypertension and Diabetes**
MV Williams, DW Baker, RM Parker, et al
Arch Intern Med, 1998; 158: 166-172

**The Role of the Medical Interview
in the Physician's Search for Meaning**
AL Suchman, WT Branch, DA Matthews
In *The Medical Interview: Clinical Care,
Education, and Research,* M Lipkin,
SM Putnam, A Lazare, eds.
New York: Springer-Verlag NY; 1995,
pp 368-375

**Righting the Medical Record:
Transforming Chronicle into Story**
WJ Donnelly
JAMA, 1988; 260:823-825

**Sex Differences in Patients' and Physicians'
Communication During Primary Care Visits**
D Roter, M Lipkin, A Korsgaard
Med Care, 1991; 29:1083-1093

**A Strategy for Improving Patient Satisfaction
by the Intensive Training of Residents
in Psychosocial Medicine: A Controlled,
Randomized Study**
RC Smith, JS Lyles, JA Mettler, AA Marshall, LF
Van Egeren, BE Stoffelmayr, et al
Acad Med, 1995; 70:729-732

**Taking Suffering Seriously: A New Role
for the Medical Case History**
WJ Donnelly
Acad Med, 1996; 71:730-737

**Talking With Patients: Is It Different When
They Are Dying?**
L Coulombe
Can Fam Physician, 1995; 41:423-437

**Teaching Cultural Aspects of Health: A Vital
Part of Communication**
PS Gill, D Adshead
Med Teacher, 1996; 18:61-64

**Temporary Matters: the Ethical
Consequences of Transient Social
Relationships in Medical Training**
Dimitri Christakis, Chris Feudtner
JAMA, Vol 278, No 9, pp 739-43

**Use and Management of Physicians'
Feelings During the Interview**
RC Smith
In *The Medical Interview: Clinical Care, Education,
and Research,* M Lipkin, SM Putnam, A Lazare, eds.
New York: Springer-Verlag, 1995, pp 104-109

**Using a Family Systems Approach
in a Balint-Style Group: An Innovative
Course for Continuing Medical Education**
RJ Botelho, SH McDaniel, JE Jones
Fam Med, 1990; 22:293-295

**Videotaped Interviewing of Non-English
Speakers: Training for Medical Students
With Volunteer Clients**
D Farnill, J Todisco, SC Hayes, D Bartlett
Med Educ, 1997; 31:87-93

**When We Talk About American Ethnic
Groups, What Do We Mean?**
Jean Phinney
American Psychologist, 1996, vol 51, no 9,
918-927

**Why Do Patients of Female Physicians
Have Higher Rates of Breast and Cervical
Cancer Screening?**
N Lurie, KL Margolis, PG McGovern, PJ Mink,
JS Slater
J Gen Intern Med, 1997; 12:34-43

**Working with Liguistically and Culturally
Different Children: Innovative Clinical
and Educational Approaches**
Sharon-Ann Gopaul-McNicol, Tania Thomas
Presswood, 1998

Reflecting 10 years of cross-cultural practice and
research with children of various linguistic and
cultural backgrounds, this volume offers an
eclectic approach to assessment, treatment,
teaching, consultation, and research with
culturally diverse children. Includes information
on the values and beliefs inherent in the child's
cultural upbringing and on using culturally
sensitive intervention strategies.

**Writing at the Margin: Discourse Between
Anthropology and Medicine**
A Kleinman
Berkeley, CA: Univ of California Press, 1995

Section III

Curriculum and Training Materials

Researchers who apply the concept of "culturally underserved and underrepresented" only to disadvantaged racial, ethnic, and socioeconomic populations lament that curriculum and training opportunities and resources are sparse. Using the term to encompass all the "invisible" cultures, with values and behaviors that affect the encounter with the health care system, produces more promising results. All of the cultural competence training resources and programs described in the following pages contain references to other helpful resources.

Assessing Cultural Competence in Managed Care Organizations

Many health care institutions are incorporating concepts related to cultural competence in multiple contexts. Kaiser Permanente's initial *Provider's Handbooks* focus on Latino, African American, and Asian populations (always emphasizing intragroup variation and individualized, nonstereotypical communication and treatment), but the organization also offers varied programs and publications that focus on sensitivity to folk medicine and other complementary practices, death and dying, and sexual and reproductive practices.

In keeping with the increased emphasis on measuring outcomes, Kaiser Permanente and others are attempting to gauge the effectiveness of efforts to provide culturally effective education and health care. *Monitoring the Managed Care of Culturally and Linguistically Diverse Populations*, by Miguel Tirado (available from primarycare@circsol.com) reports the results of a project to study issues of individual and institutional competence in large commercial managed care plans in California. Four plans were selected because of their culturally and linguistically diverse membership and their responsiveness to California's MediCal managed care cultural and linguistic contractual standards.

The resulting publication includes four cultural competence assessment tools, the methodology used to develop the tools, and a detailed explanation of each question in the tools. The four tools are being validated through an outcome-based approach during the next phase of the project, which is funded by the Health Resources and Services Administration.

Educational Programs Reflect an Inclusive Definition of Culture

The increase in educational programs addressing a broad definition of culture and diversity is reflected in the "Leader's Guide: Curriculum Transformation" section on DiversityWeb, http://www.inform.umd.edu/DiversityWeb/Leadersguide/CT/. This Web site, developed by the Association of American Colleges and Universities and the University of Maryland, in cooperation with Diversity Connections, provides specific examples of successful efforts in "curriculum transformation" at hundreds of colleges and universities. For example, the University of Arizona Diversity Action Council has developed a Diversity Action Plan that includes an "all-inclusive" definition of diversity, with goals grouped into six areas: assessment, information, training, curriculum, events, and program evaluation, all of which are applicable to medical education. Resources cited on DiversityWeb frequently include online discussion groups. Many focus on specific groups: Asian Americans; Hispanic cultures; people with different kinds of disabilities; families across cultures; women; and gays, lesbians, and bisexuals.

Cultural Competence in Medical Schools and Residency Programs

Medical education curricula are infrequently described on DiversityWeb, but Web sites for individual schools indicate increasing activity. One question in the Annual Medical School Questionnaire of the Liaison Committee on Medical Education is directly related to cultural competence, and several others about related instruction have been included since 1988.

**Instruction Relevant to Cultural Competence Covered as Part of a Required
Course in Accredited US Medical Schools, 1992-1993 and 1997-1998**

Instruction Covered as Part of a Required Course	Number of Schools in 1992/93	Number of Schools in 1997/98
Alternative Medicine	Not asked	63
Adolescent Medicine	113	Not asked
Communication Skills	Not asked	117
Death and Dying	117	121
Family Violence/Abuse	101	117
Genetic Counseling	113	110
Geriatrics	112	112
Home Health Care	75	99
Human Sexuality	106	113
Medical Humanities	74	80
Multicultural Medicine	Not asked	94
Nutrition	98	108
Organ/Tissue Procurement	75	Not asked

Source: LCME Annual Medical School Questionnaire, Part II

As indicated in the table, instruction in cultural competence issues is infused in many curriculum segments that probably would not be identified if the schools were queried about the extent to which they teach about "cultural issues" per se. For example, cultural issues are frequently included in courses as basic as humanities in medicine, nutrition, and age-related content. Some instructors incorporate cultural issues in their discussions of organ donation, genetic counseling, human sexuality, and end-of-life care.

Medical schools and residency programs are not the only sources of education and training on cultural issues. A surprising number of curriculum guides and other training materials have appeared in professional association journals, either in a series (*Academic Psychiatry*, 1994-1997), in a special issue (the *Journal of the American Medical Women's Association,* 1998), or in multiple special issues reflecting change over time.

The Association of American Medical Colleges has solicited detailed information from respondents to a survey of all LCME-accredited medical schools and residency programs in six specialties. A compendium of program outlines, information on evaluation tools, and resources for individuals is scheduled for publication in 1999.

Section Contents

This section of the *Compendium* includes examples of instruction being provided across the medical education continuum. Included are examples of assessment tools, curriculum units, training, accreditation standards, evaluation resources, and publications from organizations and individuals. Curriculum and training resources described in Section IV generally are not included here. We encourage medical schools, residency programs, and others to send us information for the next edition of this *Compendium* and for the Cultural Competence Web site; we also encourage them to submit information to the Web sites indicated in this section and in Section IX.

A. Organizations providing assessment, curriculum, training, standards, and evaluation resources

B. Educational Institutions (with relevant courses)

C. Publications by Individuals

A. Professional Organizations

American Medical Association

Policies

The following policies represent the wide range of policies and reports calling for curriculum development in areas included in this *Compendium.* Also see Section IV.

E-9.035   *Gender Discrimination in the Medical Profession*

H-20.982   *AIDS Education*

H-25.999   *Health Care for Older Patients*

H-140.977   *Residency Training in Medical-Legal Aspects of End-of-Life Care*

H-160.959   *Health Care Access for the Inner-City Poor*

H-170.974   *Update on AMA Policies on Human Sexuality and Family Life Education*

H-170.978   *Comprehensive Sexual Education*

H-200.972   *Primary Care Physicians in the Inner City*

H-210.986   *Physicians and Family Caregivers: A Model for Partnership*

H-210.991   *The Education of Physicians in Home Health Care*

H-215.985   *Child Care in Hospitals*

H-295.897   *Enhancing the Cultural Competence of Physicians*

H-295.905   *Promoting Culturally Competent Health Care*

H-295.912   *Education of Medical Students and Residents About Domestic Violence Screening*

H-295.932   *End-of-Life Care*

H-295.981   *Geriatric Medicine*

H-295.999   *Medical Student Support Groups*

H-310.971   *Resident Physician Counseling*

H-350.971   *AMA Initiatives Regarding Minorities*

H-350.977   *Indian Health Service*

H-350.979   *Increase the Representation of Minority and Economically Disadvantaged Populations in the Medical Profession*

H-350.980   *AMA's Role in Preparing Minority and Disadvantaged Youth for Careers in Medicine and the Health Professions*

H-515.983   *Physicians and Family Violence*

Publications

Alcoholism in the Elderly: Diagnosis, Treatment, Prevention
Department of Geriatric Health, 1997

In November 1992, the AMA convened an ad hoc committee to address the problems physicians face in diagnosing, treating, and preventing alcoholism in the elderly. In December 1993, the AMA House of Delegates adopted a recommendation of the AMA Council on Scientific Affairs to develop guidelines on alcoholism in the elderly for physicians. The guidelines, which have been endorsed by the American Society of Addiction Medicine, are intended to help the practicing physician establish a diagnosis, manage current emergency conditions such as acute withdrawal, and refer the elderly patient to ongoing treatment for alcoholism and for any medical or psychiatric complications.

Prevention opportunities for physicians include evaluating their elderly patients in terms of their drinking practices and behavior and paying special attention to prescribing practices with high-risk patients to avoid adverse alcohol-drug interactions or dependence on sedative-hypnotics.

Genetics in the Curricula of US Medical Schools

The AMA will publish an analysis of data on medical genetics curricula compiled from US medical schools, medical students, residents, fellows, and recently graduated physicians. The data will determine:

- What medical schools teach their students/ residents/fellows.

- What medical students/residents/fellows appear to be learning.

- Medical geneticists recommendations for what should be taught.

- Genetics medical education materials available to the practicing physician.

Annotated Catalog of Videotapes on Family Violence

An annotated catalog of videotapes on family violence intended for medical practitioners was released in 1998. The Advisory Council is now seeking to create a developmentally appropriate assessment tool for use with children who have witnessed violence or severe abuse, coordinated by psychiatric societies represented on the Council.

CEJA Reports on End-of-Life Care
Council on Ethical and Judicial Affairs, 1998

A compilation of the following reports issued from 1986 to 1987:

- *Do-Not-Resuscitate Orders* (December 1987)

- *Euthanasia* (June 1988)

- *Persistent Vegetative State and the Decision to Withdraw or Withhold Life Support* (June 1989)

- *Guidelines for the Appropriate Use of Do-Not-Resuscitate Orders* (December 1990)

- *Decisions Near the End of Life* (June 1991)

- *Decisions To Forgo Life Sustaining Treatment for Incompetent Patients* (June 1991)

- *Physician-Assisted Suicide* (June 1994)

- *Medical Futility in End-of-Life Care* (December 1996)

- *Optimal Use of Orders-Not-To-Intervene and Advance Directives* (June 1996)

Caring for the Uninsured and Underinsured: A Compendium from JAMA and the Specialty Journals of the AMA, 1991

Culturally Competent Health Care for Adolescents: A Guide for Primary Care Providers, 1994

Introduces health care providers to the complex issues involved in working with diverse populations of adolescents and outlines practical strategies for incorporating cultural issues into clinical practice.

Diagnostic and Treatment Guidelines

The AMA Campaign Against Family Violence has produced eight diagnostic and treatment guides. The *Diagnostic and Treatment Guidelines on Domestic Violence* highlights national hotlines, counseling groups, shelter directories, and publications with materials in English and other languages. This publication also briefly addresses the under-recognized issue of violence within gay and lesbian relationships.

The eighth guide, on the health aspects of firearms, was released in November 1998. Coverage includes the epidemiology of firearm injuries and deaths, as well as clinical advice for physicians about patient risk assessment and prevention counseling. The guide includes information for the safe storage, handling, and disposal of firearms in the home. Copies of the firearm guide were distributed to pediatricians and emergency physicians through joint efforts of the AMA and the relevant specialty societies. Evaluation of the guide is scheduled, supported, as was the guide itself, by the Joyce Foundation.

Educating Physicians in Home Health Care
JAMA, February 13, 1991; 265:769-771

Focus on Men's Health, 1993

Focus on Women's Health, 1993

Good Care of the Dying Patient
JAMA, February 14, 1996; 275:474-478

Guidelines for Adolescent Preventive Services (GAPS)

GAPS is a comprehensive set of recommendations that provide a framework for the organization and content of preventive services.

- **GAPS Local Implementation Training Curriculum,** 2nd edition, 1997

- **GAPS Recommendations Monograph,** 4th edition, 1997

Guidelines for the Use of Assistive Technology: Evaluation, Referral, Prescription
Department of Geriatric Health, 1996

In November 1993, the AMA convened two focus groups—one with consumers and one with allied health professionals—to address the barriers faced by physicians and their patients with disabilities when dealing with assistive technology. The concerns of the focus groups were presented to the Assistive Technology Advisory Panel in January 1994 to develop the *Guidelines for the Use of Assistive Technology: Evaluation, Referral, Prescription.*

The *Guidelines* includes both assistive technology *devices* and assistive technology *services.* An assistive technology *device* is any item, piece of equipment, or product system, whether acquired commercially off-the-shelf, modified, or customized, that is used to increase, maintain, or improve functional capability of individuals with disabilities. An assistive technology *service* is any service that directly assists an individual with a disability in the selection, acquisition, or use of an assistive technology device.

Culturally Relevant Sections

- Be sensitive to patient needs and preferences.

- Consider the social and cultural environment.

- Assess the impact of specific impairment within the patient's total environment and lifestyle.

- Continue the relationship with an interdisciplinary team that includes the patient.

- Provide individualized treatment that is sensitive to cost-effectiveness concerns.

- Be able to refer patients to local community resources for technology and support.

Culturally Relevant Advice

- Individuals often possess intimate knowledge of their goals, preferences, support systems, and functional needs for independence, which physicians must become fully aware of before treatment.

- Speak directly to the patient.

- Introduce yourself and everyone else in the room (this is especially important for patients with impaired vision).

- Face the patient when speaking and speak clearly.

- Be aware of the patient's mode of communication: oral/lip reading, American Sign Language (ASL), signed English, need for an interpreter, etc.

- Always explain what you are going to do before you do it.

- Do not assume the patient has understood what you have said; ask him or her to repeat or summarize.

The Core Knowledge and Assessment document outlines core knowledge components and provides specific patient assessment tools, including patient examination and evaluation and evaluation and prescription of assistive technology.

Office practice guidelines to meet the needs of persons with disabilities are also included.

Educational Material for Patients and Families

Additional resources include instructions for obtaining funding for assistive technology, locating state assistive technology projects, and accessing professional and interdisciplinary resources, including electronic asssistive technology resources, electronic bulletin boards, and home automation sources.

Guides to the Evaluation of Permanent Impairment, 4th edition, 1993

Health Care Needs of Gay Men and Lesbians in the United States
JAMA, May 1, 1996; 275:1354-1359

Health Literacy
JAMA, February 10, 1999; 281:552-557

Healthy Youth 2000: A Mid-Decade Review 1996

In the Mainstream: Women in Medicine in America, 1991

Medical Management of the Home Care Patient: Guidelines for Physicians, 2nd edition
Department of Geriatric Health, 1998

The first Home Care Advisory Panel, convened by the AMA in 1987 to increase the involvement of physicians in home care, produced the first edition of the *Guidelines for the Medical Management of the Home Care Patient* (1992). A second panel, convened in 1997, led to the revised second edition of the *Guidelines* (1998), endorsed by the American Academy of Home Care Physicians.

This document provides instruction in designing a curriculum in home care for education and training of physicians at all levels and in recommending an agenda for future research and development.

In describing the goals of home care, the role of the physician and the physician-patient relationship are emphasized. Physicians are reminded that in addition to overseeing fluctuating patho-physiological condition(s), they should also advise, encourage, and support self-care efforts.

Culturally Sensitive Assessment Table

The section on medical management in home care includes a two-page assessment table with cells on individualizing psychosocial assessments and interventions and observing and evaluating cultural, ethnic, or religious influences on health care behavior, beliefs, preferences, and expectations. Mental/cognitive assessments include health literacy. Information is also provided on eligibility under different payment plans.

Special Home Care Populations

Describes concerns of the elderly and populations including persons with disabilities and those requiring high-technology home care services, such as "video visits" or tele-home care. Includes step-by-step instructions for developing the care plan and for communicating with other members of the interdisciplinary team.

Emphasizes the importance of being sensitive to the emotional and physical well-being of the caregiver, the safety of others in the home and visitors, and the continued willingness of the patient to participate as a partner in the home care plan. Includes a list of patient's rights and responsibilities that reinforce patient-centered care. Describes physician responsibilities for home hospice care.

The section on community resources includes the telephone numbers of national, state, and local agencies that serve the frail elderly and other special populations, including children with special needs. The publication includes a complete list of addresses and phone numbers and fax numbers for state departments on aging, as well as hot lines.

Physicians and Family Caregivers: A Model for Partnership
JAMA, March 10, 1993; 269:1282-1284

Physician's Guide to Diagnosis and Treatment of Dementia
Rosalie J. Guttman, PhD
Projected publication date: September 1999

In late 1998, a culturally diverse expert consensus panel met to outline the forthcoming *Physician's Guide to Diagnosis and Treatment of Dementia.* The *Guide* will highlight the significance of culture, race, age, and sex on both the diagnosis and management of dementia.

Policy Compendium on Tobacco, Alcohol, and Other Harmful Substances Affecting Adolescents: Tobacco, 1993

Policy Compendium on Reproductive Health Issues Affecting Adolescents, 1996

Policy Compendium on Violence & Adolescents: Intentional Injury & Abuse, 1993

Primary Care for Persons with Disabilities: Access to Assistive Technology: Lecture Notes and Case Studies, 1995

Violence: A Compendium from JAMA and the Specialty Journals of the AMA, 1992

What is Medicare+Choice and Where Do Physicians Fit In?
Division of Health Policy Development, 1998

This 29-page booklet, one of a series of three AMA Medicare+Choice publications, contains an entry on cultural competence: "The M+C regulations include a provision of M+C plans to ensure 'cultural competency' in the provision of health care. M+C plans are required to make a particular effort to ensure that enrollees with limited English proficiency, limited education, or other socioeconomic disadvantages receive the health care to which they are entitled."

What You Can Do About Family Violence: The Federation Guide to the Physicians' Campaign Against Family Violence
1992

Work Plays: Flexible Solutions to Sexual Harassment in Health Care
1997

Note: For medical school Web sites and other electronic resources, see Section IX.

Other Organizations

Accreditation Council for Graduate Medical Education (ACGME)

515 N State St
Chicago, IL 60610
312 464-4920

General Competencies: Recommendations to the ACGME (draft)

Recommendations related to cultural competence include the following:

- Communicate effectively and demonstrate caring and respectful behaviors when interacting with patients.

- Demonstrate sensitivity and responsiveness to cultural differences, including awareness of their own and their patients' cultural perspectives.

Agency for Health Care Policy and Research

Executive Office Center
2101 E Jefferson St
Rockville, MD 20852
301 594-6662
http://www.guideline.gov

The Agency for Health Care Policy and Research (AHCPR) supports and conducts research that improves the outcomes, quality, access to, and cost and utilization of health care services. The AHCPR achieves this through health services research designed to:

- improve clinical practice,

- improve the health care system's ability to provide access to and deliver high-quality, high-value health care, and

- provide policymakers with the ability to assess the impact of system changes on outcomes, quality, access, cost, and use of health care services.

As a special focus of research across each of the major program areas, the AHCPR has identified health issues related to priority populations, including minority populations, women, and children. The AHCPR encourages women, members of minority groups, and persons with disabilities to apply as Principal Investigators.

Research activities frequently focus on nonmajority and special populations including:

- Adolescent health

- Advance directives

- Disability

- Elder health

- End-of-life treatment/issues

- Homeless

- Minority health, ethnic attitudes/differences, and treatment/access differences

- Women's health

The AHCPR priorities in research, demonstration, dissemination, and evaluation projects are to:

- Support improvements in health outcomes. Research on clinical outcomes examines the effectiveness of different strategies for preventing, diagnosing, treating, or managing conditions that are common, expensive, and for which significant variations in practice or opportunities for improvement have been demonstrated. Outcomes of clinical interventions include functional status, quality of life, patient satisfaction, and costs in addition to morbidity and mortality. A particular emphasis is on the outcomes of care provided to the elderly and those with chronic illnesses.

- Strengthen quality measurement and improvement.

- Identify strategies to improve access, foster appropriate use, and reduce unnecessary expenditures.

The AHCPR encourages partnerships with private and public organizations to facilitate development and sharing of scientific knowledge and resources, including cost-sharing mechanisms; projects that will produce results within 2-3 years; and results that can be integrated rapidly into practice or policy.

The AHCPR frequently addresses cultural competence issues in *AHCPR Research Activities*, a digest of research findings.

Healthy People 2010

The Public Health Service (PHS) is committed to achieving the health promotion and disease prevention objectives of *Healthy People 2010*, a PHS-led national activity for setting priority areas. The AHCPR encourages applicants to submit grant applications with relevance to the specific objectives of this initiative, which has a strong focus on eliminating racial and ethnic disparities in health care.

National Guideline Clearinghouse

The AHCPR's National Guideline Clearinghouse (NGC), an Internet-based repository for evidence-based clinical practice guidelines, was developed by the Agency in partnership with the AMA and the American Association of Health Plans. The NGC presents the guidelines with standardized abstracts and tables that allow for comparison of guidelines on similar topics. The tables provide information on the major areas of agreement and disagreement among the guidelines.

Racial and Ethnic Differences in Health, 1996

B Kass, R Weinick, A Monheit
Rockville (MD): Agency for Health Care Policy and Research, 1998
Pub No. 99-0001

Children's Health, 1996: Health Insurance, Access to Care, and Health Status

ME Weigers, RM Weinick, JW Cohen
Pub. No. 98-0008

E-mail: mepspd@ahcpr.gov
800 358-9295
Medicine on the Net Vol.5, #5, May 1999, p 18
http://www.meps.ahcpr.gov/publicat.htm

The AHCPR offers two chartbooks on its Web site.

Children's Health (1996) offers a summary discussion of key statistics on the health of children in America.

Racial and Ethnic Differences in Health (1996) contains estimates of health insurance coverage, access to health care, and health status for blacks, Hispanics, and whites in the United States.

With its question-and-answer format as well as charts and graphs, this chartbook compares health care differences experienced by racial and ethnic groups in 1996. Observations from the data include: more than one-third of Hispanics had no health insurance coverage; Hispanic and black Americans were more likely than white Americans to lack private, job-related health insurance coverage; and blacks were the group most likely to have only public insurance.

The Web site that includes these two chartbooks also offers a discussion of survey instruments, data, new findings, publications, work in progress, health spending projections, links to related sites, and the opportunity to join an e-mail list.

Alternative Therapies in Health and Medicine

American Association of Critical-Care Nurses
101 Columbia
Aliso Viejo, CA 92656
800 899-1712

The Fourth Annual Alternative Therapies Symposium and Exposition: Creating Integrative Healthcare (March 25-28, 1999, New York) contained sessions on addressing the needs of diverse populations, many of whom use complementary and alternative health care practices. Sponsored annually by *Alternative Therapies in Health and Medicine* and others, the symposia present information on multiple issues related to culturally effective care.

Ambulatory Pediatric Association

Marge Degnon, Executive Director
6728 Old McLean Village Dr
McLean, VA 22101
703 556-9222
703 556-8729 Fax
E-mail: info@ambpeds.org
http://www.ambpeds.org

Educational Guidelines for Residency Training in General Pediatrics

Edited by Diane Kittredge and the Ambulatory Pediatric Association (APA) Education Committee

These guidelines reference the Program Requirements for Residency Education in Pediatrics of the ACGME, which state under V.B.5, "Community Experiences," that "[T]here must be structured educational experiences that prepare residents for the role of advocate for the health of children within the community." The curriculum should include "community-oriented care with focus on the health needs of all children within a community, particularly underserved populations, [as well as] the multicultural dimensions of health care." "It is very important," the APA document continues, "that residents become sensitive to cultural and ethnic differences in their patients. Since in many programs the residents themselves come from a variety of cultures, open-ended discussions in which they discuss their own reactions to the cultural insensitivity that they have experienced may provide a means of raising the group's level of sensitivity to other cultures."

The document stresses that physicians should learn the importance of "understanding, accepting, and appreciating cultural diversity in one's patients and learn[ing] about the health-related implications of cultural beliefs and practices of groups represented in one's community."

General Pediatric Clerkship Curriculum and Resource Manual

A joint project of the APA and the Council on Medical Student Education in Pediatrics

Under "II. Professional Conduct and Attitudes," the document states, "Important personal characteristics that should be encouraged in students include, but are not limited to, caring, compassion, empathy, enthusiasm, adaptability, flexibility, patience, gentleness, cultural sensitivity, tolerance of difference, willingness to listen and explain, personal honesty, respect for privacy and confidentiality, commitment to work, and dedication to learning."

The document goes on to state that "cultural, ethnic, and socioeconomic factors also affect personal and family traits and behaviors, with varying effects on child-rearing practices. Recognition of and respect for difference are important."

Training Residents to Serve the Underserved: A Resident Education Curriculum

April 1993

Special considerations include knowledge, skills, attitudes, barriers, and advocacy in working with ethnic minorities.

American Academy of Child and Adolescent Psychiatry (AACAP)

Virginia Q Anthony, Executive Director
3615 Wisconsin Ave NW
Washington, DC 20016
202 966-7300
202 966-2891 Fax
http://www.aacap.org

Diversity and Culture Training

According to the AACAP, most regulatory governmental and nongovernmental agencies now require mental health agencies to provide special considerations in assessment and treatment of minority populations. Moreover, the program requirements for residency training in both general psychiatry and child/adolescent psychiatry include the provision of "didactic instructions and American culture" and "supervised clinical experiences with patients of a variety of ethnic, racial, social and economic backgrounds." The AACAP curriculum goals include defining cultural competence, establishing a curriculum, and evaluating the outcome of a culturally sensitive curriculum.

The curriculum outline defines cultural competence as a set of knowledge-based and interpersonal skills that enable an individual to understand and work effectively with individuals of diverse cultures (including one's own) across all categories of socioeconomic status, gender, and religious, racial, and ethnic background. Eight specific skills are described.

Experiential learning (fostering cultural awareness and sensitivity through experiential group discussions) and *didactic learning* (overview; discussion of socialization, customs, illnesses, beliefs, practices, and health care seeking behaviors of various culture groups; epidemiological findings; clinical issues; and research approaches) are included.

Evaluation/assessment of the curriculum includes didactic curriculum evaluation by the trainee and clinical applicability/case illustration evaluation by the teacher. Includes more than 60 references.

The American Board of Internal Medicine (ABIM)

510 Walnut St, Ste 1700
Philadelphia, PA 19106-3699
215 446-3500 or 800 441-2246
215 446-3590 Fax
http://www.abim.org/

Caring for the Dying: Identification and Promotion of Physician Competency—Personal Narratives

Philadelphia: American Board of Internal Medicine, 1996

American Academy of Nursing American Nurses Association

AAN/ANA
600 Maryland Ave SW, Ste 100 West
Washington, DC 20024-2571
800 274-4262
http://nursingworld.org

These associations have published many monographs related to cultural competence and diversity, including:

- *Competencies for Health Professionals: A Multicultural Perspective in the Promotion of Breast, Cervical, Colorectal, and Skin Health*

- *Cultural Diversity in Nursing: Issues, Strategies, and Outcomes*

- *Diversity, Marginalization, and Culturally Competent Health Care Issues in Knowledge Development*

- *Promoting Cultural Competence in and Through Nursing Education: A Critical Review and Comprehensive Plan for Action*

American Holistic Medical Association (AHMA)

6728 Old McLean Village Dr
McLean, VA 22101-3906
703 556-9728

The meetings and publications of AHMA frequently contain components emphasizing respect for cultural differences. The AHMA also recognizes the importance of cultural competence in its training programs.

American Medical Women's Association

801 N Fairfax St, Ste 400
Alexandria, VA 22314
703 838-0500
703 549-3864 Fax
E-mail: info@amwa-doc.org
http://www.amwa-doc.org

Conference

Advanced Curriculum on Women's Health: First International Conference, March 19–22, 1998, Miami, Florida.

Publications

In 1998, the *Journal of the American Medical Women's Association* published a supplement on *Cultural Competence and Women's Health in Medical Education* (Vol 53, No 3).

The articles in the supplement were presented at the National Conference on Cultural Competence and Women's Health Curricula in Medical Education, sponsored by the Offices of Women's Health and Minority Health of the US Public Health Service. They are available online at:
http://www.jamwa.org/vol53/toc53_3.html

Editorial: Curriculum Enhancement in Medical Education: Teaching Cultural Competence and Women's Health For a Changing Society
Elena V. Rios; Clay E. Simpson, Jr.

Required Curricula in Diversity and Cross-Cultural Medicine: The Time Is Now
Melissa Welch

Development and Evaluation of an Instrument to Assess Medical Students' Cultural Attitudes
Lynne S. Robins, Gwen L. Alexander; Fredric M. Wolf, et al

A Cultural Diversity Curriculum: Combining Didactic, Problem-Solving, and Simulated Experiences
BUK Li; Donna A. Caniano; Ronald C. Comer

Primary Care Fellowship in Women's Health
Kathleen M. Thomsen

A Women's Health Curriculum for an Internal Medicine Residency
Janice L. Werbinski; Sandra J. Hoffmann

Women's Health Curriculum at Stanford
JoDean Nicolette; Marc Nelson

American Psychiatric Association (APA)

1400 K St NW
Washington, DC 20005
202 682-6000
202 682-6353 Fax
E-mail: smirin@psych.org
http://www.psych.org

A Psychiatry Curriculum Directed to the Care of the Hispanic Patient

ES Garza-Trevino, P Ruiz, K Varegos-Samuel
Academic Psychiatry, 1997: 21:1-10

This article describes a model curriculum for psychiatric residency programs that addresses the sociodemographic, epidemiological, psychosocial, cultural, and behavioral characteristics of Hispanics. It emphasizes that faculty who are knowledgeable and sensitive about Hispanic culture should be available for the supervision and teaching of psychiatric residents during their training and that supervision should focus on cultural formulation and family dynamics and other factors of importance in clinical psychiatric practice. Includes a 29-item bibliography and 56 references.

A Psychiatric Residency Curriculum About Gender and Women's Issues

A Spielvogel, LJ Dickson, GE Robinson
Academic Psychiatry, 1995; Vol 19, no 4:187-201

Over the last 30 years, major advances have been made in our understanding of how biological factors and sociocultural influences contribute to gender differences, gender identity formation, and gendered role behavior. This article presents an outline for a curriculum in gender and women's issues, including educational objectives, learning experiences through which residents could meet these objectives, and recommended readings. It discusses potential obstacles and suggests helpful strategies for implementing the proposed curriculum. Includes 96 references and suggested core readings.

A Curriculum for Learning in Psychiatry Residencies about Homosexuality, Gay Men, and Lesbians

TS Stein
Academic Psychiatry, 1994; Vol 18, no 2:59-70

Recent research has greatly expanded knowledge about homosexuality, gay men, and lesbians. However, neither a nonpathological perspective nor this new information has been integrated into psychiatric residency curricula. This article proposes a basic model for this necessary professional training. Includes 85 references.

A Curriculum for Learning About American Indians and Alaska Natives in Psychiatry Residency Training

JW Thompson
Academic Psychiatry, 1996; Vol 20, no 1:5-14

Describes a proposed curriculum for teaching psychiatric residents about the diagnosis and treatment of American Indians and Alaska Natives. Presents the historical context, contemporary myths, and rationale for the inclusion of curriculum materials on Indians in residency programs. Briefly describes the curriculum for the 4 years of residency education and outlines the knowledge, skills, and attitudes needed by residents. The curriculum for the first and second years includes a basic history and description of Indian people, information on myths about the group, and psychiatric epidemiology and psychopathology. The third year includes clinical care and related areas such as service utilization and illness prevention. The proposed fourth year includes a seminar to discuss psychotherapy and other clinical cases. Includes 70 references.

American Psychological Association

750 First Street NE
Washington, DC 20002
202 336-5500
http://www.apa.org

APA guidelines for providers of psychological services to ethnic, linguistic, and culturally diverse populations, approved by the APA Council of Representatives, August 1990, are available online at http://www.apa.org/pi/guide.html

American Public Health Association (APHA)

1015 Fifteenth St NW
Washington, DC 20005-2605
202 789-5600
E-mail: comments@apha.org
http://www.apha.org

The APHA annual meeting, held in November, presents the latest scientific and practice information, including presentations on cross-cultural communication, culturally competent resources and research, the impact of spiritual practices and religious beliefs on health status, cross-cultural issues in death and bereavement, and the practice and teaching of alternative and complementary heath care.

Typical topics include:

- Developing a Culturally Appropriate Pain Assessment Tool: A Community Capacity Building Effort

- Tribal Involvement in the Development of Questionnaires

- The Community Tool Box: Building Capacity for Community Change

- Improving End-of-Life Care—The Case for Medicare

Annenberg Center for Health Sciences

Eisenhower Medical Center
39000 Bob Hope Dr
Rancho Mirage, CA 92270
760 340 3911

Frequently co-sponsors programs with a cultural competence track. For example,
Using Alternative and Spiritual Approaches to Healthcare (April 1-4, 1998, San Diego, CA), co-sponsored with the American Association of Critical-Care Nurses, featured several sessions related to respect for diversity.

Association for Death Education and Counseling (ADEC)

638 Prospect Ave
Hartford, CT 06105-4250
860 586-7503
860 586-7550 Fax
E-mail: info@ADEC.org
http://www.adec.org

Publications and programs frequently feature diversity issues, For example, ADEC's 21st annual conference, Embracing Our Differences in Dying and Grieving: Flowing with the River of Life, March 11-14, 1999, San Antonio, Texas, addressed culturally diverse and multidisciplinary perspectives in death, dying, loss, and bereavement.

The Forum

ADEC's bimonthly newsletter contains "Culture Corner," an editorials section devoted to multicultural issues in contemporary society. It provides information about death-related issues from various cultures and ethnic groups.

Association of American Medical Colleges (AAMC)

M Brownell Anderson, MEd
Project Director and Associate Vice President
for Medical Education
2450 N St NW
Washington, DC 20037
202 828-0400

Medical School Objectives Project

The Medical School Objectives Project is intended to guide medical schools in developing objectives that reflect an understanding of the implications for medical practice and medical education of "evolving societal needs, practice patterns, and scientific developments." The project report emphasizes that physicians must seek to understand the meaning of the patients' stories in the context of the patients' beliefs and family and cultural values. The report states that physicians must be knowledgeable of cultural factors that contribute to the development and/or continuation of maladies and must avoid being judgmental when the patients' beliefs and values conflict with their own.

Report 1: Learning Objectives for Medical Student Education—Guidelines for Medical Schools. Medical School Objectives Project, January 1998

"At all times [physicians] must act with integrity, honesty, respect for patients' privacy, and respect for the dignity of patients as persons. In all of their interactions with patients they must seek to understand the meaning of the patients' stories in the context of the patients' beliefs and family and cultural values. They must avoid being judgmental when the patients' beliefs and values conflict with their own. They must continue to care for dying patients even when disease-specific therapy is no longer available or desired."

The objectives would require physicians to "be sufficiently knowledgeable about both traditional and nontraditional modes of care to provide intelligent guidance to their patients" and to understand the economic, psychological, occupational, social, and cultural factors that contribute to the development and/or perpetuation of conditions that impair health.

The *Guidelines* state that the medical school must ensure that before graduation a student will have demonstrated, to the satisfaction of the faculty, . . . the ability to obtain an accurate medical history that covers all essential aspects of the history, including issues related to age, gender and socio-economic status."

The objectives call on medical schools to ensure that graduates have knowledge of the "important non-biological determinants of poor health and of the economic, psychological, social, and cultural factors that contribute to the development and/or continuation of maladies." They would also require of graduates a "commitment to provide care to patients who are unable to pay and to advocate for access to health care for members of traditionally underserved populations."

Health Services Research Institute

Division of Minority Health, Education, and Prevention
202 828-0579

The Health Services Research Institute, sponsored by the AAMC, with funding from the AHCPR, was established to prepare more medical school faculty to be knowledgeable about cultural competence issues. Since 1991, more than 50 minority medical school faculty members have received fellowships to research issues, such as cultural barriers affecting the patient-doctor relationship and how socio-cultural backgrounds, economic factors, and other variables are related to the prevalence of diseases.

Resources for Teaching/Evaluation

In response to the needs identified in the AAMC survey, the Division of Medical Education has solicited detailed information from a number of programs. Materials include program outlines, information on evaluation tools, and resource individuals at a number of schools and programs.

The AAMC is currently cataloguing this information and plans to have a compendium of material available in 1999. For information:
http://www.aamc.org/meded/edres/cime/start.htm.

Association of American Colleges and Universities

Leader's Guide: Curriculum Transformation

DiversityWeb
http://www.inform.umd.edu/DiversityWeb/Leaders
guide/CT/

Provides specific examples of successful efforts in "curriculum transformation" at hundreds of colleges and universities. Resources cited frequently include online discussion groups. Many focus on specific groups: Asian Americans; Hispanic cultures; people with different kinds of disabilities; families across cultures; women; and gays, lesbians, and bisexuals.

C&W Associates

825 Diligence Dr, Ste 104
Newport News, VA 23606
757 874-7208
757 874-4735 Fax
E-mail: chines@seva.net
http://www.seva.net/bus/cw.associates/

Offers customized cross-cultural training, typically 1 to 3 days, with follow-up.

California Medical Association

Jack C Lewin, MD, Executive Vice President
221 Main St, 2nd Fl
San Francisco, CA 94105
415 541-0900
415 882-5116 Fax

Cross-cultural Medicine and Cross-cultural Medicine, a Decade Later

West J Med, December 1983 (whole issue)
West J Med, September 1992 (whole issue)

Cross-cultural Communication in the Physician's Office

JD Mull
West J Med, December 1993, pp 609-613

Center for Cross-Cultural Health

410 Church St SE, Ste W-227
Minneapolis, MN 55455
612 624-4668
E-mail: ccch@tc.umn.edu
http://www.umn.edu/ccch
A clearinghouse on the role of culture in health that offers both standard and customized training packages, on-site consultation, and cultural competence assessment. Also offers community profiles for Vietnamese, Bosnian, Hmong, Nuer, Russian Jewish, and Ukranian groups in the greater Minneapolis area.

Culture and Health Project

Offers culture and health competence training on topics such as why culture matters in health care; why communication is essential for cultural competence in health care; nonverbal cross-cultural communication; working with interpreters; and specific cultural groups. Topics may be tailored to specific needs.

Caring Across Cultures: The Provider's Guide to Cross-Cultural Health Care

Cross Winds (quarterly newsletter)

Six Steps Toward Cultural Competence

Through the Eyes of Others: Cultural Competency Resources for Health Care Professionals

Center for Health Care Strategies (CHCS)

353 Nassau St
Princeton, NJ 08540

In 1997, the CHCS and Pfizer sponsored a national conference addressing the importance of functional literacy to navigate the health care system. Illiterate patients were found to be at greater risk of mis-understanding their diagnosis, prescriptions, and self-care instructions.

Connect with Spanish Language Center

PO Box 1622
Brookline, MA 02146
617 277-3181

Provides specialized Spanish language instruction. Cross-cultural medical Spanish programs are taught at Boston University School of Medicine or at physicians' offices. Offers courses in:

* Translation

* Cross-cultural medical English

* Cross-cultural medical Spanish

The Center provides the skills for communicating with Spanish-speaking patients and their families in delivering more effective medical care. Combines grammar, medical terminology, colloquial Spanish, and culture from beginner through advanced levels.

Cross-Cultural Communications

4585 48th St
San Diego, CA 92115
800 858-4478
619 583-4478
E-mail: STPhd@aol.com

Offers customized training, books, and videos.

Cross Cultural Health Care Program (CCHCP)

Pacific Medical Center
1200 12th Ave S
Seattle, WA 98144
206 621-4478
E-mail: training@pacmed.org
http://www.xculture.org

CCHCP Contacts via E-mail

Administration of CCHCP
bookdag@pacmed.org

Training Programs
training@pacmed.org

Grants and Resource Development
grants@pacmed.org

Research Projects
research@pacmed.org

Publications and Mailing Lists
rosel@pacmed.org

Resource Center
resource@pacmed.org

The CCHCP serves as a bridge between communities and health care institutions to ensure full access to quality health care that is culturally and linguistically appropriate.

The CCHCP provides training in cultural competence and language access in health and social service settings for health care professionals who provide care, administrators who coordinate the delivery of health care, and policymakers who regulate the form and manner of health care delivery.

* Provides assistance to organizations in conducting cultural competence assessment of their systems and services and in formulating workable plans for implementing change.

* Provides training for administrators and policymakers of organizations that provide, finance, and regulate health care.

- Prepares a cadre of trainers to continue the work of building culturally competent systems (3-day course).

CCHCP's approach places culture within the context of an interwoven network of relationships. The CCHCP also recognizes that health care systems and institutions operate as complex cultures, with specialized languages, traditions, and codes of conduct.

Language Services

Using bilingual and bicultural translators who are adept in both the cultures and languages concerned, the CCHCP provides interpreter and translation services in more than 50 languages for more than 25,000 patient encounters each year.

Publications

Collected Community Profiles

Contains descriptions of the culture and beliefs of Arab, Cambodian, Ethiopian, Eritrean, Lao, Mien, Oromo, Samoan, Somali, South Asian, Ukranian, and Soviet Jewish communities, as written by members of those communities.

Bilingual Medical Glossaries

Includes Cambodian, Korean, Lao, Mandarin, Russian, Vietnamese, and Spanish-English or English-Spanish.

Bridging the Gap: Basic Training for Medical Interpreters

A 40-hour CCHCP course used to prepare dedicated interpreters and bilingual medical staff who are asked to serve as interpreters. Also available are Training of Trainers, 2-3 day workshops for those who want to teach *Bridging the Gap*, as well as workshops for health care providers in working effectively through an interpreter.

Bridging the Gap Interpreter Handbook

Interpreter's Guide to Common Medications

Answers commonly asked questions about how medications work, how they are administered, and how they act.

Survey of Twenty-three Medical Interpreter Training Programs in the United States and Canada

Videos

Introduction to Interpreting in and Around Seattle

Understanding East African Communities

Understanding Latino Communities

Understanding Arab Communities

Understanding Russian Communities

East Africans and Mental Health: Delivering Bad News

Understanding Somali Communities

Communicating Effectively Through an Interpreter

Research and Resource Center

The CCHCP designs and conducts qualitative, community-centered research around issues of cross-cultural health care. Two current projects are Death and Dying in Ethnic America and Defining Cultural Competency in Medicaid Managed Care. The CCHCP has numerous resource directories on topics ranging from professional associations and community services to charitable foundations.

Education Program Associates

1 W Campbell Ave, Ste 45
Campbell, CA 95008-1039
408 374-3720
408 374-7385 Fax
E-mail: info@epa.org

The EPA includes a publications department, consulting services, and a Health Resource Center. Publications include easy-to-read (third-grade reading level and up) and culturally sensitive print and audiovisual materials about family health and multicultural health. EPA's consulting services provide training in culturally and linguistically appropriate health education materials development. The EPA's Health Resource Center, a membership service, provides access to over 7,000 health education materials in English, Spanish, and Asian languages that have been evaluated for reading level, audience, cultural appropriateness, translation quality, and content.

Fairbanks Research and Training Institute

Box 50856
Indianapolis, IN
317 842-8221
http://www.fairbankshospital.org

As a provider of professional education, consultation, and training in the field of substance abuse throughout the Midwest, the Institute has designed the Cultural Competency Action Training Project to help Indiana Managed Care Providers improve addiction treatment outcomes for the various cultural groups within their service regions.

Family Link Cultural Competence Training

The Family Link
10 W 35th St, Ste 14C3
Chicago, IL
312 326-1488

The Family Link offers both standard and customized cultural sensitive training to social service professionals, especially those who work with children and families.

Health Care Advisory Board

606 New Hampshire Ave, NW
Washington, DC 20037
202 672-5600
202 672-5700 Fax

The Health Care Advisory Board (HCAB) is a membership-based health care research firm that strives to identify innovations in health care finance and care delivery. The mission of the firm is to identify, describe, and disseminate these ideas to its members. The HCAB conducts special research services for its members and provided several entries for the sections on end-of-life care and spirituality in this publication.

Health Promotion Council of Southeastern Pennsylvania

311 S Juniper St, Ste 308
Philadelphia, PA 19107-5803
215 546-1276
215 545-1395 Fax
E-mail: hpcpa@libertynet.org
http://www.libertynet.org/hpcpa/

The Health Promotion Council promotes health to those at greatest risk through publications and training. Its pamphlets and audiovisuals for African-Americans, Latinos, and Asians, written at or below a sixth-grade reading level, currently cover blood pressure, diabetes, smoking, stress, nutrition, and use of the health care system. The Council has materials in Spanish, Cambodian, Chinese, and Vietnamese. It provides a 7- to 8-week training and curriculum for community-based hypertension and diabetes control, offered in both Spanish and English. Its Health Literacy Project offers teaching materials geared to cultural and literacy levels.

Institute of Medicine (IOM)

2101 Constitution Ave, NW
Washington, DC 20418
202 334-3300

A committee of the IOM has issued a congressionally requested report outlining ways in which the National Institutes of Health (NIH) should further explore why cancer is taking a greater toll in some groups according to race and ethnicity. The committee recommended classifying information according to ethnicity to highlight how differences in cancer incidence and mortality rates may be linked to a range of cultural factors, behaviors, health attitudes, and lifestyle conditions. The IOM published a landmark report, Approaching Death: Improving Care at the End of Life (Washington DC: National Academy Press, 1997), which includes curriculum suggestions.

Massachusetts Medical Interpreter Association in Conjunction with Education Development Center

750 Washington St
NEMC Box 271
Boston, MA 02111-1845
617 636-5479
617 636-6283 Fax
Education Development Center
800 225-4276

This project developed comprehensive medical interpreter standards based on a content analysis of interpreter skills and work responsibilities. Includes resources for interpreters around the country, guidelines for quality assessment and qualifications, and publications, videos, and training.

Medical Education Group

1 E University Pkwy, Ste 106
Baltimore, MD 21218
410 366-6212
http://www.megonline.com

Programs include customized cross-cultural training and one for physicians that awards CME credit.

Multus Inc

46 Treetop Ln, Ste 200
San Mateo, CA 94402
415 342-2040

Produces the HealthCare DIVERSOPHY Training Board Game, a training tool in cultural competence designed for the health care industry. Presents practical solutions for clinical issues involving culturally diverse patients.

National Action Plan on Breast Cancer (NAPBC)

Office of Public Health & Science
Office of Women's Health
Hubert H. Humphrey Building
200 Independence Ave, SW
Room 718E
Washington, DC 20201
202 690-7650
http://www.napbc.org

The 1999 Workshop on the Multicultural Aspects of Breast Cancer Etiology brought together breast cancer research and minority health advocacy communities to examine current knowledge concerning multicultural aspects of breast cancer etiology and to identify and prioritize future research directions. Panel discussions, question/answer sessions, and breakout sessions on specific risk factors and five racial and ethnic minority populations were included.

National Academy on Women's Health Medical Education

MCP Hahnemann University
Broad and Vine, MS 490
Philadelphia, PA 19102
215 762-4260
215 762-7301 Fax

Sponsored by MCP Hahnemann University and the American Medical Women's Association, NAWHME works to infuse women's health education into all phases of the medical education curriculum—undergraduate, graduate, and continuing—nationwide. Active participants in the group include:

- Directors of existing women's health medical education programs.

- Educators with experience in gender-related education

- Representatives of advocacy groups in women's health

- Representatives of medical professional organizations concerned with women's health

- Representatives of regulatory bodies with responsibility for medical education

National Center for Cultural Competence

307 M St NW, Ste 401
Washington, DC 20007-3935
202 687-5000

The Center is part of the Georgetown University Child Development Center, a division of Georgetown University Medical Center. This program's mission is to design, implement, and evaluate culturally competent service delivery systems for children with special health needs and their families from culturally diverse populations.

National Coalition of Hispanic Health and Human Services Organizations

1501 16th St, NW
Washington, DC 20036
202 387-5000

Proyecto Informar: A Training Program for Health Care Providers

Two-day comprehensive cross-cultural training program designed to improve access to health services by preparing health care providers to offer culturally competent health services to Hispanics, by examining their attitudes towards Hispanics and practicing new behaviors. The program's five modules include:

- Understanding Hispanics in the United States

- Understanding the role of culture in health

- Navigating cultural differences

- Navigating language differences

- Developing a culturally competent system

National Institute for Healthcare Research (NIHR)

6110 Executive Blvd, Ste 908
Rockville, MD 20852
301 231-7409

Spirituality, Cross-Cultural Issues, and End of Life Care: Curricular Development

The 1998 Conference included in-depth workshops with key information on cross-cultural issues and end-of-life care.

National MultiCultural Institute (NMCI)

3000 Connecticut Ave NW, Ste 438
Washington, DC 20008-2556
202 483-0700
http://www.nmci.org/nmci/index.html

The mission of the National MultiCultural Institute (NMCI), founded in 1983, is to increase communication, understanding, and respect among people of different racial, ethnic, and cultural backgrounds and to provide a forum for discussion of the critical issues of multiculturalism facing our society. The NMCI provides consulting service to President Clinton's Initiative on Race.

National Conferences

The NMCI has sponsored workshops on professional issues relating to diversity twice a year since 1985, designed to create a multicultural environment in which an open, cross-cultural dialogue can occur; focus on some of the unique issues that professionals face in working with culturally diverse populations; and offer an opportunity for in-depth training and skill building in multiculturalism.

Conferences generally are organized in tracks of cultural awareness, the workplace, education, and dialogue and conflict resolution and are offered in 4-day, 2-day, 1-day, and ½-day workshops.

The 13th annual spring conference, Beyond Rhetoric: Redefining Common Ground Through Diversity, May 28-31, 1998, Washington, DC, included workshops on exploring cultural assumptions, building cultural awareness, and examining cultural competence in health care.

Diversity Training and Consulting Services

The NMCI works with professional associations, hospitals, corporations, government agencies, nonprofit organizations, schools, and universities to help meet the long-term challenges of diversity. The programs focus both on individual and organizational change. Consulting services offer organizations the

opportunity to assess the climate of their working environment, heighten awareness of employees, and develop long-term plans for implementing and sustaining diversity initiatives.

The NMCI conducted an extensive organizational audit for the American Pharmaceutical Association and is designing a training program based on the results.

The NMCI also designed and delivered a series of workshops on diversity issues to train physicians at the New York Medical College and developed, designed, and delivered a Training of Trainers workshop for health care professionals at the University of California San Francisco School of Medicine.

The NMCI has provided services to other health care-related organizations, including the

- American Counseling Association

- American Medical Student Association

- Burdette Tomlin Hospital

- Cancer Information Services

- CMG Health Corporation

- Hospice of Northern Virginia

- US Food and Drug Administration

- Virginia Department of Health

Materials

Cultural Competency in Healthcare: A Guide for Trainers
Rohini Anaud

A comprehensive training manual for health care professionals on diversity issues in the workplace. Incorporating NMCI's guides for trainers, *Teaching Skills and Cultural Competency* and *Developing Diversity Training for the Workplace* (see below), it provides step-by-step guidelines for developing an experiential workshop to meet the specific needs of health care professionals, including providers and administrators. The manual includes models of cultural competence in health care, barriers to providing culturally competent care, exercises, lectures, tips for designing effective needs assessments and case studies, sample training designs, and an extensive bibliography.

Developing Diversity Training for the Workplace: A Guide for Trainers
4th edition, 1997
Lauren N. Nile

A detailed manual for diversity trainers, including sections on Trainer Readiness Self-Assessment, Managing Personal Hot Buttons, Working Effectively in a Diverse Training Team, Design Theory and Models, Elements of a One-Day Workshop, lectures, exercises, hard copy for transparencies, sample participant handouts, extensive references to resource materials (training tools, videos, exercises, and simulations), and a bibliography.

Multicultural Case Studies: Tools for Training
1998
Rohini Anaud, Laura K. Shipler

A collection of case studies to be used in diversity training for professionals in all fields. Sections include General Workplace Issues, Education, Health Care, and Mental Health. Case studies include training tips and discussion guides.

Teaching Skills and Cultural Competency: A Guide for Trainers
2nd edition, 1998
Rohini Anaud

Detailed manual for diversity trainers who want to conduct workshops that move beyond personal awareness to building specific skills and cultural competence. The manual includes sections on Models of Cultural Competence, Communication, Conflict Resolution, Team Building, Giving Effective Feedback, and Individual/Organizational Action Planning. The manual presents guidelines for trainer competencies around personal awareness, facilitation skills, and knowledge. It also provides tools for using

case studies, designing an effective needs assessment, and identifying the advantages and pitfalls of working in diverse training teams.

Cultural Diversity in the Hospital Setting Training Video

This 2-hour video, taped at a research hospital, contains lectures and questions and answers on developing cultural awareness, minimizing stereotypical thinking, and communicating more effectively across accent and language barriers. Also covered are issues relating to managing and motivating a multicultural staff. The participants are a group of culturally diverse hospital employees who bring their real-life, on-the-job questions, concerns, and experiences.

Counseling and Referral Services

The NMCI maintains information on community health resources for multilingual counseling in the Washington, DC, area. Experienced health professionals associated with the NMCI provide therapy in 25 languages to individuals and families.

Competence Assessment Tool

The NMCI will be developing an assessment tool to measure the cultural competence of providers.

North Carolina Office of Minority Health

Department of Health and Human Services
225 N McDowell St
PO Box 29612
Raleigh, NC 27626-0612
919 715-0992

The mission of the NCOMH is to bridge the health status gap between North Carolina's white and minority populations by improving the quality and availability of health information and providing cultural diversity training to public health staff.

Publications

- **Cultural Diversity Training for NC Public Health: A Facilitator's Guide**

- **An Assessment of Health Service Needs**

- **Innovative Services**

- **Health-Related Resources for the Hispanic/Latino Community in North Carolina**

- **Interpreter Services for Hispanic/Latino Clients: Report and Recommendations**

Office of Minority Health (OMH)

Rockwall II Building, Ste 1000
5600 Fishers Ln
Rockville, MD 20857
301 443-5224, 800 444-6472
http://www.omhrc.gov

The mission of the OMH is to improve the health of racial and ethnic populations through the development of effective health policies and programs that help to eliminate health disparities and gaps. These populations include blacks/African Americans, American Indians and Alaska Natives, Asian Americans, Native Hawaiians and other Pacific Islanders, and Hispanics/Latinos.

Regional minority health consultants serve as OMH representatives in the 10 HHS regional offices. The OMH works closely with established state offices of minority health and provides technical assistance, as requested, to minority community groups working to establish similar entities.

Data on Gaps in Health Care

Significant gaps still exist regarding health status, quality of life, and related risk factors for racial and ethnic minority communities. The OMH staff work with other DHHS agencies to identify health data needs for racial and ethnic minorities and develop mechanisms to address them. They provide technical assistance on research methods for racial and ethnic minority communities and the

classification of race and ethnicity. In addition, the OMH staff collaborate with state minority health offices to monitor state multiracial legislation.

The OMH staff analyze current and prospective federal activities that affect minority health and recommend program initiatives to improve the health of minorities; review the budget requests of PHS agencies to ensure that requirements are adequate and consistent with the Secretary's minority health goals and strategic plans; and plan, coordinate, and/or conduct studies and evaluations relating to the occurrence of diseases and health problems in minority populations.

Healthy People 2010 Activities

The Secretary's Council on Health Promotion and Disease Prevention Objectives for 2010 sets goals for eliminating health disparities by race, ethnicity, age, gender, income, and disability status. It focuses on promoting healthy behavior, promoting healthy and safe communities, improving systems for personal and public health, and preventing and reducing diseases and disorders.

Research, Demonstration Projects, and Grants

The OMH cooperative agreements and grants help launch research and demonstration projects. Multi-project cooperative agreements, regularly funded both by the OMH and other partners within DHHS as joint ventures, include:

- American Indian Higher Education Consortium

- Asian and Pacific Islander American Health Forum

- Association of American Indian Physicians

- Association of Asian Pacific Community Health Organizations

- Interamerican College of Physicians and Surgeons

- Minority Health Professions Foundation

- National Asian Pacific American Families Against Substance Abuse

- National Coalition of Hispanic Health and Human Services Organizations

- National Council of La Raza

- National Medical Association

The OMH encourages efforts to facilitate community linkages and strategies that maximize resources through grant programs, including:

- Minority Community Health Coalition Demonstration Grants

- Bilingual/Bicultural Service Demonstration Grant

- Program Information Technology Infrastructure Grant Program

Minority Health Network

The Minority Health Network empowers minority communities by building and strengthening viable partnerships across the public and private sectors.

Together with state Offices of Minority Health in more than 28 states and official liaisons in other states and jurisdictions, regional minority health consultants serve as the contact for federal, state, and local collaboration, technical assistance, and information exchange.

Population-Specific Initiatives

The OMH coordinates DHHS efforts to implement selected White House Initiatives and sponsors initiatives of its own.

- White House Initiative on Historically Black Colleges and Universities

- Hispanic Agenda for Action

- White House Initiative on Tribal Colleges and Universities

- Asian American and Pacific Islander Action Agenda

- American Indian/Alaska Native Initiative

As of October 1998, the Departmental Minority Initiatives Steering Committee will provide guidance and make decisions on policy issues relating to the four initiatives. The Departmental Minority Initiatives Coordinating Committee is responsible for coordinating the work of the four minority initiatives.

Minority Health Resource Center

800 444-6472
301 589-0884 Fax
301 589-0951 TDD
E-mail: info@omhrc.gov
http://www.omhrc.gov

In 1987, the OMH established the Office of Minority Health Resource Center to meet the public's need for a source of reliable, accurate, and timely information and technical assistance. The Resource Center conducts mailings inviting the public's involvement in forming health care policies. Staff conduct customized database searches, identify appropriate publications or funding sources, and make referrals to other health organizations. Services of the center are free, and Spanish-speaking information specialists are available.

Center for Linguistic and Cultural Competence in Health Care

To address language barriers in the health system faced by limited English-speaking populations, the OMH is developing the Center for Linguistic and Cultural Competency in Health Care, funds permitting. This "center without walls" will house a national database of culturally competent programs in health care and culturally competent training curricula for health care providers.

Media Projects

The OMH is a supporter of Healthfinder, the DHHS consumer information Web site. The OMH has developed a series of radio messages with basic consumer information for broadcasts in Spanish on radio stations across the United States and is collaborating with the National Council of La Raza to develop consumer health shows for Spanish-language television.

Selected Publications

Closing the Gap

Monthly newsletter that regularly reports on departmental, state, and community-based activities related to minority health. Each newsletter covers a different health topic and is available both electronically and in print.

Pocket Guide to Minority Health

Provides information on minority health resources available to the public. Aimed at consumers, professionals, and organizations, this guide details sources of information on various health-related topics and lists associations and federal clearinghouses, OMH regional minority health consultants, and state minority health contacts.

Breast Cancer Resource Guide for Minority Women

Provides a listing of information available on breast cancer, including organizations, documents, journal articles, and other resources.

Ohio Department of Mental Health

30 E Broad St, 8th Fl
Columbus, Ohio, 43266-0315
http://www.mh.state.oh.us/

Cultural Competence in Mental Health
October 1998

The Ohio Department of Mental Health (ODMH) has been engaged in activities that focus on providing mental health services that are available, accessible, acceptable, appropriate, and adaptable and that meet the needs of Ohio's ethnically diverse populations, including African-Americans, Hispanics/Latinos, American Indians, and Asian/Pacific-Americans. Particular emphasis has been placed in developing new approaches of service delivery that address cultural differences.

During fiscal years 1994-1995 and 1996-1997, the ODMH funded ADAMH/CMH Boards to develop nine culturally competent programs to encourage the provision of cultural sensitivity training to the mental health community and to develop nontraditional and culturally sensitive service delivery methods. As of October 1998, four of these programs have been evaluated.

The evaluation focused on three basic questions that tried to ascertain the changes in:

- client's use of mental health services

- staff knowledge and skills in how services are provided

- policy development to reflect cultural competence

Data were obtained from many sources, including:

- Local data gathered at each site

- Evaluation data from internal program evaluation efforts

- Data maintained at ODMH from project reports, site visits, and anecdotal information

- On-site data obtained from standardized protocols used during site visits

- ODMH staff who monitored the status of data collection

- Written, open-ended survey questionnaire mailed to each site

- Information obtained from consumers

The key findings and cross-program commonalities were used to develop a model for Organizational Cultural Competence. The final report is organized into four parts:

Evaluation of Programs—includes a description of the evaluation approach used to assess the nine programs; a description of each program; a discussion of cross-program observations, including similarities and differences across the nine programs; and a delineation of key findings and important concepts that evolved from the evaluation.

Organizational Cultural Competence Model— introduces the guiding framework used to formulate the recommendations.

Recommendations—reflect the changes needed to continue to improve the delivery of effective mental health services to ethnically diverse persons.

Appendices—provide a checklist of materials collected from the programs, the survey questionnaire, and other materials central to the project.

Picker Institute

1295 Boylston St, Ste 100
Boston, MA 02215
617 667-2388
http://www.picker.org

The Institute sponsors an annual symposium, Through the Patient's Eyes. The 1997 symposium focused on Envisioning Culturally Competent Health Care. The 1999 symposium, Improvement Tools for the New Millenium, featured presentations and interactive breakout sessions on end-of-life care, shared decisionmaking, the relationship between employee and patient satisfaction, and public reporting of data. Tools and strategies for improving health care from the patient's perspective were presented. Topics included:

- Correlating patients' perspectives with clinical outcomes

- The impact of patient-centered processes on outcomes

- Using the Baldrige criteria to help create a patient-focused environment

- End-of-life care from the family's perspective

- Using technology to improve patients' experiences and outcomes

President's Initiative on Race

http://www.whitehouse.gov/Initiatives/OneAmerica/america.html

In 1997, President Clinton announced *One America in the 21st Century: The President's Initiative on Race.* Among its stated goals was "to have a diverse, democratic community in which Americans respect, even celebrate their differences, while embracing the shared values that unite them." To reach that goal, the President has asked all Americans to join him in a national effort to deal openly and honestly with our racial differences. One of the central features of this program is a series of thoughtful discussions aimed at helping Americans understand the causes of racial tension and the steps communities might take to relieve them.

The Initiative has recently published a compilation of race relations programs that includes a framework to assess strengths and weaknesses of diversity initiatives.

Regional Health Education Center

1000 4th St SW
Mason City, IA 50401
515 422-7100

A partnership between the North Iowa Mercy Health Center and North Iowa Area Community College offers the following classes for health care professionals:

- Spanish for Health Care Workers

- Assisting the Hispanic Client in Health Care, which is designed to increase the participant's awareness of the health care needs of the Hispanic client, including the values and beliefs of Hispanic culture that may have an impact on health care.

Resources for Cross Cultural Health Care (RCCHC)

Julia Puebla Fortier, Director
8915 Sudbury Rd
Silver Spring, MD 20901
301 588-6051
http://www.diversityrx.org

A national network of individuals and organizations in ethnic communities and health care organized to offer technical assistance and information on linguistic and cultural competence in health care.

Programs are designed to help policymakers, health care administrators and practitioners, and consumer representatives deliver quality health care services to ethnically diverse populations. The RCCHC provides information, resources, and technical assistance to design and implement linguistically and culturally appropriate health care programs and policies.

Areas of Expertise

- Medical interpretation program design and training

- Cross-cultural assessment and training

- Development of linguistically and culturally competent health care programs, policies, and laws, especially Medicaid managed care policy and Title VI enforcement

Services

- Program design

- Policy development and analysis

- Research

- Community advocacy

- Onsite and telephone technical assistance, consultation services, and referrals

- Custom informational packets for individuals and organizations representing federal, state, and local governments; public health departments; community-based organizations; managed care organizations; hospitals and clinics; universities; and advocacy groups

Policy Research and Development

Includes a DHHS-sponsored project to evaluate federal, state, and private-sector measures of linguistic and cultural competence and to develop a draft national standard and accompanying research agenda.

Information Dissemination

- *Diversity Rx* Web site (www.diversityrx.org) is a comprehensive clearinghouse of information on model programs, policies, and legal issues related to cross-cultural health, in collaboration with the National Conference of State Legislatures and the Kaiser Family Foundation.

- *Cross Currents* (quarterly newsletter) includes news and analysis of cross cultural health issues; program profiles; training and curriculum reviews; and forums on topics of current interest.

Online Interactive Forums

The RCCHC sponsors online interactive forums for policymakers, managed care organizations, medical interpreters, and researchers interested in sharing information and best practices on linguistically and culturally appropriate health care.

Conferences

Offers conference development and workshops, presentations, and poster sessions on a variety of cross-cultural health topics for meetings and institutional training seminars. The RCCHC cosponsored, with the New York Academy of Medicine and the OMH, a widely attended national conference on quality health care for culturally diverse populations (New York, October 1998).

Western Interstate Commission for Higher Education (WICHE)

PO Box 9752
1540 30th St, RL-2 (third floor)
Boulder, CO 80301
303 541-0200

Cultural Competence Standards in Managed Mental Health Care

The WICHE and the Center for Mental Health Services of the Substance Abuse and Mental Health Services Administration

Standards, guidelines, and cultural competencies for managed behavioral health services for racial/ethnic populations were produced by four national panels. These documents, which emphasize that consumers should be viewed within the context of their cultural group, include:

- a core set of standards for delivering culturally competent services and

- ethnic-specific system and clinical standards and guidelines for African Americans, Asian and Pacific Islander Americans, Latinos, and Native Americans

Core Cultural Competence Standards

Cultural Competence Standards in Managed Mental Health Care for Four Underserved/ Underrepresented Racial/Ethnic Groups

Ethnic-specific Cultural Competence Standards

Consumer-driven Standards and Guidelines in Managed Mental Health for Populations of African Descent

Cultural Competence Standards in Managed Care Mental Health Services for Asian and Pacific Islander American Populations

Cultural Competence Standards in Managed Care Mental Health Services for Latino Populations

Cultural Competence Standards in Managed Care Mental Health Services for Native American Populations

Cultural Competence Assessment Tools

Developing Culturally Competent Systems of Care for State Mental Health Services

Includes:

- A patient satisfaction survey containing suggested modifications

- A service provider version of a cultural competence self-assessment questionnaire

- Clinical performance assessment

- Cultural competence assessment instrument focusing on organizational environment, public relations, community work, human resources, and clinical issues

- Program and administration self-assessment survey for cultural competence

- Administrative performance assessment

- A community survey on cultural competence

B. Educational Institutions

California

Stanford University School of Medicine

Senior Associate Dean for Education and Student
Affairs
300 Pasteur Dr
Stanford, CA 94305
415 725-3900
http://www-med3.stanford.edu

"Physicians and Patients (Doctoring): Focus on
Cultural Issues and Nutrition" exposes students to
interdisciplinary topics related to health and disease
to give them an understanding of some of the
complex interactions between the patient, the
doctor, and society.

University of California
at San Francisco
Division of General Internal Medicine
San Francisco General Hospital

Helen Chen, MD
SFGH Medical Clinic
http://www.medicine.ucsf.edu/dgimsfgh/
residency.html

The primary care internal medicine residency
program incorporates into practice the humanistic
aspects of patient care. This includes the
psychosocial aspects of medical care as well as the
relationship of a person's physical, cultural, social,
and economic environment to health. In the first
year a module, "Improving Cultural Competence,"
is offered, which includes experiential training and
segments on medical treatment issues with specific
ethnic groups. In the third year a core month focuses
on alternative medicine, which includes clinical site
visits to practitioners of acupuncture, Chinese
medicine, and biofeedback and addresses the
integration of spiritual/religious beliefs into
medicine.

Connecticut

Yale University School of Medicine

Robert H. Gifford, MD
Deputy Dean for Education
Yale University School of Medicine
Director, Office of Education
367 Cedar St/ESH 21
New Haven, CT 06510-8046
203 785-3800
203 737-4911 Fax
E-mail: robert.gifford@yale.edu

A year-long course, "Doctor-Patient Encounter,"
required for all first-year medical students, introduces
issues of multiculturalism in realistic clinical
encounters between physicians and patients through
case studies and small group discussions. Focuses on
racial/ethnic and sexual orientation issues; some
coverage of religion, alternative/complementary
medicine, linguistic barriers/interpretation, and
reproductive choices.

District of Columbia

Georgetown University Child
Development Center

National Technical Assistance Center for Children's
Mental Health
3307 M St NW, Ste 401
Washington, DC 20007-3935
202 687-5000

Offers training institutes and workshops to provide
in-depth, practical information on developing and
operating community-based systems of care,
including Operationalizing Cultural Competence
and Culturally Competent Systems of Care.

Georgia

Morehouse School of Medicine

Department of Community Health and Preventive
Medicine
Associate Dean for Student Affairs and Curriculum
720 Westview Dr SW
Atlanta, GA 30310
404 752-1500
http://www.msm.edu/chpmdept.html

Aspects of the humanities in medicine curriculum
have been integrated into five required courses to
expose students to more empathetic interactions
with patients, particularly among the poor and
elderly. The first year of the 2-year "Human Values
in Medicine" course introduces medical students to
current ethical dilemmas and human values issues
explored from clinical, public health, psychosocial,
and cultural perspectives.

The public health and preventive medicine
residency program includes content related to
cultural competence.

Hawaii

University of Hawaii
John A. Burns School of Medicine

Associate Dean for Student Affairs
1960 East-West Road
Honolulu, Hawaii 96822
808 956-8287
http://medworld.biomed.hawaii.edu/Prog.html

Special features of the program include an emphasis
on primary care medicine and cross-cultural
psychiatry.

Illinois

Cook County Hospital

Department of Family Practice
1900 W. Polk St, 13th Floor
Chicago, IL 60612
312 633-8587

The family practice residency program utilizes the
video training program *Shared Understanding:
Bridging Racial and Socioeconomic Differences in
Doctor-Patient Communication*, a 40-minute
instructional video based on a cross-cultural medical
interview, and a bound manual.

Loyola University Medical Center
Stritch School of Medicine

Associate Dean of Educational Affairs
2160 S First Ave
Maywood, IL 60153
708 216-9000
http://www.meddean.luc.edu

"Introduction to the Practice of Medicine II"
explores the various psychosocial, cultural,
economic, and spiritual facets of illness. Each
student also goes on rounds with a chaplain at
Loyola University Medical Center, an experience
designed to help students understand the personal
and spiritual impact of illness in a patient's life.

Iowa

University of Iowa College of Medicine

Office of Student Affairs and Curriculum
100 Medicine Administration Bldg
Iowa City, IA 52242-1101
319 335-8050
http://www.medicine.uiowa.edu/OSAC/
Medcurric.htm

The curriculum strives to orient medicine in the larger
societal context, so that students appreciate the impact
of patients' beliefs and personal environments on
disease processes, as well as their response to
treatment.

Massachusetts

Harvard Medical School

Department of Continuing Education
25 Shattuck St
Boston, MA 02115
617 432-1000

Offers "Mind/Body Training in Optimism, Humor, and Cognitive Restructuring" and CME programs around the country.

Michigan

University of Michigan Medical School

Associate Dean for Student Programs
1301 Catherine Rd
Medical Science Building I
Ann Arbor, MI 48100-0624
313 763-9600
http://www.med.umich.edu

Students in the "Introduction to the Patient" course discuss medical ethics, medical economics, and social and cultural issues. Students rotating through the required family practice clerkship gain experience in comprehensive care of individuals and their families in the context of their psychosocial, economic, and community environments.

Minnesota

Mayo Medical School

Associate Dean for Student Affairs
200 First St SW
Rochester, MN 55905
507 284-3671
http:/www.mayo.edu/education/mms/year4.htm

As part of the Patient, Physician, and Society curricular unit, fourth-year students elect at least one of their clerkships in the area of social medicine/cultural diversity.

Nebraska

Creighton University School of Dentistry

Associate Dean for Academic Affairs
2500 California Plaza
Omaha, NE 68178
402 280-2881
http://jonah.creighton.edu/aboutsccnet.htm

The Socio-Cultural Competence NET at Creighton has an online tutorial to sensitize dental students and other health professionals to distinctive issues concerning access and dental care delivery in a diverse sociocultural environment. The information is organized into three modules: education, research, and links to other sites. The education module contains an interactive multimedia program, including the general principles of sociocultural competence, a literature review, and case studies.

New Jersey

New Jersey Medical School

Associate Dean for Education
185 S Orange Ave
Newark, NJ 07103-2714
201 982-4300
http://www.umdnj.edu/njmsweb/educ/course/artmed.htm

The Art of Medicine module introduces first-year students to clinical medicine, including the impact of economic, cultural, and legal/political influences on the American health care system. A session on patient education/cross-cultural medicine is offered during the winter/spring semester.

New York

University of Medicine and Dentistry of New Jersey-Robert Wood Johnson Medical School

Center for Healthy Families and Cultural Diversity
Department of Family Medicine
1 Robert Wood Johnson Pl
New Brunswick, NY 08903
732 235-7662
E-mail: like@umdnj.edu

Offers half- to full-day customized cross-cultural training.

New York University School of Medicine

New York Task Force on Immigrant Health
Office of Minority Affairs and Student Services
550 First Ave
New York, NY 10016
212 263-8949
http://www.med.nyu.edu/MINORITY.html

Established in 1989, the Task Force facilitates the delivery of culturally and epidemiologically sensitive health services for immigrants. Membership includes health practitioners, social scientists, community advocates, and policy makers. The integrated, interdisciplinary approach to immigrant health includes research, education, training, information dissemination, and program policy development. Publications include:

Cross-cultural Care Giving in Maternal and Child Health: A Trainer's Manual, 1995

Presents techniques to conduct immigrant health training sessions for maternal and child health care providers. Topics include:

- working with interpreters

- the cross-cultural medical interview and history taking

- maternal child health beliefs and practices across cultures

- family dynamics and domestic violence

Epidemiologic Information on Immigrants and Minority Groups in New York, 1980-1993: An Annotated Bibliography, 1994

Presents results of computerized literature searches of Medline, Psylit, Cancerlit, Health Administration, Sociological Abstracts, and Doctoral Dissertation Abstracts to locate all New York immigrant and Puerto Rican epidemiological data published since 1980. Annotations of 93 articles are classified by disease categories.

Access Through Medical Interpreter and Language Services Research Findings and Recommendations, 1997

Intended to enhance the ability of limited and non-English speaking persons to obtain quality health care services; includes an overview of legal mandates and survey findings of interpreter models in several states.

An Introduction to Medical Interpreter and Language Services Research Findings and Recommendations, 1997

Basic principles of interpreting for individuals working in medical settings.

Integrated Maternal and Child Health Care for Immigrant and Refugee Populations, 1993

Proceedings from a December 1993 symposium that explored the provision of culturally competent health services to various immigrant communities. Topics include cross-cultural training curricula, health beliefs, domestic violence, and prenatal care.

Health Belief Fact Sheets, 1997

Fact sheets describing the health beliefs and practices of Bangladeshi, Chinese, Haitian, Korean, Mexican, Puerto Rican, and West African immigrant groups.

North Carolina

University of North Carolina at Chapel Hill School of Medicine

Associate Dean of Academic Affairs
Chapel Hill, NC 27599
919 966-4161
http://www.med.unc.edu/wrkunits/ldean/acadaff/
descript/program.htm

The medical school curriculum emphasizes the social, cultural, ethical, and economic issues as well as humanities and social and behavioral sciences that influence medicine. The "Medical Practice and the Community I and II" courses emphasize the doctor-patient relationship and the role of the community in health care. The "Medicine and Society" course highlights how illness and healing take place in a cultural context. The "Community Health Project" has medical students working in direct contact with the people of a defined community on health-related issues. The students gain an understanding of the cultural, social, and personal experiences that influence an individual's health and the use of community resources.

Oklahoma

University of Oklahoma Health Sciences Center

Irwin H. Brown
Office of Continuing Medical Education
800 NE 15th St
PO Box 26901
ROB 202
Oklahoma City, OK 73190
888 682-6348

Offers courses in "Enhancing Patient-Physician Communication: The Therapeutic Sequence," "Traditional and Non-Traditional Approaches to Diabetes in Native Communities," and "New Horizons in Women's Health Care."

Oregon

Research and Training Center on Family Support and Children's Mental Health

Portland State University
PO Box 751
Portland, OR 97207-0751
503 725-5558 or 503 725-4040
503 725-4180 Fax

The Center has the overall goal of improving services for families whose children have serious mental, emotional, or behavioral disabilities. All programs of research and training are designed to promote services that are community-based, family-oriented and culturally appropriate. Two of the center's projects relating to cultural diversity are Multicultural Perspectives of Empowerment and Increasing Multicultural Parent Involvement.

Cultural Competence Self-Assessment Questionnaire: A Manual for Users, 1995

Developed to help child and family-serving agencies assess their cross-cultural strengths and weaknesses in order to design specific training activities or interventions that promote greater competence across cultures.

Focal Point

The bulletin of the Portland State Minority Research and Training Center on Family Support and Children's Mental Health reports on culturally competent organizations and projects.
http://www.rtc.pdx.edu

An Introduction to Cultural Competence Principles and Elements: An Annotated Bibliography
JL Mason, K Braker, TL Williams-Murphy
1995

About 115 abstracted listings exemplify aspects of the Child and Adolescent Service System Program's cultural competence model, emphasizing care of children and youth with serious emotional disabilities. Citations are categorized under:

• Cultural Self-Assessment

- Dynamics of Difference

- Valuing Diversity

- Adaptation to Diversity

- Incorporation of Cultural Knowledge

Understanding Cultural Identity in Intervention and Assessment
RH Dana
1998

Presents a model for effective culture-specific services that emphasizes the description and understanding of cultural/racial identity and the use of this information to develop cultural formulations to increase the accuracy of diagnoses, with four chapters devoted to discussions of mental health services.

Pennsylvania

MCP♦Hahnemann School of Medicine

Janet Fleetwood, PhD
Director, Division of Medical Humanities
3300 Henry Ave
Philadelphia, PA 19129
215 842-6540
http://www.auhs.edu/medschool/educprog.html

The mission of the school is to prepare medical graduates to be competent, caring physicians who can collect clinical information as well as communicate and build rapport with patients in order to facilitate diagnosis and therapy. The Medical Humanities Program, administered by the Department of Community and Preventive Medicine, offers a required curriculum in medical ethics for all students and directs skills training in cultural competence.

West Chester University

School of Health Sciences
Department of Health
West Chester, PA 19383
610 436-2300

Offers courses on transcultural health and alternative medicine.

Transcultural Health: Principles and Practices
Contact Roger Mustalich, PhD, 610 436-2101

- Provides an overview of the role of culture in health and sickness.

- Addresses the influence of culture on the health status of individuals and societies.

- Presents the role of culture in access and use of health care in the United States and other nations.

- Considers special issues, such as women's health, infant health, mental health, alternative medicine, and death and dying in the context of cultural, racial, and ethnic diversity.

- Highlights how beliefs and values stemming from one's culture can affect the provision and use of health care services.

Tennessee

Meharry Medical College

1005 Dr DB Todd Jr Blvd
Nashville, TN 37208
615 327-6204
http://www.mmc.edu/sofm.htm

As the largest single private institution for the education of black health professionals in the United States, Meharry trains physicians and dentists who practice largely in medically underserved inner-city and rural areas. In 1999, Meharry and Vanderbilt University Medical Center formed an alliance to create joint residency programs, engage in cross-faculty appointments, and work to improve diversity.

Institute on Health Care for the Poor and Underserved

In 1988, to further focus attention on the health of and health care for underserved populations, Meharry formed the nonprofit Institute.

The Institute aims to solve problems by bringing together health professionals, disseminating critical information, and serving as a focal point for research news. The scope of the Institute encompasses diverse concerns such as the cost of health care; law; service delivery and access; bureaucratic regulations and procedures; and individual and group behaviors. Principle activities of the Institute include:

- Operating a national clearinghouse

- Convening annual conferences and meetings

- Publishing a quarterly journal

- Establishing and supporting local demonstration projects

- Engaging in health services research

University of Texas Medical Branch at Galveston

301 University Blvd
Galveston, TX 77555
409 747-2150
http://www.meded.utmb.edu

The Dr. Hector P. Garcia Cultural Competence Award recognizes a student's application of cross-cultural skills in better serving patients.

Virginia

Northern Virginia Area Health Education Center

5105-P Backlick Rd
Annandale, VA 22003
703 750-3248
703 750-3072 Fax
E-mail: Envahec@aol.com

Offers cross-cultural health education and consultation programs for health care practitioners in northern Virginia and throughout the state. Also operates a health care interpreter service, with trained interpreters available in 10 languages.

Texas

Baylor College of Medicine

Department of Family and Community Medicine
5510 Greenbriar
Houston, TX 77005
713 798-4951
http://chico.rice.edu/projects/HispanicHealth/excourse.html

The Hispanic Health Course, offered on the Internet, is designed for understanding the health needs of Hispanic subpopulations in the United States and abroad. Included in the 10 modules are the social, cultural, economic, environmental, and genetic factors associated with differences in disease frequency between Hispanics and other groups.

Wisconsin

Medical College of Wisconsin and the University of Wisconsin Medical School Milwaukee Campus

Milwaukee AHEC
2220 E North Ave
Milwaukee, WI 53202
414 226-2432
http://www.biostat.wisc.edu/ahec/mahec.html

MCW and UWMS have been collaborating with the Milwaukee Area Health Education Center to develop educational programming in cultural competence, including study in area community health centers, cultural competence seminars, and community cultural rounds.

C. Publications by Individuals

Assessing and Treating Culturally Diverse Clients: A Practical Guide
Freddy Paniagua
Sage, 1998

Becoming a Clinician: A Primer for Students
Shirley Neitch, Maurice Mufson, eds.
McGraw Hill, 1998

Discusses common patient presentations useful in physical diagnosis and interviewing courses. Offers practical advice, such as how medical students should introduce themselves to patients.

Breaking the Silence: A Guide to Help Children with Complicated Grief: Suicide, Homicide, AIDS, Violence, and Abuse
Linda Goodman
Brunner/Mazel, 1996

Provides specific ideas and techniques for working with children in various stages of grief. Addresses suicide, homicide, and violent crime; AIDS and abuse. Lists national support resources and an extensive annotated grief bibliography.

Calibrating the Physician: Personal Awareness and Effective Patient Care
DH Novack, AL Suchman, W Clark, et al, for the Working Group on Promoting Physician Personal Awareness, American Academy on Physician and Patient
JAMA, 1997; 278:502-9

The four-part proposed curriculum to enhance physician personal awareness helps to define cultural competence and the training to achieve it, especially the materials related to core beliefs,

attitudes, and personal philosophy; influences from family of origin, gender, and socioeconomic status; feelings and emotional response in patient care; and physician self-care.

Cross-Cultural Practice: Assessment, Treatment, and Training
Sharon-Ann Gopaul-McNicol and Janet Brice-Baker, 1997, 224 pages.

Describes culturally sensitive assessment and intervention models for psychological assessment, intervention, and training. Introduces a new technique for culturally sensitive assessment and treatment of patients and families, a multi-cultural, multi-modal, multi-systems (Multi-CMS) model, which provides a framework for clinical interventions with diverse patient populations. Numerous case examples are included.

Cross-Cultural Primary Care: A Patient-Based Approach
J. Emilio Carrillo, Alexander R. Green, Joseph R. Betancourt
Ann Intern Med 1999; 130:829-834
Also available at http://www.acponline.org

Points out that assuring quality health care for all persons requires physicians to understand how each patient's sociocultural background affects his or her health beliefs and behaviors. Because existing cross-cultural curricula are not widely used in medical education and because some curricula take a potentially stereotypic approach to "cultural competence" that links patients of certain cultures to a set of specific unifying characteristics, the authors developed a patient-based cross-cultural curriculum for residents and medical students that teaches a framework for analyzing the individual patient's social context and cultural health beliefs and behaviors. The curriculum consists of five thematic units taught in four 2-hour sessions, including:

- Focus on the individual patient

- Case-based learning

- Exploration of both social and cultural factors

- Teaching techniques

- Progressive curriculum

- Use of simple, direct questions and recognition of "hot-button issues" through 10 to 15 minute interviews with medical actors

Culturally Effective Pediatric Care: Education and Training Issues
Pediatrics, 1999; 103:167-170

This policy statement from the American Academy of Pediatrics' Committee on Pediatric Workforce "defines culturally effective health care and describes its importance for pediatrics." The statement also defines cultural effectiveness, cultural sensitivity, and cultural competence and describes the importance of these concepts for training in medical school, residency, and continuing medical education. The statement is based on the premise that culturally effective health care is important and that the knowledge and skills necessary for providing culturally effective health care can be taught and acquired through:

- educational courses developed specifically to address cultural competence and/or cultural sensitivity and

- educational components on cultural competence and/or cultural sensitivity incorporated into medical school, residency, and CME curricula.

On the basis of this policy statement, the Academy recommends that the pediatric community "develop and evaluate curricular programs in medical schools and residency programs to enhance the provision of culturally effective health care [and] to develop continuing medical education materials for pediatricians and nonpediatricians with the goal of increasing culturally effective health care."

Culture and Child Behavior and Psychosocial Development
Lee M. Pachter, Robin L. Harwood
In: *Developmental and Behavioral Pediatrics*, 1996

Presents the "complex interrelationship between cultural patterns of thought and behavior and child behavior and psychosocial development," which requires "theoretical models that take into account the many levels on which cultural values, beliefs, and practices play a role." Studies from the fields of psychology, anthropology, and medicine should help health care practitioners recognize these issues and in turn use their knowledge to deliver culturally competent health care. "Future research should incorporate the knowledge of cultural variation within the clinical practice of behavioral medicine."

Culture and Psychopathology: A Guide to Clinical Assessment
Wen-Shing Tseng, Jon Streltzer, eds.
Brunner/Mazel, 1997

Offers a theoretical framework for the analysis of cultural factors that shape symptoms and may contribute to the creation of mental disorder, with practical case examples. Assessment is presented as an interactive dynamic between patient and clinician.

Culture and the Clinical Encounter: An Intercultural Sensitizer for the Health Professions
RC Gropper
Intercultural Press, 1996

Presents some 45 real-life incidents of cross-cultural conflict or difficulty in a clinical context to alert the reader to common intercultural misperceptions and their outcomes. The reader can choose the best of four possible explanations, then read the proposed solutions to gain additional knowledge about the 23 represented cultures.

Death Attitudes and the Older Adult
Adrian Tomer
Brunner/Mazel, January 2000

Bridges the fields of gerontology and thanatology; attitudes toward the dying process, end-of-life decision making, and death itself are explored. Contributors' backgrounds include gerontology, death education, and general psychology.

Developing Intercultural Communication Skills
V Ricard
Krieger Publishing Co, 1993

Identifies human responses to commonality and diversity; promotes intercultural communication and interaction skills in valuing, observing, listening, thinking, speaking, and gesturing; recognizes the influence of human values on the interaction process; and uses a practical, flexible framework for ongoing learning and personal development in the area of intercultural communication and interaction.

Diagnostic and Statistical Manual of Mental Disorders, 4th edition
American Psychiatric Association

Highlights the importance of considering the patient's ethnic and cultural context in the evaluation of each of the DSMMD-IV axes, including the cultural identity of the patient; cultural explanations of the patient's illness; cultural factors related to psychosocial environment and levels of functioning; cultural elements of the relationship between the individual and the psychiatrist; and overall cultural assessment for diagnosis and care. Emphasizes the importance of spirituality.

Enhancing Awareness of Diversity and Cultural Competence: A Workshop Series for Department Chairs and Course Directors
M Welch
Academic Medicine, 1997; 72:461-462

The Ethnic/Minority Focus Unit as a Training Site in Transcultural Psychiatry
Douglas F. Zatzick, Francis G. Lu
Academic Psychiatry, 1991; vol 25, no 4, 218-225

Handbook of Multicultural Counseling
JG Ponterotto
Sage Publications, 1995

Presents theory, research, practice, and training in the field of multicultural counseling and examines racial/ethnic identity and acculturation theory.

Honoring Differences: Cultural Issues in the Treatment of Trauma and Loss
Kathleen Nader, Nancy Dubrow, Beth Hudnall Stamm, eds.
Brunner/Mazel, 1999

Describes cultural beliefs that may interact with traumatic reactions within the United States and several international communities.

Improving Cross-Cultural Skills of Medical Students Through Medical School—Community Partnerships
LM Nora, SR Daugherty, A Mattis-Peterson, et al
Western Journal of Medicine, 1994; 161:144-147

Increasing Multicultural Understanding: A Comprehensive Model
Don Locke
Sage, 1998

Masculine Patterns of Grief
Kenneth J Doka, Terry L Martin
Brunner/Mazel, November 1999

Includes clinical strategies for assisting masculine bereavement, as well as contemporary research on gender-related differences.

Measuring Diversity Results, Managing Organizational Change

Edward E. Hubbard
Petaluma, CA: Global Insights, 1997

Highlights step-by-step processes, tools, techniques, and methods to assist, evaluate, and monitor diversity efforts in numerical, qualitative, and financial terms.

Medical Interviewing and Interpersonal Skills Teaching in US Medical Schools: Progress, Problems, and Promise

DH Novack, G Volk, DA Drossman, et al
JAMA, 1993; 269:2101-2105

Monitoring the Managed Care of Culturally and Linguistically Diverse Populations

Miguel Tirado
National Clearinghouse for Primary Care
Information
2070 Chain Bridge Road, Ste 450
Vienna, VA 22182
800 400-2742 or 703 902-1248
703 821 2098 Fax
E-mail: primarycare@circsol.com

Includes four cultural competence assessment tools, the methodology used to develop the tools, and a detailed explanation of each question included in the tools. The four tools are being validated during the next phase of the project, funded by the Health Resources and Services Administration.

Multicultural Counseling Competencies and Standards: A Call to the Profession

Sue W Derald, Patricia Arredondo, Roderick J McDavis
J CounselDevelop, 1992; 70: 477-486

Multicultural/Multimodal/Multisystems Approach to Working with Culturally Different Families

Sharon-Ann Gopaul-McNicol, 1997

Nelson Textbook of Pediatrics

15th edition
Ricard E Behrman, Waldo E Nelson, MD, eds.
WB Saunders Co, 1995

Chapter 4, "Cultural Issues in Pediatric Care," by Lee M. Pachter, highlights the three steps necessary to providing culturally sensitive health care. The pediatrician must "become aware of the commonly held cultural beliefs and culturally normative interactive styles in the patient population. . . , to assess the effects of these beliefs and behaviors on a particular patient or family. . .[, and] to negotiate between the ethnocultural beliefs and practices of the patient and the culture of biomedicine for the benefit of the child." Also included is a discussion of specific issues, such as intracultural diversity, sickness and its causes, folk illness and folk healers, physician-patient interaction, and compliance.

Palliative Care in Undergraduate Medical Education: Status Report and Future Decisions

JA Billings, S Block
JAMA, 1997; 278:7333-7338

Promoting Health in Multicultural Populations: A Handbook for Practitioners

Robert M Huff and Michael V Kline, eds.
Sage Publications, 1999

Key aspects involving health promotion programs for ethnic minorities in the United States, including theory, needs assessment, planning, implementation, evaluation, and ethical considerations. Research and practice on effective strategies to address disease prevention among African-Americans, Hispanics, American Indians, Asian-Americans, and Pacific Islanders are reviewed.

Recommended Core Curriculum Guidelines on Culturally Sensitive and Competent Health Care

RC Like, RP Steiner, AJ Rubel
Family Medicine, 1996; 27:291-297

Refocusing on History-Taking Skills During Internal Medicine Training
GP Schechter, L Blank, HA Godwin, et al
Am J Med, 1996; 101:210-216.

Serving My People: Cultural Competence in Human Service
David Wiley Campt, PhD
University of California, Berkeley, 1997
Department of City and Regional Planning
333 pages

Includes *A Theoretical Framework for Understanding Cultural Competency* and 12 pages of bibliographical references.

Teaching Cultural Sensitivity in Medical Schools: Discounting Diversity, or Drowning in the Melting Pot?
DW Gee, G Flores
Washington, DC: Pediatric Academic Societies
Meeting, May 1997

Section IV

Specific Populations: Needs and Resources

Attention to the health care needs of identified populations began to appear in medical journals and other publications in the late 1950s, as researchers presented the results of studies of health and disease in specific racial and ethnic groups. By 1981, Alan Harwood was able to cite more than 100 references in the introductory chapter to *Ethnicity and Medical Care*, including 16 he identified as "Guidelines for Culturally Appropriate Health Care." Each of the contributed chapters (on urban Black Americans, Chinese Americans, Haitian Americans, Italian Americans, Mexican Americans, Navajos, and Mainland Puerto Ricans) addressed culture-specific health beliefs and behaviors.

In "Recognizing Intraethnic Variation in Clinical Care," Harwood identifies those aspects of ethnic subcultures that are still most likely to bear heavily on medical care: "concepts of disease and illness, folk and popular traditions of health care, problems of language and translation, dietary practices, interactional norms, and the role of the family in compliance with long-term treatment" (p 505). Harwood's suggested procedures for responding to the various factors that make folk and popular concepts of disease relevant to medical delivery are applicable nearly 20 years later.

Cautions Against Generalizing, Stereotyping

Harwood, like most authors who have developed culture-specific guides of any kind, repeatedly reminds readers not to use research results or other materials in any way that reflects stereotypical interpretations, that ignores variation within ethnic groups, or that fails to account for individual patient preferences and needs. Similar cautions against stereotyping were provided in Elaine Geissler's 1994 *A Pocket Guide to Cultural Assessment*: "The reader is strongly cautioned against assuming that people from one country or geographic area . . . hold the same beliefs as those held by their neighbors." But she also makes the important point that "[n]ot to use a guide such as this for fear of stereotyping impedes movement toward delivery of culturally relevant health care."

Inclusive Definition of "Culture"

Our use of "cultural competence" and "culturally competent health care" reflects an inclusive definition of the word "culture"—any group of people who share experiences, language, and values that permit them to communicate knowledge not shared by those outside the culture. Physicians reflect many individual cultural attributes, but they also participate to some extent in the culture of medicine, with its special shared language, values, and experiences. Within this macro physician culture are the numerous subcultures related to specialty/subspecialty and practice type and location.

Patient-Centered Care

To be culturally competent in accord with either the inclusive or narrow definition, physicians must be able to provide patient-centered care by adjusting their attitudes and behaviors to the needs and desires of different patients, including accounting for the impact of emotional, cultural, social, and psychological issues on the main biomedical ailment. This in turn requires complex integration of knowledge (including knowledge of the effects of culture on others' beliefs and behavior and on one's own beliefs and behavior), attitudes (of the patient as well as the physician), and skills (with communication skills as important as technical skills). The importance of communication skills in conducting a patient-centered trust-promoting method of inquiry is reflected in Section II.

Determining Categories for the *Compendium*

The categories for this section of the *Compendium* were determined as we proceeded with our search for materials related to cultural competence and as we learned of AMA initiatives that had or could have a cultural competence component.

The first category, underserved and underrepresented racial, ethnic, and socioeconomic groups, has the most entries because it encompasses the most common definition of cultural competence. The AMA has extensive policy and reports addressing health disparities among these groups. Ironically, it may also be the category in which medical educators and professional associations need to do the most work, because many of the materials are either too generic or too specific to meet the needs of students, employees, or patients associated with a particular educational or health care institution or a specific health care specialty.

Resources in the second category, people with physical or mental illnesses or disabling conditions, are intended to help educators and practitioners understand the special communication skills required to provide the most effective care to people with serious or chronic illness, with mental illness, or with a disability. For example, some physicians still refer to "the crippled kid in bed 3," "the CP," or "the spastic." While groups representing people with disabilities do not always agree on terms, dozens of groups agree that terms should focus on the person, rather than the disability—"people with disabilities," "a person with cerebral palsy." The AMA has produced several publications and other resources to assist physicians in improving their ability to communicate respectfully with patients in this category.

Children and adolescents are included because the Centers for Disease Control and Prevention has reported that "adolescents are among the most underserved groups medically" (*Sacramento Bee*, March 10, 1999) and because the AMA and the American Academy of Pediatrics, among others, have specific materials to assist in providing appropriate care for children and adolescents.

The Florida Medical Association recognizes the importance of including women in considerations of culturally competent care. In "Women's Health Care: Cross-Cultural Encounters within the Medical System" (*Journal of the Florida Medical Association*, August/September 1997), authors Lieberman, Stroller, and Burg emphasize the relationship between cultural competence and patient outcomes: "The more a physician knows of the patient's beliefs, communication style, and daily patterns of behavior, the more effective and appropriate the physician-patient encounter will be." Education and training in women's health is being examined by AMA councils for medical education and for scientific affairs, and professional associations for women are playing a leadership role in developing resources to assist physicians in improving women's health.

Older adults are treated separately to indicate that although they may fall into several other categories, they have very special concerns, including health literacy, which decreases regardless of education, general health, or socioeconomic status. In addition, issues of end-of-life care, domestic violence, and sexuality are very different for older adults than for other age groups.

Caring for people at the end of life, as indicated by the AMA project for Educating Physicians in End of Life Care (EPEC), requires special sensitivity and communication skills on such topics as age, the cause of approaching death, and even the site of death. Issues related to race, ethnicity, and spirituality may require more consideration at the end of life than at any other time.

Four of the five categories grouped under special issues—domestic violence, genetic conditions, organ donation, and sexuality—were selected because they all have special cultural considerations in either the inclusive or narrow sense. For example, the 106th Congress may consider legislation prohibiting genetic discrimination in health insurance or employment or legislation protecting medical records privacy. In January 1998, the Department of Labor released a report outlining recommendations to protect employees from genetic discrimination in the workplace. Along the same lines, the National Human Genome Research Institute (NHGRI) and the National Bioethics Advisory Commission sponsored a meeting on November 23, 1998, on "Involving Diverse Communities in Genetics Research," particularly NHGRI research, education, and policy development activities. Homelessness was selected because homeless people are perhaps the most underserved of all groups.

Section Contents

Most of the resources categorized in the "Specific Populations" segments could generally be assigned to three or more groups. To assist readers in identifying populations in which they have the most interest, we have attempted to place resources in the two most specific categories; readers looking for citations related to older African American women with a mental illness should review all four categories. We have also cited many relevant references from other sections (for example, literacy, spirituality, complementary practices, consumer resources, and self-help groups) that apply to specific populations below, but those sections should also be reviewed for references that do not appear in this section.

A. Underserved and Underrepresented Racial, Ethnic, and Socioeconomic Groups

B. People with Physical or Mental Illnesses or Disabling Conditions

C. Children and Adolescents

D. Women

E. Older Adults

F. People at the End of Life

G. Special Issues

- Domestic Violence

- Genetic Conditions

- Homelessness

- Organ Donation

- Sexuality

A. Underserved and Underrepresented Racial, Ethnic, and Socioeconomic Groups

Organizations and Their Resources

American Medical Association

Contact

See Section I for comprehensive information about AMA activities and specific AMA units for individuals with responsibilities related to Section IV.

Policies

B-1.50	*Discrimination*
E-9.03	*Gender Discrimination in the Medical Profession*
E-9.065	*Caring for the Poor*
E-9.12	*Physician-Patient Relationship: Respect for Law and Human Rights*
E-9.121	*Racial Disparities in Health Care*
H-20.974	*AIDS Prevention Through Educational Materials Directed at Minority Populations*
H-65.990	*Civil Rights Restoration*
H-65.999	*Equal Opportunity*

H-160.934	*Use of Chaperones During Physical Exams*
H-160.959	*Health Care Acces for the Inner-City Poor*
H-200.972	*Primary Care Physicians in the Inner City*
H-350.971	*AMA Initiatives Regarding Minorities*
H-350.972	*Improving the Healthcare of Black and Minority Populations in the United States*
H-350.973	*Sickle Cell Anemia*
H-350.974	*Racial and Ethnic Disparities in Health Care*
H-350.975	*Improving the Healthcare of Hispanic Populations in the United States*
H-350.976	*Improving the Healthcare of American Indians*
H-350.977	*Indian Health Service*

H-350.978	Minorities in the Health Professions	H-370.977	The Inclusion of Advance Directives Concerning Organ Donation in Living Wills
H-350.979	Increase the Representation of Minority and Economically Disadvantaged Populations in the Medical Profession	H-370.978	The Use of Minors as Organ and Tissue Sources
H-350.980	AMA's Role in Preparing Minority and Disadvantaged Youth for Careers in Medicine and the Health Professions	H-370.979	Financial Incentives for Organ Procurement Ethical Aspects of Future Contracts for Cadaveric Donors
H-350.981	AMA Support of American Indian Health Career Opportunities	H-370.980	Strategies for Cadaveric Organ Procurement Mandated Choice and Presumed Consent
H-350.982	Project 3000 by 2000—Medical Education for Under-Represented Minority Students	H-370.982	Ethical Considerations in the Allocation of Organs and Other Scarce Medical Resources Among Patients
H-350.983	Federal Guidelines for Standardization of Race/Ethnicity	H-370.983	Tissue and Organ Donation
H-350.985	Physicians' Role in Preparing Minority and Disadvantaged Youth for Careers in Medicine and the Health Professions	H-370.984	Organ Donation Education
		H-370.986	Donor Tissues and Organs for Transplantation
H-350.989	Continued AMA Support for Minority Health Improvement	H-370.987	Transplant Centers
H-350.992	Indian Health Service Contract Care Program	H-370.994	Sale of Donor Organs for Transplant
H-350.993	Minority Physician Manpower	H-370.995	Organ Donor Recruitment
H-350.994	Funding for Affirmative Action Programs	H-370.996	Organ Donor Recruitment
		H-370.999	Computerized Donor Registry
H-350.995	Minority and Economically Disadvantaged Representation in the Medical Profession	H-385.963	Physician Review of Accounts Sent for Collection
H-370.974	Working Toward an Increased Number of Minorities Registered as Potential Bone Marrow Donors	H-500.992	Tobacco Advertising Directed to Children, Minorities and Women
		H-555.982	Participation of Minorities in Organized Medicine
H-370.975	Ethical Issues in the Procurement of Organs Following Cardiac Death		See Section X for the complete text of these policies, including references to related reports.

AMA Reports

Most of the above policies emanated from reports of the same title. See Section X for the complete text of selected reports. See Section I for the titles and dates of many of these reports. Three of the most relevant reports are cited below.

Black-White Disparities in Health Care
JAMA, May 2, 1990; 263(17):2344-6, Review

Hispanic Health in the United States
Council of Scientific Affairs of the American Medical Association
JAMA, 1991; 15:248-252

Racial and Ethnic Disparities In Health Care
Board of Trustees Report, 50-I-95

Minority Affairs Consortium

Women and Minority Services
515 North State St
312 464-4392
312 464-5845
E-mail: mps@ama-assn.org
http://www.ama-assn.org/mem-data/mimed/mihome.htm

The AMA Minority Affairs Consortium (MAC) functions as the AMA conduit for minority concerns, from the grassroots level to the Board of Trustees. It provides a national forum for advocacy on minority health issues and for addressing the professional concerns of minority medical students and physicians. E-mail and the AMA Web site are the primary means through which MAC conducts its member communications and outreach and educational activities.

The nine-member MAC Governing Committee includes formal representation from the National Medical Association, National Hispanic Medical Association, and Association of American Indian Physicians. The primary MAC goal is to build an interorganizational, grassroots communication network to educate, inform, and advocate for underrepresented medical students and physicians across the nation.

MAC provides a structural framework for physicians committed to addressing minority issues at the national, state, and local levels by developing and supporting efforts to:

- eliminate minority health disparities;

- assist all physicians to become better prepared to deliver culturally effective health care;

- recruit and retain more minority students to promote diversity in the profession;

- increase the membership and leadership participation of minority physicians in organized medicine; and

- advocate on minority health issues at local, state, and national levels.

Membership is free to any interested AMA-member physicians or medical students. Non-AMA members may join on a 1-year introductory basis.

Recent MAC recommendations include urging (1) the AMA Foundation to support programs geared toward increasing diversity, (2) the AMA to explore state medical society/AMA partnerships to increase diversity, and (3) medical schools to weigh the likelihood of service to underserved populations as an admission criterion. MAC has recommended that the AMA Advocacy Resource Center be authorized to assist in these efforts.

Robert Wood Johnson Foundation "Reach Out" Initiative

The AMA and organized medicine are involved with the Robert Wood Johnson Foundation initiative "Reach Out: Physicians' Initiative to Expand Care to Underserved Americans." Reach Out mobilizes private physicians to improve care for the underserved at the local level. Ten of the 22 initial grants and 14 of the 37 second-phase grants were awarded to local medical societies.

Organ Donation Initiative

Karen Goraleski, Professional Standards
312 464-4840
E-mail: karen_goraleski@ama-assn.org

Although organ transplants increased by approximately 600 and tissue transplants increased by 14,000 in 1998, the transplant waiting list also increased, from more than 56,000 registrants in 1997 to more than 64,000 in 1998. Donor trends among whites and Hispanics increased by 6.6% and 7.8%, respectively, while those for African American donors remained relatively unchanged, and Asian donors decreased by 8.4%. Concerned about low donor rates in general and within African American populations in particular, the AMA is intensifying activities to implement its organ donation policies.

"Live and Then Give"

"Live and Then Give," an organ donation program modeled after the Texas Medical Association program of the same name, is intended to encourage physicians to become organ donors and to present information to their patients. It was launched with a special 11-minute video during the December 1998 Interim Meeting. The June 1999 Annual Meeting included several organ donation awareness events sponsored by the Medical Student Section and the Minority Affairs Consortium (MAC), covering cultural barriers and general awareness of organ and transplant issues and particularly aimed at increasing organ donations in minority communities. Activities included a Minority Issues Forum, a Public Rally for Organ Donation Awareness, and a MAC Consensus Panel/Forum, which provided CME credit.

Campaign Manual and Ready-to-Use Materials

Materials supporting "Live and Then Give" are available in formats that give Federation partners the flexibility to develop a campaign unique to their own needs and responsive to the diverse populations they serve. The campaign manual is supplemented by camera-ready artwork, question and answer brochures, two donor cards, and a poster.

Medical Student Section Program Module

Organ Donation Awareness
National Service Project
800 262-3211, ext 4742
E-mail: mss@ama-assn.org

The AMA Department of Medical Student Services developed the 1999 National Service Project Organ & Tissue Donor Awareness Program Module (February 1999), with assistance from the United Network for Organ Sharing, to encourage Medical Student Section chapters to apply for a policy promotion grant to set up an Organ Donation Awareness National Service Project.

The module includes sections on community and professional education, fact sheets on organ donation and transplantation, understanding the organ procurement process, dispelling fears about organ donation, and religious/spiritual views on donations and transplantation. Specific program activities are suggested, from donor days to appearing on TV and radio programs. The module also includes information about state and regional organ procurement organizations.

Giving Life: Share Your Decision To Be an Organ and Tissue Donor

Mi Young Hwang
(posted on *JAMA* Patient Page, AMA Health Insight, at http://www.ama-assn.org/
public/journals/jama/ppindex9.htm)

This two-page discussion of the need for organ and tissue donation and how to indicate willingness to be a donor may be reproduced by physicians to share with patients.

Collaborations Sought

The AMA is developing collaborative relationships and projects with the Illinois chapter of the National Medical Association, the Regional Organ Bank of Illinois, and other groups committed to cooperative efforts in the areas of policy development, education, technology, and assessment related to advancing organ availability and transplantation. *See Section IV G for a list of national organizations.*

American Psychiatric Association (APA)

Steve Mirin, MD, Medical Director
1400 K St NW
Washington, DC 20005
202 682-6000
202 682-6353 Fax
E-mail: smirin@psych.org
http://www.psych.org

The APA Council on National Affairs has been involved with developing curricula for psychiatric residents in six major minority or underrepresented groups. Four articles have been published.

Psychiatry Residency Curricula

A Psychiatry Curriculum Directed to the Care of the Hispanic Patient

ES Garza-Trevino, P Ruiz, K Varegos-Samuel
Academic Psychiatry, 1997: 21:1-10

This article describes a model curriculum for psychiatric residency programs that addresses the sociodemographic, epidemiological, psychosocial, cultural, and behavioral characteristics of Hispanics. It emphasizes that faculty who are knowledgeable and sensitive about Hispanic culture should be available for the supervision and teaching of psychiatric residents during their training and that supervision should focus on cultural formulation and family dynamics and other factors of importance in clinical psychiatric practice. Includes a 29-item bibliography and 56 references.

A Psychiatric Residency Curriculum About Gender and Women's Issues

A Spielvogel, LJ Dickson, GE Robinson
Academic Psychiatry, 1995:Vol 19, no 4:187-201

Over the last 30 years, major advances have been made in our understanding of how biological factors and sociocultural influences contribute to gender differences, gender identity formation, and gendered role behavior. This article presents an outline for a curriculum in gender and women's issues, including educational objectives, learning experiences through which residents could meet these objectives, and recommended readings. It discusses potential obstacles and suggests helpful strategies for implementing the proposed curriculum. Includes 96 references and suggested core readings.

A Curriculum for Learning in Psychiatry Residencies about Homosexuality, Gay Men, and Lesbians

TS Stein
Academic Psychiatry, 1994:Vol 18, no 2:59-70

Recent research has greatly expanded knowledge about homosexuality, gay men, and lesbians. However, neither a nonpathological perspective nor this new information has been integrated into psychiatric residency curricula. This article proposes a basic model for this necessary professional training. Includes 85 references.

A Curriculum for Learning About American Indians and Alaska Natives in Psychiatry Residency Training

JW Thompson
Academic Psychiatry, 1996:Vol 20, no 1:5-14

Describes a proposed curriculum for teaching psychiatric residents about the diagnosis and treatment of American Indians and Alaska Natives. Presents the historical context, contemporary myths, and rationale for the inclusion of curriculum materials on Indians in residency programs. Briefly describes the curriculum for the 4 years of residency education and outlines the knowledge, skills, and attitudes needed by residents. The curriculum for the first and second years includes a basic history and description of Indian people, information on myths about the group, and psychiatric epidemiology and psychopathology. The third year includes clinical care and related areas such as service utilization and illness prevention. The proposed fourth year includes a seminar to discuss psychotherapy and other clinical cases. Includes 70 references.

California Center for Health Improvement (CCHI)

1321 Garden Hwy, Ste 210
Sacramento, CA 95833-9576
916 646-2149
policymatters@cchi.org
www.policymatters.org

The CCHI is an independent, impartial, not-for-profit, prevention-focused health policy center. The CCHI is committed to improving the health of the public by disseminating objective, accurate and easily understood information about community health and health care issues and policies to diverse audiences. Through CCHI's Survey Reports, Policy Briefs and Policy Notes, the Center analyzes and synthesizes complex health research and policy information.

Institute of Medicine (IOM)

2101 Constitution Avenue, NW
Washington, DC 20418
202 334-3300
http://www4.nas.edu/IOM/IOMHome.nsf

According to *AMNews* (February 8, 1999), growing awareness of persistent disparities between majority and nonmajority populations has resulted in IOM efforts to improve service to underserved groups. An IOM committee has issued a congressionally requested report outlining ways in which the National Institutes of Health (NIH) should further explore why cancer is taking a greater toll in some racial and ethnic groups. The committee recommended classifying information according to ethnicity to highlight how differences in cancer incidence and mortality rates may be linked to a range of cultural factors, behaviors, health attitudes, and lifestyle conditions.

The IOM issued the following recommendations to the National Cancer Institute (NCI) to increase its cultural competence:

- Expand cancer data collection and classifications to better measure the influence of ethnicity on incidence and mortality rates.

- More accurately assess and increase the NCI research sources dedicated to studies targeted to minority and medically underserved groups.

- Establish a formal system to report to Congress about the amount of minority targeted research included in overall cancer research.

- Improve minority participation in clinical trials by addressing barriers created by current informed consent processes.

- Tap cancer survivors in minority groups as a resource for educating others in the community about their risks.

Institute on Health Care for the Poor and Underserved

Meharry Medical College
1005 Dr DB Todd, Jr Blvd
Nashville, TN 37208
615 327-6204

The Institute was established to address the fact that, in a country that devotes more money per capita to health care than any other nation, more than 30 million people lack adequate health protection. The Institute aims to solve problems by bringing together health professionals, disseminating critical information, and serving as a focal point for research news. The broad scope of the Institute encompasses diverse concerns such as the cost of health care; federal, state, and local laws; service delivery and access; bureaucratic regulations and procedures; and individual and group behaviors. Principle activities include:

- Operating a national clearinghouse

- Convening annual conferences and meetings

- Publishing a quarterly journal

- Establishing and supporting local demonstration projects

- Engaging in health services research

Publications

Journal of Health Care for the Poor and Underserved

The Institute's quarterly journal addresses the health of, and health care for, low-income and other medically underserved communities to health care practitioners, policy makers, and community leaders. Pertinent issues include access to and quality and cost of health care. Articles in the special *Journal* supplement *Language Barriers to Health Care* issue, Vol 9, 1998, include:

- *Language Barriers to Health Care: An Overview*
  Pancho H. Chang, Julia Puebla Fortier

  Provides a context for the discussion of language issues in health care by reviewing federal and state laws and related initiatives; discussing the case history of language access in Seattle, Washington; and surveying the expansion of managed care. Also describes different models of language services and raises issues in the delivery, financing, and regulation of language services in a managed care environment.

- *The Pervading Role of Language on Health*
  Roberto E. Torres

  Highlights the complex and multidimensional nature of language barrier problems relative to the health status of US ethnic groups and to health care delivery in the United States and identifies the challenges faced by the US health care system to overcome these barriers. Illustrates the multiple facets of this public health issue by examining current literature, focusing on how ethnic groups such as Latino, Asian Pacific Islander, and Arab Americans are affected by these impediments. Calls for creating effective systems to improve communication between providers and people with English-language limitations.

- *Improving Access for Limited English-Speaking Consumers: A Review of Strategies in Health Care Settings*
  Sherry Riddick

Describes models and strategies currently used in various health care settings to improve health care access for limited English-proficient (LEP) individuals and examines a spectrum of strategies that overcome barriers to care. Recommended strategies include the use of bilingual providers, bilingual/bicultural community health workers, and professional and nonprofessional interpreters; the role of written translations; and new technological approaches to interpretation. Also considers how these strategies are applied in community health centers, public health departments, hospitals, and managed care organizations. Reviews recommendations to assist institutions in improving the provision of health care for LEP populations.

- *Legal Protections to Ensure Linguistically Appropriate Health Care*
  Jane Perkins, Yolanda Vera

  Points out that the health care delivery system is confronted with providing adequate translation services for the 32 million people in the United States (13.8 percent of the population) who depend on a language other than English. Describes how hospitals relying on untrained employees, friends, or family members to translate frequently do not meet interpreter and translation needs. Outlines federal and state laws that impose legal obligations on health care providers to offer minimally adequate translation services and discusses the need to ensure linguistically appropriate care in the emerging managed care delivery system. Includes 118 references.

- *Language Barriers to Health Care: Federal and State Initiatives, 1990-1995*
  Julia Puebla Fortier, Christoper Strobel, Esther Aguilera

  Focuses on the legislative and oversight activities of the US Congress from 1990 to 1995—a period of significant activity on the issue of access to health care for underserved and minority populations—and examines a three-step process leading to the development of federal policy on language barriers to health care. Includes an overview of the initial

legislation developed on language access to
health care and an analysis of its implemen-
tations, followed by a review of additional
legislative actions in 1994. Analyzes the
potential limitations of government
mechanisms in reducing language barriers.

Kaiser Permanente National Diversity Program

1950 Franklin St
Oakland, CA 94612
510 987-1000

Kaiser Permanente has developed a series of
handbooks with learning modules on culturally
competent care that summarize epidemiologic data,
health beliefs, and cultural characteristics that have
implications for service delivery to special
populations. Kaiser also conducts monthly
educational lunches to work with clinical staff on
developing and implementing cultural competence
efforts; a physician/patient communication training
project; a self-guided reading list/tour on utilizing
interpreters and analyzing demographics; and model
programs.

The first handbook in the series is summarized
below. Kaiser Permanente publishes additional
Provider's Handbooks on African American and
Asian/Pacific Islander populations.

A Provider's Handbook on Culturally Competent Care: Latino Population
Kaiser Permanente National Diversity Council,
1996

This handbook includes:

- Sections devoted to demographic information:

  - Mexican Americans living primarily in the
    Southwest

  - Puerto Ricans living primarily in the
    Northeast

  - Cubans living primarily in Dade County,
    Florida

  - Other Latinos and Central and South
    Americans living primarily in California.

- Cultural characteristics of the groups, with
  attention to the unique factors that shape health-
  related beliefs and behaviors.

- Health profiles for the groups that summarize
  the following risk factors and disease states:

  - Substance abuse/chemical dependency

  - Obesity and centralized fat distribution

  - Diet and nutrition

  - Diabetes mellitus

  - End stage renal disease

  - Gallbladder disease

  - Cardiovascular diseases

  - Cancer

  - Cerebrovascular disease

  - Infectious diseases: tuberculosis, AIDS,
    measles

  - Childbirth and breastfeeding

- A helpful discussion of the implications of the
  data for health providers.

Latin International Network of Mental Health

6551 W North Ave
Oak Park, IL 60302

The Latin International Network of Mental Health
publishes *Psychline: Inter-Transdisciplinary
Journal of Mental Health,* which examines cultural
issues and guides organizations in assessing and
improving the cultural competence of their

organization in order to meet the diverse needs of clients and communities. See the cultural assessment chart in the introduction to the *Compendium*.

Latino Coalition for a Healthy California and California Pan-Ethnic Health Network

1535 Mission St
San Francisco, CA 94103
415 431-7430

Formed to promote multi-cultural issues in the health care reform debate. Both groups developed principles to evaluate health care reform legislation to assess whether it meets the needs of California's diverse communities.

Minnesota Department of Health Community Health Services

717 Delaware St, SE
Minneapolis, MN 55400-9441
651 296-9619
barbara.kizzee@health.state.mn.us

The Minnesota Department of Health's unit on Community Health Services exemplifies the types of programs and resources provided by departments of health.

Healthy Minnesotans: Public Health Improvement Goals for 2004

Includes 18 goals designed to achieve three priorities: increase healthy years of life, eliminate disparities in health status affecting certain populations (especially communities of color), and assure a strong foundation for health protection.

National Coalition of Hispanic Health and Human Services Organizations (COSSMHO)

1501 16th St NW
Washington, DC 20036
202 387-5000

The organization's mission is to network with communities and create change to improve the health and well-being of Hispanics in the United States.

The COSSMHO Reporter

Examines how conditions such as diabetes and arthritis affect Hispanics.

Delivering Preventive Health Care to Hispanics: A Manual for Providers

A manual intended to assist health providers in responding more effectively to the growing needs of Hispanics for greater access and utilization of health services. It addresses many of the barriers Hispanics face in obtaining health care, including language gaps between patient and provider, cultural misunderstandings, Hispanics' distrust of the medical system, cost, and institutional policies that are not sensitive to Hispanics' cultural values.

Chapters cover:

- the diversity of Hispanic groups in the United States

- Hispanic health status, risk factors, and patterns of seeking care

- cultural values and beliefs affecting Hispanics' health

- cultural and language considerations affecting patient-provider interactions

- techniques for bridging the gaps inherent to direct service and community-wide interventions

- references, resources, and list of Spanish-language publications

Proyecto Informar: A Training Program for Health Care Providers

This comprehensive cross-cultural training program is designed to improve access to health services by preparing health care providers to offer culturally competent health services to Hispanics. The 2-day training allows participants to actively gain knowledge about delivering health services to Hispanics, examine their attitudes towards Hispanics, and have opportunities to practice new behaviors. The program's five modules include:

- Understanding Hispanics in the United States

- Understanding the role of culture in health

- Navigating cultural differences

- Navigating language differences

- Developing a culturally competent system of care

National Public Health and Hospital Institute (NPHHI)

1212 New York Ave NW, Ste 800
Washington, DC 20005
202 408-0229

Conducts policy research and education programs related to vulnerable populations, their communities, and the providers who serve them. Recent work includes investigations of urban and social health issues in US cities, interpreter services in teaching hospitals, and cultural diversity and cross-cultural competence in health care.

New York Task Force on Immigrant Health

NYU School of Medicine
Division of Primary Care
550 First Ave
New York, NY 10016

The Task Force has several publications on interpreting, including:

Access Through Medical Interpreter and Language Services: Research and Recommendations, 1997

An Introduction to Medical Interpretation: A Trainer's Manual, 1997

US Department of Health and Human Services Office of Health Promotion and Disease Prevention

Hubert H Humphrey Bldg
200 Independence Ave, SW, Rm 738G
Washington, DC 20201
202 401-6295
800 367-4725

HHS Initiative to Eliminate Racial and Ethnic Disparities in Health

http://raceandhealth.hhs/gov

Priorities of this comprehensive national initiative include:

- getting people to take responsibility for their own health

- eliminating health disparities related to race and minority status, and

- encouraging the inclusion of women's health curricula in medical education and health professions training.

Valuable statistics and charts are maintained and disseminated in conjunction with this initiative

Healthy People 2010

http://www.health.gov/healthypeople

Healthy People 2010, of which the AMA is a partner, continues the major national collaboration project designed to focus national and local efforts on eliminating health disparities by race, ethnicity, age, gender, income, and disability status.

Organizations, agencies, and individuals are provided with information and resources to:

- promote healthy behavior;

- promote healthy and safe communities;

- improve systems for personal and public health; and

- prevent and reduce diseases and disorders.

The comprehensive campaign has a strong consumer outreach, involving hundreds of disease-related associations and self-help groups. The DHHS recognizes he untapped resources available through consumer groups to support behavior change.

Books

Children of Color: Psychological Interventions with Minority Youth

JT Gibbs, LN Huang, eds.
San Francisco, CA: Jossey-Bass Publishers, 1989

Cultural Competence for Evaluations: A Guide for Alcohol and Other Drug Abuse Prevention Practitioners Working With Ethnic/Racial Communities

MA Orlandi, R Weston, LG Epstein
Rockville, MD: OSAP, US Department of Health and Human Services, 1992

Directing Health Messages Towards African Americans: Attitudes Toward Health Care and the Mass Media

JL Sylvester
Garland Publishing, 1998

Explores diversity and similarities between white and African-American populations with specific information on how health messages can be effectively communicated to African Americans. Includes chapters on communication theories and crafting an effective health campaign.

Ethnic Minority Health: A Selected Annotated Bibliography

Craig Haynes
Medical Library Association, 1997

Focuses on Native Americans/Alaskan Natives, African Americans, Hispanic Americans, Asian/Pacific Islander Americans, the elderly, women, children, the poor, immigrants, refugees, and people with disabilities.

Materials on ethnic minority health are organized under the following broad topics and material types:

* Bibliographies
* Directories
* Medicine
* Mental health
* Medical education
* Health professions
* Research
* Service delivery and access
* Prevention and health promotion
* Law
* Legislation
* Congressional hearings
* Dissertation and theses
* Multimedia
* Serials

Ethnicity and Family Therapy

M McGoldrick, JK Pearce, J Giordano, eds.
New York: Guilford Press, 1996

Ethnicity and Medical Care

Alan Harwood
Harvard University Press, 1981

Harwood's book appears in the reference lists of many of the books and articles in the *Compendium*. The chapters on urban Black Americans, Chinese Americans, Haitian Americans, Italian Americans, Mexican Americans, Navajos, and Mainland Puerto Ricans contain information and suggestions of use to today's health care providers. Harwood was among the first to emphasize that, "[a] personal commitment by health-care personnel to improve face-to-face interactions in health-care situations can make a significant contribution toward greater patient satisfaction and more effective medical care."

Harwood felt that clinicians must become capable in the following areas to deliver culturally competent care:

- Address class and professional barriers to ethnically appropriate health care.

- Elicit the patient's model of the problem and treating the illness.

- Make medical treatment more comfortable with the patient's lifestyle.

- Improve the articulation between mainstream and nonmainstream sources of health care.

Harwood warns against using cultural-specific information to obscure the individual patient, which "can occur if the health-care provider treats the information stereotypically and acts as if all members of an ethnic category must behave and believe in the same fashion." Harwood further advises health care providers to apply their "expanded knowledge of ethnic health beliefs and practices with due attention to the needs of the individual patient."

In "Guidelines for Culturally Appropriate Health Care," Harwood notes that "[r]ecurrent issues allow for the development of general guidelines for the delivery of health services to ethnic groups" (482). These recurrent issues in clinical care include:

Recognizing intraethnic variation

- Exposure to biomedical and popular standards of health care

- Income, occupation, and religion

- Area of origin in the mother country

- Implications for the clinician

Ethnic concepts of disease and illness

- Eliciting the patient's concept of disease

- Identifying and managing discrepancies between patients' and practitioners' concepts of disease or illness

- Working with common ethnic concepts of disease etiology

- Treating culture-specific syndromes

Becoming ill: how patients' evaluation of symptoms affect treatment

- Variables precipitating the illness experience

- Women as interpreters of symptoms

- Relief of pain or other symptoms

- Anxiety-provoking symptoms

- Fear of treatment

- Interference with role responsibilities and valued activities

Coping with illness outside the mainstream medical system

- Home treatment: implications for mainstream health care

- Incorporating preferred modes of treatment into standard regimens

- Self-medication as a possible health hazard

- Alternative healers: implications for mainstream health care

  While recognizing that in some cases alternative forms of therapy may interfere with biomedical diagnosis and treatment, Harwood reported data demonstrating that, more often than not, alternative healers complement the delivery of mainstream medical services and frequently refer their clients to mainstream sources of care.

Ethnic factors in encounters with and adherence to mainstream medicine

- Language and patient expectations

- Interactional norms

- Behavioral ethics

- Therapeutic diets

Helping familes during recovery, rehabilitation, and terminal illness

Access to biomedical knowledge

Access to biomedical knowledge remains a crucial issue for many ethnic patients. The sections on Virtual Resources (IX) and Patient Resource Materials (VII) are intended to assist providers in making this information more readily available.

The aspects of ethnic subcultures identified by Harwood as likely to bear most heavily on medical care—ethnic concepts of disease and illness, folk and popular traditions of health care, problems of language and translation, dietary practices, interactional norms, and the role of the family in compliance with long-term treatment—continue to be identified by researchers at the turn of the century.

Family Therapy with Ethnic Minorities

MK Ho, ed.
Newbury Park, CA: Sage Publications, 1992

Healing Latinos: Realidad y Fantasia—The Art of Cultural Competence in Medicine

D Hayes-Bautista, R Chiprut
Cedar-Sinai Health System, 1999

Provides health care professionals with understanding of the Latino community's cultural approach to health, disease, and health care. Chapters include personal accounts of experiences with Latino clients by the authors and other contributors on the topics of culture, the meaning of death, spirituality and religion, and complementary practices.

Health Issues for Women of Color: A Cultural Diversity Perspective

DL Adams, ed.
University of Maryland, 1995

Multidisciplinary and multifaceted approach to the major health concerns of women of color, focusing on African American, Hispanic/Latina, Asian/Pacific Islander, Middle Eastern, and American Indian/Alaskan Native women. Identifies emerging health concerns, research needs, and key policy issues. Also addresses topics such as homelessness, mental health, and drug abuse.

Latino Health in the US: A Growing Challenge

C Molina, M Aguirre-Molina, eds.
American Public Health Association, 1994

Comprehensive volume reflecting the research, knowledge, and expertise of nationally recognized Latino researchers, scholars, educators, and activists. Includes:

- Profiles of Latinos in the health care system
- Life cycle and family health
- Patterns of chronic disease
- Occupational health
- Alcohol, drug, and mental health issues

Minority Children and Adolescents in Therapy

MK Ho
Newbury Park, CA: Sage Publications, 1992

Nuestra Cultura, Nuestra Salud: A Handbook of Information on Latin American Health Beliefs and Practices

Centro San Bonifacio, 1997
1332 N Greenview
Chicago, IL 60622
773 252-9098

Compiled by Centro San Bonifacio, Erie Family Health Center, and Midwest Latino Health Research Training and Policy Center of the University of Illinois at Chicago, to build greater understanding, respect, and communication between providers and their patients. Topics include hot and cold classification of disease, traditional health beliefs and practices, and home treatments for folk illnesses.

One America in the 21st Century: Forging a New Future

President's Initiative on Race
Washington, DC: September 1998

Complete text available at:
http://www.whitehouse.gov/Initiatives/OneAmerica/cevent.html

Reflects the results of a 15-month effort by seven board members, chaired by John Hope Franklin, to discover the role race plays in civil rights enforcement, education, poverty, employment, housing, stereotyping, the administration of justice, health care, and immigration.

Cultural Competence of Providers

The 121-page report contains a section on "Cultural Competency of Providers," which addresses structural inequities and provider discrimination, as well as other causes of racial disparities in health care access.

Recommendations to reduce these disparities include strategies similar to those espoused by the AMA:

- Continue advocating for broad-based expansions in health insurance coverage.

- Continue advocacy of increased health care access for underserved groups.

- Continue pushing for full funding of the race and ethnic health disparities initiative.

- Increase funding for existing programs targeted to underserved and minority populations.

- Enhance financial and regulatory mechanisms to promote culturally competent care.

- Emphasize importance of cultural competence to institutions training health care providers.

The report urges the Department of Health and Human Services to strongly encourage medical training institutions and accrediting associations to require that students receive some training in cultural competency.

Palliative Care: Patient and Family Counseling Manual

Aspen Publishers Inc, June 1996
200 Orchard Ridge Dr
Gaithersburg, MD 20878
800 638-8437
http://www.aspenpublishers.com

- Provides information on end-of-life care that includes segments related to many of the special populations included in this *Compendium*.

- Includes handouts for patients and family and practical applications for practitioners.

- Provides guidance on training volunteers to deal effectively and caringly with patients from all cultural backgrounds and deciding who to listen to if the parents and partner of a gay patient offer conflicting instructions.

- Includes recommendations and policies from the AMA's Elements of Quality of Care for Patients in the Last Phase of Life, as well as:

Patient and family issues
- Education tools
- Final stages of life
- General patient education
- Patient planning guide
- General family education

General guidelines for caregiving
- Pain management
- Grief
- Psychosocial issues
- Spiritual care
- Nutrition in terminal care
- Professional concerns/volunteer training
- Financial/legal issues
- HIV/AIDS issues (patient and family)

A Pocket Guide to Cultural Assessment

Elaine Geissler
Mosby-Year Book, 1994

An invaluable compilation of information on dozens of cultural variables for 170 countries, including:

- major languages
- ethnic groups, religions
- predominant sick care practices
- family role in hospital care
- pain reactions
- ethnic/race specific or endemic diseases
- dominance patterns
- eye contact practices
- touch practices
- perception of time
- birth and death rites

- food practices and intolerances
- infant feeding practices
- child rearing practices
- national childhood immunizations

Psychopharmacology and Psychobiology of Ethnicity

K Lin, R Poland, G Makasaki, eds.
Washington DC: American Psychiatric Press, 1993

Societal Forces Reshaping American Medicine: Implications for Internal Medicine and the Board

American Board of Internal Medicine (ABIM)
50 Walnut St
Philadelphia, PA 19106
215 446-3562

Several presentations from the 1997 ABIM Summer Conference addressed issues on cultural competence, including complementary care and a multicultural society. Contains "Cultural Competence: Addressing a Multicultural Society," with a 77-item bibliography centered on the significance of disparities in care to nonmajority populations.

Transcultural Child Development

G Johnson-Powell, J Yamamoto, GE Wyatt,
W Arroyo, eds.
New York, John Wiley and Sons, 1997

The Ultimate Multi-Ethnic Resource for Chicago

C Linton, ed.
Illinois Ethnic Council, 1998

Includes information on 450 ethnic organizations, 120 ethnic media outlets and area scholars, and translation services for the Chicago area. The Illinois Ethnic Council also published *Ethnic Handbook: A Guide to the Cultures and Traditions of Chicago's Diverse Communities*.

Journals and Journal Articles

Analysis of Quality Care for Patients Who Are Black or Poor in Rural and Urban Settings

KL Kahn, ML Pearson, ER Harrison, et al
RAND, 1993

Assessing Multicultural Counseling Competence: A Review of Instrumentation

JG Ponterotto, BP Rieger, A Barrett, et al
Journal of Counseling and Development;
Jan-Feb 1994, Vol 72:316-322

Black-White Disparities in Health Care, AMA Council on Ethical and Judicial Affairs

JAMA, May 2, 1990; 263(17):2344-2346

Cancer Studies Fail Minorities

S Stapleton
AMNews, Feb 8, 1999

Cardiovascular Risk Factors in Mexican American Adults: A Transcultural Analysis of NHANES III, 1988-1994

Jan Sundquist, Marilyn Winkleby
American Journal of Public Health, May 1999,
Vol 89, No 5

Examines the extent to which cardiovascular disease risk factors differ among subgroups of Mexican Americans living in the United States. Findings illustrate the heterogeneity of the Mexican -American population and identify a new group at substantial risk for cardiovascular disease and in need of effective heart disease prevention programs. Includes 75 references.

The Clinical Use of Interpreters

W Arroyo
In *Handbook of Child and Adolescent Psychiatry*,
Vol 7, New York: John Wiley and Sons, 1997

A Comparative Analysis of Three Cross-Cultural Training Approaches: In Search of Cross-Cultural Competency

R Salcido, JA Garcia
Arate 1997;Vol 22, No 7:35-49

The Concept of Race and Health Status in America

DR Williams, R Lavizzo-Mourey, RC Warren
Public Health Rep, 1994; 109:26-41

A Conceptual Framework for Assessing and Treating Minority Youth

JT Gibbs, LN Huang
In *Children of Color: Psychological Interventions with Minority Youth*, pp 1-29
JT Gibbs, LN Huang, eds.
San Francisco, CA: Jossey-Bass Publishers, 1989

Cross-cultural Mental Health Treatment

L Comas-Diaz
In *Clinical Guidelines in Cross-cultural Mental Health*, pp 337-361
New York: John Wiley & Sons, 1988

Cultural Aspects of Treatment: Conceptual, Methodological, and Clinical Issues and Directions

AJ Marsella, J Westermeyer
In *Treatment of Mental Disorders,* pp 391-420
N Sartorius, et al, eds.
American Psychiatric Press, World Health
Organization, 1993

Cultural Assessment of Black American Men Treated for Prostate Cancer: Clinical Case Studies

ME Cooley, K Jennings-Dozier
Oncol Nurs Forum, 1998;25:1729-1736

Presents the importance of beliefs about health and
illness, use of a lay referral system, use of folk
treatments, and the importance of family,
community, and spiritual support.

Cultural-Specific Methods, Techniques, and Skills in Individual Therapy

MK Ho
In *Family Therapy with Ethnic Minorities,*
pp 119-149, MK Ho, ed.
Newbury Park, CA: Sage Publications, 1992

Differences by Race in the Rates of Procedures Performed in Hospitals for Medicare Beneficiaries

AM McBean, M Gornick
Health Care Financing Review, Summer 1994; 77

Effect of an Intensive Educational Program for Minority College Students and Recent Graduates on the Probability of Acceptance to Medical School

JC Canter, MA Bergeisen, LC Baker
JAMA, 1998;280:772-776

The Effect of Race and Sex on Physicians' Recommendations for Cardiac Catheterization

Kevin A Schulman, Jesse A Berlin, William
Harless, et al
NEJM, February 25,1999, Vol 340, No 8, 618-626

Effects of Race and Income on Mortality and Use of Services among Medicare Beneficiaries

ME Gornick, PW Eggers, TW Reilly, et al
NEJM, 1996; 335:791-799

The Entry of Underrepresented Minority Students into US Medical Schools: An Evaluation of Recent Trends

DM Carlisle, JE Gardner, H Liu
Am J Public Health, 1998;88:1314-1318

Ethnic Minorities and Health Promotion: Developing a Culturally Competent Agenda

BWK Yee, GD Weaver
Generations, Spring 1994;18(1):39-44

Ethnic Variation in Cardiovascular Disease Risk Factors Among Children and Young Adults. Findings from the Third National Health and Nutrition Examination Survey, 1988-1994

MA Winkleby, TN Robinson, J Sundquist,
HC Kraemer
JAMA, March 17, 1999;281:1006-1013

Family Medicine Journal

Society of Teachers of Family Medicine
Box 8729
8880 Ward Parkway
Kansas City, MO 64114
800 274-2237
http://stfm.org

The March 1998 issue of the journal was dedicated
to minority health.

Health Care for Black and Poor Hospitalized Medicare Patients

KL Kahn, ML Pearson, ER Harrison, et al
JAMA, 1994; 271:1169-1174

Implications of Race/Ethnicity for Health and Health Care Use: Racial/Ethnic Differences in Health Care Utilization of Cardiovascular Procedures: A Review of the Evidence

ES Ford, RS Cooper
Health Services Research, April 1995; 30:1, Part II,
237

Income, Race, and Surgery in Maryland

AM Gittelsohn, J Halpern, RL Sanchez
American Journal of Public Health, 1991; 1435

Journal of Health Care for the Poor and Underserved

Meharry Medical College
1005 Dr. D B Todd, Jr. Blvd
Nashville, TN 37208

Published four times a year by the Institute on
Health Care for the Poor and Underserved at
Meharry Medical College. Disseminates
information on the health of, and health care for,
low-income and other medically underserved
communities to health care practitioners, policy
makers, and community leaders who are in a

position to effect meaningful change. Pertinent
issues include access to, quality of, and cost of
health care. See *Language Barriers to Health Care*
issue, Vol 9 Supplement, 1998, above.

Multicultural Counseling Competencies and Standards: A Call for the Profession

DW Sue, P Arredondo, RJ McDavis
Journal of Counseling and Development,
1992;70:477-486

National Comparative Survey of Minority Health Care

The Commonwealth Fund, 1995

A Paradigm for Culturally-Based Care in Ethnic Minority Populations

Marjorie Kagawa-Singer, Rita Chi-Ying Chung
Journal of Community Psychology, April 1994,
Vol 22, 192-208

Pew: Encourage Minority Physicians

J Greene
AMNews, Dec 28, 1998

Physician Race and Care of Minority and Medically Indigent Patients

E Moy, BA Bartman
JAMA, 1995;273:1515-1520

Physician Service to the Underserved: Implications for Affirmative Action in Medical Education

JC Cantor, EL Miles, LC Baker, DC Barker
Inquiry, 1996;33:167-180

Race and Health Care—An American Dilemma?

HJ Geiger
NEJM, 1996; 335:815-816

Race Differences in Estimates of Sudden Coronary Heart Disease Mortality, 1980-1988: The Impact of Ill-defined Death

D Armstrong, S Wing, HA Tyroler
J Clin Epidemiol, 1996; 49:2147-1251

Racial Differences in Cerebrovascular Disease Hospitalizations

AL Klatsky, MA Armstrong, GD Friedman
Stroke, 1991; 22:299-304

Racial Differences in the Delivery of Hemodialysis

RA Sherman, RP Cody, JC Solanchick
Am J Kidney Dis, 1993; 21:632-634

Racial Differences in the Elderly's Use of Medical Procedures and Diagnostic Tests

JL Escarce, KR Epstein, DC Colby, et al
American Journal of Public Health, 1993:948

Racial Differences in the Use of Drug Therapy for HIV Diseases in an Urban Community

RD Moore, D Stanton, R Gopalan, et al
NEJM, 1994:763

Black patients were significantly less likely than whites to receive anti-retroviral therapy or PCP prophylaxis when first referred to an HIV clinic.

Racial Differences in the Use of Invasive Cardiovascular Procedures in the Department of Veterans Affairs Medical System

J Whittle, J Conigliaro, CB Good, et al
NEJM, 1993;621

The authors found race-related inequities in the Veterans Administration system when studying the use of invasive cardiovascular procedures. White patients were more likely than blacks to undergo invasive cardiac procedures, including cardiac catherization, PTCA, and CABG. Similar findings were present in the Ford and Cooper study of the private sector, published in 1995.

Racial Variation in Cardiac Procedure Use and Survival Following Acute Myocardial Infarction in the Department of Veterans Affairs

ED Peterson, SM Wright, J Daily, et al
JAMA, 1994; 271(15):1175-1180

Refugee and Immigrant Information Outline

The Tennessee Department of Human Services has prepared a packet of materials describing issues related to refugee and immigrant health, including information on state regions where refugees settle and their access to care in those areas. Approximately 3,500 to 5,000 legal immigrants and 1,400 refugees are admitted annually to Tennessee, and the Hispanic population in middle Tennessee is estimated as high as 26,000. The packet includes materials on mental health issues of southeast Asian refugees, the magnitude of culture gaps and differing world views, and strategies to build trust for a successful physician-patient relationship.

Relationship Between Patient Race and the Intensity of Hospital Service

J Yergan, AB Flood, JP LoGerfo, et al
Medical Care, 1987; 592

Roles of Race and Socioeconomic Factors in Health Service Research

KA Schulman, LE Rubenstein, FD Chesley, et al
Health Services Research, 1995

Training Psychiatrists for Working with Blacks in Basic Residency Programs

WH Bradshaw
American Journal of Psychiatry,
1978;135(12):1520-1523

Zeroing in on Cancer

AMNews, Feb 8, 1999

B. People with Physical or Mental Illnesses or Disabling Conditions

Organizations and Their Resources

American Medical Association

See Sections I and II for AMA staff contact and policies related to people with physical or mental illnesses or disabling conditions.

Publications

The Americans with Disabilities Act: A Practice of Accommodation

American Medical Association, 1998

This guide, produced by the American Medical Association and the American Academy of Physical and Medical Rehabilitation, is aimed at health care professionals and facilities with the goal of eliminating barriers that may prevent people with disabling conditions from obtaining and accessing quality health care and employment.

Alcoholism in the Elderly: Diagnosis, Treatment, Prevention

Department of Geriatric Health
American Medical Association, 1997

In November 1992, the AMA convened an ad hoc committee to address the problems physicians face in diagnosing, treating, and preventing alcoholism in the elderly. In December 1993, the AMA House of Delegates adopted a recommendation of the AMA

Council on Scientific Affairs to develop guidelines on alcoholism in the elderly for physicians. The guidelines, which have been endorsed by the American Society of Addiction Medicine, are intended to help the practicing physician establish a diagnosis, manage current emergency conditions such as acute withdrawal, and refer the elderly patient to ongoing treatment for alcoholism and for any medical or psychiatric complications.

Prevention opportunities for physicians include evaluating their elderly patients in terms of their drinking practices and behavior and paying special attention to prescribing practices with high-risk patients to avoid adverse alcohol-drug interactions or dependence on sedative-hypnotics.

Guidelines for the Use of Assistive Technology: Evaluation, Referral, Prescription

Department of Geriatric Health
American Medical Association, 1996

In November 1993, the AMA convened two focus groups—one with consumers and one with allied health professionals—to address the barriers faced by physicians and their patients with disabilities when dealing with assistive technology. The concerns of the focus groups were presented to the Assistive Technology Advisory Panel in January

1994, and *Guidelines for the Use of Assistive Technology: Evaluation, Referral, Prescription* was published in 1996.

The *Guidelines* include both assistive technology *devices* and assistive technology *services*. An assistive technology *device* is any item, piece of equipment, or product system, whether acquired commercially off-the-shelf, modified, or customized, that is used to increase, maintain, or improve functional capability of individuals with disabilities. An assistive technology *service* is any service that directly assists an individual with a disability in the selection, acquisition, or use of an assistive technology device.

Culturally Relevant Sections

Physicians are advised to:

- Be sensitive to patient needs and preferences.

- Consider the social and cultural environment.

- Assess the impact of specific impairment within the patient's total environment and lifestyle.

- Continue the relationship with an interdisciplinary team *that includes the patient.*

- Provide individualized treatment that is sensitive to cost-effectiveness concerns.

- Be able to refer patients to local community resources for technology and support.

Culturally Relevant Advice

Physicians are also advised to become fully aware of the patients' intimate knowledge of their goals, preferences, support systems, and functional needs for independence.

In collecting this information, physicians should:

- Speak directly to the patient.

- Introduce themselves and everyone else in the room (this is especially important for patients with impaired vision).

- Face the patient when speaking and speak clearly.

- Be aware of the patient's mode of communication: oral/lip reading, American Sign Language (ASL), signed English, need for an interpreter, etc.

- Always explain what they are going to do before doing it.

- Ask the patients to repeat or summarize what they think they have heard the physician say.

The Core Knowledge and Assessment document outlines core knowledge components and provides specific patient assessment tools, including patient examination and evaluation and evaluation and prescription of assistive technology. Office practice guidelines to meet the needs of persons with disabilities are also included.

Educational Material for Patients and Families

Additional resources include instructions for obtaining funding for assistive technology, locating state assistive technology projects, and accessing professional and interdisciplinary resources, including electronic asssistive technology resources, electronic bulletin boards, and home automation sources.

Medical Management of the Home Care Patient: Guidelines for Physicians

2nd Edition
Department of Geriatric Health
American Medical Association, 1998

The first Home Care Advisory Panel, convened by the American Medical Association in 1987 with the goal of increasing the involvement of physicians in home care, produced the first edition of the *Guidelines for the Medical Management of the Home Care Patient* (1992). A second panel, convened in 1997, led to the revised second edition of the *Guidelines* (1998), which are endorsed by the American Academy of Home Care Physicians.

This document provides instruction in designing a curriculum in home care for education and training of physicians at all levels and in recommending an agenda for future research and development.

The role of the physician and the physician-patient relationship are emphasized in the section describing the goals of home care. Physicians are reminded that in addition to overseeing frequently fluctuating pathophysiological condition(s), they should also advise, encourage, and support the patient's efforts in self-care.

Culturally Sensitive Assessment Table

The section on medical management in home care includes a two-page assessment table with cells on individualizing psychosocial assessments and interventions and observing and evaluating cultural, ethnic, or religious influences on health care behavior, beliefs, preferences, and expectations. Mental/cognitive assessments include health literacy. Information is also provided on eligibility under different payment plans.

Special Home Care Populations

The document describes special concerns of other populations, including persons with disabilities and those requiring high-technology home care services, such as "video visits" or tele-home care. Step-by-step instructions are provided for developing the care plan and for communicating with other members of the interdisciplinary team.

The publication emphasizes the importance of being sensitive to the emotional and physical well-being of the caregiver, the safety of others in the home, and visitors, and the continued willingness of the patient to participate as a partner in the home care plan. It also includes a list of patient's rights and responsibilities that reinforce patient-centered care. Home hospice care is described, including physician responsibilities.

The section on community resources includes (a) the telephone numbers of national, state, and local agencies that serve the frail elderly and other special populations, including children with special needs, and (b) complete list of addresses and phone numbers and fax numbers for state departments on aging. When available, hot lines are included.

A systematic literature review produced 61 references. The document concludes with a CME questionnaire that provides up to 3 hours of AMA Physician's Recognition Award category 1 credit.

Physician's Guide to Diagnosis and Treatment of Dementia

American Medical Association, September 1999 (projected publication date)
Rosalie Guttman, PhD
312 464-5069

Produced by a culturally diverse expert consensus panel, the *Guide* will highlight the significance of culture, race, age, and sex on both the diagnosis and management of dementia.

American Psychiatric Association (APA)

Steve Mirin, MD, Medical Director
1400 K St NW
Washington, DC 20005
202 682-6000
202 682-6353 Fax
E-mail: smirin@psych.org
http://www.psych.org

The APA Council on National Affairs has been involved with developing curricula for psychiatric residents in six major minority or underrepresented groups; four have been published.

A Psychiatry Curriculum Directed to the Care of the Hispanic Patient

ES Garza-Trevino, P Ruiz, K Varegos-Samuel
Academic Psychiatry, 1997: Vol 21:1-10

Describes a model curriculum for psychiatric residency programs that addresses the sociodemographic, epidemiological, psychosocial, cultural, and behavioral characteristics of Hispanics. It emphasizes that faculty who are knowledgeable and sensitive about Hispanic culture should be available for the supervision and teaching of psychiatric residents during their training and that supervision should focus on cultural formulation and family dynamics and other factors of importance in clinical psychiatric practice. Includes a 29-item bibliography and 56 references.

A Psychiatric Residency Curriculum About Gender and Women's Issues

A Spielvogel, LJ Dickson, GE Robinson
Academic Psychiatry, 1995: Vol 19, no 4:187-201

Over the last 30 years, major advances have been made in our understanding of how biological factors and sociocultural influences contribute to gender differences, gender identity formation, and gendered role behavior. This article presents an outline for a curriculum in gender and women's issues, including educational objectives, learning experiences through which residents could meet these objectives, and

recommended readings. It discusses potential obstacles and suggests helpful strategies for implementing the proposed curriculum. Includes 96 references and suggested core readings.

A Curriculum for Learning in Psychiatry Residencies about Homosexuality, Gay Men, and Lesbians

TS Stein
Academic Psychiatry, 1994: Vol 18, no 2:59-70

Recent research has greatly expanded knowledge about homosexuality, gay men, and lesbians. However, neither a nonpathological perspective nor this new information has been integrated into psychiatric residency curricula. This article proposes a basic model for this necessary professional training. Includes 85 references.

A Curriculum for Learning About American Indians and Alaska Natives in Psychiatry Residency Training

JW Thompson
Academic Psychiatry, 1996: Vol 20, no 1:5-14

Describes a proposed curriculum for teaching psychiatric residents about the diagnosis and treatment of American Indians and Alaska Natives. Presents the historical context, contemporary myths, and rationale for the inclusion of curriculum materials on Indians in residency programs. Briefly describes the curriculum for the 4 years of residency education and outlines the knowledge, skills, and attitudes needed by residents. The curriculum for the first and second years includes a basic history and description of Indian people, information on myths about the group, and psychiatric epidemiology and psychopathology. The third year includes clinical care and related areas such as service utilization and illness prevention. The proposed fourth year includes a seminar to discuss psychotherapy and other clinical cases. Includes 70 references.

Center for Research on Women with Disabilities (CROWD)

Baylor College of Medicine
Department of Physical Medicine and
Rehabilitation
One Baylor Plaza
Houston, TX 77030
Task Force on Health Care for Adults with
Developmental Disabilities
713 798-4951

CROWD is a research center that focuses on issues related to health, aging, civil rights, abuse, and independent living.

Institute for Health & Disability

Department of Pediatrics
University of Minnesota
Box 721, 420 Delaware St SE
Minneapolis, MN 55455-0392
http://www.cyfc.umn.edu/NRL/

Health Issues: For Children & Youth & Their Families

Newsletter reporting on issues pertinent to improving the health and functioning of children and youths up to 24 years old within their families and communities, which addresses cultural diversity issues.

National Resource Library

Database of information about children and adolescents with disabilities.

Latin International Network of Mental Health

6551 W North Ave
Oak Park, IL 60302

The Latin International Network of Mental Health publishes *Psychline: Inter-Transdisciplinary Journal of Mental Health,* which examines cultural issues and guides organizations in assessing and improving the cultural competence of their organization in order to meet the diverse needs of clients and communities. See the cultural assessment chart in the introduction to Section IV.

Midwest Bioethics Center

1100 Pennsylvania Ave, Ste 4041
Kansas City, MO 64105
816 221-1100
E-mail: midwestbio@aol.com.

Health Care Treatment Decision-Making Guidelines for Adults with Developmental Disabilities

Midwest Bioethics Center and University of Missouri-Kansas City Institute for Human Development Task Force on Health Care for Adults with Developmental Disabilities
Bioethics Forum, Fall 1996;1-8

National Institute of Child Health and Human Development (NICHD)

Box 3006
Rockville, MD 20847
800 370-2943
301 984-1473 Fax
E-mail: NICHDClearinghouse@iqsolutions.com
http://www.nih.gov/nichd

Features a toll-free number, on-line ordering of publications through the NICHD Web site, and an information and referral service.

National Organization on Disability (NOD)

910 16th St NW, Ste 600
Washington, DC 20006
202 293-5960
E-mail: ability@nod.org
http://www.nod.org

NOD promotes the full and equal participation of America's 54 million men, women, and children with disabilities in all aspects of like. NOD was founded in 1982 at the conclusion of the United Nations International Year of Disabled Persons. NOD is the only national disability network organization concerned with all disabilities, all age groups, and all disability issues.

1998 NOD/Harris Survey of Americans with Disabilities

Includes *Closing the Gaps: 1998.*

The National Rehabilitation Information Center (NARIC)

1010 Wayne Ave, Ste 800
Silver Spring, MD 20910-3319
301 562-2400
http://www.naric.com/naric/index.html

For 20 years, the National Rehabilitation Information Center (NARIC) has collected and disseminated the results of federally funded research projects. NARIC's literature collection, which also includes commerically published books, journal articles, and audiovisuals, averages around 200 new documents per month.

NARIC is funded by the National Institute on Disability and Rehabilitation Research (NIDRR) to serve anyone, professional or lay person, who is interested in disability and rehabilitation, including consumers, family members, health professionals, educators, rehabilitation counselors, students, librarians, administrators, and researchers. NARIC provides:

- *Inhouse services*: information and referral, customized database searches, document delivery, NARIC products.

- *On-line services*: 60,000 disability-related records in five searchable and browsable databases: literature, organizations, timely information, the latest research.

- *NIDRR Project Area*: Projects funded by the National Institute on Disability and Rehabilitation Research.

Parent Advocacy Coalition for Educational Rights (PACER)

PACER Center
4826 Chicago Ave S
Minneapolis, MN 55417-1098
612 827-2966
http://www.pacer.org

Publishes *Pacesetter*, by and for parents of children and young adults with disabilities, which frequently addresses racial/ethnic and other diversity issues.

Portland State University Research and Training Center on Family Support and Children's Mental Health

Regional Research Institute for Human Services
Box 751
Portland, OR 97207-0751
503 725-4040
http://www-adm.pdx.edu/user/rri/rtc

Works to improve services for families whose children have serious mental, emotional, or behavioral disabilities. All programs of research and training are designed to promote services that are community-based, family-oriented, and culturally appropriate.

Multicultural Perspectives of Empowerment
and
Increasing Multicultural Parent Involvement

Two of the Center's many projects looking at multicultural issues. Other themes and topics include family-centered outreach strategies for diverse populations.

Cultural Competence Self–Assessment Questionnaire: A Manual for Users
1995

The *Cultural Competence Self-Assessment Questionnaire* was developed to help child and family-serving agencies assess their cross-cultural strengths and weaknesses in order to design specific training activities or interventions that promote greater competence across cultures.

Focal Point

The bulletin of the Portland State Minority Research and Training Center on Family Support and Children's Mental Health reports on culturally competent organizations and projects.
http://www.rtc.pdx.edu

An Introduction to Cultural Competence Principles and Elements: An Annotated Bibliography

JL Mason, K Braker, TL Williams-Murphy
Portland State University, 1995

About 115 abstracted listings exemplify aspects of the Child and Adolescent Service System Program's (CASSP) cultural competence model, Emphasizing care of children and youth with serious emotional disabilities. Citations are categorized under the headings of Cultural Self Assessment, Dynamics of Difference, Valuing Diversity, Adaptation to Diversity, Incorporation of Cultural Knowledge.

Understanding Cultural Identity in Intervention and Assessment

RH Dana
Portland State University, 1998

Presents a model for effective culture-specific services that emphasizes the description and understanding of cultural/racial identity and the use of this information to develop cultural formulations to increase the accuracy of diagnoses, with four chapters devoted to discussions of mental health services.

Publications

Bio-Ecological Approach to Cognitive Assessment

E Armour-Thomas, SA Gopaul-McNicol
Cultural Diversity and Mental Health, 1997:Vol 3, No 2:131-144

A Critique on Cultural Competence

A Noboa-Rios
Psychline, 1998;2(4):18-19

Includes an organizational assessment tool.

Cross-Cultural Issues in Psychiatric Treatment

CA Gonzales, EEH Griffith, P Ruiz
In *Treatment of Psychiatric Disorders,* 2nd ed,
Vol 1, pp 55-85
GO Gabbard, ed.
Washington, DC: American Psychiatric Press, 1995

Cultural Competence in Child Psychiatry

AJ Pumariega, TL Cross
In *Handbook of Child and Adolescent Psychiatry,*
pp 473-484
NE Alessi, ed.
New York: John Wiley & Sons, 1997

Cultural Considerations in the Classification of Mental Disorders in Children and Adolescents

G Canino, I Canino, W Arroyo
In *DSM-IV Sourcebook, Volume 3,* 873-883
TA Widiger, AJ Frances, HA Pincus, et al, eds.
Washington, DC: American Psychiatric
Association, 1996

Culture, Ethnicity and Mental Illness

AC Gaw
Baltimore, MD: American Psychiatric Press, 1992

Depression Following Spinal Cord Injury: A Clinical Practice Guideline for Primary Care Physicians

Consortium for Spinal Cord Medicine, 1998

Provides treatment recommendations on everything from assessment to social support systems, including consumer and family education and evaluation and modification of treatment plans. Important because it establishes practice guidelines in physical and psychological co-morbidities.

Disability, Difference, Discrimination: Perspectives on Justice in Bioethics and Public Policy

A Silvers, et al
Rowman and Littlefield, 1999
http://www.rowmanlittlefield.com

Disability Discrimination in America: HIV/AIDS and Other Health Conditions

Lawrence O Gostin, Chai Feldblum, David W Webber
JAMA, February 24, 1999; Vol 281, No 8

Includes 78 references, many to articles in *JAMA.*

Gerontology, Perspectives and Issues

Kenneth Ferraro, ed.
New York: Springer, 1997

Designed as a text for graduate and advanced graduate studies; includes a chapter on "Cross-Cultural Comparisons of Aging" by CL Fry.

Health Issues for Women of Color: A Cultural Diversity Perspective

DL Adams, ed.
University of Maryland, 1995

Includes a multidisciplinary and multifaceted approach to the major health concerns of women of color, focusing on African American, Hispanic/Latina, Asian/Pacific Islander, Middle Eastern, and American Indian/Alaskan Native women. Identifies emerging health concerns, research needs, and key policy issues and addresses topics such as homelessness, mental health, and drug abuse.

Living in the Community with Disability—Service Needs, Use, and Systems

Susan M Allen, Vincent Mor
New York: Springer, 1998

Experts in the fields of six disability populations review the past and current state of health services to project what is needed within the context of the emerging health care delivery system to meet the medical and supportive service needs of this growing population.

Methodological Challenges in Cross-Cultural Research of Childhood Psychopathology

G Canino, HR Bird, IA Canino
In *Evaluating Mental Health Services,* Vol 3, pp 259-277
CT Nixon, DA Northrup, eds.
Thousand Oaks, CA: Sage Publications, 1997

Multicultural Clinical Interactions

MH Fitzgerald
J Rehabilitation, 1992 Apr-Jun;58(2):38-42

Physician's Guide to Diagnosis and Treatment of Dementia

American Medical Association, September 1999 (projected publication date)
Rosalie Guttman, PhD
312 464-5069

Produced by a culturally diverse expert consensus panel, the *Guide* will highlight the significance of culture, race, age, and sex on both the diagnosis and management of dementia.

Toward a Culturally Competent System of Care: A Monograph on Effective Services for Minority Children Who Are Severely Emotionally Disturbed

TL Cross, BJ Bazron, KW Dennis, et al
Washington, DC: CASSP Technical Assistance Center, George Washington University Child Development Center, 1989

Toward a Culturally Competent System of Care, Volume II

MR Isaacs, MP Benjamin
Washington, DC: CASSP Technical Assistance Center, Georgetown University Child Development Center, 1991

The Unique Challenges Faced by Psychiatrists and Other Mental Health Professionals Working in a Multicultural Setting

TL Chiu
Int J Soc Psychiatry, Spring 1994;40(1):61-74

C. Children and Adolescents

Organizations and Their Resources

American Medical Association

Contact

Missy Fleming, Program Director
Child and Adolescent Health Program
American Medical Association
515 N State St
Chicago, IL 60610
312 464-5315

Policies

E-9.12	*Physician-Patient Relationship: Respect for Law and Human Rights*
H-60.974	*Children and Youth with Disabilities*
H-165.877	*Universal Coverage for Prenatal Care, Children and Adolescents*
H-215.985	*Child Care in Hospitals*
H-245.986	*Infant Mortality in the United States*
H-420.962	*Perinatal Addiction—Issues in Care and Prevention*
H-420.972	*Prenatal Services to Prevent Low Birthweight Infants*
H-420.978	*Access to Prenatal Care*

H-420.995	*Medical Care for Indigent and Culturally Displaced Obstetrical Patients and Their Newborns*
H-430.990	*Bonding Programs for Women Prisoners and Their Newborn Children*
H-500.992	*Tobacco Advertising Directed to Children, Minorities and Women*
H-515.981	*Family Violence—Adolescents as Victims and Perpetrators*
H-515.983	*Physicians and Family Violence*
H-515.994	*Child Abuse and Neglect*
H-515.993	*Child Sexual Abuse*
H-515.997	*AMA Diagnostic and Treatment Guidelines Concerning Child Abuse and Neglect*

Published Reports

Adolescents as Victims of Family Violence
JAMA, October 20, 1993; 1850-6

Confidential Health Services for Adolescents
JAMA, March 17, 1993; 269:1420-4

American Medical Association Adolescent Health Online

http://www.ama-assn.org/adolhlth/adolhlth.htm

Designed to provide information to physicians, other health care providers, researchers, parents, and teenagers on important adolescent health issues. Regularly updated with the latest scientific information in the field of adolescent health. Provides information on the Guidelines for Adolescent Preventive Services (GAPS) and an extensive list of links to other organizations working to improve the health status of young people.

Information about cultural competence resources developed by the Child and Adolescent Health Program are viewable on the Web site. Adolescent Health Online is supported through a cooperative agreement from the Health Services and Resources Administration, Maternal and Child Health Bureau's (MCHB's) federal Office of Adolescent Health.

Child and Adolescent Health Program

Partners in Program Planning for Adolescents Health (PIPPAH)

The AMA was awarded a cooperative agreement from the Health Resources and Services Administration (HRSA) and the MCHB's federal Office on Adolescent Health in 1996. The cooperative agreement supports the Partners in Program Planning for Adolescent Health (PIPPAH) initiative. The seven partners include the American Medical Association, American Bar Association, American Dietetic Association, American Nurses Association, American Psychological Association, National Assembly on School-Based Health Care, and National Association of Social Workers.

Project goals are to:

- Promote increased clinical advocacy efforts of physicians and other health professionals to improve the health status of adolescents.

- Enhance the programmatic and advocacy efforts of national, state, and local public and private organizations regarding adolescent health.

Activities include:

- **Advocacy Packets**
  Information packets produced through a collaborative effort between PIPPAH staff and the Society for Adolescent Medicine provide health professionals with information on the health status of young people, adolescent health and managed care, and information for parents and guardians regarding their teenager's health.

- **Survey of State Medical Societies**
  The survey collected information about adolescent health activities that state medical societies are directing as well as any work they are doing interdisciplinarily with other professional organizations.

- **Professional Conferences**
  PIPPAH partners have presented panel discussions of respective projects at annual MCHB grantee meeting, and at meetings of some of the partners.

Future PIPPAH activities include identification of adolescent health problems to which all partners may contribute to develop a unified, interdisciplinary perspective.

National Coalition on Adolescent Health

A forum for multidisciplinary, coordinated activities on behalf of youth in the United States, the coalition is made up of 40 member organizations, including national specialty societies in medicine, psychiatry, allied health professions, public health and education organizations, private foundations, and federal agencies. Major initiatives include the development and distribution of policy compendia that have focused on:

- Confidential health services for adolescents
- Violence and intentional injury
- Tobacco

- Alcohol and other harmful substances
- Reproductive health issues

The coalition assisted with the initiation of the Healthy Youth 2000 project, which established the 3,000-member National Adolescent Health Promotion Network. Its biannual meetings are organized around emerging issues and feature presentations by experts who address the most current medical, legal, psychological, and policy issues facing today's adolescents. The activities of the coalition are supported in part by the PIPPAH cooperative agreement with HRSA/MCHB.

Child Health Initiative

Contact: Beth Lipa-Glaysher
312 464-4944

Under the guidance and direction of a steering committee composed of representatives of national organizations with a commitment to, and expertise in, child and adolescent health, this initiative will enhance healthy lifestyles of children and youth and reduced health risk behaviors. The overarching goal of the initiative is to develop a continuum for enhancing infant, child, and adolescent health by identifying culturally consistent strategies for physician, family, and community implementation. Project activities will be directed at identifying the relationship between genetic and environmental factors that influence health behaviors and resulting health status of infants, children, and adolescents during critical periods of growth and development and developing, implementing, and evaluating recommendations for health promotion strategies that support children and adolescents, families, and communities. Special attention will be paid to health-related sociocultural differences of individuals, families, and communities in order to maximize program impact.

Publications

Healthy Youth 2000: A Mid-Decade Review, 1996

Culturally Competent Health Care for Adolescents: A Guide for Primary Care Providers
American Medical Association, 1994

Introduces health care providers to the complex issues involved in working with diverse populations of adolescents and outlines practical strategies for incorporating cultural issues into clinical practice.

Guidelines for Adolescent Preventive Services (GAPS)

GAPS is a comprehensive set of recommendations that provide a framework for the organization and content of preventive services. The GAPS publications include:

GAPS Recommendations Monograph, 1997-1998

Recommendation 2: "Preventive services should be age and developmentally appropriate, and should be sensitive to individual and sociocultural differences."

GAPS Implementation Forms
* *Also available in Spanish*

Contains the following reproducible forms:

- * *Parent/Guardian Questionnaire*. Collects adolescent and family health history and parents concerns about their adolescent.

- * *Early Adolescent Questionnaire*. For the younger adolescent (aged 11-14), this form collects medical history and screens for health risk behaviors and biomedical problems.

- * *Initial Adolescent Questionnaire*. For the new patient, this form collects medical history and screens for health risk behaviors and biomedical problems.

- ** Periodic Adolescent Questionnaire*. For the established patient, this form collects an abbreviated medical history and screens for health risk behaviors and biomedical problems.

- *Height, Weight, and Body Mass Index (BMI)*. Chart to measure BMI, which indicates an adolescent's risk for obesity.

- *Blood Pressure by Age*. Chart to provide the normal range of blood pressure readings according to age and gender.

- *Master Checklist*. Form to track preventive services provided to adolescents and parents.

- *Provider Prompt Sheet for Health Guidance and Screening*. Form to summarize recommended health guidance and screening activities.

- *Preventive Health Services by Age and Procedure*. Chart to show the recommended periodicity for preventive services.

- *Adolescent Physical Examination Form*. Form to record the results of a physical examination.

The Parent Package, 1997
(Also available in Spanish)

Contains 15 reproducible tip sheets for parents/guardians of adolescents. Topics include growth and development, parenting, nutrition, injury prevention, sex, tobacco, alcohol and other drugs, HIV/AIDS, immunizations, and more. The Parent Package corresponds with the list of "for more information" topics on the GAPS Parent/Guardian Questionnaire.

Web Sites

AMA Health Insight
http://www.ama-assn.org/
insight/h_focus/adl_hlth/teen/teen.htm

American Academy of Pediatrics (AAP)

Joe M. Sanders Jr, MD, Executive Director
141 North West Point Blvd
PO Box 927
Elk Grove Village, IL 60007
847 228-5005
847 228-5097 (Fax)
E-mail: jsanders@aap.org
http://www.aap.org

Policies

Culturally Effective Pediatric Health Care: Education and Training Issues (Committee on Pediatric Workforce policy statement)

Reports

Report of the AAP Task Force on Minority Children's Access to Pediatric Care
American Academy of Pediatrics, 1994

The Task Force addresses impediments to the physical well-being of all children, especially those that affect minority group children. The report deals with and makes recommendations in five major areas: Health Status, Access Barriers (among those addressed is cultural insensitivity/racism/classism), Workforce (includes a section on the cultural competence of pediatric care providers), Organizational Response, and the Academy's Role. Includes 131 references.

Association for the Care of Children's Health

19 Mantua Rd
Mount Royal, NJ 08061
609 224-1742
609 423-3420
acchhq@talley.com
http://www.acch.org/

- Promotes family-centered care policies and practices that are responsive to the unique developmental and psychosocial needs of children, youth, and their families.

- Produces educational materials that provide greater understanding of psychosocially sound, developmentally supportive, family-centered care and practical knowledge to make it a reality.

- Conducts an annual conference, bringing together members and others to share knowledge, skills, and experiences. Plans and coordinates Children and Healthcare Week™ each year to focus attention on the unique needs of children and families as they interact with the health care system.

- Publishes *Children's Health Care*, a quarterly research-based journal; a newsletter, *ACCH News*; and an annual membership directory.

- Provides opportunities for parents and professionals to work together to develop key practices and guidelines for implementing family-centered care.

- Provides information, referral, and support to professionals and families of children with disabilities and life-threatening illnesses

Institute for Health and Disability

Department of Pediatrics
University of Minnesota
Box 721, 420 Delaware Street SE
Minneapolis, MN 55455-0392

Health Issues: For Children and Youth and Their Families

The Institute's newsletter addresses issues pertinent to improving the health and functioning of children and youths up to 24 years old within their families and communities; frequently includes cultural diversity issues.

National Resources Library

The Institute also maintains a database of information, the National Resource Library, about children and adolescents with disabilities.
http://www.cyfc.umn.edu/NRL/

National Adolescent Health Information Center (NAHIC)

University of California, San Francisco
School of Medicine
Division of Adolescent Medicine
1388 Sutter St, Ste 605A
San Francisco, CA 94109
415 476-9000

Established with funding from the Maternal and Child Health Bureau in 1993 to promote linkages among key sectors of the health care system that affect the health of adolescents. Major activities have focused on:

- Promoting collaborative networks

- Information collection, analysis, and dissemination (including studies to synthesize research and policy trends)

- Technical assistance, consultation, and continuing education

The NAHIC has a variety of products that address adolescent health issues, including a set of 11 fact sheets and multiple reports covering topics such as managed care, health care reform, and policy recommendations for improving adolescent health.

Fact Sheet Topics

- Investing in Preventive Health Services for Adolescents
- Adolescent Demographics
- Adolescent Morality
- Adolescent Suicide
- Adolescent Injury
- Adolescent Substance Abuse
- Adolescent Sexuality
- Adolescent Pregnancy Prevention: Effective Strategies
- Adolescent Health Care Utilization
- Out-of-Home Youth

Improving Adolescent Health: An Analysis and Synthesis of Policy Recommendations

CD Brindis, EM Ozer, M Handley, et al
San Francisco, CA: NAHIC, 1998

National Technical Assistance Center for Children's Mental Health

Georgetown University Child Development Center
3307 M St NW, Ste 401
Washington, DC 20007-3935
202 687-5000
202 687-8899 Fax

Towards a Culturally Competent System of Care

Terry Cross, Karl Dennis, Mareasa Isaacs, Barbara Bazron
Washington, DC: Georgetown University Child Development Center, 1989

- Describes the goals and principles of cultural competence and the nine principles that govern the development of culturally competent programs.

- Emphasizes the need to develop cultural competence at the policymaking level, at the administrative level, and at the services level.

- Advises programs to

  ➢ assess their level of cultural competence;

  ➢ develop support for change throughout the organization and community;

  ➢ identify the leadership and resources needed to change;

  ➢ devise a comprehensive cultural competence plan with specific action steps and deadlines for achievements; and

  ➢ commit to an ongoing evaluation process and a willingness to respond to change.

Parent Advocacy Coalition for Educational Rights (PACER)

PACER Center
4826 Chicago Ave S
Minneapolis, MN 55417-1098
612 827-2966
http://www.pacer.org

Pacesetter

The PACER newsletter, by and for parents of children and young adults with disabilities, which frequently addresses racial/ethnic and other diversity issues.

Portland State University Research and Training Center on Family Support and Children's Mental Health

Regional Research Institute for Human Services
Box 751
Portland, OR 97207-0751
503 725-4040
http://www-adm.pdx.edu/user/rri/rtc
http://www.rtc.pdx.edu

The Center has the overall goal of improving services for families whose children have serious mental, emotional, or behavioral disabilities. All programs of research and training are designed to promote services that are community-based, family-oriented and culturally appropriate.

Multicultural Perspectives of Empowerment
and
Increasing Multicultural Parent Involvement

Two examples of the Center's many projects looking at multicultural issues. Other themes and topics include family-centered outreach strategies for diverse populations.

Publications

Cultural Competence Self–Assessment Questionnaire: A Manual for Users
Regional Research Institute for Human Services, 1995

Instrument to assist child- and family-serving agencies assess cross-cultural strengths and weaknesses in order to design specific training activities or interventions that promote greater competence across cultures.

An Introduction to Cultural Competence Principles and Elements: An Annotated Bibliography
JL Mason, K Braker, TL Williams-Murphy
Portland State University, 1995

About 115 abstracted listings exemplify aspects of the Child and Adolescent Service System Program's (CASSP) cultural competence model, emphasizing care of children and youth with serious emotional disabilities. Citations are categorized under:

- Cultural Self Assessment
- Dynamics of Difference
- Valuing Diversity
- Adaptation to Diversity
- Incorporation of Cultural Knowledge

Understanding Cultural Identity in Intervention and Assessment
RH Dana
Portland State University, 1998

Presents a model for effective culture-specific services that emphasizes the description and understanding of cultural/racial identity and the use of this information to develop cultural formulations to increase the accuracy of diagnoses, with four chapters devoted to discussions of mental health services.

Focal Point

The bulletin of the Research and Training Center on Family Support and Children's Mental Health; reports on culturally competent organizations and projects.

Publications

Children of Color: Psychological Interventions with Minority Youth

JT Gibbs, LN Huang, eds.
San Francisco, CA: Jossey-Bass Publishers, 1989

Cultural Competence in Child Psychiatry

AJ Pumariega, TL Cross
In *Handbook of Child and Adolescent Psychiatry*
NE Alessi, JD Noshpitz, eds.
New York: John Wiley & Sons, Inc, 1997,
pp 473-484

Cultural Considerations in the Classification of Mental Disorders in Children and Adolescents

G Canino, I Canino, W Arroyo
DSM-IV Sourcebook, Volume 3
TA Widiger et al, eds.
Washington, DC: American Psychiatric
Association, 1996, pp 873-883

Culturally Diverse Children and Adolescents: Assessment, Diagnosis, and Treatment

I Canino, J Spurlock
New York: Guilford Press, 1994

Culturally Effective Pediatric Care: Education and Training Issues

American Academy of Pediatrics Committee on
Pediatric Workforce
Pediatrics, January 1999;103(1):167-70

Ethnic Variation in Cardiovascular Disease Risk Factors Among Children and Young Adults: Findings from the Third National Health and Nutrition Examination Survey, 1988-1994

MA Winkleby, TN Robinson, J Sundquist, HC
Kraemer
JAMA, March 17, 1999;281:1006-1013

Handbook of Child and Adolescent Psychiatry: Varieties of Culture and Ethnicity

JD Noshpitz, N Alessi, eds.
New York: John Wiley and Sons, 1997

Methodological Challenges in Cross-Cultural Research of Childhood Psychopathology

G Canino, HR Bird, IA Canino
In *Evaluating Mental Health Services,* Vol 3
CT Nixon, DA Northrup, eds.
Thousand Oaks, CA: Sage Publications, 1997,
pp 259-277

Minority Children and Adolescents in Therapy

MK Ho
Newbury Park, CA: Sage Publications, 1992

Toward a Culturally Competent System of Care: A Monograph on Effective Services for Minority Children Who Are Severely Emotionally Disturbed

TL Cross, BJ Bazron, KW Dennis, et al
Washington, DC: CASSP Technical Assistance
Center, George Washington University Child
Development Center, 1989

Toward a Culturally Competent System of Care, Volume II

MR Isaacs, MP Benjamin
Washington, DC: CASSP Technical Assistance
Center, Georgetown University Child Development
Center, 1991

The Transcultural Child

IA Canino
*Handbook of Clinical Assessment of Children and
Adolescents*, vol 11
C Kestenbaum, D Williams, eds.
New York University Press, 1988, pp. 1025-1042

Transcultural Child Development

G Johnson-Powell, J Yamamoto, et al, eds.
New York: John Wiley and Sons, 1997

D. Women

Organizations and Their Resources

American Medical Association

Contact

Phyllis Kopriva
Women in Medicine
American Medical Association
515 N State St
Chicago, IL 60610
312 464-4392

Policies

E-9.035   *Gender Discrimination in the
Medical Profession*

E-9.12   *Physician-Patient Relationship:
Respect for Law and Human Rights*

E-9.122   *Gender Disparities in Health Care*

H-30.943 *Alcoholism and Alcohol Abuse
Among Women*

H-20.977 *Reducing Transmission of Human
Immunodeficiency Virus (HIV)*

H-55.984 *Screening and Treatment for Breast
and Cervical Cancer*

H-165.877 *Universal Coverage for Prenatal
Care, Children and Adolescents*

H-420.962 *Perinatal Addiction—Issues in Care
and Prevention*

H-420.972 *Prenatal Services to Prevent Low
Birthweight Infants*

H-420.978 *Access to Prenatal Care*

H-420.995 *Medical Care for Indigent and
Culturally Displaced Obstetrical
Patients and Their Newborns*

H-430.990 *Bonding Programs for Women
Prisoners and Their Newborn
Children*

H-500.992 *Tobacco Advertising Directed
to Children, Minorities and Women*

H-515.983 *Physicians and Family Violence*

H-525.991 *Inclusion of Women in Clinical Trials*

H-515.985 *Identifying Victims of Adult
Domestic Violence*

H-515.986 *A Proposed AMA National Campaign
Against Family Violence*

H-515.998 *Violence Against Women*

H-525.990 *Gender Disparities in Clinical
Decision-Making*

Published and Unpublished Reports

Alcoholism and Alcohol Abuse Among Women
LN Blum, NH Nielsen, JA Riggs
Journal of Women's Health, September 1998;
7:861-71

**Alternative Therapies for the Symptoms
of Menopause**
Report of the Council on Scientific Affairs, 4 – I-96

Gender Discrimination in the Medical Profession
Women's Health Issues, Spring 1994; 4(1):1-11

Gender Disparities in Clinical Decision Making
JAMA, July 24-31, 1991; 266(4):559-62

**Improving Education and Training
in Women's Health**
Joint Report of the Council on Scientific Affairs and
the Council on Medical Education
June 1995

Violence Against Women
JAMA, June 17, 1992; 267:3184-9

Publications

Complete Guide to Women's Health
Kathleen Cahill Allison, Ramona I Slupik, MD
New York: Random House, 1996

Provides pertinent health information for each of
four age ranges—puberty to 18, 18 to 40, 40 to 60,
and over 60.

Part 4, "Health Concerns of Women," the largest
section of the book, covers health problems that
have a unique impact on women, including coronary
artery disease, urinary tract infections, osteoporosis,
stroke, eating disorders, thyroid problems,
autoimmune diseases, and cosmetic surgery. Special
chapters also address death and bereavement, as
well as sexual assault and family violence.

Part 1, "Staying Healthy for Life," emphasizes
preventive health, nutrition, body weight, routine

health care (including how to choose a doctor), and
how to avoid risky behavior and manage stress.

Part 2, "Sexual and Reproductive Health," discusses
puberty, the reproductive system, birth-control
options, sexually transmitted diseases, and
menopause.

Part 3, "Pregnancy," also covers infertility, delivery
options, and breast-feeding. Also includes:

- more than 750 pages and 700 illustrations,
  graphs, and charts

- full-color atlas of the body

- "What You Can Do for Your Body Now"—top
  health priorities for four major stages of a
  woman's life

- "Practical Guides"—fully illustrated double-
  page features with the essential facts to take
  action on such concerns as early detection of
  breast cancer, hormone replacement, aging
  successfully, recognizing a heart attack, and
  controlling blood pressure

- Symptom charts—easy-to-follow flow charts
  identifying the possible causes of many
  common symptoms, from difficulty sleeping
  and painful periods to chest pain, headaches,
  and depression

- "One Woman's Story"—first-person accounts
  of coping with important health concerns

- "Pros and Cons"—the advantages and
  disadvantages of many medical treatments

- "Questions Women Ask"—answers to
  concerns about pressing health problems

Essential Guide to Menopause
Angela R Perry, ed.
Pocket Books, 1998

Provides objective discussions of hormone
replacement therapy, osteoporosis prevention, and
lifestyle changes. Helps women make informed
decisions about their health.

American Medical Women's Association (AMWA)

801 North Fairfax St, Ste 400
Alexandria, VA 22314
703 838-0500
703 549-3864 Fax
E-mail: info@amwa-doc.org
http://www.amwa-doc.org

The 10,000-member American Women's Association (AMWA) functions at local, national, and international levels to advance women in medicine and improve women's health by providing and developing leadership, advocacy, education, expertise, mentoring, and strategic alliances. When AMWA was founded in 1915, women physicians were an underrepresented minority. As of 1996, 21% of all practicing physicians were women.

Policy and Activities

AMWA's policy agenda includes a focus on affirmative action, tobacco control and prevention, reproductive health, and managed care. Some of the women's health issues AMWA has worked to improve include smoking prevention and cessation, osteoporosis, violence against women, heart disease, gender equity, breast cancer, and reproductive health. AMWA has worked to improve gender equity in medical education.

Journal of the American Medical Women's Association

In 1998, the *Journal of the American Medical Women's Association* published a supplement on *Cultural Competence and Women's Health in Medical Education* (Vol 53, No 3).

Available online at:
http://www.jamwa.org/vol53/toc53_3.html.

The articles in the supplement were presented at the National Conference on Cultural Competence and Women's Health: Curricula in Medical Education, sponsored by the Offices of Women's Health and Minority Health of the US Public Health Service.

Curriculum Enhancement in Medical Education: Teaching Cultural Competence and Women's Health for a Changing Society (editorial)
Elena V. Rios, Clay E. Simpson, Jr.

Required Curricula in Diversity and Cross-Cultural Medicine: The Time Is Now
Melissa Welch

Development and Evaluation of an Instrument to Assess Medical Students' Cultural Attitudes
Lynne S. Robins, Gwen L. Alexander, Fredric M. Wolf, et al

A Cultural Diversity Curriculum: Combining Didactic, Problem-Solving, and Simulated Experiences
B. U. K. Li, Donna A. Caniano, Ronald C. Comer

Primary Care Fellowship in Women's Health
Kathleen M. Thomsen

A Women's Health Curriculum for an Internal Medicine Residency
Janice L. Werbinski, Sandra J. Hoffmann

Women's Health Curriculum at Stanford
JoDean Nicolette, Marc Nelson

Jacobs Institute for Women's Health

409 12th St SW
Washington, DC 20024-2188
202 863-4990
http://www.jiwh.org

The Institute:

- Identifies and studies women's health care issues involving the interaction of medical and social systems.

- Facilitates informed dialogue and fosters awareness among consumers and providers alike.

- Promotes problem resolution, interdisciplinary coordination and information dissemination at the regional, national, and international levels.

Publications

State Profiles on Women's Health

Jacqueline A Horton
Washington, DC: Jacobs Institute for Women's Health, 1998

Outlines the status of women's health in all 50 states and the District of Columbia. Includes variables ranging from family income and risk factors for illness to health care coverage and use of preventive services.

The Women's Health Data Book, 2nd edition

Jacqueline A. Horton, ed.
Washington, DC: Jacobs Institute for Women's Health, 1995

Women's Health Issues

212 633-3730
6 issues per year

Journal devoted to women's health at the medical/social interface. Intended for health professionals, social scientists, policy makers, and others concerned with the complex facets of health care delivery to women. Publishes peer-reviewed articles, position papers, and reports.

National Action Plan on Breast Cancer (NAPBC)

US Public Health Service
Office on Women's Health
200 Independence Ave SW, Rm 718F
Washington, DC 20201
202 401-9587
http://www.napbc.org

The NAPBC sponsored a 1999 workshop on the Multicultural Aspects of Breast Cancer Etiology, bringing together breast cancer research and minority health advocacy communities to examine the current state of knowledge concerning multicultural aspects of breast cancer etiology and to identify and prioritize future research directions. Panel discussions, question and answer sessions, and breakout sessions addressed specific risk factors and five racial and ethnic minority populations.

National Academy on Women's Health Medical Education (NAWHME)

NAWHME
MCP Hahnemann University
Broad and Vine, MS 490
Philadelphia, PA 19102
215 762-4260
215 762-7301 Fax

Sponsored by MCP Hahnemann University and the American Medical Women's Association, NAWHME works to infuse women's health education into undergraduate, graduate, and continuing medical education nationwide. In 1995, NAWHME published *Women's Health in the Curriculum: A Resource Guide for Faculty*, edited by G.D. Donoghue.

Active participants in the group include:

- Directors of existing women's health medical education programs

- Educators with experience in gender-related education

- Representatives of advocacy groups in women's health

- Representatives of medical professional organizations concerned with women's health

- Representatives of regulatory bodies with responsibility for medical education

National Centers of Excellence in Women's Health

US Public Health Service
Office on Women's Health
200 Independence Ave SW, Rm 718F
Washington, DC 20201
202 401-9587

The program to fund National Centers of Excellence in Women's Health was established by the US

Public Health Service's Office on Women's Health in 1996. The Centers are based in 18 academic medical institutions across the country:

- Boston University Medical Center
- Harvard University
- Indiana University School of Medicine
- Magee-Women's Hospital
- MCP Hahnemann University
- Ohio State University Medical Center
- Tulane University and Xavier University of Louisiana
- University of California - Los Angeles
- University of California - San Francisco
- University of Illinois at Chicago
- University of Maryland - Baltimore
- University of Michigan Health System
- University of Pennsylvania Medical Center and Health System
- University of Puerto Rico
- University of Washington
- University of Wisconsin - Madison
- Wake Forest University
- Yale University School of Medicine

Each medical institution works to establish and evaluate a model health care system that unites women's health research, medical training, clinical care, public health education, community outreach, and the promotion of women in health professions around a common mission—to improve the heath status of diverse women across the life span.

Center of Excellence at Harvard Medical School

Julie Rabinovitz, MPH, Program Administrator
Harvard Medical School's Center of Excellence
in Women's Health
75 Francis St, PBB5
Boston, MA 02115
617 732-5881
617 264-5210 Fax
E-mail: jrabinovitz@rics.bwh.harvard.edu

The Harvard Medical Center of Excellence in Women's Health exemplifies the fundamental themes of the National Centers for Excellence project as it strives to:

- Develop best practice models for health care for all women.

- Broaden the use of outcome measures and patient surveys to evaluate clinical services and patient satisfaction.

- Expand the use of community-based primary and preventive health care services.

- Encourage more research into women's health, particularly issues related to minority women's health, through expanded collaboration across institutions.

- Create better programs and culturally sensitive materials in women's health to educate the public.

- Strengthen the role of minority women in its institutions.

- Develop mechanisms to ensure the career advancement of women in its institutions.

- Develop better curricula in women's health for both medical students and house staff, emphasizing the use of new information technologies.

Minority Women Issues

Issues related to care of minority women are also integrated into the Harvard Center of Excellence in Women's Health program. Specific objectives include:

- *Clinical Care*
  Working with community health centers across the system to develop programs to address all phases of the female life cycle, with a special emphasis on minority women's health.

- *Medical Education*
  Identifying knowledge, skills, and attitudes required for physicians to be competent in the care of minority women and develop educational methods for training students and physicians.

- *Community Education*
  Developing a community health agenda and plan in order to expand minority women's knowledge about their health and to increase minority women's influence on policies that impact their health.

  ➢ Identify issues of concern for minority women and design culturally appropriate educational opportunities and materials.

  ➢ Develop and maintain linkages and partnerships with various community organizations.

- *Research*
  Identifying ways to address barriers to enrolling minority women into clinical trials, develop a minority women's health research agenda, and increase research in minority women's health.

National Women's Health Information Center

800 944-9662
http://www.4woman.org

Provides access to information from Federal health clearinghouses and hundreds of private sector organizations.

Publications

Ethnic and Socioeconomic Differences in Cardiovascular Disease Factors: Findings for Women from the Third National Health and Nutrition Examination Survey, 1988-1994

MA Winkleby, HC Kramer, DK Ahn, et al
JAMA, 1998; 15:39-67

Health Issues for Women of Color: A Cultural Diversity Perspective

DL Adams, ed.
University of Maryland, 1995

Includes a multidisciplinary and multifaceted approach to the major health concerns of women of color, focusing on African-American, Hispanic/Latina, Asian/Pacific Islander, Middle Eastern, and American Indian/Alaskan Native women. The book identifies emerging health concerns, research needs, and key policy issues and addresses topics such as homelessness, mental health, and drug abuse.

The Healthy Heart Handbook for Women

NHLBI Information Center, Box 30105
Bethesda, MD 20825-0105
301 251-1222
fax 301 251-1223
Can be downloaded free from
http://www.nhlbi.nih.gov

100 pages of the latest information on preventing cardiovascular diseases, such as coronary heart diseases, heart attack, high blood pressure, stroke, and chest pain.

Introduction of a New Curriculum in Women's Health in Medical Education: A Framework for Change

J Searle
Women's Health Issues, 1998;8(6):382-388

Women and Medicine: Fifth Report

Council on Graduate Medical Education
Rockville, Maryland: DHHS, July 1995

Women in Clinical Trials: An FDA Perspective

LA Sherman, R Temple, RB Merkatz
Science, 1995;269:793-795

Women's Health in the Curriculum: A Resource Guide for Faculty

GD Donoghue, ed.
Philadelphia: National Academy on Women's Health Medical Education, 1995

Women's Health in the Medical School Curriculum: Report of a Survey and Recommendation

Health Resources and Services Administration, National Institutes of Health, 1996

Women's Health-Related Behaviors and Use of Clinical Preventive Services

ER Brown, R Wyn, WG Cumberland, et al
Los Angeles: The Commonwealth Fund Commission on Women's Health, 1995

Women's Health: Report of the Public Health Service Task Force on Women's Health Issues: Volume II

Washington, DC, DHHS publication #PHS 85-50206, May 1985

The Women's Health Track: A Model for Training Internal Medicine Residents

MM Roberts, FJ Frank, GM Beriner, Jr
Journal of Women's Health, 1995;4(3):313-318

E. Older Adults

Organizations and Their Resources

American Medical Association

Contact

Joanne Schwartzberg, MD
Integrated Clinical and Public Health
American Medical Association
515 N State St
Chicago, IL 60610
312 464-5355

Policies

E-9.12	*Physician-Patient Relationship: Respect for Law and Human Rights*
H-25.994	*Increased Liaison, Communication, and Educational Efforts with the Elderly*
H-25.999	*Health Care for Older Patients*
H-30.952	*Alcoholism in the Elderly*
H-85.966	*Hospice Coverage and Underutilization*
H-85.967	*Good Care of the Dying Patient*
H-140.966	*Decisions Near the End of Life*
H-160.931	*Health Literacy*

H-210.986	*Physicians and Family Caregivers—A Model for Partnership*
H-210.991	*The Education of Physician in Home Health Care*
H-210.992	*Tax Deduction for Individuals Rendering Home Care to Family Members with a Long-Term Illness*
H-295.981	*Geriatric Medicine*
H-515.983	*Physicians and Family Violence*
H-515.984	*Violence Against Women*
H-515.985	*Identifying Victims of Adult Domestic Violence*
H-515.986	*A Proposed AMA National Campaign Against Family Violence*
H-515-991	*Elder Abuse and Neglect*
H-515.992	*Abuse of Elderly Persons*

Published Reports

Alcoholism in the Elderly
JAMA, March 13, 1996; 275:797-801

Decisions Near the End of Life
JAMA, April 22-29, 1992; 267(16):2229-33

Educating Physicians in Home Health Care
JAMA, February 13, 1991;265:769-71

Good Care of the Dying Patient
JAMA, February 14, 1996; 275:474-8

Health Literacy
JAMA, February 10, 1999; 281:552-7

Physicians and Family Caregivers: a Model for Partnership
JAMA, March 10, 1993;269:1282-4

Publications

Alcoholism in the Elderly: Diagnosis, Treatment, Prevention

Department of Geriatric Health, American Medical Association, 1997

In November 1992, the AMA convened an ad hoc committee to address the problems physicians face in diagnosing, treating, and preventing alcoholism in the elderly. In December 1993, the AMA House of Delegates adopted a recommendation of the AMA Council on Scientific Affairs to develop guidelines on alcoholism in the elderly for physicians. The guidelines, which have been endorsed by the American Society of Addiction Medicine, are intended to help the practicing physician establish a diagnosis, manage current emergency conditions such as acute withdrawal, and refer the elderly patient to ongoing treatment for alcoholism and for any medical or psychiatric complications.

Prevention opportunities for physicians include evaluating their elderly patients in terms of their drinking practices and behavior and paying special attention to prescribing practices with high-risk patients to avoid adverse alcohol-drug interactions or dependence on sedative-hypnotics.

Guidelines for the Use of Assistive Technology: Evaluation, Referral, Prescription

Department of Geriatric Health
American Medical Association, 1996

In November 1993, the AMA convened two focus groups—one with consumers and one with allied health professionals—to address the barriers faced by physicians and their patients with disabilities when dealing with assistive technology. The concerns of the focus groups were presented to the Assistive Technology Advisory Panel in January 1994, and *Guidelines for the Use of Assistive Technology: Evaluation, Referral, Prescription* was published in 1996.

The *Guidelines* include both assistive technology *devices* and assistive technology *services*. An assistive technology *device* is any item, piece of equipment, or product system, whether acquired commercially off-the-shelf, modified, or customized, that is used to increase, maintain, or improve functional capability of individuals with disabilities. An assistive technology *service* is any service that directly assists an individual with a disability in the selection, acquisition, or use of an assistive technology device.

Culturally Relevant Sections

- Be sensitive to patient needs and preferences.
- Consider the social and cultural environment
- Assess the impact of specific impairment within the patient's total environment and lifestyle.
- Continue the relationship with an interdisciplinary team that includes the patient.
- Provide individualized treatment that is sensitive to cost-effectiveness concerns.
- Be able to refer patients to local community resources for technology and support.

Culturally Relevant Advice

Physicians are also advised to become fully aware of the individual's intimate knowledge of goals, preferences, support systems, and functional needs for independence.

In collecting this information, physicians should:

- Speak directly to the patient.
- Introduce themselves and everyone else in the room (this is especially important for patients with impaired vision).
- Face the patient when speaking and speak clearly.
- Be aware of the patient's mode of communication: oral/lip reading, American Sign Language (ASL), signed English, need for an interpreter, etc.
- Always explain what they are going to do before doing it.
- Ask the patients to repeat or summarize what they think they have heard the physician say.

The Core Knowledge and Assessment document outlines core knowledge components and provides specific patient assessment tools, including patient examination and evaluation and evaluation and prescription of assistive technology.

Office practice guidelines to meet the needs of persons with disabilities are also included.

Educational Material for Patients and Families

Additional resources include instructions for obtaining funding for assistive technology, locating state assistive technology projects, and accessing professional and interdisciplinary resources, including electronic asssistive technology resources, electronic bulletin boards, and home automation sources.

Medical Management of the Home Care Patient: Guidelines for Physicians

2nd edition
Department of Geriatric Health
American Medical Association, 1998

The first Home Care Advisory Panel, convened by the AMA in 1987 with the goal of increasing the involvement of physicians in home care, produced the first edition of the *Guidelines for the Medical Management of the Home Care Patient* (1992). A second panel, convened in 1997, led to the revised second edition of the *Guidelines* (1998), which are endorsed by the American Academy of Home Care Physicians.

This document provides instruction in designing a curriculum in home care for education and training of physicians at all levels and in recommending an agenda for future research and development.

The role of the physician and the physician-patient relationship are emphasized in the section describing the goals of home care. Physicians are reminded that in addition to overseeing frequently fluctuating pathophysiological condition(s), they should also advise, encourage, and support the patient's efforts in self-care.

Culturally-Sensitive Assessment Table

The section on medical management in home care includes a two-page assessment table with cells on individualizing psychosocial assessments and interventions and observing and evaluating cultural, ethnic, or religious influences on health care behavior, beliefs, preferences, and expectations. Mental/cognitive assessments include health literacy. Information is also provided on eligibility under different payment plans.

Special Home Care Populations

The document describes special concerns of other populations, including persons with disabilities and those requiring high-technology home care services, such as "video visits" or tele-home care. Step-by-step instructions are provided for developing the care plan and for communicating with other members of the interdisciplinary team.

The publication emphasizes the importance of being sensitive to the emotional and physical well-being of the caregiver, the safety of others in the home, and visitors, and the continued willingness of the patient to participate as a partner in the home care plan. It also includes a list of patient's rights and responsibilities that reinforce patient-centered care. Home hospice care is described, including physician responsibilities.

The section on community resources includes telephone numbers of national, state, and local agencies that serve the frail elderly and other special populations, including children with special needs. A complete list of addresses and phone numbers and fax numbers for state departments on aging and, when available, hot lines are available.

A systematic literature review produced 61 references. The document concludes with a CME questionnaire that provides up to 3 hours of AMA Physician's Recognition Award category 1 credit.

Physician's Guide to Diagnosis and Treatment of Dementia

American Medical Association, September 1999 (projected publication date)
Rosalie Guttman, PhD
312 464 5069

Produced by a culturally diverse expert consensus panel, the *Guide* will highlight the significance of culture, race, age, and sex on both the diagnosis and management of dementia.

Administration on Aging, US Department of Health and Human Services

330 Independence Ave, SW
Washington, DC 20201
202 619-0724
http://www.aoa.dhhs.gov/aoa/dir/intro.html

Serves older people and their families, health and legal professionals, social service providers, and others with an interest in the field of aging.

Resource Directory for Older People
Published periodically by the Administration on Aging.

Alzheimer's Association

Alzheimer's Association National Office
919 N Michigan Ave, Ste 1000
Chicago, Illinois 60611-1676
800 272-3900
312 335-8700
312 335-1110 Fax
http://www.alz.org

The Alzheimer's Association focuses on eliminating Alzheimer's disease through the advancement of research and on enhancing care and support services for individuals and their families.

The Association has numerous projects designed to:

* Mobilize worldwide resources, set priorities, and fund select projects for biomedical, social and behavioral research.

* Promote, develop, and disseminate educational programs and training guidelines for health and social service professionals.

* Increase public awareness and concern for Alzheimer's disease and the magnitude of its impact on individuals, families, and our diverse society.

* Expand access to services, information, and optimal care techniques to maximize care and support for individuals and their families.

* Build organizational capability throughout the association to ensure the most effective and efficient foundation for carrying out the mission.

The American Geriatrics Society

770 Lexington Ave, Ste 300
New York, NY 10021
212 308-1414
http://www.americangeriatrics.org

Professional organization of health care providers dedicated to improving the health and well-being of all older adults.

American Society on Aging

833 Market St., Suite 511
San Francisco, CA 94103
E-mail: info@asa.asaging.org
http://www.asaging.org

Members of the American Society on Aging (ASA) comprise the largest multidisciplinary national community of professionals working with and on behalf of older people. The membership includes representatives of the public and private sectors; researchers and educators; advocates, policy makers, and planners; and health, allied health, social service, managed care, long-term care, and mental health professionals.

For over 40 years, the ASA has served professionals in aging and aging-related fields who want to enhance their ability to promote the well-being of aging people and their families. ASA seeks to:

* Foster a sense of community among professionals working with and on behalf of the aging.

- Provide high-quality professional education and training.

- Promote research and disseminate information.

- Facilitate innovative approaches to service delivery.

- Promote a public image of aging that respects the wisdom, dignity, experience and independence of aging people.

- Influence social and public policies and structures by facilitating debate about new and developing issues.

- Enhance and increase the involvement of ethnic, racial and other minorities in the field of aging.

- Collaborate with other organizations to enhance the well-being of older people and their families.

To help professionals achieve these goals, the ASA offers publications, training programs, conferences, and special projects and initiatives. Educational offerings include:

- The Summer Series on Aging, a 2-day to week-long series of intensive seminars on a wide variety of subjects, held each year in five to seven cities.

- ASA's National Learning Center, which offers online access to training, useful Web sites, publications, multimedia, products and services, and much more.

- A biennial International Conference on Long Term Care Case Management, which brings together experts and practitioners from all over the world.

- Special programs held in conjunction with the annual meeting targeted to topics and settings that are emerging as crucial issues or new constituencies in the spectrum of services to older people.

- New technologies, such as CD-ROMs and the Internet, that make interactive learning cost-effective and flexible to meet the needs of a wide range of professional staff.

Publications

Generations has a national reputation as one of the most authoritative and informative quarterly journals in the field.

Aging Today, a widely praised bimonthly newspaper, provides continuous national coverage of developments in public policy, innovative practice, and research in aging.

Forums and Networks

The ASA provides members the opportunity to join constituent units—Forums and Networks—that provide specialized newsletters and programming in a particular area of interest.

Publications

Alzheimer's Education and Training Research Catalog

Ben Lucero, ed.
Geriatric Resources, Inc, August 1998
Box 239
Radium Springs, NM 88054
800 359-0390
505 524-0254 Fax
E-mail: GRI@zianet.com
http://www.geriatric-resources.com

Features more than 150 publications and videos on Alzheimer's disease.

Alzheimers.Com

http://www.alzheimers.com

A gateway to information about Alzheimer's disease on the Internet; features selected publications and videos. Content is reviewed by an advisory board of people—neurologists, social workers, and caregivers—who specialize in Alzheimer's disease.

Comfort Care
Video series, 1993-1997

Geriatric Resources, Inc
20 hours of specific dementia training and dementia-specific policies and procedures.

Elderly Men: Special Problems and Professional Challenges

Jordan Kosberg, Lenard Kaye
New York: Springer, 1997

An interdisciplinary overview of common and unique features of elderly men that illustrates the diversity within this population and highlights ethnicity, religion, and important sociodemographic variables. The volume presents elderly men as a forgotten minority in need of critical examination.

Gerontology, Perspectives and Issues, 2nd Edition

Kenneth F. Ferraro, ed.
New York, Springer, 1997

Designed as a text for graduate and advanced graduate studies. Includes a chapter on "Cross-Cultural Comparisons of Aging."

Health Literacy Among Medicare Enrollees in a Managed Care Organization

Julie A Gazmararian et al
JAMA, February 10, 1999, Vol 281, No 6, pp 545-551

Refers to literacy problems of older adults.

Journal of Aging and Ethnicity

Kyriakos S. Markides, PhD, ed.
Department of Preventive Medicine and
Community Health
University of Texas Medical Branch
Galveston, TX 77550

An interdisciplinary forum for research findings
and scholarly exchange in aging and health.
Articles cover social and behavioral factors related
to health and aging. Disciplines represented include
the behavioral and social sciences, public health,
epidemiology, demography, health services
research, nursing, social work, medicine, and
related disciplines.

Racial Differences in the Elderly's Use of Medical Procedures and Diagnostic Tests

JL Escarce, KR Epstein, DC Colby, et al
American Journal of Public Health, 1993;948

Self-Care in Later Life: Research, Program, and Policy Issues

Marcia G. Ory, Gordon H. DeFriese
New York: Springer, 1998

Assesses the efficacy of self-care in maintaining
autonomy. Includes a range of behaviors
undertaken by individuals, families, and
communities to enhance health, prevent disease,
limit illness, and restore health. Contains a section
titled "Cultural Origins and Beliefs About Self-
Care in Minority and Ethnic Populations."

F. People at the End of Life

Organizations

American Medical Association

Contact

Reed V. Tuckson, PhD, MD
Senior Vice President, Professional Standards
American Medical Association
515 N State St
Chicago, IL 60610
312 464-4370

Policies

E-8.18	*Informing Families of a Patient's Death*
E-9.12	*Physician-Patient Relationship: Respect for Law and Human Rights*
H-85.966	*Hospice Coverage and Underutilization*
H-85.967	*Good Care of the Dying Patient*
H-85.968	*Patient Self-Determination Act*
H-85.971	*Resource on Death and Dying*
H-85.972	*The Compassionate Care of the Terminally Ill*
H-85.979	*Informing Families of a Patient's Death: Guidelines for the Involvement of Medical Students*
H-140.948	*Medical Futility in End-of-Life Care*
H-140.966	*Decisions Near the End of Life*
H-140.970	*Decisions to Forgo Life-Sustaining Treatment for Incompetent Patients*
H-140.977	*Residency Training in Medical-Legal Aspects of End-of-Life Care*
H-295.932	*End-of-Life Care*
H-385.963	*Physician Review of Accounts Sent for Collection*

Selected Reports

Decisions Near the End of Life
JAMA, April 22-29, 1992; 267(16):2229-33

Developing Medical Education Curriculum for End-of-Life Care
Council on Medical Education Report 4-I-94

Summarizes AMA activities related to palliative medicine, including resolutions related to end-of-life care, Council on Scientific Affairs resources, and Council on Judicial and Ethical Affairs reports and publications. Describes ongoing collaborations with the Education Development Center's Decisions Near the End of Life project and with the American Institute of Life Threatening Illness and Loss.

Good Care of the Dying Patient
JAMA, February 14, 1996; 275:474-8

Medical Education for End-of-Life Care

Summarized AMA reports and recommendations from 1994 to 1996, summarized the status of AMA activities to improve education related to end-of-life care, described plans to improve the education of medical students, resident physicians, and physicians on end-of-life care (including patient-centered care in various settings), and reported on a strategy for communicating with deans and program directors about the importance of education related to quality care for dying patients.

Medical Futility in End-of-Life Care
JAMA, March 10, 1999; 281(10):937-41

Trends from the United States with End-of-Life Decisions in the Intensive Care Unit
D Teres
Intensive Care Med, 1993;19(6):316-22, Review

CEJA Reports on End of Life Care

AMA Council on Ethical and Judicial Affairs, 1998

Compiles the following reports issued by the Council on Ethical and Judicial Affairs from:

- *Do-Not-Resuscitate Orders* (December 1987)

- *Euthanasia* (June 1988)

- *Persistent Vegetative State and the Decision to Withdraw or Withhold Life Support* (June 1989)

- *Guidelines for the Appropriate Use of Do-Not-Resuscitate Orders* (December 1990)

- *Decisions Near the End of Life* (June 1991)

- *Decisions To Forgo Life Sustaining Treatment for Incompetent Patients* (June 1991)

- *Physician-Assisted Suicide* (June 1994)

- *Medical Futility in End-of-Life Care* (December 1996)

- *Optimal Use of Orders-Not-To-Intervene and Advance Directives* (June 1996)

Education for Physicians on End-of-Life Care (EPEC)

Damon Marquis
312 464-4609
http://www.ama-assn.org/EPEC

Improved care for patients at the end of life is the focus of a curriculum developed by the AMA's Institute for Ethics. Regional conferences were held in conjunction with the Institute's EPEC Project. The Project, funded by the Robert Wood Johnson Foundation, uses a "train-the-trainer" approach. EPEC participants are encouraged to use the same materials to teach other physicians. The curriculum consists of four general sessions and 12 small-group modules, includes videotapes that depict physicians and patients discussing issues associated with end-of-life care, including talking to health patients about the need for advance care directives, comforting dying patients in their families, and helping sick patients cope with their pain. Many of the examples include culturally sensitive issues.

LCME Accreditation Standard on End-of-Life Care

The Liaison Committee on Medical Education, jointly sponsored by the AMA and the Association of American Medical Colleges, has issued an accreditation requirement that clinical education for the MD degree must now include experience in palliative care, pain management, and end-of-life care. In 1998, 121 medical schools indicated that end-of-life care subject matter was part of required course content; of these schools, four had a separate required course. Thirty-five offered separate elective courses.

American Institute of Life-Threatening Illness and Loss

Austin Kutscher, MD
Columbia-Presbyterian Medical Center
630 W 168th St
New York, NY 10032
718 601-4453
718 549-7219 Fax

For more than 30 years American Institute programs have reflected respect for cultural diversity in everything from the planning process to selecting presenters. The September 24-26, 1999, Symposium on Palliative Care for Advanced Chronic Pulmonary Disease contains a segment and a future planning session on cultural competence and end-of-life care.

The American Institute has a special focus on palliative geriatric medicine (as opposed to geriatric end-of-life care). The Institute emphasizes treatment approaches to diseases of differing etiologies, as experienced in both a general and geriatric medicine context, and is establishing for each disease its own general parameters and geriatric medical management specifics. Chronic obstructive pulmonary disease, depression, and the pitfalls of polypharmacy are being presented in conjunction with geriatric medicine.

Association for Death Education and Counseling (ADEC)

342 N Main St
West Hartford, CT 06117-2507
860 586-7503
http://www.ADEC.org

ADEC is a nonprofit educational and professional organization dedicated to promoting excellence in death education, bereavement counseling, and care of the dying. It sponsors a reception for various racial and ethnic groups at its annual meetings. ADEC has developed a brochure to encourage cultural diversity and to improve the quality of the individual membership experience.

The Forum

ADEC's newsletter, published six times per year, contains a section with information of interest about death-related issues from various cultures and ethnic groups.

Center to Improve the Care of the Dying

Joanne Lynn, MD
The George Washington University Medical Center
1001 22nd St NW, Ste 820
Washington, DC 20037
202 467-2222
E-mail: lynn@hcs.gwumc.edu

Colorado Collaboration on End-of-Life Care (CCELC)

Program in Health Care Ethics, Humanities, and Law
University of Colorado Health Sciences Center
Campus Box B137
4200 E 9th Ave
Denver, CO 80262

Contacts
Judy Hutchinson
303 315-2558
Mary Fletcher
303 695-3399

Seeks out others in Colorado who want to understand the barriers to improving care at the end of life and want to build networks for mutual assistance. CCELC emphasizes consideration of religious and cultural traditions.

Many Voices, Many Choices

The CCELC newsletter focuses on diversity issues.

Commission on Aging with Dignity

Box 11180
Tallahassee, FL 32303-1180

The Commission on Aging with Dignity produces its Five Wishes living will guidelines in Spanish. *Five Wishes* and *Cinco Deseos* contain 38 questions, ranging from the basics such as "I do (or do not) want a tube placed in my nose or mouth and connected to a machine," to "I wish to have others by my side praying for me when possible." It includes:

- The Kind of Medical Treatment You Want or Don't Want

- How Comfortable You Want to Be

- How You Want People to Treat You

- What You Want Your Loved Ones to Know

- Which Person You Want to Make Health Care Decisions for You When You Can't Make Them

Considered the first consumer-friendly living will form encouraging families to explore the spiritual side of terminal care, the free document is accepted in at least 32 states.

Hospice Foundation of America

777 17 St #401
Miami Beach, FL 33139
800 854-3402
305 538-0092 Fax

Hospital Palliative Care Initiative

The 3-year, $2.2 million Hospital Palliative Care Initiative, commissioned and financed by the United Hospital Fund, is assessing and fundamentally changing how 12 New York City hospitals address terminal care issues. The initiative involves research and analysis of the needs of patients and their families related to palliative care in the acute care hospital. Palliative care models are being researched and 2-year demonstration projects are being funded.

Inter-Institutional Collaborative Network on End-of-Life Care

See Last Acts—Care and Caring at the End of Life.

Last Acts—Care and Caring at the End of Life

The Robert Wood Johnson Foundation
Route 1 and College Rd East
Box 2316
Princeton, NJ 08543-2316
609 452-8701
E-mail: mail@rwjf.org
http://www.rwjf.org

The Last Acts Campaign was established with initial funding from the Robert Wood Johnson Foundation. The Campaign quarterly newsletter, published by the Robert Wood Johnson Foundation, reports on such issues as the challenge of patient diversity and how cultural difference is relevant to clinical decision making at the end of life. Major themes include enhancing end-of-life care through communication and decision making, changing health care and health care institutions, and changing American attitudes toward death.

Task forces focus on the family, palliative care, service providers, provider education, and financing. Resource committees focus on communication, diversity, spirituality, standards and guidelines, and evaluating outcomes.

In conjunction with the Last Acts Campaign, a national meeting will be conducted to address the issues of cultural diversity in improving end-of-life care. Marian Secundy, PhD, will spearhead this initiative with event planning and programming support from Stewart Communications, one of three agencies working on the Last Acts Campaign. The conference is being planned for the first quarter of 2000 in Tuskegee, Alabama.

Diversity and Palliative Care
http://growthhouse.net/~lastacts

The Last Acts Campaign is expanding the dialogue and collaboration among readers, partners, and allies by joining the Inter-Institutional Collaborative Network on End-of-Life Care, sponsored by Growth House, Inc. This service utilizes state-of-the-art Internet technologies and encourages networking, debate, dialogue, collaboration, and live chat among hundreds if not thousands of end-of-life professionals around the world. Last Acts is hosting a specially focused discussion on "Diversity and Palliative Care."

Last Acts Partners

The Last Acts coalition includes major national interest organizations (including the AMA) and local groups. Last Acts Partners share the following goals:

- Improve communications between dying people and their loved ones, and between dying people, families, and health professionals

- Reshape the medical care environment to better support high-quality end-of-life care

- Change American culture so that people can more comfortably face death and the issues raised by care of the terminally ill

Partners have the opportunity to:

- Demonstrate leadership in end-of-life care

- Network with other concerned organizations and individuals through in-person conferences and on-line discussions

- Have the Last Acts Web site hotlink to your organization's Web site

- Receive quarterly newsletters, weekly e-mail newsletters, policy updates, special mailings of reports and materials, and invitations to meetings and workshops

- Receive up-to-date information about end-of-life issues readily usable in their newsletters or Web sites

- Get help in planning meeting sessions around end-of-life care

- Obtain high-quality materials about end-of-life issues—caregiving, diversity bereavement, palliative care, policy—to share with their boards, committees, or membership

- Promote their organization's activities related to the end of life through articles in the Last Acts electronic and print newsletters or by listings in the online Resources Directory

- Tap into the Last Acts network to locate experts and models of action in end-of-life care

National Hospice Organization

1901 N Moore St, Ste 901
Arlington, VA 22209-1714
703 243-5900
703 525-5762 Fax
http://www.nho.org

Project on Death in America (PDIA)

Open Society Institute
400 West 59th St
New York, NY 10019
212 548-0150
212 548-4613 Fax
pdia@sorosny.org
http://www.soros.org/death/

The PDIA is part of the Open Society Institute in New York, a private foundation created by George Soros. Directed by Kathleen M. Foley, MD, the project supports a broad-based approach including research on pain control, art exhibits, and explorations of the role of spirituality. One program links physicians-in-training with dying patients to put them in a better position to help patients die comfortably.

The *PDIA Newsletter* discusses general end-of-life and palliative care issues and issues of care for specific populations.

PDIA Faculty Scholars Program

The PDIA Faculty Scholars Program identifies outstanding clinical faculty who are making a commitment to improving end-of-life care. The program provides support for disseminating existing models of good care, developing new models for improving care for the dying, and developing new approaches for educating health professionals on the care of dying patients and their families. Fellowship recipients receive up to $70,000 per year for 2 years for projects aimed at improving end-of-life care. Currently 50 PDIA Faculty Scholars are located in 33 medical schools and two nursing schools in the United States and four Canadian medical schools.

Supportive Care of the Dying: A Coalition for Compassionate Care

Sylvia McSkimming, PhD, RN
Providence Health System
4805 NE Glisan St 2E07
Portland, OR 97213
503 215-5053
503 215-5054 Fax
E-mail: smcskimming@providence.org

The Coalition's Model Operations Project included the goal of conducting focus groups with ethnically diverse communities and creating community-based supportive care models. The final report on its findings is available.

The Coalition's newsletter, *Supportive Voice*, discusses Coalition activity and frequently includes items of general interest in the area of end-of-life care.

Veteran's Administration

http://www.va.gov/oaa/flp/

The Veteran's Administration Faculty Leaders Project for Improved Care at the End of Life offers a Web site under the auspices of the Office of Academic Affiliations. The Web site is a significant resource for physician and nurse educators who teach palliative medicine in academic and clinical settings.

West Chester University

Roger Mustalich, PhD
School of Health Sciences
Department of Health
West Chester, PA 19383
610 436-2101

Offers a course on Transcultural Health: Principles and Practices, which considers special issues, such as women's health, infant health, mental health, alternative medicine, and death and dying in the context of cultural, racial, and ethnic diversity.

Books

Approaching Death: Improving Care at the End of Life

Committee on the Care at the End of Life, Institute of Medicine, 1997

Considers the experience of dying in hospitals, nursing homes, and other settings and the role of interdisciplinary teams and managed care. Offers perspectives on quality measurement and improvement, the role of practice guidelines, cost concerns, and legal issues such as assisted suicide. Proposes how health professionals can become better prepared to care for those who are dying and to understand that these are not patients for whom "nothing more can be done."

Breaking the Silence: A Guide to Help Children with Complicated Grief: Suicide, Homicide, AIDS, Violence, and Abuse

Linda Goodman
Brunner/Mazel, 1996

Provides specific ideas and techniques to work with children in various areas of complicated grief. Addresses suicide, homicide, violent crime, AIDS, and abuse at length. Lists national support resources and an extensive annotated bibliography of books grouped by grief category.

Death Attitudes and the Older Adult

Adrian Tomer
Brunner/Mazel, January 2000 (scheduled)

Will bridge the fields of gerontology and thanatology in exploring attitudes toward the dying process, end-of-life decision making, and death itself. Contributors' backgrounds include gerontology, death education, and general psychology.

Ethnic Variations in Dying, Death and Grief

Donald P. Irish, Kathleen F. Lundquist, Vivian Jenkins Nelsen, eds.
Taylor & Francis, 1993

Instructive presentation of beliefs about death and the burial and mourning practices of a variety of ethnic and religious groups.

Facing Death: Where Culture, Religion, and Medicine Meet

HM Spiro et al, eds.
Yale University Press, 1996

Covers many of the controversial issues surrounding death, such as issues of death in the gay world, euthanasia, hospice care, dignity of dying, and death as a medical proprietorship.

Healing Latinos: Realidad y Fantasia— The Art of Cultural Competence in Medicine

D Hayes-Bautista, R Chiprut
Cedar-Sinai Health System, 1999

Provides health care professionals with understanding of the Latino community's cultural approach to health, disease, and health care. Chapters include personal accounts of experiences with Latino clients by the authors and other contributors on the topics of culture, the meaning of death, spirituality and religion, and complementary practices.

Helping Adults with Mental Retardation Grieve a Death Loss

Charlene Luchterhand, Nancy E. Murphy
Accelerated Development, 1998

Serves as a guide for those taking an active role in assisting this special population to grieve. Presents general information on the grieving process, outline features unique to these grieving situations, and provides concrete ideas for interacting with and supporting grief-stricken adults with mental retardation.

Honoring Differences: Cultural Issues in the Treatment of Trauma and Loss

Kathleen Nader, Nancy Dubrow, Beth Hudnall Stamm, eds.
Brunner/Mazel, 1999

Describes cultural beliefs within the United States and several international communities that may interact with traumatic reactions.

How We Die: Reflections on Life's Final Chapter

SB Nuland
New York: Random House Large Print, in association with Alfred A. Knopf, 1994

Life to Death: Harmonizing the Transition

R Boerstler, H Kornfeld
Compassion Books
704 675-9670

Authors teach a co-meditation process that ameliorates fear and anxiety to help dying patients and their families face death with dignity and conscious awareness.

Masculine Patterns of Grief

Kenneth J. Doka, Terry L. Martin
Brunner/Mazel, November 1999

Includes clinical strategies for assisting masculine bereavement, as well as contemporary research on gender-related differences.

Palliative Care: Patient and Family Counseling Manual

Aspen Publishers Inc, June 1996
200 Orchard Ridge Dr
Gaithersburg, MD 20878
800 638-8437
http://www.aspenpublishers.com

Provides information on end-of-life care that includes segments related to many of the special populations. Includes numerous handouts for patients and family and practical applications for practitioners. Provides guidance on training volunteers to deal effectively and caringly with patients from all cultural backgrounds and deciding who to listen to if the parents and partner of a gay patient offer conflicting instructions.

Includes the latest policies and recommendations from the AMA's Elements of Quality of Care for Patients in the Last Phase of Life.

Contents include:

Patient and family issues
- Education tools
- Final stages of life
- General patient education
- Patient planning guide
- General family education

General guidelines for caregiving
- Pain management
- Grief
- Psychosocial issues
- Spiritual care
- Nutrition in terminal care
- Professional concerns/volunteer training
- Financial/legal issues
- HIV/AIDS issues (patient and family)

Peaceful Dying: The Step-by-Step Guide to Preserving Your Dignity, Your Choice, and Your Inner Peace

Daniel R. Tobin
Perseus Books: New York, 1999

Presents a 26-step program to guide people throughout the final stages of life, from "recognizing individuality of disease, individuality of choice," to "dying with tranquility." Uses a conversational story-telling style in providing specific tips for taking care of physical, emotional, and spiritual needs in order to live fully and well though the very end of life. Describes techniques for preventing pain and isolation.

The Rights of the Dying: A Companion for Life's Final Moments

David Kessler
HarperCollins: New York, 1997

Uses 17 "rights of the dying" principles as a framework for guiding people dealing with life-challenging diseases and their supporters in communicating with one another and with physicians and hospital staff. Stresses the importance of allowing dying people to participate in all decisions and express their feelings and emotions.

Series in Trauma and Loss

Charles R Figley, Therese A Rando, eds.
Warwick, RI: Institute for the Study and Treatment of Loss

Journals and Journal Articles

Cross-cultural Variation in the Experience, Expression, and Understanding of Grief

PC Rosenblatt
In *Ethnic Variations in Dying, Death, and Grief*
Washington DC: Taylor & Francis, 1993, pp 13-19

Crossing the Cultural Divide

R Kreier
AMNews, Jan 25, 1999

Cultural Diversity Meets End-of-Life Decision-Making

B Jennings
Hospitals and Health Networks, Sept 20, 1994,
p 72

Culture and Ethnicity in Clinical Care

Archives of Internal Medicine, Oct 26, 1998,
Vol 158, pp 2085-2090

Deterrents to Access and Service for Blacks and Hispanics: The Medicare Hospice Benefit, Healthcare Utilization, and Cultural Barriers

A Gordon
Hospice J, 1995; 10:65-83

Diverse Cultural Beliefs and Practices About Death and Dying in the Elderly

M Kagawa-Singer
In *Cultural Diversity and Geriatric Care*
New York, 1994, pp 101-116

Hispanic American Elders: Caregiving Norms Surrounding Dying and the Use of Hospice Services

M Tamalamantes, W Lawler, D Espino
Hospice J, 1995; 10:35-49

Hispanics Getting Help with Death; Popular Living Will Available in Spanish

D Lade
Sun-Sentinel, April 20, 1998

Holding Their Own with Pediatric Hospice

C Tobin
Caring, 1993; 12:56-57

Hospice and Minorities: a National Study of Organizational Access and Practice

A Gordon
Hospice J, 1995; 11:49-70

Hospice: What Gets in the Way of Appropriate and Timely Access

Charlotte B Johnson
Holistic Nursing Practice, October 1998

In 1987, the National Hospice Organization (NHO) identified the barriers to minority access to hospice care. The barriers described in the article include limited information about hospice targeted toward nonwhite populations, a general lack of financial resources for medical care among minority populations, and lack of understanding of cultural variables related to death and dying on the part of the predominantly white, middle-class hospice staff. Additional significant barriers include lack of referral, lack of a primary caregiver, and lack of a relationship with an attending physician.

The NHO formulated interventions to address these barriers, and implementation continues today for African-American and Hispanic, infants and children, and diagnostic populations (AIDS, dementia, etc).

The article also relates the Medicare hospice benefit to how it helps and hinders nonmajority populations and describes efforts of the NHO to reduce the barriers.

Identifying and Meeting Needs of Ethnic Minority Patients

B Noggle
Hospice J, 1995; 10:85-93

Illness, Crisis and Loss

Sage Publications
Box 5084
Thousand Oaks, CA 91359
805 499-9774.

The quarterly interdisciplinary journal from the Center for Death Education and Bioethics deals with psychosocial and ethical issues of life-threatening illness, grief work, and crisis.

Influence of Ethnicity on Advance Directives and End-of-Life Decisions

LJ Romero et al
JAMA, 1997;277:298

Informed Consent, Cultural Sensitivity, and Respect for Persons

LO Gostin
JAMA, 1995;274:844-845

Jewish Tradition in Death and Dying

MedSurg Nursing, October, 1998

Judaism approaches dying with some unique views that can differ from other religious traditions. The article relates these differences to the concept of the near-death state known as "goses" and describes how the differences affect treatment decisions, including organ donation. Health care professionals are reminded that "death is approached in unique, but powerful ways in Judaism and in all religious and ethnic traditions." Some dying people use religious traditions to cope with death, while others reject those traditions.

Many Immigrants' Views of Death Are Out of United States Mainstream

Seth Mydans
New York Times, September 12, 1995

Mutual Support among Nurses Who Provide Care to Dying Children

D Papadatou, I Papazoglou, D Petraki, et al
Illness, Crisis and Loss, January 1999; Vol 7, No 1

Physician-Patient Communication. The Primary Care Relationship with Malpractice Claims Among Primary Care Physicians and Surgeons

W Levinson, DL Roter, JP Mullooly, et al
JAMA, 1997; 277:533-9

Report from the National Task Force on Access to Hospice Care by Minority Groups

B Harper
Hospice J, 1995; 10:1-9

Terminally Ill Children in Hospice

M Amenta
Home Healthcare Nurse, 1994; 12:66-67

Understanding Cultural Difference in Caring for Dying Patients

Barbara A Koenig, Jan Gates-Williams
West J Med 1995; 163:244-249

Describes how experiences of illness and death, as well as beliefs about the appropriate role of healers, are profoundly influenced by patients' cultural background. Points out that cultural difference is a central feature of many clinical interactions and that knowledge about how patients experience and express pain, maintain hope in the face of a poor prognosis, and respond to grief and loss will aid health professionals.

Suggests how many patients' or families' beliefs about appropriate end-of-life care may be easily accommodated in routine clinical practice. Cautions that because expected deaths are increasingly the result of explicit negotiation about limiting or discontinuing therapies, the likelihood of serious moral disputes and overt conflict increases.

The authors suggest a way to assess cultural variation in end-of-life care, arguing that culture is only meaningful when interpreted in the context of a patient's unique history, family constellation, and socioeconomic status. They warn that efforts to use racial or ethnic background as simplistic, straightforward predictors of beliefs or behavior will lead to harmful stereotyping of patients and culturally insensitive care for the dying.

Understanding the Mourner's Spiritual Needs: A Guide for Caregivers

Alan D Wolfelt
Centerpiece, Spring 1999, pp 1-2

Presents grief as "the ultimate spiritual struggle," because it challenges people to question the meaning of life and the possibilities for life after death. Advises bereavement caregivers to gather information to form a religious-spiritual understanding of clients, maintaining an attitude of empathy, respect, and nonjudgment at all times.

Questions include:

- Can you help me understand how faith or spirituality is a part of your life?

- Do you have a specific clergyperson or spiritual guide you turn to for support?

- What spiritual practices are important to you?

- What religious or spiritual symbols are important to you?

- Is there anything you would like to tell me that would help me better understand your religious and/or spiritual needs?

Bereavement caregivers are advised to write a plan for integrating a religious-spiritual care plan into the care of the bereaved person.

Western Journal of Medicine

September 1995

The California Medical Society devoted a special issue of *The Western Journal of Medicine* to Caring for Patients at the End of Life.

G. Special Issues

Domestic Violence

Genetic Conditions

Homelessness

Organ Donation

Sexuality

Domestic Violence

American Medical Association

Contact

Roger Brown
Science and Public Health Advocacy
American Medical Association
515 N State St
Chicago, IL 60610
312 464-5476

Policies

H-515.969	*Domestic Violence Intervention*
H-515.970	*Campaign Against Family Violence: Annual Update*
H-515.971	*Public Health Policy Approach for Preventing Violence in America*
H-515.972	*Violence Toward Men*
H-515.975	*Alcohol, Drugs and Family Violence*
H-515.976	*Mental Health Consequences of Interpersonal and Family Violence*
H-515.979	*Violence as a Public Health Issue*
H-515.980	*Update on the AMA's National Campaign Against Family Violence*
H-515.981	*Family Violence—Adolescents as Victims and Perpetrators*
H-515.983	*Physicians and Family Violence*
H-515.984	*Violence Against Women*
H-515.985	*Identifying Victims of Adult Domestic Violence*
H-515.986	*A Proposed AMA National Campaign Against Family Violence*

Published Reports

Adolescents as Victims of Family Violence
JAMA, October 20, 1993; 1850-1856

Physicians and Domestic Violence: Ethical Considerations
JAMA, June 17, 1992;267(23):3190-3

Violence Against Women
JAMA, June 17, 1992; 267:3184-3189

National Campaign Against Family Violence

Board of Trustees Report 22-A-99 provides the 1999 update of ongoing activities related to the AMA public health Campaign Against Family Violence. Relevant resolutions passed at the 1998 Annual and Interim Meetings included encouraging news organizations not to reveal the identities of sexual assault victims; concerns about depictions of violence in the media; review of laws on stalking; school violence issues; and encouraging health care facilities to adopt policies that would "reduce and prevent workplace violence and abuse."

Coalition of Physicians Against Family Violence

Nearly 10,000 people have joined the Coalition since its inception in 1992, with about 10 physicians and physician partners enrolling each month. Membership is free to AMA members. Coalition members continue to receive a poster, a button ("It's OK to talk to me about family violence"), and all AMA diagnostic and treatment guidelines, as they are issued.

National Advisory Council on Family Violence

The Advisory Council, with representatives from some 40 state and specialty medical societies and several collaborating members, including the American Bar Association and the Centers for Disease Control and Prevention (CDC), is chaired by AMA trustee Timothy T. Flaherty, MD. The Advisory Council meets twice a year to enable members to share information about their family violence activities and review and comment on AMA activities.

The American College of Occupational and Environmental Medicine and the American College of Preventive Medicine jointly hosted the March 1999 meeting. The Advisory Council urged AMA support for a monograph aimed at decreasing abuse in the medical workplace, funding family violence research by the National Institutes of Health and the CDC, and the development and distribution of materials to help physicians better address sensitive topics with their patients or deal with fears of reprisals for providing care. The Council is also studying reimbursement for mental health care that can be provided through the Victims of Crime Assistance Act.

Annotated Catalog of Violence Videotapes

An annotated catalog of videotapes on family violence intended for medical practitioners was released in 1998. The Advisory Council is now seeking to create a developmentally appropriate assessment tool for use with children who have witnessed violence or severe abuse, coordinated by the psychiatric societies represented on the Council.

Diagnostic and Treatment Guidelines

The AMA Campaign Against Family Violence has produced eight diagnostic and treatment guides. The *Diagnostic and Treatment Guidelines on Domestic Violence* highlights national hotlines, counseling groups, shelter directories, and publications with materials in English and other languages. This publication also briefly addresses the under-recognized issue of violence within gay and lesbian relationships.

The eighth guide, on the health aspects of firearms, was released in November 1998. Coverage includes the epidemiology of firearm injuries and deaths, as well as clinical advice for physicians about patient risk assessment and prevention counseling. The guide includes information for the safe storage, handling, and disposal of firearms in the home. Copies of the firearm guide were distributed to pediatricians and emergency physicians through joint efforts of the AMA and the relevant specialty societies.

Internet and Child Safety

In November 1998, the AMA brought together medical, advocacy, and regulatory groups to discuss child safety and the Internet. Chaired by AMA trustee John C. Nelson, MD, the meeting covered inaccurate and misleading information, child predators, privacy, commercial exploitation, pornography, and inappropriate material promoting violence, suicide, drug use, and hate. Participants suggested that the AMA might be able to facilitate the development of a coalition of the diverse parties to create such messages.

Stop America's Violence Everywhere

The AMA Alliance is dedicated to making America a safer place by stopping America's violence everywhere through its SAVE initiative. Through the SAVE program, Alliance volunteers teach schoolchildren conflict resolution skills and assist domestic abuse victims living in shelters. See Section I.

Centers for Disease Control and Prevention

National Center for Injury Prevention and Control
4770 Buford Highway NE
Atlanta, GA 30341-3724
770 488-4362

Has several ongoing projects dealing with family violence, particularly violence against women.

Family Violence Prevention Fund

383 Rhode Island St, Ste 304
San Francisco, CA 94103
415 252-8900
415 252-8991 Fax
800 313-1310

Operates a health resource center on domestic violence with resource materials, technical assistance, and library services designed to improve the health care response to domestic violence.

New York Academy of Medicine

1216 5th Ave
New York, NY 10029-5293
212 822-7202
212 996-7826

Is studying the possibility of establishing a coalition of clinical medical societies that would address issues of handgun injuries and safety with a more coherent voice.

Publications

Recognizing Abuse in Culturally Diverse Clients

R Davidhizar, S Dowd, JN Giger
Health Care Superv. 1998;17:10-20.

Discusses the problem of abuse among ethnically diverse persons; describes the Giger-Davidhizar Model of Transcultural Assessment as a tool to assess the client who is abused.

Genetic Conditions

American Medical Association

Contact

Michael J. Scotti, Jr., MD
Vice President for Medical Education
American Medical Association
515 N State St
Chicago, IL 60610
312 464-4804

Policies

E-2.12	*Genetic Counseling*
E-2.132	*Genetic Testing by Employers*
E-2.135	*Insurance Companies and Genetic Information*
E-2.137	*Ethical Issues in Carrier Screening of Genetic Disorders*
E-2.138	*Genetic Testing of Children*
E-2.139	*Multiplex Genetic Testing*
H-140.965	*Ethical Issues in Carrier Screening for Cystic Fibrosis and Other Genetic Disorders*
H-185.972	*Genetic Information and Insurance Coverage*
H-315.983	*Patient Privacy and Confidentiality*
H-350.998	*Sickle Cell Disease*
H-420.965	*Carrier Screening for Cystic Fibrosis*
H-420.992	*Genetic Counseling and Prevention of Birth Defects*

H-440.911   *Medicine/Public Health Initiative*

Policies related to genetics were identified after Sections I and II were completed and are not listed in those Sections. These policies, as well as additional policies related to other components of this *Compendium*, will be included in the 2000 edition of this publication.

Published Reports

Ethical Issues Related to Prenatal Genetic Testing
The Council on Ethical and Judicial Affairs
Arch Fam Med, Jul 1994; 3(7):633-42

Use of Genetic Testing by Employers
JAMA, Oct 2, 1991; 266(13):1827-30

Genetics Initiative

Contact
Priscilla Short, MD
312 464-4547

The AMA Genetics Initiative spans many cultural competence issues, including discrimination against patients simply because they have genetic disorders. The adverse health effects of this discrimination are intensified if patients also share racial or ethnic characteristics of traditionally underserved groups. The Genetics Initiative is undertaking a broad spectrum of existing and planned activities to address barriers to effective care, including projects in partnership with a national organization for self-help groups related to genetic conditions, the Alliance of Genetic Support Groups (see below for additional information about the Alliance).

Study of Discrimination Against Patients with Genetic Disorders

The AMA recognizes that the findings of the Human Genome Project have already changed the day-to-day practice of medicine. As the genome is mapped, discrimination on the basis of genetic findings may be an unfortunate by-product. The AMA is studying patterns of discrimination that patients with genetics disorders have experienced.

Using neurofibromatosis (NF) as a model, AMA staff are cataloging incidents of discrimination experienced by patients and their families in education, health and life insurance, employment, and medical care to determine patterns of discrimination.

Family History Tool

Using AMA volunteer employees, Genetics Initiative staff will determine which aspects of family history individuals deem important and compare questionnaire findings and end results based on a variety of family history instruments.

Analyze Data on Medical Genetics in the Curricula of US Medical Schools

The AMA is analyzing data that physicians on medical genetics curricula compiled from US medical schools, medical students, residents, fellows, and recently graduated physicians. The data will determine:

- What medical schools teach their students/ residents/fellows.

- What medical students/residents/fellows appear to be learning.

- Medical geneticists recommendations for what should be taught.

- Genetics medical education materials available to the practicing physician.

Gene Shop II

A proposed *Gene Shop II* is intended as the AMA's vehicle for accomplishing goals of the Genetics Awareness Campaign (GAC) and for providing useful information to the public and the medical community. An informational kiosk at a public Chicago location will promote ongoing education on the impact of genetics on health and disease. This project is conceived as a collaborative effort. Although the initial educational focus is genetics, the information kiosk could rotate coverage to other AMA programs with cultural competence elements, including domestic violence, adolescent health, and alcohol or tobacco use.

National Institute on Drug Abuse Modular Workshop on Addiction and Genetics

The AMA is initiating conversations with the National Institute on Drug Abuse (NIDA) about facilitating workshops to increase awareness in the medical community of prenatal counseling for risks related to recreational drug and alcohol use and the genetics of addiction.

Alliance of Genetic Support Groups

The AMA is working with the Alliance of Genetic Support Groups to create "standardized genetic patients" to facilitate the education of medical students and resident physicians in interviewing and examining patients with genetic disorders. Tasks include surveying schools on use of standardized patients and working with the Alliance and the regional genetic networks to match patients with specific curricula.

Web-based Interactive Module

An online continuing medical education module on colorectal cancer screening and the availability of genetic markers for different forms of familial colon cancer is under development in partnership with the the Society of Colorectal Surgeons. In the interactive module, the physician manages the patient through genetic testing and other traditional interventions with variable outcomes.

GenEthics

A consumer-oriented site on genethics is scheduled
for posting on the AMA Health Insight Web site in
1999. The project is a collaboration between the
AMA's Institute for Ethics and the Science,
Technology, and Public Health Standards group.

Alliance of Genetic Support Groups

4301 Connecticut Ave, Ste 404
Washington, DC 20008
800 336-5557 or 202 966-5557
E-mail: info@geneticalliance.org
http://www.geneticalliance.org

A June 1985 symposium, Genetic Support Groups: Volunteers and Professionals as Partners, examined how a "professional-voluntary" partnership could "promote maximum health care and social and psychological functioning for genetically affected individuals and their families." Tracks devoted to self-help groups as an emerging social resource were permeated with the concept of networking to communicate with health professionals and the public about the value of self-help groups and to have an impact on policies related to genetic disorders.

Subsequent to the meeting, the Mid-Atlantic Regional Human Genetics Network (MARHGN) and the National Organization for Rare Disorders (NORD) brought together groups related to a number of disorders to strengthen communication with health professionals and the public. The symposium also created a new coalition of voluntary organizations and professionals, the Alliance of Genetics Support Groups, which continues to function as a clearinghouse.

The Alliance sponsored the 1990 National Conference on Peer Support Training, which brought consumers and professionals together to "strengthen critical working relationships." As indicated by the current cooperative project with the AMA, the Alliance supports a variety of regional and national projects. The Alliance publishes an information sheet that promotes policies supportive of genetic services and of the role of self-help groups in those services.

Alliance Alert

The Alliance communicates with its constituents, state groups, federal agencies, and the public through its Web site (see above) and its newsletter, *Alliance Alert*. The newsletter contains information about relevant legislation, meetings, and publications, including Web sites with legislative and genetics information.

Partnership for Genetic Services Pilot

Since 1997 the Alliance, through its Partnership for Genetic Services Pilot Program, has conducted surveys and focus groups with consumers and professionals in three broad US regions to determine what consumers consider essential to the delivery of quality family-centered, culturally sensitive health care services to people affected by genetic conditions. The fundamental elements of the Partnership Program include the value that "peer support provides valuable resources and emotional nourishment" and that "consumer and provider collaboration is the basis for an *effective* care team."

Working with 12 Midwest medical schools, the Partnership offers students and consumers an opportunity for dialogue outside the clinical setting and sensitizes providers-in-training to the needs of consumers and to community resources. The Partnership also cooperates with Kaiser Permanente's Northwest and mid-Atlantic regions, Group Health Cooperative of Puget Sound, and NYLCare Health Plans to offer educational and service interventions to managed care providers.

Culturally Sensitive Consumer Indicators of Quality Genetic Services

Consumer Indicators of Quality Genetic Services will be used through the Partnership Program with managed care providers and medical students. One of the activities is to "improve provider access to quality consumer-oriented support group resources—resources that can support, supplement, and enhance services." Indicator 9 relates most specifically to cultural competence:

"Information about genetic conditions is provided to each consumer in a manner best suited to their needs and culture, which may include:

- their primary language;

- an appropriate educational level; and

- more than one medium."

Council of Regional Networks for Genetic Services

Emory University School of Medicine
Pediatrics/Medical Genetics
2040 Ridgewood Dr
Atlanta, GA
http://www.healthfinder.gov

Publishes materials related to genetic conditions.

Publications

Genetic Services: Developing Guidelines for the Public's Health

SB Freeman, CF Hinton, LJ Elsas II, eds.
1996
The outcome of a February 1996 conference, this publication includes presentations on the Human Genome Project and national, regional, and state guidelines for genetic services. Includes a section on cultural diversity, "Making Genetic Services and Education Culturally Relevant" (JS Lin-Fu).

Homelessness

American Medical Association

Contact

Roger Brown
Science and Public Health Advocacy
American Medical Association
515 N State St
Chicago, IL 60610
312 464-5476

Policies

E-9.065	*Caring for the Poor*
H-160.959	*Health Care Access for the Inner-City Poor*
H-160.978	*The Mentally Ill Homeless*
H-295.912	*Education of Medical Students and Residents About Domestic Violence Screening*
H-385.963	*Physician Review of Accounts Sent for Collection*

Published Reports

Caring for the Poor
Council on Ethical and Judicial Affairs
JAMA, May 19, 1993; 269(19):2533-7

American Public Health Association

Box 753
Waldorf, MD 20604-0753
301 893-1894
http://www.apha.org

Homelessness in America

APHA Reprint Series #3 contains research on the
problem of homelessness and specific conditions
associated with it.

Health Care for the Homeless Information Resource Center

Policy Research Associates
262 Delaware Ave
Delmar, NY 12054
888 439-3300
http://www.prainc.com/hch

Health Care for the Homeless Directory
1998

Provides information on government and private
agencies that serve homeless people.

National Coalition for the Homeless

1012 14th Street NW, Ste 600
Washington, DC 20005-3410
202 737-6444

Mourning in America: Health Problems, Mortality, and Homelessness

Washington, DC: National Coalition for the
Homeless, 1991

Publications on Homelessness

Causes of Death in Homeless Adults in Boston

SW Hwang, EJ Orav, JJ O'Connell, et al
Ann Intern Med, 1997;126:625-628

Gender, Ethnicity, and Homelessness: Accounting for Demographic Diversity on the Streets

S Baker
Am Behav Sci, 1994;37:476-504

Health Issues for Women of Color: A Cultural Diversity Perspective

DL Adams, ed.
University of Maryland, 1995

Includes a multidisciplinary and multifaceted
approach to the major health concerns of women of
color, focusing on African-American,
Hispanic/Latina, Asian/Pacific Islander, Middle
Eastern, and American Indian/Alaskan Native
women. The book identifies emerging health
concerns, research needs, and key policy issues and
addresses topics such as homelessness, mental
health, and drug abuse.

Mortality Among Homeless Shelter Residents in New York City

Susan M Barrow, Daniel B Herman, Pilar Cordova,
et al
Am J Public Health, 1999;89:529-534

The authors point out that, "for homeless shelter
users, chronic homelessness itself compounds the
high risk of death associated with disease/disability
and intravenous drug use. Interventions must address
not only the health conditions of the homeless but
also the societal conditions that perpetuate
homelessness." Includes 51 references related to
deficiencies in health care for homeless persons.

Organ Donation

American Medical Association

Contact

Karen Goraleski, Professional Standards
American Medical Association
515 N State St
Chicago, IL 60610
312 464 4840
E-mail: karen_goraleski@ama-assn.org

Policies

H-370.974	*Working Toward an Increased Number of Minorities Registered as Potential Bone Marrow Donors*
H-370.975	*Ethical Issues in the Procurement of Organs Following Cardiac Death*
H-370.977	*The Inclusion of Advance Directives Concerning Organ Donation in Living Wills*
H-370.978	*The Use of Minors as Organ and Tissue Sources*
H-370.979	*Financial Incentives for Organ Procurement: Ethical Aspects of Future Contracts for Cadaveric Donors*
H-370.980	*Strategies for Cadaveric Organ Procurement Mandated Choice and Presumed Consent*
H-370.982	*Ethical Considerations in the Allocation of Organs and Other Scarce Medical Resources Among Patients*
H-370.983	*Tissue and Organ Donation*

H-370.984	*Organ Donation Education*
H-370.986	*Donor Tissues and Organs for Transplantation*
H-370.987	*Transplant Centers*
H-370.994	*Sale of Donor Organs for Transplant*
H-370.995	*Organ Donor Recruitment*
H-370.996	*Organ Donor Recruitment*
H-370.999	*Computerized Donor Registry*

Published Reports

Ethical Considerations in the Allocation of Organs and Other Scarce Medical Resources Among Patients
Arch Intern Med, Jan 9, 1995; 155(1):29-40
Review

Organ Donation Initiative

Although organ transplants increased by approximately 600 and tissue transplants increased by 14,000 in 1998, the transplant waiting list also increased, from more than 56,000 registrants in 1997 to more than 64,000 in 1998. Donor trends among whites and Hispanics increased by 6.6% and 7.8%, respectively, while those for African-American donors remained relatively unchanged, and Asian donors decreased by 8.4%. Concerned about low donor rates in general and within African-American populations in particular, the AMA is intensifying activities to implement its organ donation policies.

"Live and Then Give"

"Live and Then Give," an organ donation program modeled after the Texas Medical Association program of the same name, is intended to encourage physicians to become organ donors and to present information to their patients. The December 1998 Interim Meeting featured an 11-minute video. The June 1999 Annual Meeting included several organ donation awareness events sponsored by the Medical Student Section and the Minority Affairs Consortium (MAC), covering cultural barriers and general awareness of organ and transplant issues and particularly aimed at increasing organ donations in minority communities. Activities included a Minority Issues Forum, a Public Rally for Organ Donation Awareness, and a MAC Consensus Panel/Forum, which provided CME credit.

Campaign Manual and Ready-to-Use Materials

Materials supporting "Live and Then Give" are available in formats that allow Federation partners the flexibility to develop a campaign unique to their needs and responsive to the diverse populations they serve. The campaign manual is supplemented by camera-ready artwork, question and answer brochures, two donor cards, and a poster.

Medical Student Section Program Module

Organ Donation Awareness National
Service Project
800 262-3211, ext 4742
E-mail: mss@ama-assn.org

The AMA Department of Medical Student Services developed the 1999 National Service Project Organ & Tissue Donor Awareness Program Module (February 1999), with assistance from the United Network for Organ Sharing, to encourage Medical Student Section chapters to apply for a policy promotion grant to set up an Organ Donation Awareness National Service Project.

The module includes sections on community and professional education, fact sheets on organ donation and transplantation, understanding the organ procurement process, dispelling fears about organ donation, and religious/spiritual views on donations and transplantation. Specific program activities are suggested, from donor days to appearing on TV and radio programs. The module also includes information about state and regional organ procurement organizations.

Giving Life: Share Your Decision to Be an Organ and Tissue Donor
Mi Young Hwang
(posted on *JAMA Patient Page* AMA Health Insight at
http://www.ama-assn.org/
public/journals/jama/ppindex9.htm)

A two-page discussion of the need for organ and tissue donation and how to indicate willingness to be a donor that may be reproduced by physicians to share with patients.

Collaborations Sought

The AMA is developing collaborative relationships and projects with the Illinois chapter of the National Medical Association, the Regional Organ Bank of Illinois, and other groups committed to cooperative efforts in the areas of policy development, education, technology, and assessment related to advancing organ availability and transplantation. See Section IV for a list of national organizations.

American Association of Tissue Banks

1350 Beverly Rd, Ste 220-A
McLean, VA 22101
703 827-9582

American Society for Transplant Surgeons

University of Texas Health Sciences Center
Department of Surgery
6431 Fannin, Ste 6.240 MSMB
Houston, TX 77030
713 500-7400

Association of Organ Procurement Agencies

1714 Hayes St
Nashville, TN 37203
615 321-3003

Coalition on Donation

800 355-74273
http://www.shareyourlife.org

Children's Organ Transplant Association

2501 Cota Dr
Bloomington, IN 47403
812 336-8872
E-mail: cota@cota.org

Health Resources and Services Administration's Division of Transplantation

Division of Transplantation
5600 Fishers Lane, Room 4-81
Rockville, MD 20857
http://www.hrsa.dhhs.gov/osp/dot/

Regional Organ Bank of Illinois

Jackie Lynch
800 S Wells St, Ste 190
Chicago, IL 60607-4529
312 431-3600
E-mail: jlynch@robi.org

Texas Medical Association "Live and Then Give"

Laurie Reece
401 West 14 St
Austin, TX 78701-1680
512 370-1422
E-mail: laurie_r@texmed.org

Transplant Recipient International Organization

800 875-6386
http://www.primrenet.com/~trio

United Network for Organ Sharing

1100 Boulders Pkwy, Ste 500
Box 13770
Richmond, VA 23225-8770

Professional Education Resources: 804 330-8541
Patient and Public Information: 888 895-6361
Data Requests: 804 330-8576
News Bureau: 804 327-1432

Sexuality

American Medical Association

Contact

John Henning, PhD
Integrated Clinical and Public Health
American Medical Association
515 N State St
Chicago, IL 60610
312 464-4566

Policies

B-1.50	*Discrimination*
E-3.08	*Sexual Harassment and Exploitation Between Medical Supervisors and Trainees*
E-9.122	*Gender Disparities in Health Care*
E-9.131	*HIV-Infected Patients and Physicians*
H-65.983	*Nondiscrimination Policy*
H-65.984	*Gender Discrimination in the Medical Profession*
H-65.990	*Civil Rights Restoration*
H-65.992	*Continued Support of Human Rights and Freedom*
H-160.991	*Health Care Needs of the Homosexual Population*
H-170.973	*Teaching Sexual Restraint to Adolescents*
H-170.974	*Update on AMA Policies on Human Sexuality and Family Life Education*

H-170.978	*Comprehensive Sexual Education*
H-180.980	*Sexual Orientation as Health Insurance Criteria*
H-210.986	*Physicians and Family Caregivers—A Model for Partnership*
H-270.997	*Legal Restrictions on Sexual Behavior Between Consenting Adults*
H-295.969	*Nondiscrimination Toward Medical School and Residency Applicants on the Basis of Sexual Orientation*
H-310.976	*Gender-Based Questioning in Residency Interviews*
H-525.990	*Gender Disparities In Clinical Decision-Making*

Some of these policies were identified after Sections I and II were completed and are not listed in those Sections. These policies, as well as additional policies related to other components of this Compendium, will be included in the 2000 edition of this publication.

Published Reports

Gender Discrimination in the Medical Profession
Council on Ethical and Judicial Affairs
Womens Health Issues, Spring 1994; 4(1):1-11

Gender Disparities in Clinical Decision Making
Council on Ethical and Judicial Affairs
JAMA, July 24-31, 1991; 266(4):559-62

Health Care Needs of Gay Men and Lesbians in the United States
Council on Scientific Affairs Report
JAMA. 1996:275:1354-1359

Web Sites

AMA Health Insight
http://www.ama-assn.org/consumer.htm

Includes a wealth of consumer information on a variety of health issues, from HIV/AIDS to breast cancer, domestic violence, depression, insomnia, back pain, and more. Divided into four main sections: Specific Conditions, General Health, Family Focus, and Interactive Health.

Hepatitis C
http://www.ama-assn.org/med-sci/98oct13b.htm

JAMA Information Centers
http://www.ama-assn.org/special/

Easy-to-use, peer-reviewed collections of resources on specific conditions, including HIV/AIDS, asthma, migraine, and women's health.

Minority Physicians Services Web Site
http://www.ama-assn.org/mem-data/joint/sex001.htm

Contains a section on "Talking to Patients about Sex: Training Programs for Physicians," developed at the AMA. Cultural competence is one of the sections.

Gay and Lesbian Medical Association

459 Fulton St, Ste 107
San Francisco, CA 94102
415-255-4547
info@glma.org
http://www.glma.org

A 2,000 member organization founded in 1981 to combat homophobia and to foster quality health care for the groups it serves. The *Journal of the Gay and Lesbian Medical Association* frequently references diversity issues affecting gay, lesbian, bisexual, and transgendered physicians, medical students, and their supporters.

Publications on Sexuality

Ethnic and Cultural Concerns in Sexual Function Assessment

JR Heiman, KA Schloredt
Int J Impot Res, 1998;10(suppl):S134-S137

Examines respect, beneficence, and justice as they might relate to sexual dysfunction assessment in clinical trials. Describes the need for investigators to conduct research assessment that respects ethical principles and cultural values. Recommends including proportional ethnic groups as well as non-heterosexual participants in research projects.

Handbook of Sexuality-Related Measures

Clive Davis, William Yarber, et al
Sage Publications, Thousand Oaks, CA: 1998

Contains more than 200 instruments to assist researchers, clinicians, and educators in evaluating, measuring, and assessing human sexual expression. Includes information for practical application in a variety of settings. Each chapter describes the development and appropriate use of the featured instrument, providing information on timing, scoring, and interpretation. Reliability and validity data are summarized and referenced.

Lesbian Health: Current Assessment and Directions for the Future

Institute of Medicine
2101 Constitution Ave, NW
Washington, DC 20418
202 334-3300
800 624-6242
http://www.nap.edu

Contains Institute of Medicine recommendations for more research on the specific health needs of lesbians at a time when few large mainstream medical organizations had addressed the issue of lesbian health. Lesbians are at risk because: certain diseases, such as breast cancer, may be more common among lesbians; fear of discrimination may keep lesbians from seeking routine medical care; and stress associated with homophobia may adversely affect their health.

Race, Gender, and Health

Marcia Bayne-Smith, ed
Sage Publications: Thousand Oaks, CA, 1996

Explores the influence of race and gender on the health status of a diverse group of nonwhite women in the US, as well as structural and cultural factors that affect women's health issues. Examines four groups of women: African-American, American Indian and Alaska Native, Asian/Pacific Islander American, and Latinas in detail.

Treating Lesbians and Bisexual Women: Challenges and Strategies for Health Professionals

Elisabeth Paige Gruskin
Sage Publications: Thousand Oaks, CA, 1998

Provides an integrated critical analysis of lesbian and bisexual women's health. Integrates material from a wide array of disciplines, including medicine, nursing, sociology, psychology, anthropology, and epidemiology

Section V

Complementary and Spiritual Practices and Their Impact on Effective Care

Interest in complementary and spiritual practices and their impact on effective health care has been stimulated by establishment of the Office of Alternative Medicine (now the National Center for Complementary and Alternative Medicine), National Institutes of Health and by national consensus conferences, such as the 1997 conference announcing the effectiveness of acupuncture for some conditions. Increasing numbers of policies, reports, and publications are encouraging physicians to become more knowledgeable about practices used by their patients. These sources include references to the increasing evidence that (1) respectful communication about patient preferences and practices is crucial for adherence to biomedical treatment and (2) health care belief systems are critical to the patient's healing process.

At the same time, schools of medicine, nursing, and other health professions have added or are adding curriculum in areas such as mind/body interventions, nonbiomedical systems, diet and nutrition, bioelectromagnetic applications, manual healing techniques, and herbal medicines and remedies. The 1988 Liaison Committee for Medical Education survey found that acupuncture was covered by eight US medical schools as part of a required course, by six as a separate elective course, and by 12 as part of an elective course.

This increased activity parallels research results since the 1970s documenting the ways in which the biomedical approach is perceived as failing to adequately address personal and social concerns. Researchers and others have theorized that failure to address these concerns is part of the reason patients are increasingly using health care practices outside mainstream Western biomedicine. Patients may also choose to use complementary practices simply because they are part of their family or national background or because they believe such practices are less harmful than biomedicine.

The emphasis of managed care organizations on low-risk interventions, self-care, and prevention also appears to be boosting interest in and increasing access to nonbiomedical treatments. More clinics, group practices, and other settings are offering multiple modalities through an "integrative medicine" unit. Varied options for reimbursement are available as insurance companies and managed care plans incorporate complementary providers in their networks. This trend is likely to continue as mainstream publications, such as the November 1998 issues of *JAMA* and the *Archives* journals, report the results of clinical studies demonstrating the efficacy and cost-effectiveness of specific techniques.

Complementary Health Care Practices Defined and Exemplified

In this *Compendium*, the term " complementary" refers to interventions for improving, maintaining, and promoting health and well-being, preventing disease, or treating illnesses that are not part of a standard North American biomedical regimen of health care or disease prevention. The term "health care practices" is used instead of "medicine" because many widely used practices are not part of a medical system. Spirituality is included in this section because it is frequently included in books and articles on complementary practices.

Spiritual beliefs and practices are receiving increased attention in connection with "comfort care" and decision making at the end of life. Studies also suggest an association between spiritual practices and improved outcomes in nonterminal situations. Herbert Benson, MD, professor of medicine at Harvard Medical School and chief of the Division of Behavioral Medicine at Beth Israel Deaconess Medical Center, has declared that spiritual practices clearly complement traditional medicine and that "we should make every effort to incorporate our patient's spirituality to promote healing" (Mark Moran, *AMNews*, April 12, 1999). Since 1997, the National Institute for Healthcare Research and the John Templeton Foundation have awarded grants to 19 medical schools to develop curricula in spirituality and medicine, beginning with $25,000 grants to eight schools. More than 50 US medical schools now offer elective courses in spirituality. Opinions differ about whether to introduce a spiritual dimension into the clinical encounter; proponents argue that even a militant atheist should be able to identify resources to meet patients' spiritual needs. But as reported by David Larson, MD, president of the National Institute for Healthcare Research, "nearly 90% of physicians do not address their patients' spiritual needs" (*Minnesota Medicine*, December 1996).

With the growth of centers for spiritual care and healing and lunchtime lectures on spirituality, physician resistance to addressing patients' spiritual needs may be weakening. Children's Health Care in St. Paul, Minnesota, permits shamans for Hmong families, tribal elders for Native Americans, and food and rituals important to Hasidic Jewish families. The Catholic Health Association of Wisconsin has developed a 6-hour program, including a training manual used by more than a dozen major health care systems across the country. Information about the increase in programs on spirituality is presented at the Annual Alternative Therapies Symposium and Exposition, "Integrating Alternative and Spiritual Approaches in Healthcare," with continuing medical education credits designated by the Annenberg Center for Health Sciences. "Spirituality, Cross-Cultural Issues and End of Life Care: Curricular Development," sponsored annually since 1997 by the National Institute for Healthcare Research and the Association of American Medical Colleges, emphasizes the clinical relevance of patients' belief systems and cultural backgrounds to treatment and care and the importance of integrating these patient factors in medical school curricula. Annual meetings of the American Public Health Association include many presentations related to spirituality and health care.

Representative Complementary Categories and Selected Practices

The following categories and selected practices are presented only to indicate the variety and inclusiveness of topics presented in the resources described in the following pages. The list does not include many widely used modalities.The list is not to be used to indicate any type of recognition or endorsement of any of the categories or selected practices by the American Medical Association. AMA policies related to alternative medicine and other alternative and complementary practices are included in Section X.

Some categories have similar entries. For example, spirituality is included as a mind/body intervention (prayer and mental healing) and as a nonbiomedical system (anthroposophic medicine).

Mind/Body Interventions
Aromatherapy
Art therapy
Biofeedback
Dance and movement therapy
Hypnosis
Imagery
Meditation
Music therapy
Prayer and mental healing
Qigong (t'ai chi chuan/chih)
Self-help and support groups
Yoga

Nonbiomedical Systems
Acupuncture
Anthroposophic medicine
Ayurveda
Latin American community
　health care
Native American health care
Homeopathy
Naturopathy
Traditional Oriental/Chinese
　medicine

Diet and Nutrition
Cultural diets
- Macrobiotic
- Mediterranean
- Traditional Native
  American
Diet modification regimens
Supplemental therapies
- Amino acids
- Minerals
- Vitamins (eg,
  antioxidants)
- Enzymes

Bioelectromagnetic Applications
Electroacupuncture
Neuromagnetic stimulation
Transcranial electrostimulation

Manual Healing Techniques
Biofield therapeutics
- Healing touch
- Polarity therapy
- Reiki
- SHEN physioemotional
  release therapy
- Therapeutic touch
Chiropractic
Massage & related techniques
- Deep tissue massage
- Manual lymph drainage
- Neuromuscular massage

Postural reeducation therapies
- Alexander technique
- Feldenkrais method
Pressure point therapies
Trager psychophysical
　integration
Sports massage

Herbal Medicines and Remedies
European botanical medicines
Latin American herbal
　remedies
Native American herbal agents
Oriental herbal agents
Chinese
Japanese-Kampo

Pharmacologic and Biologic Treatment Agents
Antineoplastons
Bee venom
Cartilage products
Ethylene diamine tetraacetic
　acid (EDTA) chelation
　therapy
Hoxsey method
Immunoaugmentive therapy
Ozone therapy

Section Contents

A. Organizations

B. Educational Institutions

C. Health Care Providers and Insurers

D. Publications and Audiotapes

- Books

- Journals, Newsletters, and Articles

- Audiotapes

E. Web Sites

A. Organizations

American Medical Association

515 N State St
Chicago, IL 60610

Contact

Hannah L. Hedrick, PhD
312 464-4697
312 464-5830 Fax
E-mail: hannah_hedrick@ama-assn.org
http://www.ama-assn.org

Policies

H-295.902   *Alternative Medicine*

H-480.964   *Alternative Medicine*

H-480.967   *Alternative Therapies for the*
             Symptoms of Menopause

H-480-973   *Unconventional Medical Care in the*
             United States

Reports and Publications

Alternative Medicine
Council on Scientific Affairs Report 12-A-97;
amended by Res. 525-A-98

Alternative Therapies for the Symptoms of
Menopause
Council on Scientific Affairs Report 4-I-96

Encouraging Medical Student Education on
Alternative Health Care Practices
Council on Medical Education Report 2-I-97

Inclusion of Complementary Health Care Practices
in the Medical Curriculum
Council on Medical Education Report 2-I-98

Unconventional Medical Care in the United States
Board of Trustees Report 15-A-94

American Medical News

What Is the Role of Spirituality in Medicine?
Mark Moran
April 12, 1999

Reports that more than 50 U.S. medical schools now offer elective courses in spirituality, including 19 that have been awarded grants from the National Institute for Healthcare Research to develop curricula in spirituality and medicine. Describes the increasing number of studies suggesting an association between religious practice and health and quotes Herbert Benson, MD: "Spiritual practices clearly are a complement to traditional medicine, and we should make every effort to incorporate our patient's spirituality to promote healing." Points out that although opinions differ about how to address ethical issues surrounding the introduction of religion into the clinical encounter, proponents argue that even a militant atheist should be able to identify resources to meet patients' spiritual needs.

Special Theme Issues of *JAMA* and the Archives Journals

JAMA: Alternative Medicine
November 11, 1998, Vol 280, No 18
http://www.ama-assn.org/jama

This issue of *JAMA* and the annual coordinated theme issues of the nine AMA *Archives* journals published on alternative medicine (listed below) represent a planned, concerted effort by the editors to provide physicians and other health care professionals with clinically relevant, reliable, fresh scientific information on alternative therapies.

Archives of Dermatology: Alternative Medicine and Dermatology
November 1998, Vol 134, No 11
http://www.ama-assn.org/derm

Archives of Family Medicine:
Alternative/Complementary Medicine
November/December 1998, Vol 7, No 6
http://www.ama-assn.org/family

Archives of General Psychiatry
November 1998, Vol 55, No 11
http://www.ama-assn.org/psych

Archives of Internal Medicine:
Alternative and Complementary Medicine
November 9, 1998, Vol 158, No 20
http://www.ama-assn.org/internal

Archives of Neurology:
Alternative Neurology
November 1998, Vol 55, No 11
http://www.ama-assn.org/neuro

Archives of Ophthalmology
November 1998, Vol 116, No 11
http://www.ama-assn.org/ophth

Archives of Otolaryngology—
Head and Neck Surgery
November 1998, Vol 124, No 11
http://www.ama-assn.org/oto

Archives of Pediatrics and Adolescent Medicine
November 1998, Vol 152, No 11
http://www.ama-assn.org/peds

Archives of Surgery:
Surgical Infection Society/Alternative Medicine
November 1998, Vol 133, No 11
http://www.ama-assn.org/surgery

AiC Worldwide

29 W 35th St, 3rd Fl
New York, NY 10001
212 952-1899
800 409-4242
212 248-7374 Fax
http://www.aic-usa.com

Manages annual events with detailed "how to" sessions on integrating complementary practices within health care institution structures.

Integrating Alternative & Complementary Medicine with Conventional Medicine

An annual event promoted as an opportunity to learn how to "increase competitiveness and generate new revenue streams." Includes detailed case studies of how well-established facilities have implemented alternative therapies, from integrated medicine clinics to outpatient alternative medicine clinics.

American Public Health Association (APHA)

1015 Fifteenth St NW
Washington DC 20005-2605
202 789-5600
202 789-5661 Fax
E-mail comments@apha.org
http://www.apha.org

Founded in 1872, the APHA is the largest organization of public health professionals in the world, representing more than 50,000 members and affiliates from over 50 public health occupations, including researchers, practitioners, administrators, educators, and health workers.

Units Addressing Complementary Practices and Spirituality

Alternative and Complementary Health Practices Special Primary Interest Group (ACHP SPIG)

Founded in 1994, the ACHP SPIG sponsors multiple sessions at the APHA annual meeting, focusing on topics such as Cross-Cultural Communication, Integrating and Synthesizing Alternative and Complementary Health Practices into Western Medical Practice, Attitudes of the Medical Community, Practicing and Teaching Alternative and Complementary Health Care, and Value of Outcomes Research to Assess Efficacy, Effectiveness, and Cost-effectiveness of Alternative Medicine.

Other Sections and Interest Groups

Other APHA sections and interest groups, such as those for Chiropractic Health Care, Community Health Planning and Policy Development, Food and Nutrition, International Health, Public Health Nursing, and Social Work, also consider issues related to cultural competence.

Publications

American Journal of Public Health

Monthly peer-reviewed journal that frequently addresses diversity issues, including those related to complementary practices and spirituality.

The Nation's Health

Reports on legislation and policy issues affecting all public health professionals.

Association of American Medical Colleges (AAMC)

2450 M St NW
Washington, DC 20037-1127
202 828-0412
202 828-0972 Fax
http://www.aamc.org

Alternative and Complementary Medicine Special Interest Group

Patricia A. Muehsam, MD
212 946-5700
E-mail: pm2@doc.mssm.edu

The AAMC Alternative and Complementary Medicine Special Interest Group (ACM SIG) has a current membership mailing list of more than 160 individuals. The ACM SIG is working in three areas:

- Practical steps for developing integrative curricula

- Networking within the AAMC

- Formalizing regional SIG activities

Developing Integrative Curricula

Sample proposed approaches include integrating alternative and complementary medicine principles into the following curriculum areas:

Undergraduate basic sciences

- Anatomy—Include surface anatomy relevant to osteopathy, acupuncture, massage, etc

- Pharmacology—Include botanical medicine, homeopathy, and biologic and pharmacologic approaches

- Behavioral medicine—Include mind-body approaches

Clinical and graduate medical education training

- Students rotate to other training institutions, eg, acupuncture, massage, naturopathy, chiropractic

- Students share rotations with complementary and alternative practitioners

- Students from complementary and alternative medicine training institutions rotate through undergraduate, clinical, and graduate medical education sites

- Involve "CAM" preceptors in clinical rounds

Sample proposed approaches for expanding the current curriculum include:

- Evaluating current curriculum for conceptual limits, ie, is the biomedical model incompatible with alternative and complementary practices?

- Developing an expansive integrative model that would facilitate interface between the biomedical model and complementary practices.

- Developing practical steps for expanding the concepts of self-care for physicians in training.

- Exposing medical students and residents to mind-body techniques, eg, stress-reduction, meditation, yoga.

Concurrent activities could include:

- Educating faculty in self-care practices, including those categorized as complementary and alternative.

- Interfacing with other interdisciplinary endeavors, such as cross-cultural studies and ethics.

- Involving students at all levels of planning and implementation.

Networking Within the AAMC

The ACM SIG considers networking within the AAMC as essential to meaningful endeavors in integrative curriculum approaches. The first SIG objective is to provide medical educators with information about complementary and alternative health care practices; to provide a greater historical, social, cultural, and scientific context for biomedicine; and to present the concept of integration as part of the broader context for Western medicine. Complementary and alternative practices are planned for inclusion in the AAMC Medical School Objectives Project, part 3 or 4.

Formalizing Regional Activities

The ACM SIG is working through regional interest groups, all AAMC organized units, student groups, list serves, and Web sites to communicate its objectives. Individuals have volunteered to convene regional SIGs, and regional meetings have had venues for addressing curriculum development.

Cedars-Sinai Integrative Medicine Medical Group

444 S San Vicente Blvd, #600
Los Angeles, CA 90048

Part of:
Cedars-Sinai Medical Center
8700 Beverly Blvd
Los Angeles, CA 90048
310 855-3674
Fax 310 657-9614

The Integrative Medicine Medical Group will offer the following services: acupuncture, massage, T'ai chi, traditional Chinese medicine, chiropractic, mind—body interventions, yoga, nutritional counseling, lifestyle modification

Center for Mind-Body Medicine

5225 Connecticut Ave NW, Ste 414
Washington, DC 20015
202 966-7338
http://healthy.net/othersites/mindbody/center.htm

The Center addresses the mental, emotional, social, spiritual, and physical dimensions of health and illness. It emphasizes the uniqueness of each person and the centrality of therapeutic partnerships. The Center is committed to the development of new models of care; to the education of medical students and those who teach them; and to service to the poor, children, the elderly, the chronically ill, and the institutionalized. The Center is involved in demonstrating the cost-effectiveness and universal appropriateness of mind-body medicine and in making it a shaping force in the current debate on health care reform. The Center's first annual conference, Comprehensive Cancer Care: Integrating Complementary and Alternative Therapies was held on June 12-14, 1998, in Arlington, VA. The second annual Comprehensive Cancer Care conference was held on June 11-13, 1999.

National Center for Complementary and Alternative Medicine

(formerly the Office of Alternative Medicine)

PO Box 8218
Silver Spring, MD 20907-8218
888 644-6226 (voice and TTY)
301 495-4957 Fax
http://altmed.od.nih.gov/nccam/

The National Center for Complementary and Alternative Medicine (NCCAM) of the National Institutes of Health conducts and support basic and applied research and training and disseminates information on complimentary and alternative medicine to practitioners and the public. The NCCAM is funded for approximately $50 million per year to establish clinical data on outcomes for complementary medical treatments. More than a dozen coordinating clinical research centers are now operating, with each one counting 10 clinical intake sites.

Park Ridge Center for the Study of Health, Faith, and Ethics

211 E Ontario, Ste 800
Chicago, IL 60611-3215
312 266-2222
312 266-6086 fax

Contact

Bernice Chantos
312 266-2222 ext 255

The Park Ridge Center sponsors intensive courses on Spiritual Issues in Health Care.

Aging and Spirituality Program

The Park Ridge Center for the Study of Health, Faith, and Ethics has developed a program on "The Challenges of Aging: Retrieving Spiritual Traditions for the Elderly," designed for those who work with the elderly in hospitals, nursing homes, home care settings, and congregations and for those interested in the spiritual possibilities of the aging process. Challenging contemporary cultural notions about aging, this program emphasizes using the wisdom of religious traditions to explore aging as a spiritual journey. The education packet consists of:

- Two 20-minute videos presenting spiritual aging through the observations of elderly people themselves

- A *Leader's Guide* for those leading a study group

- *Participant's Workbook* for following the leader and keeping a personal journal

- A handbook with historical and scriptural background on the perspectives of Christianity, Judaism, Islam, Buddhism, and Hinduism on the meaning and purpose of aging.

Spirituality in Health Care

The Park Ridge Center conducted a workshop to address the following questions of practitioners and patients:

- How does a patient's spirituality enter into his or her experience of sickness and health?

- What role does the spirituality of health care practitioners play in their medical responsibilities?

- How are the resources of spiritual traditions made available to patients and practitioners?

A book on *Spirituality in Healthcare Settings*, by John Shea, is forthcoming.

T'ai Chi Chih Center

3107 Eubank NE Ste 19
Scottsdale Village
Albuquerque, NM 78111
505 299-2095
http://www.taichichih.org

The national headquarters for an easy-to-learn form of t'ai chi originated in 1974 by Justin Stone, the center offers classes, Justin Stone's *Joy Though Movement* video and book, and instructional and practice video for Seijaku (an advanced form based on t'ai chi chih). Also has information about the videotapes created in conjunction with the PBS t'ai chi chih program that is still being aired throughout the country. Described as "meditation in motion," t'ai chi chih has been found to improve balance, reduce the risk of falls, reduce stress, and improve muscle tone. It is taught widely in health care institutions, self-help groups for survivors of life-threatening illnesses, retirement centers, recreation centers for older adults of persons with disabilities, educational institutions from grade school through college, prisons, and recreation programs sponsored by the YMCA and park districts. The Folsom prison program has introduced more than 400 inmates to t'ai chi chih and has been credited with breaking down barriers between inmates from different ethnic and racial backgrounds.

B. Educational Institutions

American College for Advancement in Medicine

23121 Verdugo Dr/Ste 242
Laguna Hills, CA 92653
714 583-7666

Courses include Nutritional Intervention in Cancer Prevention and Treatment: Shifting the Paradigm.

Case Western Reserve University School of Medicine

10900 Euclid Ave
Cleveland, OH 44106-4915
216 368-2825

Offers continuing physician professional development courses at various locations, especially in homeopathy (core curriculum and for physicians).

Harvard Medical School

Department of Continuing Education
Harvard MED-CME
Box 825
Boston, MA 02117-0825
617 432-1525
617 432 1562 Fax
www.med/harvard.edu/conted/
www.bdmc.harvard.edu/medicine/camr/
projects.html

Beth Israel Deaconess Medical Center, Harvard Medical School, is one of 12 research centers funded by the National Institutes of Health National Center for Complementary and Alternative Medicine. The Center has a number of ongoing complementary and alternative therapies projects, including a clinical trial on low back pain, a survey of complementary medicine providers around the country, and a survey of use among cancer patients.

In exploring the relationship between spirituality and healing in medicine, the courses:

- give perspectives from world religions

- present the neurological and psychological effects of healing resulting from spirituality

- explore similarities and differences among long-standing religious practices from objective scientific research as well as from subjective points of view

Data on spirituality and healing and the power and biology of belief are discussed.

The "relaxation response" is presented as effective therapy for diseases such as hypertension, cardiac rhythm irregularities, many forms of chronic pain, insomnia, infertility, the symptoms of cancer and AIDS, premenstrual syndrome, anxiety, and mild and moderate depression.

Courses include:

- Alternative Medicine: Implications for Clinical Practice

- Clinical Training in Mind/Body Medicine

- Mind/Body Training in Optimism, Humor and Cognitive Restructuring

- Spirituality and Healing in Medicine

Mount Sinai School of Medicine of the City University of New York

One Gustave L Levy Pl
New York, NY 10029-6574
212 946-5700

Courses include:

- Integrative Approaches to Health Care: A Survey Course in CAM

- Integrative Approaches in Clinical Practice

- Integrating Clinical Experience in Oriental Medicine

Rush-Presbyterian-St. Luke's Medical Center

Department of Family Medicine
600 S Paulina/Rm 764 AF
Chicago, IL 60612
312 942-7083

Offerings include mind/body medicine.

University of Arizona

PO Box 245018
Tucson, AZ 85724-5018
520 626-6214

In addition to the residency program on integrative medicine, the University of Arizona features conferences on Integrative Medicine: Integrating Conventional and Alternative Medicine.

University of California, Los Angeles School of Medicine

Office of Continuing Medical Education
10833 Le Conte Ave, 12-138 CHS
Los Angeles, CA 90024-1722
310 825-6373; 310 206-5046 Fax

Courses include Acupuncture for Physicians.

University of Vermont College of Medicine

Given E-109 Bldg
Burlington, VT 05405
802 656-2292
802 656-8577 Fax
E-mail: frymoyer@salus.med.uvm.edu

Courses include The Scientific Basis for Using Holistic Medicine to Treat Chronic Disease.

West Chester University

School of Health Sciences
Department of Health
West Chester, PA 19383
610 436-2300

Courses include:

Transcultural Health: Principles and Practices
Roger Mustalich, 610 436-2101

- Provides an overview of the role of culture in health and sickness

- Addresses the influence of culture on the health status of individuals and societies

- Presents the role of culture in access and use of health care in the United States and other nations

- Considers special issues, such as women's health, mental health, and alternative medicine

- Highlights how beliefs and values stemming from one's culture can affect the provision and use of health care services

Alternative Medicine
Betty Boyle, 610 436-3357

- Explores alternative and/or complementary medical systems and practices in the United States from a consumer and personal viewpoint

- Investigates such topics as homeopathy, chiropractic, acupuncture, naturopathy, hands-on healing, herbal medicine in terms of health and medical, legal, and social issues

C. Health Care Providers and Insurers

Complementary Healthcare Plans (CHP)

Richard Brinkley
President and CEO
5319 SW Westgate Dr, Ste 130
Portland, OR 97221-2430
503 203-8333 or 800 449-9479
503 203-8522 Fax
E-mail: inquiries@comphcplans.com
http://www.chiro-net.com

Complementary Healthcare Plans (CHP), a Portland-based preferred provider organization, is the exclusive contractor for complementary medical services in Oregon and Southwest Washington state for PacifiCare, Regence Blue Cross and Blue Shield of Oregon, Kaiser Foundation Health Plan of the Northwest, and Providence Health Plans. The CHP provides chiropractic, acupuncture, and naturopathic services, including acupuncture services to 18,000 of PacifiCare of Oregon's 138,000 commercial members.

According to President Brinkley, the CHP exceeds National Committee for Quality Assurance (NCQA) standards, putting its providers through five credentialing steps (primary source verification of professionals credentials, site visits to office to check against NCQA, an economic profile, a general practice profile, and a practitioner questionnaire) and sending them periodic comparative utilization reports highlighting inconsistencies.

Lifestyle Center of America

Route 1, Box 4001
Sulphur, OK 73086
800 213-8955 or 405 993-2327
http://www.lifestylecenter.com

Uses a comprehensive lifestyle approach to control chronic diseases that have their origins in the way people live. The Center's programs, all physician-supervised, focus on physical, mental, and spiritual health. After medical evaluations, health guests receive individual programs incorporating health lectures, nutritional guidance, therapeutic exercise, hydrotherapy, massage, stress management, and counseling. Most health guests choose the 19-day extended intervention program. Three-day diabetes education seminars are also available. Smokers are offered a weeklong smoking cessation program.

PacificCare Health Systems of Oregon, Southwest Washington

Offers members chiropractic, acupuncture, and naturopathic services for employer premiums of approximately $6.50 per member per month and a patient copay of either $10 per visit/$1,500 cap or $15 per visit/$2,500 cap.

Sloans Lake Managed Care

1355 S Colorado Blvd, Ste 902
Denver, CO 80222
303 691-2200

The Sloans Lake Health Plan HMO has developed a "Spiritual Care" program designed to address the emotional issues surrounding a person's illness or ailment. Patients accessing the program are counseled on emotional issues within a spiritual or religious context. The program provides counseling and direction in those areas not covered under a mental health program, even though many of the practitioners of this field can perform a broader set of services.

The program focuses on:

- Spiritual direction/guidance and development

- Short-term crisis intervention (bereavement counseling, religious injury counseling, marriage and family counseling for terminal illness, and other issues)

- Direction to community resources

The program allows for six visits per year with a $10 co-pay per visit.

D. Publications

Books

Alternative Remedies: CD-ROM
Steve Blake
St. Louis, MO: Mosby, 1998

Describes when and how natural remedies are recommended worldwide in the treatment of more than 5,700 medical conditions, from asthma to yellow fever. Includes more than 1,200 supplements, over 1,000 supplement actions, over 6,600 herb names, and over 15,000 chemical and organic constituents. Search by health condition, action, continent, or name. Biochemistry, dosages, and warnings are cross-referenced for products from vitamins to Chinese and Ayurvedic herbs.

Alternative Therapies: Expanding Options in Health Care
Rena J. Gordon, Barbara Cable Nienstedts, Wilbert M. Gesler
Springer Publishing Co, 1998
536 Broadway
New York, NY 10012-3955

Contributions from specialists from a wide diversity of academic disciplines, including geography, anthropology, engineering, health economics, public policy, public administration, epidemiology, and marketing, give this book a multi-layer view of the alternative medicine movement. While describing the history, present status, principles, research, and clinical applications of specific treatment modalities, this book also provides the cultural, social, demographic, political, economic, and legal implications of alternative therapies. Of particular relevance to physicians are "The Changing Medical Marketplace," "Social and Cultural Aspects of Alternative Therapies," "Biomedical Physicians Practicing Holistic Medicine," and "Medical Education: Changes and Responses."

The American Holistic Health Association Complete Guide to Alternative Medicine
William Collinge
Warner Books, 1996
1271 Avenue of the Americas
New York, NY 10020

Provides an overview of eight major complementary and alternative health care practices. Case examples of each are designed to help readers decide which might suit their needs and how to use them with conventional medicine. Evidence of scientific support, strengths and limitations, and guidelines for selecting a practitioner are included for each approach. Readers are cautioned against using the remedies on their own and are advised to consult their health care professionals. Included are concrete data on procedures and principles for:

- Chinese medicine
- Ayurveda
- Naturopathic medicine
- Mind/body medicine
- Osteopathic medicine
- Chiropractic
- Massage therapy and bodywork

Celebrating Diversity: Approaching Families Through Their Food
National Center for Education in Maternal and Child Health, 1994

Provides information on how specific foods mean different things in different cultures. Health promotion can be greatly enhanced when health care professionals are aware of the significance of food and preparation by their patients. Many cultural groups use foods as medicine or to promote health, and included is a chart with examples of medicinal uses of food by various ethnic groups.

Complementary & Alternative Medicine: Legal Boundaries and Regulatory Perspectives
Michael Cohen
Johns Hopkins University Press, 1998

Concise summation of the history and current status of the legal underpinnings of complementary and alternative medicine. Covers areas of regulation, scope of practice, informed consent, and malpractice and describes some of the alternative providers and treatments. Includes case studies and related literature. Cohen advocates for regulating providers of complementary treatments in a way that protects patients yet preserves freedom of choice.

Complementary/Alternative Medicine: An Evidence-Based Approach
John Spencer and Joseph Jacobs, eds.
(33 contributors)
St. Louis, MO: Mosby, 1998

Extensive review of trials performed on a number of popular alternative treatments and other tools to assess their effectiveness. Organized by major medical disciplines (allergies/asthma, cardiovascular disease, diabetes mellitus, cancer, neurological disorders, psychiatric illness, and alcohol and addictions) and populations (women, children, the elderly).

Encounters With Qi
David Eisenberg, Thomas Lee Wright
Viking Penguin, 1985
40 W 23rd St
New York, NY 10010

David Eisenberg, MD, learned acupuncture, massage, and herbal techniques as the first US medical exchange student to the People's Republic of China, where he worked beside his teachers in Chinese clinics. Dr. Eisenberg is director of Harvard's undergraduate and continuing medical education programs on alternative medicine and director of the Center for Alternative Medical Research, established to assess the efficacy, safety, and cost-effectiveness of alternative medicine.

He has published two landmark surveys on alternative medicine use in the United States and is a member of the US National Institutes of Health Alternative Medicine Program Advisory Council. In addition, he served as principal consultant to the PBS series, "Healing and the Mind with Bill Moyers." Dr. Eisenberg's *Encounters with Qi* was one of the first books by a physician recounting his personal benefits from "energy medicine."

The book explores how—and if—acupuncture, herbal remedies, and psychic healing actually work effectively as medical treatments. Dr. Eisenberg probes the mysteries of ancient Chinese skills with skepticism and open-mindedness. The book discusses how techniques thousands of years old compare with the West's modern views of healing ailments, relieving pain, and curing disease. It also indicates new frontiers for the interrelation of Chinese and Western medicine. The readable style includes case histories, human interest, dialogue, and local color.

Encyclopedia of Complementary Health Practices
Carolyn Chambers Clark, ed.
Springer Publishing Co, 1999

Encyclopedia of Natural Remedies
C. Norman Shealy
Element Books, 1993
160 N Washington St
Boston, MA 02114

C. Norman Shealy, a neurosurgeon, is the founder of the American Holistic Medical Association and director of the Shealy Institute in Springfield, Missouri, a center for health care and pain and stress management. *Natural Remedies* covers natural remedies from eight complementary and alternative health practices:

- Ayurveda
- Chinese herbal medicine
- Traditional home and folk remedies
- Herbalism
- Aromatherapy
- Homeopathy
- Flower remedies
- Vitamins and minerals

The book describes the techniques and practice of each therapy and lists the remedy sources they use, the ailments they treat, and the effects they have been reported to have on health and well-being. It also includes a long list of common ailments and more than 1,000 natural remedies and treatments, as well as a glossary and a comprehensive list of useful addresses and contacts. Illustrated in full color throughout.

The Encyclopedia of Alternative Medicine

Jennifer Jacobs
Journey Editions, 1996
153 Milk St
Boston, MA 02109

Describes the innate self-healing capacity of the body, called "chi" in Chinese medicine and the "vital force" in homeopathic medicine. This ability of the body to heal itself was first recognized by the Greek physician Hippocrates as *vis medicatrix naturae*. Dr. Jacobs contends that this healing energy can be stimulated and enhanced, either directly through therapies such as homeopathy and acupuncture, or indirectly through such practices as nutrition and herbs.

The book includes information on the origins, techniques, safety, practical application, and typical visits for a number of modalities that have not been extensively covered in other publications, including chapters on Natural Healing, The Power of Plants, Nutrition and Diet, Mobility and Posture, The Mind, Massage and Touch, and Eastern Therapies.

Facing Death: Where Culture, Religion, and Medicine Meet

HM Spiro et al, eds.
Yale University Press, 1996

Covers many of the controversial issues surrounding death, such as issues of death in the gay world, euthanasia, hospice care, dignity of dying, and death as a medical proprietorship.

The Four Pillars of Healing

Leo Galland
New York: Random House, 1997

Healing and the Mind

Bill Moyers
Bantam Doubleday Dell, 1993
666 Fifth Ave
New York, NY 10103

This companion volume to the PBS series from journalist Bill Moyers and David Grubin explores the healing connections between the mind and the body. Bill Moyers spoke with physicians, scientists, therapists, and patients about the meaning of sickness and health. In a series of interviews, he discusses their search for answers to how emotions translate into chemicals in our bodies, how thoughts and feelings influence health, and how we can collaborate with our bodies to encourage healing. Small private clinics and large public hospitals are examined for how they apply advances in mind/body medicine.

The case studies from neonatal care to geriatrics and from day surgery to the treatment of chronic illness describe the experiences of medical professionals practicing the "new medicine." They found that their patients healed faster, left the hospital sooner, and did better once they got home. A segment on the People's Republic of China explores implications of that country's fusion of Western practices with traditional Chinese medicine, including acupuncture, massage, herbal potions, and "chi."

Healing Traditions: Alternative Medicine and the Health Professions

BB O'Connor
University of Pennsylvania Press, 1995

Holistic Health Promotion and Complementary Therapies: A Resource for Integrated Practice

Aspen Publishers
7201 McKinney Circle
Frederick, MD 21704
800 234-1660

A practical manual that shows how to incorporate holistic and complementary therapies into a traditional medical practice. Contains step-by-step guidelines and ready-to-use tools on topics including relaxation, meditation, and guided imagery; manual healing methods; spirituality-focused interventions; homeopathy; herbal medicine; and acupuncture. Also includes relationship-centered care and communication, including culturally relevant interventions and models on integrating patient spirituality into health care.

Foundations gives a concise overview of essential concepts and terminology and sets out the major components of the integrative approach.

Modalities presents the rationale for a variety of complementary techniques and cites research studies supporting their efficacy and appropriateness. Provides many protocols, guidelines, and examples for implementing the modalities.

Applications explores options and presents tools for implementing the integrative approach according to specific conditions, patient groups, and types of care settings.

Integrative Practice Development offers insights and protocols for program planning and design, including detailed descriptions of integrative initiatives across the country.

Relationship-Centered Care contains a section which includes an example of how the biomedical methods of diagnosing and treating a disease process compare with those of other health belief systems. It also includes direction for promoting wellness through culturally relevant interventions in the areas of communication, family and kinship networks, and access to and acceptance of interventions.

Medical Acupuncture: A Western Scientific Approach

J Filshie, A White, eds.
Churchill Livingstone, 1998

Twenty active medical acupuncture practitioners from the United States, the United Kingdom, and Europe provide a comprehensive introduction to acupuncture and its practical medical applications.

Practical Reviews: Complementary and Alternative Medicine

Oakstone Medical Publishing
6801 Cahaba Valley Rd
Birmingham AL 35242
800 633-4743
205 995-1926 Fax

Audiotape reviews articles on evidence-based approaches to complementary and alternative medicine from 53 medical publications, including those for family physicians, obstetricians and gynecologists, clinical nutritionists, sports medicine, endocrinology and metabolism, pediatrics, and reproductive medicine. Also covers *JAMA*, *Lancet*, *the New England Journal of Medicine*, the *British Medical Journal*, and the major alternative medicine publications.

Each audiotape includes 12-15 summarized articles, along with expert commentary and critiques and self-assessment quizzes. Each tape also has a corresponding pocketsize abstract card reviewing the materials on the tape and including citation and reprint information. The QuickFlash Review Cards come with a color-tabbed filing system for review or sharing.

The subscription price includes the option for up to 36 hours of AMA PRA category 1 credit through the Albert Einstein College of Medicine and the American Holistic Medical Association for completing monthly quizzes.

Radical Healing: Integrating the World's Great Therapeutic Traditions to Create a New Transformative Medicine

Rudolph Ballentine
Harmony Books, 1999
201 East 50th St
New York, NY 10022

Radical Healing blends the primary holistic schools of healing, allowing readers to understand their common elements. Drawing on 30 years of medical study and practice, Dr. Ballentine integrates the wisdom of the great traditional healing systems (especially Ayurveda, homeopathy, traditional Chinese medicine, and European and Native American herbology) with nutrition, psychotherapy, and bodywork. *Radical Healing* covers the spectrum from plants, natural substances, diet, exercise, and cleansing to principles of spiritual and psychological interventions. Includes case studies and examples.

Societal Forces Reshaping American Medicine: Implications for Internal Medicine and the Board

ABIM Report, 1997-1998

Selected presentations from the 1997 American Board of Internal Medicine Summer Conference address issues on cultural competence, including complementary care and a multicultural society. Has a 77-item bibliography centered on the significance of disparities in care to nonmajority populations.

Stories That Heal: Kitchen Table Wisdom

Rachel Naomi Remen
Riverhead Books, New York, 1996

The Way of Qigong: The Art and Science of Chinese Energy Healing

Kenneth S. Cohen
New York: Ballantine Books, 1997

World Medicine: The East West Guide to Healing Your Body

Tom Monte and the editors of *EastWest Natural Health*
New York: Tarcher/Putnam, 1993

Journals, Newsletters, and Articles

Alternative and Complementary Therapies: An Agenda for Otolaryngology

John H. Krouse
Archives of Otolaryngology - Head and Neck Surgery, Nov 1998;124:1199

Alternative and Complementary Therapies

Mary Ann Liebert
2 Madison Ave
Larchmont, NY 10538
914 834-3100
800-M-LIEBERT
http://www.liebertpub.com

Intended for health care practitioners. The "Web Watch" section *in Alternative and Complementary Therapies* provides regular updates on electronic resources related to complementary and alternative health care practices.

Alternative Health Practitioner: The Journal of Complementary and Natural Care

Springer Publishing
536 Broadway
New York, NY 10012

Alternative Medicine and the Conventional Practitioner

Wayne Jonas
JAMA, 1998;279:708-709

Succinct description of major issues and summary of research conducted by the National Center for Complementary and Alternative Medicine.

Alternative Medicine Business News

Atlantic Information Services
1100 17th St NW, Ste 300
Washington DC
202 775-9008 or 800 521-4323
www.aispub.com

Available electronically on PTS Newsletter Database/Information Access Company
800 321-6388

Reports on issues such as which practices are covered by the nation's largest HMOs, insurer/provider fee schedules and capitation, summaries of state activities, and arrangements for discounts between insurance companies and pharmacies.

Alternative Therapies in Health and Medicine

American Association of Critical-Care Nurses
101 Columbia
Aliso Viejo, CA 92656
800 899-1712

The bimonthly *Alternative Therapies in Health and Medicine,* which is indexed in *Index Medicus* and *Medline,* provides a forum for developing and sharing information about alternative therapies in preventing and treating disease, healing illness, and promoting health. It publishes a variety of methods, including scientific research, and encourages the integration of alternative therapies with conventional medical practices.

Complementary Medicine in the Surgical Wards

Mehmet C. Oz, GC Whitworth, EH Liu
JAMA, 1998;279:710-711

Courses Involving Complementary and Alternative Medicine at US Medical Schools

MS Wetzel, DM Eisenberg, TJ Kaptchuk
JAMA, 1998;280(9):784-787

Creating a Spirituality Curriculum for Family Practice Residents

HD Silverman
Alternative Therapies in Health and Medicine, 1997;3:54-61

Cultural Diversity, Folk Medicine, and Alternative Medicine

DJ Hufford
Alternative Therapies in Health and Medicine,
1997;3:78-80

Cultural Influences in "Noncompliant" Behavior and Decision Making

CV Charonko
Holistic Nursing Practice, 1992;6:73-78

Cultural Perspectives on Mental Health

M Kohl
Alternative & Complementary Therapies, 1998
Aug; 4(4):236-240

Culture and Clinical Care: Folk Illness Beliefs and Behaviors and Their Implications for Health Care Delivery

LM Pachter
JAMA, 1994;271(9):690-694

Current Trends in the Integration and Reimbursement of Complementary and Alternative Medicine by Managed Care, Insurance Carriers, and Hospital Providers

Kenneth Pelletier, Ariane Marie, et al
American Journal of Health Promotion
November/December 1997, Vol 12, No.2, 112-122

Based on a literature review and information search, telephone interviews were conducted with a definitive sample of 18 insurers and a representative subsample of seven hospitals. A majority of the insurers interviewed offered some coverage for nutrition counseling, biofeedback, psychotherapy, acupuncture, preventive medicine, chiropractic, osteopathy, and physical therapy. Twelve insurers reported that market demand was their primary motivation for coverage. Factors determining whether insurers offered coverage included potential cost-effectiveness based on consumer interest, demonstrable clinical efficacy, and state mandates. Contains a table summarizing treatments offered by four health care institutions.

Evaluating the Alternatives

JH Lin
JAMA, 1998;279:706

Federation Bulletin: The Journal of Medical Licensure and Discipline

Federation Place
400 Fuller Wiser Rd, Ste 300
Euless, TX 76039-3855
Vol 84, No 3, 1997

Articles in the 1997 issue of the quarterly journal of the Federation of State Medical Boards include:

- The National Institutes of Health Office of Alternative Medicine

- The Role of Alternative Medicine

- Report of the Special Committee on Health Care Fraud

- Alternative/Complementary Medicine: Keeping Tabs on the Legislative Record

Folk Medical Beliefs and Their Implications for Care of Patients: A Review Based on Studies Among Black Americans

LF Snow
Annals of Internal Medicine, 1974;81:82-96

The Healing Power of Spirituality

Katie Colon
Minnesota Medicine, December 1996

Reports the 1996 finding by David Larson, MD, president of the National Institute for Healthcare Research, that in spite of mounting evidence of a positive link between a patient's spirituality and the ability to recover or cope with illness, "nearly 90% of physicians do not address their patients' spiritual needs."

Homeopathy: Another Tool in the Bag

MA Johnson
JAMA, 1998;279:707

Integrated Chinese/Western Therapies in the Treatment of Cancer, Part 1

Irene Serenson
Alternative & Complementary Therapies
December 1997; 3(6):441-446.

Uses some of the most recently published traditional Chinese medicine sources on the treatment of cancer that recommend an integrated approach, comparing the treatments afforded by both modalities and attempting to highlight how and when each modality excels in its particular treatment of cancer.

The Integrative Medicine Consult: The Essential Guide to Integrating Conventional and Complementary Medicine

43 Bowdoin St
Boston, MA 02114
617 720-4080
http://www.onemedicine.com
Seventeen annual issues

The January 1, 1999, issue contained a two-page Special Report on "Highlights from *JAMA*'s Alternative Medicine Issue," referring to it as "an impressive compilation of studies, editorial perspectives, and other presentations."

Integrative Medicine: Integrating Conventional & Alternative Medicine

Elsevier Science
PO Box 945
New York, NY 10159-0945
888 437-4636
http://www.elsevier.com/locate/intmed

Peer-reviewed quarterly journal integrates the concepts and techniques of a wide variety of health care practices.

Introducing Students to the Role of Folk and Popular Health Belief Systems in Patient Care

HL Rubenstein, JD Bonnie, B O'Connor, et al
Acad Med, 1992;67:566-568

Journal of Alternative and Complementary Medicine: Research on Paradigm, Practice, and Policy

Mary Ann Liebert
2 Madison Ave
Larchmont, NY 10538
800 M-LIEBERT

This peer-reviewed journal for research in nontraditional medical therapies includes observational and analytical reports to assess the therapeutic value of therapies outside the realm of conventional medicine. It covers current concepts in clinical care, including case reports, for physicians and other health care professionals seeking to evaluate and integrate these therapies into patient care protocols. Aims to establish rigorous research methodologies to support effective and reliable measurement, data collection, and analysis.

MD Programs in the United States with Complementary and Alternative Medicine Education: An Ongoing Listing

Bhaswati Bhattacharya
J Alternative and Complementary Med, 1998; 4(3):325-335.

Native American Medicine: Traditional Healing

C Avery
JAMA, 1991;265:2271-2273

Pediatricians' Experience With and Attitudes TowardComplementary/ Alternative Medicine (CAM)

Anju Sikand, Marilyn Laken
Arch Pediatr Adolesc Med, Nov 1998;Vol 152:1059

A majority of pediatricians sampled believed a small percentage of their patients were seeking alternatives to conventional medicine. Half of the pediatricians would consider referring patients for CAM, and most were interested in CME courses on CAM. Larger studies surveying pediatricians, along with more education and research on CAM therapies, were recommended.

The Philosophical, Cultural, and Historical Aspects of Complementary, Alternative, Unconventional, and Integrative Medicine in the Old World

Oumeish Youssef Aoumeish
Arch Dermatol, Nov 1998; 134:1373-1386

The author reports that complementary medicine is a formal method of health care in most countries of the Old World and is expected to become integrated in the modern medical system and to be part of medical education programs. He believes that issues of efficacy and safety of complementary medicine have become increasingly important, that supervision of the techniques and procedures used is required, and that more research studies are needed to understand and use this type of medicine.

Prevalence and Patterns of Physician Referral to Clergy and Pastoral Care Providers

Timothy P. Daaleman, Bruce Frey
Arch Fam Med, Nov/Dec 1998; 7:548-553

More than 80% of physicians responding to a survey reported that they refer or recommend their patients to clergy and pastoral care providers, with more than 30% reporting that they refer more than 10 times a year. Most physicians—75.5%—chose conditions associated with end-of-life care (ie, bereavement, terminal illness) as reasons for referral. Marital and family counseling were cited by 72.8%. Physicians who reported a greater degree of religiosity had a small increased tendency to refer to these providers. In addition, physicians who were in practice for more than 15 years were more likely to refer to clergy.

Religion and Spirituality in Medicine: Research and Education

JS Levin, DB Larson, CM Puchalski
JAMA, 1997; 278:792-793

Tapping the Soul's Healing Potential: An Interview With Carlos Warter

Anne H. Coulter
Alternative & Complementary Therapies
Sept/Oct 1996;Vol 2, No 5:283-287

According to the author, a number of physician alternative practitioners who have emphasized the importance of spirituality in healing, including Larry Dossey, Deepak Chopra, and Andrew Weil, have published widely and are beginning to be acknowledged within mainstream medicine. Carlos Warter believes that healing, in any tradition, can be facilitated by reestablishing individual connection with the soul (the self or animus) that is the center of wellness. He has developed an 11-step patient-interviewing technique to help physicians integrate spiritual considerations in their practice.

Trends in Alternative Medicine Use in the United States, 1990-1997

DM Eisenberg, et al
JAMA, Nov 11, 1998; Vol 280, No 18:1569-1575

A survey conducted by the authors confirmed that alternative medicine use and expenditures have increased dramatically from 1990 to 1997. The authors advise federal agencies, corporations, foundations, and academic institutions to become more proactive about implementing clinical and basic science research; developing relevant educational curricula, credentialing, and referral guidelines; improving quality control of dietary supplements; and establishing postmarket surveillance of drug-herb (and drug-supplement) interactions. Includes 29 references.

Understanding the Mourner's Spiritual Needs: A Guide for Caregivers

Alan D. Wolfelt
Centerpiece, Spring 1999; 1-2

Presents grief as "the ultimate spiritual struggle" because it challenges people to question the meaning of life and the possibilities for life after death. Advises bereavement caregivers to gather information to form a religious-spiritual understanding of clients, maintaining an attitude of empathy, respect, and nonjudgment at all times.

Questions include:

- Can you help me understand how faith or spirituality is a part of your life?

- Do you have a specific clergyperson or spiritual guide you turn to for support?

- What spiritual practices are important to you?

- What religious or spiritual symbols are important to you?

- Is there anything that would help me better understand your religious/spiritual needs?

Bereavement caregivers are advised to write out a plan for integrating a religious-spiritual care plan into the care of the bereaved person.

Use of Native American Healers Among Native American Patients in An Urban Native American Health Center

AM Marbella, MC Harris, S Diehr, G Ignace
Department of Family and Community Medicine
Medical College of Wisconsin
Arch Fam Med 1998; 7:182-185

Reports the results of semistructured interviews at an urban Indian Health Service Clinic in Milwaukee, Wisconsin, of a convenience sample of 150 patients. The authors found that 38% of the patients see a healer, and of those who do not, 86% would consider seeing one in the future. Most patients report seeing a healer for spiritual reasons. More than one third of the patients seeing healers received different advice from their physicians and healers. The patients rate their healer's advice higher than their physician's advice 61.4% of the time. Only 14.8% of the patients seeing healers tell their physicians about this activity. The authors conclude that physicians should be aware that their Native American patients may be using alternative forms of treatment.

Use of Traditional Health Practices by Southeast Asian Refugees in a Primary Care Clinic

D Buchwald, S Panwala, TM Hooton
Western Journal of Medicine, 1992;156:507-511

Why Patients Use Alternative Medicine: Results of a National Study

John A. Astin
JAMA, May 20, 1998; Vol 279, No 19:1548-1553

The author reports that along with being well educated and reporting poor health status, the majority of alternative medicine users appear to be doing so largely because they find these health care alternatives to be more congruent with their own values, beliefs, and philosophical orientations toward health and life than conventional medicine.

Women's Health: Alternative Medicine Report

Mary Ann Liebert
2 Madison Ave
Larchmont, NY 10538

Audiotapes

The Way of Chi Kung

Ken Cohen
Sounds True Audio
735 Walnut St
Boulder, CO 80302
303 449-6229

For more than 2,000 years, *chi kung* has been a cornerstone of traditional Chinese healing. This noninvasive, preventive healing system is viewed by millions of Chinese as a way of mastering the energy—the *chi*—that permeates all of nature and humanity. Ken Cohen's *The Way of Chi Kung* consists of 5 audiotapes covering *chi kung* theory and practice, including 25 meditation exercises with specific instructions for breathing, postures, and visualizations.

E. Web Sites

Alternative Medicine Connection
http://arxc.com/arxchome.htm

Alternative Medicine Digest
http://www.alternativemedicine.com

Alzheimer's Web Home Page
http://dsmallpc2.path.unimelb.edu.au/ad.html

American Academy of Pain Management
http://www.aapainmanage.org

American Association of Naturopathic Physicians
http://www.aanp.com

American Association of Oriental Medicine
http://www.aaom.org

American Chiropractic Association
http://www.amerchiro.org

American Holistic Health Association
http://www.healthworld.com/ahha

American Holistic Nurses Association
http://www.ahna.org

American Massage Therapy Association
http://www.amtamassage.org

American Oriental Bodywork Therapy Association
http://www.healthy.net/pan/pa/bodywork/
index.html

American Polarity Therapy Association
http://www.polaritytherapy.org

Ask Dr. Weil
http://cgi.pathfinder.com/drweil

Organized by keywords relating to diseases and treatments

Botanical Medicine Resources
http://cpmcnet.columbia.edu/dept/rosenthal/About_
RHRC.html

Center for Complementary and Alternative (CAM) Research in Women's Health
http://cpmcnet.columbia.edu/dept/rosenthal/
welcome_women.html

Feldenkrais-Somatic Options Home Page
http://www.somatic.com

HealthWorld Online
http://www.healthy.net/womenshealth

Lifestyle Center of America
http://www.lifestylecenter.com

The Mining Company: Women's Health— Alternative Medicine Net Links
http://altmedicine.miningco.com/msub9.htm

Links to a collection of articles on alternative approaches to a range of women's health problems

National Women's Health Resource Center
http://www.healthywomen.org

Physician's Association for Anthroposophical Medicine
http://www.healthy.net/pan/pa/paam/index.html

Qigong Institute Database
http://www.healthy.net/qigonginstitute/
database.htm

Bibliography of articles, many from China, on qigong and antiaging and on qigong and cancer.

Wellness Web Women's Health Center
http://www.wellweb.com/women/women.htm

WorldWide Wellness
http://www.wholeliving.com

Section VI

Relevant Materials from Nursing and Other Professional Organizations

A number of health-related professional associations have formulated strategies to develop and assess cultural awareness programs for their staff, leadership, and membership. A few associations have produced independent study modules, including tools that enable practitioners to consider their own individual, family, and professional health beliefs, as well as those of their patients, when they are conducting interviews. Several other health care professional organizations have also developed multicultural resources and programs related to issues special or unique to the profession.

Nursing has clearly devoted more attention to cultural competence than most other professions. Many nursing resources can be used as they are or adapted for other professions.

Section Contents

American Academy of Nursing

American Nurses Association

American Academy of Physician Assistants

Association of Physician Assistant Programs

American Association for Respiratory Care

American Dental Hygienists' Association

American Humane Association

American Occupational Therapy Association

American Physical Therapy Association

American Psychological Association

American Society of Association Executives

American Society of Radiologic Technologists

American Speech-Language-Hearing Association

Center for Cross-Cultural Research

International Association for Cross-Cultural Psychology

National Association of Hispanic Nurses

National Association of Social Workers

National Black Nurses Association

Philippine Nurses Association of America

Transcultural Nursing Society and Other Transcultural Publications

American Academy of Nursing (AAN)

American Nurses Association (ANA)

600 Maryland Ave SW, Ste 100 West
Washington, DC 20024-2571
800 274-4262
http://nursingworld.org

AAN/ANA Monographs

These associations have published many monographs related to cultural competence and diversity, including

- *Competencies for Health Professionals: A Multicultural Perspective in the Promotion of Breast, Cervical, Colorectal, and Skin Health*

- *Cultural Diversity in Nursing: Issues, Strategies, and Outcomes*

- *Diversity, Marginalization, and Culturally Competent Health Care Issues in Knowledge Development*

- *Health Policy for America's Emerging Majority: Proceedings from the Minority Health Policy Conference*

- *Promoting Cultural Competence in and Through Nursing Education: A Critical Review and Comprehensive Plan for Action*

- *Strategies for Recruitment, Retention, and Graduation of Minority Nurses in Colleges of Nursing*

- *Successful Postdoctoral Research Training for African American Nurses*

American Academy of Physician Assistants (AAPA)

Association of Physician Assistant Programs (APAP)

950 N Washington St
Alexandria, VA 22314-1552

Contacts

Shelley L. Hicks, MA
Assistant Vice President, Special Projects
AAPA
703 836-2272 ext. 3402
703 684-1924 fax
E-mail: shelley@aapa.org

Timi Agar Barwick, Director
APAP
703 548-5538
703 684-1924 Fax
E-mail: timi@aapa.org

Organizational Units Addressing Cultural Competence

- AAPA and APAP Board of Directors

- Minority Affairs Committee

APAP Reports

- Minority Retention Programs, 1997

- Minority Attrition Data on Nine Physician Assistant Programs

- Annotated Bibliography on Minority Student Attrition, 1995

AAPA Board Strategic Directive

Continue to promote human diversity within the physician assistant profession and increase sensitivity to diversity-related issues that affect patient care.

Minority Population Health Care Issues

AAPA—Recruitment of minorities to the profession and delivery of culturally sensitive care to diverse populations.

APAP—Recruitment of minority faculty, retention of minority students, and access to education for minority students.

Programs and Activities

- Cultural diversity training workshops have been conducted for senior staff, Board of Directors, and Minority Affairs Committee members (AAPA), and a cultural competence program for members-at-large is being developed (AAPA).

- Several government contracts had cultural diversity issues as primary and/or indirect goals, including a component of faculty development initiatives (APAP).

AAPA and APAP Project Access

National minority recruitment activities were organized in each annual conference location. Physician assistants of various ethnicities and cultural backgrounds visit secondary schools and junior colleges in the conference city to discuss the PA profession. Several constituent chapters organized similar activities in their own areas.

AAPA Mentor Program

The Student Minority Affairs Committee and the Minority Affairs Committee have organized a mentor program. The APAP has assisted with recruitment through Health Care Opportunity Program.

AAPA and APAP Project Access

- Central Application Service to begin in 2000

- Individual institution/program initiatives

Publications

AAPA MAC Insider (Minority Affairs Committee Quarterly Newsletter) and the *APAP Minority Affairs Committee Newsletter*

American Association for Respiratory Care (AARC)

Sam Giordano, Executive Director
11030 Ables Ln
Dallas TX 75229-4593
972 243-2272
972 484-2720 Fax
E-mail: infor@aarc.org
http://www.aarc.org

Contact

Carl P. Wiezalis, Vice President, AARC
Professor and Chair
Department of Cardiorespiratory Sciences
SUNY Health Science Center
750 E Adams St
Syracuse NY 13210
315 464-5580
315 464-6876 Fax

The AARC, a 36,000-member professional society for respiratory care therapists worldwide, is primarily focused on supporting entry-level and continuing education and research in respiratory care. The American Respiratory Care Foundation, which sponsors the International Fellowship Program described later, supports research, education, and charitable purposes to further the art, science, quality, and technology of respiratory care.

Organizational Units Addressing Cultural Competence

- Cultural Diversity Committee

- AARC International Committee

- Education Committee

- Program Committee

- Committee on Cultural Awareness

Cultural Diversity Action Agenda

1. Develop cultural awareness and diversity strategies for use by the Chartered Affiliates, House of Delegates, and Board of Directors.

2. In collaboration with the Membership and Public Relations Committee, include these strategies in membership recruitment and retention activities.

3. Review and revise, as necessary, the cultural awareness/diversity information presented at the Chartered Affiliate Leadership Workshop.

4. Develop and present cultural awareness/ diversity information to the House of Delegates and Board of Directors.

5. Review, revise as necessary, and forward to the Position Statement Committee the position statement on Cultural Diversity.

6. Recommend strategies to enact and promote the Association's commitment to cultural awareness and diversity.

7. In collaboration with the Executive Office, develop and include in the *AARCTimes* a "Culture Calendar" and other articles and information on cultural awareness and diversity.

8. Publish a "How To" article in the *AARCTimes* on issues such as how to become active within the Chartered Affiliate, the AARC Committee structure, the House of Delegates, and the Board of Directors.

9. Conduct a "How do you measure up as a multicultural team member?" survey.

10. In collaboration with the Education Committee, address the inclusion of this cultural awareness training in entry-level and graduate respiratory care training programs.

Mission and Position Statements

The following documents have been developed and promoted by AARC in the past 10 years.

Mission Statement on Cultural Diversity
The American Association for Respiratory Care is an organization whose membership includes professional men and women each with cultural heritage, ethnicity, and national origins. AARC recognizes that it is enhanced by its cultural diversity and seeks to assist its members in the accomplishment of their professional aspirations as well as to strengthen their cultural uniqueness and value to the Association. It shall be the mission of the Cultural Diversity Committee to guide the AARC toward the recognition of the role of culturally diverse professionals by focusing on their exceptional accomplishments, supporting their cultural group identity, and utilizing their cultural potentials to advance the goals of the Association and the respiratory care profession.

Position Statement on Cultural Diversity
The American Association for Respiratory Care is committed to the advancement of cultural diversity among our members as well as in our leadership. This commitment entails:

- Being sensitive to the professional needs of all our members.

- Promoting appreciation for, communication between, and understanding among people with different beliefs, colors, genders, and backgrounds.

- Recruiting strong leadership candidates from under-represented groups for leadership and mentoring programs.

Programs and Activities

International Fellowship Program
Since its establishment in 1990, the AARC International Fellowship Program has hosted more than 70 professionals from more than 35 countries during 2-week stays. Participants spend a week in each of two US cities where they interact with multi-national colleagues in an apolitical, humanitarian context. Participants observe the practice of respiratory care in large and small hospitals and other sites at which health care is delivered, such as home care organizations, rehabilitation centers, and hospices. For information, contact the AARC executive office or visit http://www.aarc.org/internatinal.

International Council for Respiratory Care
The AARC is the founder and primary supporter of this worldwide organization of respiratory care practitioners.

Independent Study Package

The ARRC distributes an independent study package, "Towards Culturally Competent Respiratory Care," developed by Enid Sepulveda, MA, RCP. The document is intended to give practitioners a basic knowledge of the differing health and illness belief models, help practitioners inquire about a patient's health beliefs and practices, and help them incorporate and negotiate approaches to care that best serve the patient and the provider. The package is divided into modules separated by self-tests. It includes basic information about such concepts as culture-bound illnesses, traditional and folk remedies for common conditions, a "culturally sensitive interview and assessment" guide based on the Berlin LEARN method, and questions practitioners can use to explore their own family's health beliefs and folklore. The AARC also distributes Sepulveda's "Impact of Culture and Poverty on Health and Illness."

Proposed Collegiate Unit of Instruction on Cultural Competence

The Education and Cultural Diversity committees are working on a recommended unit of instruction addressing multiculturality and pluralism for collegiate respiratory care programs.

Patient Assessment Course

A 16-hour course with significant content on diversity and end-of-life issues.

Cultural Calendar

The AARC and its Committee on Cultural Awareness have designated 1999-2000 a Multicultural Year, to celebrate the diversity of its members. Each month a different ethnic group will be profiled in *AARCTimes*, and translations into several languages of commonly used respiratory care terminology will be available through the AARC Web site.

American Dental Hygienists' Association

Rosetta Gervasi, Director of Communications
444 N Michigan Ave, Ste 3400
Chicago, IL 60611
312 440-8900
312 440-8929 Fax
http://www.adha.org

Has several publications and projects with a cultural competence angle:

- Oral Diseases Prevention Kits and Needs Assessment for Targeted Populations: A Study of Oral Health Literacy and Need in This Nation's Community and Migrant Health Centers

- Preventing Dental Diseases in Children With Disabilities

- English-to-Spanish Chairside Translator

- Enhancing Patient Care Through Internet Resources

American Humane Association

63 Inverness Dr E
Englewood, CO 80112-5117
303 792-9900

The Children's Division of the Association, which is dedicated to the protection of children from abuse and neglect, has developed an annotated bibliography of resources on cultural competence and cultural diversity in child welfare/child protection services.

American Occupational Therapy Association (AOTA)

Penny Kyler, MA, OT/L
1383 Piccard Dr
Box 1725
Rockville, MD 20849-1725
301 948-9626

Reports

- *Nondiscrimination and Inclusion Regarding Members of the Occupational therapy Professional Community*

- *Occupational Therapy and the Americans with Disabilities Act*

- *Human Immunodeficiency Virus*

Policies

- 1.41—Inclusion of Ethical and Cross-Cultural Concerns/Issues in All Appropriate AOTA Documents and Publications

- 3.12—Diverse and Inclusive Membership

- 5.13—Accessibility of AOTA-sponsored Events and Activities

Relevant Minority Population Health Care Issues

Accessibility of Minority and Diverse Populations to Occupational Therapy Services

Programs and Activities

Partners for Professional Growth/Mentoring Program

Workshops at Annual Conference

Disability Forum: Issues of practitioners with disabilities as they related to practice, education, and research

Diversity Forum: Issues of cultural diversity as they related to practice, education, and research

Books

Functional Terms in Occupational Therapy
Carla M. Iwata, Charlene D. Harvey
Spanish and German versions

A Guide to Reasonable Accommodation for OT Practitioners With Disabilities
Shirley A. Wells, Sandy Hanebrink

Multicultural Education and Resource Guide for Occupational Educators and Practitioners
Shirley A. Wells

Continuing Education Materials

Video:
Creating a Multicultural Approach and Environment

"Workshop on a Disk:"
Children's Wellness: Relevance of Cultural Differences on Intervention

American Physical Therapy Association (APTA)

1111 N Fairfax St
Alexandria, VA 22314
703 684-2782
703 684-7343 Fax
http://www.apta.org

Contact

Johnette L. Meadows, MS, PT
703 706-3143
E-mail: johnettemeadows@APTA.org

Units Addressing Cultural Competence

- Department of Minority/International Affairs

- Advisory Panel on Minority Affairs (advisory group to the Board of Directors)

Policies

The APTA House of Delegates has passed policies on affirmative action, equal opportunity, and nondiscrimination.

Relevant Minority Population Health Care Issues

Providing physical therapy services to minorities and other underserved populations.

Programs and Activities

- Develops materials emphasizing that understanding a person's cultural background should be part of any clinical interaction, even when that background may appear similar to that of the clinician.

- Offers workshops on cultural diversity and health care.

- Promotes the development of physical therapy educational curricula that include cultural competence.

Resources

- The newsletter, *Spectrum*, frequently features cultural diversity issues

- Bibliography and videography on cultural competence

- *Plan to Foster Minority Representation and Participation in Physical Therapy* (video)

- *Cultural Diversity in Physical Therapy* (video)

American Psychological Association (APA)

750 First Street NE
Washington, DC 20002
202 336-5500
http://www.apa.org

Publications

Guidelines for Culturally Diverse Populations

APA guidelines for providers of psychological services to ethnic, linguistic, and culturally diverse populations, approved by the APA Council of Representatives in August 1990, are available online at http://www.apa.org/pi/guide.html.

Psychology's Cultural Competence, Once "Simplistic," Now Broadening
Scott Sleek
APA Monitor, 1998; vol 29

American Society of Association Executives (ASAE)

1575 I Street, NW
Washington, DC 20005
202 626-2723

Contact

Cookie Cottrell, CAE
202 626-2789
E-mail: ccottrell@asaenet.org

Unit Addressing Cultural Competence

National Diversity Committee

Diversity Policy Statement

In principle and practice, the ASAE values and seeks diverse and inclusive participation within the field of association management. The ASAE will promote involvement and expand access to leadership opportunity, regardless of race, ethnicity, gender, religion, age, sexual orientation, nationality, disability, appearance, geographic location, or professional level. The association will provide leadership and commit time and resources to accomplish this objective while serving as a model for other associations engaged in such endeavors.

Programs and Activities

- Various programs address diversity issues

- Quarterly article in *Association Management* presents information to members on key diversity and inclusion issues, trends, and strategies

- ASAE Diversity Executive Leadership Program

American Society of Radiologic Technologists (ASRT)

15000 Central Ave SE
Albuquerque, NM 87123-3917

Contact

Greg Morrison
505 298-4500
505 298-5063 fax
http://www.asrt.org

The ASRT addresses cultural competence issues through a number of activities, including lectures and workshops dealing with age-specific needs and people at the end of life, continuing education courses on age-specific competencies, and relevant articles in its scholarly journals (see example below).

Managing Cultural Diversity: The Art of Communication
Radiologic Technology
January/February 1998

American Speech-Language-Hearing Association (ASHA)

10801 Rockville Pike
Rockville, MD 20852
301 897-5700
http://www.asha.org

Units Addressing Cultural Competence

- Multicultural Affairs Department—lends many ASHA documents

- Five cultural caucuses provide information and materials

Resources Respect Differences

ASHA has extensive resources to help speech-language-hearing professionals understand the implications that cultural differences have for treatment. In these resources, ASHA emphasizes the importance of recognizing and showing respect for differences.

Multicultural Resource Center

ASHA's multicultural resource center remains alert to issues such as the choice of foods for use during swallowing training because they might conflict with a patient's dietary customs and therefore adversely affect clinical outcomes. Speech therapists unfamiliar with common dialects might embarrass and frustrate clients by insisting on a particular pronunciation in connection with therapy following a stroke.

Web Site

- reading lists

- a multicultural history and demographic profile of US regional and social dialects

- cultural differences in communication and learning styles

- bibliographies on specific ethnic groups

Center for Cross-Cultural Research (CCCR)

Psychology Department
Miller Hall, Room 328
Western Washington University
Bellingham, WA 98225-9089
360 650-3574

The CCCR was established within the Department of Psychology at Western Washington University in 1969 in response to the Euro-American bias in psychological theory, research, and practical applications common at that time. Activities of the CCCR and its associates include contributions to the curriculum, research and scholarship, and publications.

Curriculum

Two undergraduate courses are devoted to cross-cultural topics and issues: Psychology and Culture, an entry-level introduction to cross-cultural psychology open to all students; and Seminar in Cross-Cultural Psychology, required of some graduate students and open to graduate students from other areas. Another graduate course, Professional, Legal, and Cultural Issues, addresses relevant cultural and ethnic topics that are especially important for applied psychologists. Both undergraduate and graduate students can emphasize cross-cultural psychology.

Research and Scholarship

Associates of the Center have conducted research in many areas, both in other countries and among various ethnic groups in the United States.

Publications

The bimonthly *Journal of Cross-Cultural Psychology (JCCP),* with subscribers in more than 75 countries and an Editorial Advisory Board of experts from 25 countries, is the only psychology journal in the world completely devoted to cross-cultural psychology. *JCCP* has been an official publication of the International Association for Cross-Cultural Psychology since 1972.

Cross-Cultural Psychology (Sage Publications) is the longest-standing book series in this area in the world.

International Association for Cross-Cultural Psychology (IACCP)

Theodore Singelis
Department of Psychology
California State University - Chico
Chico, CA 95929-0234
530 898-4009
http://www.fit.edu/CampusLife/clubs-org/iaccp

The IACCP is an organization of some 700 psychologists from about 75 countries established in 1972.

National Association of Hispanic Nurses

1501 16th St, NW
Washington, DC 20006
202 393-6870

National Association of Social Workers (NASW)

750 First St NE, Ste 700
Washington, DC 20002-4241
202 408-8600
http://www.socialworkers.org

The NASW, the largest organization of professional social workers (155,000 members), has a strong affirmative action program that applies to national and chapter leadership and staff. It supports three national committees on equity issues:

- National Committee on Women's Issues

- National Committee on Racial and Ethnic Diversity

- National Committee on Gay, Lesbian, and Bisexual Issues

Materials are available under the categories of Affirmative Action, Black History, and Women's Issues.

Press Resources

- *Workplace and Diversity*

- *Multicultural Issues in Social Work*

Books

Cultural Competence in Substance Abuse Prevention, 1997
Joanne Philleo, Frances Brisbane, Leonard Epstein

Ethnicity & Race: Critical Concepts in Social Work, 1988
Carolyn Jacobs, Dorcas Bowles, eds.

Lesbian and Gay Issues: A Resource Manual for Social Workers, 1985
Hilda Hidalgo, Travis Peterson, Natalie Woodman, eds.

Multicultural Issues in Social Work, Vols I & II,
1996 and 1999
Patricia L. Ewalt, Edith M. Freeman, et al, eds.

National Black Nurses Association

8630 Fenton St, Ste 330
Silver Spring, MD
301 589-3200

Philippine Nurses Association of America

320 E 23rd St, #15-G
New York, NY 10010
212 995-6047

Transcultural Nursing Society and Other Transcultural Publications

College of Nursing and Health
36600 Schoolcraft Rd
Livonia, MI 48150-1173
888 432-5470
http://www.tcns.org/

This society serves as a forum to bring nurses together worldwide with common and diverse interests to improve health care to culturally diverse people.

Founder's Focus: Transcultural Nursing Administration: An Imperative Worldwide
MM Leininger
Journal of Transcultural Nursing
1996; 8(1):28-33

Transcultural Concepts in Nursing Care, 3rd ed
Margaret M. Andrews, Joyceen S. Boyle
Lippincott-Raven Publishers, 1998

Transcultural Perspectives in Nursing Administration
Margaret M. Andrews
Journal of Nursing Administration
November 1998;30-45,53

Nurse administrators are responding to the population demographics reshaping the health care work force with respect to race, ethnicity, gender, national origin, sexual orientation, age, handicap, disability, and related factors as national sensitivity to various forms of diversity grows. They are developing skills in transcultural administration as they manage diversity and identify the cultural origins of conflict in the workplace. This article explores how culture influences the manner in which administrators, staff, and patients percieve, identify, define, and solve problems and examines the complex and interrelated factors that influence workplace diversity. Excellent explanations of cultural perspectives on the meaning of work; on conflict; on space, distance, and touch; on etiquette and interpersonal relationships; on time orientation; on gender and sexual orientation; on family obligations; on moral and religious beliefs; on personal hygiene; on clothing and accessories; and on corporate cultures and organizational climate, cultural values, and cross-cultural communication.

Section VII

Patient Support Materials, Including Self-Help Group Resources

Many of the general physician associations, specialty and state societies, and other organizations in the preceding sections prepare and distribute patient support materials related to specific health conditions and population groups. Some of these materials have culturally sensitive content or are printed in various languages. Please contact the organizations listed in previous sections for information about their culturally relevant patient support materials. These organizations may also be able to provide you with information about consumer groups related to specific diseases or special populations.

This section provides background information on American Medical Association (AMA) policies and activities and describes some patient support materials, especially self-help group resources, with which physicians may not be familiar. Physicians can contact the American Self-Help Clearinghouse for information about national consumer and self-help groups. Local clearinghouses, such as the Illinois Self-Help Coalition, can provide information about local groups.

Self-help groups have been recognized by federal agencies and health care and educational institutions as important sources of patient/public information and support. A recent survey conducted by Tom Ferguson, MD (doctom@doctom.com) indicates that more and more consumers are consulting online with people with the same condition, not only for emotional support but also for information and treatment options. *Unfortunately, racial, ethnic, and socioeconomically underserved and underrepresented nonmajority populations have limited access to self-help groups and the special kinds of support they provide.*

Although some professionals express concern about the possibility that self-help groups may discourage members from seeking needed medical attention and may encourage the use of unhealthy complementary practices, research studies do not support these concerns. Dr. Ferguson suggests ways in which physicians can cooperate with self-help and other consumer groups to improve patient-centered care and encourage appropriate self-care.

The AMA and Self-Help Groups

The AMA, while acknowledging concerns about the safety and efficacy of self-help groups, has included references to the importance of peer support in several policies, including those related to the environment of medical education. In past years, the National Leadership Development Conference has featured self-help groups for a variety of conditions, and *AMNews* has published numerous articles about the benefits of peer support, including groups specifically for physicians.

In 1986, AMA staff approached then-Surgeon General C. Everett Koop, MD, about devoting one of his Surgeon General's Workshops to the need for improving communication between professionals and self-help groups to maximize the benefits of this underutilized army of volunteers. A self-help group advocate from his early days in practice, when he organized support groups for staff dealing with the loss of pediatric patients, Dr. Koop had incorporated self-help groups in several of his workshops, some of which were attended by AMA leadership. The 1987 Surgeon General's Workshop on Self-Help and Public Health culminated in a publication and a symposium in 1989, cosponsored by the Illinois Self-Help Center and the AMA. The 16 Surgeon General's recommendations continue to serve as a blueprint for encouraging greater understanding of the contributions of self-help groups and their potential for improving the health of the public.

Dr. Koop also supported the organization of the National Council on Self-Help and Public Health, which, during his tenure, succeeded in incorporating self-help group awareness in all eight public health agencies. Several of the agencies now include self-helpers on the panels that determine priorities and funding directions. The National Council was also successful in getting specific objectives related to self-help groups and clearinghouses included in *Healthy People 2000: Objectives for the Nation*. The AMA role in these and others efforts is summarized in *Self-Help Concepts and Applications*, Charles Press, 1992.

Peer Support Stronger Than Willpower

National organizations and federal agencies are continuing to recognize the contributions of peer education and support. A panel established to review how the culture and programs of the National Cancer Institute (NCI) and the National Institutes of Health (NIH) address the needs of ethnic minorities concluded that the agencies fall short in their efforts. The panel recommended that the NCI and NIH tap cancer survivors in ethnic minority groups "as important resources for educating others in the community about cancer" and for providing information about cancer to patients, clinicians, and others in ethnic minority and underserved populations.

The same techniques used to help members cope with the health challenges that drew them together—sharing stories, offering constructive advice, and mentoring—have been found to promote healthy behaviors that can have a positive effect on disease states. The findings of Dean Ornish, MD, about the benefits of meeting with peers with heart disease have been widely publicized through professional and popular media. Many professional associations associated with addictive behavior, from drinking and drug abuse to gambling, have policies indicating the value of 12-step and other types of groups. Physicians appear to be referring patients in ever larger numbers to such groups.

Hundreds of groups exist throughout the nation for most of the specific populations categorized in this Compendium. A case in point is domestic violence. Some groups, such as Parents Anonymous (PA), focus primarily on presenting very specific techniques parents can use to replace their abusive behavior. PA has a long history of testimony and research about how it has reduced risks related to domestic violence and how it educated the public as well as members. The National Committee for Prevention of Child Abuse is among the national organizations that have praised PA for its role in reducing the propensity for future abuse.

The benefits of self-help groups go far beyond stopping harmful or unhealthy behavior. Groups for arthritis, stroke, and diabetes are known for their disease prevention activities, both for their members and for people unaffected by these conditions. Many other groups also sponsor presentations, demonstrations, and even ongoing programs on physical activity, healthy food choices, and other self-care techniques that can improve general health.

Groups formed to help people affected by HIV/AIDS have been recognized by Population Reports (September 1989) as providing the "knowledge, emotions, and skills [that] reinforce healthful changes" and for persuading people "to change their behavior and to maintain new behavior."

Technology Increases Communication Opportunities

Although it is unlikely that electronic communication will replace the mutual support of face-to-face contact, self-helpers have been among the most aggressive consumers in using online information sources and connections. To supplement their time together during meetings—or as the main source of support for those unable to attend meetings—self-help group members regularly use private online mail sent between two or more individuals; contact discussion list members through broadcast mail; attend online meetings with numerous people signing on to a "chat group" at the same time; access Web-based health information produced by professionals and consumers; use hyperlinks to move to a site with additional health information; consult local clearinghouse listings to find out when and where groups meet locally; or use combinations of the above to organize a group to meet specific needs or respond to a tragedy.

Section Contents

A. The AMA and Other Organizations

B. Consumer and Self-Help Publications

C. Web Sites

- General Web Sites

- Specific Web Sites

A. The AMA and Other Organizations

American Medical Association

Policies and Reports

H-20.977   *Reducing Transmission of Human*
            Immunodeficiency Virus (HIV)
            (CSA Rep. C, A-88; amended: BOT
            Rep. I-93-34)

H-25.999   *Health Care for Older Patients*
            (Committee on Aging Report, I-60)

H-85.967   *Good Care of the Dying Patient*
            (*JAMA,* February 14, 1996;
            275:474-478)

H-210.986   *Physicians and Family Caregivers—*
            A Model for Partnership
            (*JAMA,* March 10, 1993;
            269:1282-1284)

H-295.897   *Enhancing the Cultural Competence*
            of Physicians

H-295.999   *Medical Student Support Groups*

Consumer Books

The emphasis of all consumer books published by or in cooperation with the AMA is on prevention—advocating a working partnership between physicians and patients and showing patients how to take responsibility for their health and well-being. The books also include health information specific to various ethnic and racial groups, such as the incidence of particular diseases within different groups and the risk factors for those groups.

AMA Essential Guides
New York: Pocket Books, 1998
800 223-2336

A series of books that explores one medical topic per volume. Current titles in the series offer consumers information about asthma, depression, hypertension, and menopause. Published by Pocket Books, each guide is easy to read and provides comprehensive information ranging from diagnosis and symptoms to treatments and prevention.

Complete Guide to Women's Health
Kathleen Cahill Allison, Ramona I. Slupik
New York: Random House, 1996

Provides pertinent health information for each of four age ranges—puberty to 18, 18 to 40, 40 to 60, and over 60. Covers health problems that have a unique impact on women, including coronary artery disease, urinary tract infections, osteoporosis, stroke, eating disorders, thyroid problems, autoimmune diseases, and cosmetic surgery. Special chapters also address death and bereavement, as well as sexual assault and family violence.
For a more detailed description, see Section IV.

Complete Guide to Your Children's Health
Donna Kotulak, Dennis Connaughton
New York: Random House, 1996

Includes 700 pages of information on child and adolescent health. Part I, "Your Healthy Child from Birth Through Adolescence," discusses fundamentals such as nutrition, exercise, and developmental milestones at every stage of a child's life. Part 2, "Caring for Your Child's Health," explains how to keep kids safe, find quality child care, and help children learn to deal with stress. The third and largest part of the book, "Childhood Diseases and Disorders," is an illustrated A-Z encyclopedia of the most common childhood illnesses. Easy-to-read symptom charts suggest the possible causes and significance of many common symptoms and suggest appropriate measures.

Encyclopedia of Medicine
Charles B. Clayman, MD, ed.
New York: Random House, 1989

Almost 1,200 pages, with 5,000 listings; 2,000 illustrations; descriptions of 2,200 common and uncommon disorders, diseases, conditions, and cures; over 300 symptoms; 2,500 drugs in generic, brand-name, and major groupings; and 600 tests, procedures, and surgical operations. Extensively indexed and cross-referenced.

Family Medical Guide, Third Edition
Charles B. Clayman, MD, ed.
New York: Random House, 1994

Nearly 900 pages of essential health information in one volume, divided into four sections. Part I, "Your Healthy Body," contains specific preventive self-care tips, with advice on diet, exercise, weight loss, stress reduction, and stopping smoking. Part II, "Symptoms and Self-Diagnosis," provides unique diagnostic charts with clear yes/no questions to help users determine what their symptoms mean. Part III, "Diseases, Disorders, and Other Problems," includes detailed articles on more than 650 medical problems. Part IV, "Caring for the Sick," covers the basics of professional medical care, home nursing, and care giving.

JAMA Patient Page

Printed on the last page in each issue of *JAMA*, the *JAMA* Patient Page provides consumer information on a topic related to the content of the particular issue. Recent editions have covered such topics as sickle cell anemia, stroke, blood pressure, and exercise. Also available online at
http://www.ama-assn.org/
public/journals/jama/ppindex9.htm

AMA Web Sites

AMA Adolescent Health On-Line
http://www.ama-assn.org/adolhlth/adolhlth.htm

Adolescent Health On-Line, the Web site for the AMA's Child and Adolescent Health Program, is designed to provide information to physicians, health care providers, researchers, parents, and

teenagers on important adolescent health issues. The Web site is regularly updated with the latest scientific information in the field of adolescent health and provides information on the Guidelines for Adolescent Preventive Services (GAPS). It also offers extensive links to other organizations working to improve the health status of young people, as well as information about cultural competence resources developed by the Child and Adolescent Health Program. Adolescent Health On-Line will continue to include more information for adolescents, their parents or guardians, and health care providers striving to provide culturally competent health care.

The site is supported through a cooperative agreement from the Health Services and Resources Administration, Maternal and Child Health Bureau's federal Office of Adolescent Health.

AMA Health Insight
http://www.ama-assn.org/consumer.htm

Extensive information for consumers.

JAMA Information Centers
http://www.ama-assn.org/special/

Easy-to-use, peer-reviewed collections of resources on specific conditions, including HIV/AIDS, asthma, migraine, and women's health.

Hepatitis C
http://www.ama-assn.org/med-sci/98oct13b.htm

Resources on Alcohol and Tobacco
http://www.ama-assn.org/special/aos/

See Section IX for a complete list of AMA and other organizations' Web sites.

Alliance of Genetic Support Groups

4301 Connecticut Ave, Ste 404
Washington, DC 20008
800 336-5557 or 202 966-5557
E-mail: info@geneticalliance.org
http://www.geneticalliance.org

A June 1985 symposium, Genetic Support Groups: Volunteers and Professionals as Partners, examined how a professional-voluntary partnership could "promote maximum health care and social and psychological functioning for genetically affected individuals and their families." Tracks devoted to self-help groups were permeated with the concept of networking to communicate with health professionals and the public about the value of self-help groups and to impact on policies related to genetic disorders.

The Mid-Atlantic Regional Human Genetics Network and the National Organization for Rare Disorders subsequently brought together groups related to a number of disorders to strengthen communication with health professionals and the public. The symposium also created a new coalition of voluntary organizations and professionals, the Alliance of Genetics Support Groups. It provides "minority scholarships" to promote participation of diverse ethno-cultural communities at the Alliance Annual Conference.

The Alliance sponsored the 1990 National Conference on Peer Support Training, which brought consumers and professionals together to "strengthen critical working relationships." The Alliance publishes an information sheet that promotes policies supportive of genetic services and of the role of self-help groups in those services.

Alliance Alert

The Alliance communicates with its constituents, state groups, federal agencies, and the public through its Web site (see above) and its newsletter, *Alliance Alert*. The newsletter contains information about relevant legislation, meetings, and publications, including Web sites with legislative and genetics information.

Partnership for Genetic Services Pilot Program

Since 1997 the Alliance, through its Partnership for Genetic Services Pilot Program, has conducted surveys and focus groups with consumers and professionals in three broad US regions to determine what consumers consider essential to the delivery of quality family-centered, culturally sensitive health care services to people affected by genetic conditions. The fundamental elements of the Partnership Program include the value that "peer support provides valuable resources and emotional nourishment" and that "consumer and provider collaboration is the basis for an *effective* care team."

Working with 12 Midwest medical schools, the Partnership offers students and consumers an opportunity for dialogue outside the clinical setting and sensitizes providers-in-training to the needs of consumers and to community resources. The Partnership also cooperates with Kaiser Permanente's Northwest and mid-Atlantic regions, Group Health Cooperative of Puget Sound, and health plans to offer educational and other service interventions to managed care providers.

Culturally Sensitive Consumer Indicators of Quality Genetic Services

Consumer Indicators of Quality Genetic Services, which contains 12 indicators, will be used through the Partnership Program with managed care providers and medical students. One of the activities is to "improve provider access to quality consumer-oriented support group resources— resources that can support, supplement, and enhance services." Indicator 9 relates most specifically to cultural competence:

"Information about genetic conditions is provided to each consumer in a manner best suited to their needs and culture, which may include:

- their primary language

- an appropriate educational level

- more than one medium"

American Academy of Child and Adolescent Psychiatry

Virginia Q. Anthony, Executive Director
3615 Wisconsin Ave NW
Washington, DC 20016
202 966-7300
202 966-2891 Fax
http://www.aacap.org

Your Child: What Every Parent Needs to Know: What's Normal, What's Not, and When to Seek Help
David B. Pruitt, ed.
New York: Harper Collins, 1998
800 242-7737
http://www.parentshandbooks.org

A comprehensive guide to emotional, behavioral, and cognitive development from infancy through preadolescence. Guides readers through the developmental milestones of childhood, discussing specific questions and concerns and examining more troublesome problems. Covers topics from choosing a pediatrician to dealing with sleep problems, from monitoring behavior to helping a child develop self-esteem.

Your Adolescent: What Every Parent Needs to Know: What's Normal, What's Not, and When to Seek Help
David B. Pruitt, ed.
New York: Harper Collins, 1999
800 242-7737
http://www.parentshandbooks.org

Addresses everyday issues such as peer influence, dating, sexuality, independence, separation anxiety, and responsibility, as well as violent behavior, substance abuse, suicide, and eating disorders.

American Medical Association Alliance

Hazel Lewis, Executive Director
515 N State St
Chicago, IL 60610
312 464-4470
http://www.ama-assn.org/alliance

The American Medical Association Alliance (AMA Alliance) is a national grassroots organization of 50,000 physician spouses. As the proactive volunteer voice of the AMA, it promotes the good health of America and the family of medicine. For more than 75 years, Alliance members have participated in numerous local activities and projects that reflect a commitment to health care for diverse populations. The AMA Alliance strongly supports AMA efforts to enhance the ability of physicians to provide culturally effective care.

Programs and Activities

SAVE: Stop America's Violence Everywhere

Since its inception in 1995, the SAVE initiative has been implemented at the grassroots level by more than 700 local Alliances. These programs are tailored to the communities they serve, but all assist victims of violence or teach violence prevention. For the 1999-2000 AMA Alliance year, SAVE activities will focus on situations that threaten the health and safety of children daily—violence in our schools. To help address this growing problem, the AMA Alliance has developed a SAVE Schools from Violence campaign. It encourages Alliances nationwide to adopt a school in their community and provide those students with conflict resolution materials that teach nonviolent behaviors and enhance self-esteem. With the support of the community and the country, the AMA Alliance believes the SAVE program can help break the cycle of violence.

Consumer Education and Resources

Alliance volunteers educate their communities about health-related issues by distributing AMA Alliance publications and resources. Alliance consumer resources include:

Hands Are Not for Hitting—conflict resolution activity book and place mat

Teaches preschool through third grade children positive, nonviolent activities and acceptable ways to treat others. "Hands" identifies what children's hands should and should not do.

Monitor the Media

Series of brochures that provide suggestions on ways to supervise a child's television viewing, video game playing, and Internet surfing. Each contains startling statistics and provides a realistic look at what is really coming into your living room through your television and computer.

Shape Up for Life

Series of brochures that address specific health issues and concerns such as child abuse, stress, teen suicide, elder abuse, eating disorders, and drug abuse.

Project Bank: The Encyclopedia of Public Health and Community Projects

Contains more than 500 projects conducted by state and county Alliances nationwide from 1994-1998. Project ideas range from domestic violence posters to teen health fairs, medical marriage seminars to medical textbook collections, and HIV awareness campaigns to elder care programs.

Physician Spouse Series

Series of pamphlets that addresses the needs of physicians' spouses. Topics include impairment and well-being, marriage, medical family support, working in a spouse's office, and retirement.

American Self-Help Clearinghouse

Edward Madara, Director
Northwest Covenant Medical Center
Denville, NJ 07834-2995
973 625-9565
http://www.cmhc.com/selfhelp

The American Self-Help Clearinghouse serves as a repository and distribution center for information about national self-help organizations, regional clearinghouses, and innovations in online self-help. Founder and director Edward Madara, along with Tom Ferguson, MD, has supported the extensive development of online self-help groups and has provided hundreds of groups with technical assistance. The Clearinghouse has dozens of guides for assisting in developing and maintaining groups.

The Self-Help Sourcebook: Your Guide to Community and Online Support Groups

Published annually by the American Self-Help Clearinghouse. Provides information on more than 800 national groups and networks addressing issues such as abuse, addictions, bereavement, disabilities, rare illnesses, mental health, and parenting.

Forging Connections: An Ethno-Cultural Self-Help Conference

416 487-4355
E-mail: kevin.gosine@utoronto.ca
http://www3.sympatico.ca/shrc/ethno.html

This conference serves as a model for collaboration. It was organized by the Self-Help Resource Centre of Greater Toronto; the Anti-Racism, Multiculturalism, and Native Issues Centre (AMNI); and the Ontario Self-Help Network (OSHNET). Each of those organizations can provide specific information related to individual and collaborative efforts to increase access to self-help groups in Canada.

Health Promotion Council of Southeastern Pennsylvania

311 S Juniper St, Ste 308
Philadelphia, PA 19107-5803
215 546-1276
215 545-1395 Fax
E-mail: hpcpa@libertynet.org
http://www.libertynet.org/hpcpa/

The Health Promotion Council promotes health to those at greatest risk through publications and training. Pamphlets and audiovisuals for African Americans, Latinos, and Asians, written at or below a sixth-grade reading level, currently cover blood pressure, diabetes, smoking, stress, nutrition, and use of the health care system. The Council has materials in Spanish, Cambodian, Chinese, and Vietnamese. It offers a 7- to 8-week training and curriculum for community-based hypertension and diabetes control in both Spanish and English. Its Health Literacy Project offers teaching materials geared to specific cultural and literacy levels.

Illinois Self-Help Coalition

Daryl Holtz Isenberg, PhD
Wright College South
3400 N Austin Ave
Chicago, IL 60634
773 481-8837
773 481-8917 Fax
http://www.selfhelp-illinois.org

For nearly 3 decades, the Illinois Self-Help Coalition (formerly the Illinois Self-Help Center) has been instrumental in planning and conducting national and international forums for promoting understanding and acceptance of self-help groups. Founder Leonard Borman, PhD, attended the 1978 meeting on mental health convened by then-President Carter, and the current director provided administrative support for the 1987 Surgeon General's Workshop on Self-Help and Public Health. The Illinois Self-Help Coalition promotes the development of and access to self-help groups in the state and throughout the nation by:

- publishing a directory guiding consumers in identifying groups that meet their needs (see below)

- partnering with community college and university research and development efforts

- conducting cooperative training sessions for self-help group leaders

- maintaining Web-based resources, including group lists and a newsletter

- providing workshops and in-service training about these and other Web-based resources

- educating health and human service professionals about the utility and availability of groups

- conducting research to fill in the gaps in the support provided by self-help groups, such as enhancing their ability to provide care at the end of life and motivating members to adopt healthy behaviors

Typical projects include partnering with the Rehabilitation Institute of Chicago to provide a variety of self-help options, including Web-based groups and resources, for substance abuse prevention for persons with disabilities.

The Insiders' Guide to Self-Help Groups in Illinois

Includes tips on selecting appropriate self-help groups and provides contact information for more than 2,500 groups for 500 problems. National listings provide access to information about thousands of other groups.

The 43-page narrative introductory section, "The Power of Self-Help," contains titles on topics designed to help newcomers overcome their fears and reservations, such as "You Are Not Alone," "Taking Charge," "Is This Group for Me?," "Supporting Vulnerable Members," "Complementary and Alternative Health Practices," and "Information Age Self-Care."

Last Acts—Care and Caring at the End of Life

The Robert Wood Johnson Foundation
Route 1 and College Road East
Box 2316
Princeton, NJ 08543-2316
609 452-8701
E-mail: mail@rwjf.org
http://www.rwjf.org

The Last Acts campaign was established with initial funding from the Robert Wood Johnson Foundation. The campaign's quarterly newsletter, published by the Foundation, reports on such issues as the challenge of patient diversity and how cultural difference is relevant to clinical decision making at the end of life. Major themes include enhancing end-of-life care through communication and decision making, changing health care and health care institutions, and changing American attitudes toward death. Task forces focus on the family, palliative care, service providers, provider education, and financing. Resource committees focus on communication, diversity, spirituality, standards and guidelines, and evaluating outcomes.

Diversity and Palliative Care

http://growthhouse.net/~lastacts

The Last Acts Campaign is expanding the dialogue and collaboration among readers, partners, and allies by joining the Inter-Institutional Collaborative Network on End-of-Life Care, sponsored by Growth House, Inc.

This service utilizes state-of-the-art Internet technologies and encourages networking, debate, dialogue, collaboration, and live chat among hundreds if not thousands of end-of-life professionals around the world. Includes a specially focused discussion on "Diversity and Palliative Care."

Last Acts Partners

The Last Acts coalition includes major national organizations, including the AMA, and local groups. Last Acts Partners share the following goals:

- Improve communication between dying people and their loved ones and between dying people, families, and health professionals

- Reshape the medical care environment to better support high-quality end-of-life care

- Change American culture so that people can more comfortably face death and the issues raised by care of the terminally ill.

Partners have the opportunity to:

- demonstrate leadership in end-of-life care

- network with other concerned organizations and individuals through in-person conferences and on-line discussions

- have the Last Acts Web site hotlink to your organization's Web site

- receive quarterly newsletters, weekly e-mail newsletters, policy updates, special mailings of reports and materials, and invitations to meetings and workshops

- receive up-to-date information about end-of-life issues readily usable in their newsletters or Web sites

- get help in planning meeting sessions around end-of-life care

- obtain high-quality materials about of end-of-life issues—caregiving, diversity bereavement, palliative care, policy—to share with their boards, committees, or membership

- promote their organization's activities related to the end of life through articles in the Last Acts electronic and print newsletters, or by listings in the online Resources Directory

- tap into the Last Acts network to locate experts and models of action in end-of-life care

Multi-Cultural Educational Services

Charles LaRue, President
832 104th Lane NW
Coon Rapids, MN 55433
612 767-7786
E-mail: service@mcedservices.com
http://www.mcedservices.com

Organization specializing in translating, publishing, and distributing information, including health promotion material, to members of the refugee and immigrant community who have not gained competency in English language skills.

National Mental Health Consumer's Self-Help Clearinghouse

Joseph A. Rogers
1211 Chestnut St, Ste 1000
Philadelphia, PA 19107
800 553-4538
E-mail: infor@mhselfhelp.org
http://www.mhselfhelp.org

Funded by the Center for Mental Health Services, the clearinghouse focuses on training and on organizing consumers and survivors to form a collective voice with which to influence such issues as:

- protection of the Americans with Disabilities Act

- consumer rights in managed care

- involuntary commitment and other issues of rights, protection, and advocacy

- the future of community-based systems of care, particularly those managed by consumers

The Clearinghouse has contact information for other consumer-based mental health groups, such as the National Empowerment Center of Lawrence, Massachusetts, and the West Virginia Mental Health Consumers Association in Charleston, West Virginia. Publishes a quarterly newsletter, *The Key*.

National Osteoporosis Foundation Osteoporosis Patient Information Center (OPIC)

1150 17th St NW, Suite 500
Washington, DC 20036-4603
202 223-2226 (9:00am-4:30pm EST)
202 223-2237 Fax
http://www.nof.org

The National Osteoporosis Foundation (NOF) is a nonprofit, voluntary health organization dedicated to reducing the widespread prevalence of osteoporosis through programs of research, education, and advocacy. Founded in 1986, the NOF is used by patients, health professionals, and the public for osteoporosis information, programs, and services.

NIH Osteoporosis and Related Bone Diseases - National Resource Center

1232 22nd St NW
Washington, DC 20037-1292
800 624-2663
http://www.osteo.org

The NIH Osteoporosis and Related Bone Disease National Resource Center links patients, health professionals, and the public to resources and information. The Center collects information on materials, programs, and support services on metabolic diseases and disseminates this information widely through publications, online services, professional and patient meetings, and general media outreach. The Center has developed fact sheets and annotated bibliographies on osteoporosis for African Americans, Latinos, and Asian Americans, some of which are in Spanish.

National Patient Safety Foundation

515 N State St
Chicago, IL 60610
312 464-4848
312 464-4154
E-mail: npsf@ama-assn.org
http://www.npsf.org

Founded in 1997, the National Patient Safety Foundation (NPSF) is an independent, nonprofit research and education organization dedicated to the measurable improvement of patient safety in the delivery of health care. Through the NPSF, health care clinicians, institutional providers, health product manufacturers, researchers, legal advisors, patient/consumer advocates, regulators, and policy makers are working together to make health care safer for patients.

The NPSF Communications Program will explore ways to raise awareness of the influence of cultural competence on patient safety. Activities toward this goal will include an article in the NPSF quarterly newsletter, *Focus on Patient Safety*. NPSF staff are also recommending that cultural competence be addressed at NPSF regional forums, which bring together community and health care leaders for candid discussions of patient safety. Local planners of the Wisconsin regional forum, for example, are considering the topic for a breakout session.

In addition to the NPSF quarterly newsletter, *Focus on Patient Safety*, other resources include the *News Brief*, a semimonthly glance at patient safety activities occurring nationwide; the NPSF Clearinghouse, a repository of information on patient safety and related topics; and the NPSF Web site, an online resource for patient safety literature, activities, and related Web sites.

National Women's Health Information Center

800 994-9662
http://www.4woman.org

Provides access to information from federal health clearinghouses and hundreds of private sector organizations.

T'ai Chi Chih Center

3107 Eubank NE, Ste 19
Scottsdale Village
Albuquerque, NM 78111
505 299-2095
http://www.taichichih.org

The national headquarters for an easy-to-learn form of t'ai chi originated in 1974 by Justin Stone, offers classes, Justin Stone's Joy Though Movement video and book, and instructional and practice video for Seijaku (an advanced form based on t'ai chi chih), and information about the videotapes created in conjunction with the PBS t'ai chi chih program that is still being aired throughout the country. Described as "meditation in motion," t'ai chi chih has been found to improve balance, reduce the risk of falls, reduce stress, and improve muscle tone. It is taught widely in health care institutions, self-help groups for survivors of life-threatening illnesses, retirement centers, recreation centers for older adults of persons with disabilities, educational institutions from grade school through college, prisons, and recreation programs sponsored by the YMCA and park districts. The Folsom prison program has introduced more than 400 inmates to t'ai chi chih and has been credited with breaking down barriers between inmates from different ethnic and racial backgrounds.

B. Consumer and Self-Help Publications

The American Holistic Health Association Complete Guide to Alternative Medicine
William Collinge
Warner Books, 1996
1271 Avenue of the Americas
New York, NY 10020

Provides an overview of eight major complementary and alternative health care practices. Case
examples of each are designed to help readers
decide which might suit their needs and how to use
them in conjunction with conventional medicine.
Evidence of scientific support, strengths and
limitations, and guidelines for selecting a
practitioner are included for each approach.
Readers are cautioned against using the remedies
on their own and are advised to consult their health
care professionals. Included are concrete data on
procedures, techniques, and principles for:

- Chinese medicine

- Ayurveda

- Naturopathic medicine

- Mind/body medicine

- Osteopathic medicine

- Chiropractic

- Massage therapy and bodywork

Bereavement Support Group Program for Children
Beth Haasl, Jean Marnocha
Brunner/Mazel, 1990

Includes a *Leader Manual* and *Participant
Workbook*. This comprehensive resource received
the National Hospice Organization Award for
Excellence.

Consumer Bill of Rights and Responsibilites: Report to the President of the United States
Advisory Commission on Consumer Protection and
Quality in the Health Care Industry
November 1997

The Advisory Commission on Consumer
Protection and Quality in the Health Care Industry
was appointed by President Clinton on March 26,
1997, to "advise the President on changes
occurring in the health care system and recommend
measures as may be necessary to promote and
assure health care quality and value and protect
consumers and workers in the health care system."
As part of its work, the President asked the
Commission to draft a "consumer bill of rights."
The eight areas of consumer rights and
responsibilities includes one on "Respect and
Nondiscrimination," which states that:

- "Consumers have the right to considerate,
  respectful care from all members of the health
  care system at all times and under all
  circumstances. An environment of mutual
  respect is essential to maintain a quality health
  care systems.

- "Consumers must not be discriminated against
  in the delivery of health care services . . . as
  required by law based on race, ethnicity,
  national origin, religion, sex, age, mental or
  physical disability, sexual orientation, genetic
  information, or source of payment.

- "Consumers who are eligible for coverage
  under the terms and conditions of a health plan
  or program or as required by law must not be
  discriminated against in marketing and
  enrollment practices based on race, ethnicity,
  national origin, religion, sex, age, mental or
  physical disability, sexual orientation, genetic
  information, or source of payment."

Directory of National Helplines: A Guide to Toll-Free Helplines, FaxLines, Web Sites, and Other Public Service Numbers, 1998

Consumers Index
Box 1808
Ann Arbor, MI 48106
800 678-2435
http://www.pierianpress.com

Many organizations and agencies sponsor toll-free public service helplines in order to provide assistance to persons in need of support and advice. This specialized directory contains nearly 300 social, economic, health, and environmental helplines.

Dr. Tom Linden's Guide to Online Medicine

Tom Linden
New York: McGraw-Hill, 1995

Encyclopedia of Complementary Health Practices

Carolyn Chambers Clark, ed
Springer Publishing Co, 1999

Encyclopedia of Natural Remedies

C. Norman Shealy
Element Books Inc, 1993
160 N Washington St
Boston, MA 02114

C. Norman Shealy, a neurosurgeon, is the founder of the American Holistic Medical Association and director of the Shealy Institute in Springfield, Missouri, a center for health care and pain and stress management. *Natural Remedies* covers natural remedies from eight complementary and alternative health practices:

- Ayurveda

- Chinese herbal medicine

- Traditional home and folk remedies

- Herbalism

- Aromatherapy

- Homeopathy

- Flower remedies

- Vitamins and minerals

The book describes the techniques and practice of each therapy and lists the remedy sources they use, the ailments they treat, and the effects they have been reported to have on health and well-being. It also includes a long list of common ailments and more than 1,000 natural remedies and treatments, as well as a glossary and a comprehensive list of useful addresses and contacts. Illustrated in full color throughout.

The Encyclopedia of Alternative Medicine

Jennifer Jacobs
Journey Editions, 1996
153 Milk St
Boston, MA 02109

Describes the innate self-healing capacity of the body, called "chi" in Chinese medicine and the "vital force" in homeopathic medicine. This ability of the body to heal itself was first recognized by the Greek physician Hippocrates as *vis medicatrix naturae*. Dr. Jacobs contends that this healing energy can be stimulated and enhanced, either directly through therapies such as homeopathy and acupuncture, or indirectly through such practices as nutrition and herbs.

The book includes information on the origins, techniques, safety, practical application, and typical visit for a number of modalities that have not been extensively covered in other publications. Includes chapters on Natural Healing, The Power of Plants, Nutrition and Diet, Mobility and Posture, The Mind, Massage and Touch, and Eastern Therapies.

1996 Guide to Health Care Resources on the Internet

John W Hoben
New York: Faulkner and Gray, 1996

Health Online: How to Find Health Information, Support Groups, and Self-Help Communities in Cyberspace
Tom Ferguson
Addison-Wesley, 1996

This print source opens the door to a universe of technical and personal help, reflecting the author's decades of trying to expand access to resources through interactive telecommunications. The author's profound respect for peer support, which transforms participants from passive victims to empowered helpers, is apparent throughout the book. In preparation for a consumer-centered health care system, the book provides a guided tour of the virtual self-help communities through which thousands of volunteer self-helpers are assisting one another with a wide range of problems. The organization of the book is logical, and the contents are clearly presented. *Health Online* also provides detailed instructions on how to access newsgroups, which permit people to exchange messages. Most of the book is directed to consumers, but professionals are addressed in a small section toward the end, "A Note to Health and Computer Professionals." These four pages present Ferguson's vision for improving and maintaining an effective consumer health information system.

How to Use the Internet
Mark Butler
Berkeley: Ziff-Davis Press, 1994

Palliative Care: Patient and Family Counseling Manual
Aspen Publishers Inc
200 Orchard Ridge Dr
Gaithersburg, MD 20878
800 638-8437
http://www.aspenpublishers.com

Features segments on end-of-life care related to many of the special populations included in this *Compendium*. Includes numerous handouts for patients and families and practical applications for practitioners. Provides guidance on training volunteers to deal effectively and caringly with patients from all cultural backgrounds. Covers special issues such as deciding who to listen to if

the parents and partner of a gay patient offer conflicting instructions. Includes:

- Patient and family issues
    - Final stages of life
    - General patient and family education
    - Patient planning guide
    - General guidelines for caregiving

- Pain management

- Grief and psychosocial issues

- Spiritual care

- Nutrition in terminal care

- Professional concerns/volunteer training

- Financial/legal issues

- HIV/AIDS issues

Patient Education in the Medical Encounter: How to Facilitate Learning, Behavior Change, and Coping
UJ Grueninger, FD Duffy, MG Goldstein
In *The Medical Interview: Clinical Care, Education, and Research*
M Lipkin, SM Putnam, A Lazare, eds.
New York: Springer-Verlag; 1995; pp 122-133

Patient Resources on the Internet: A Provider to Patient Resource for On-line Disease Management and Personal Health, 1998-1999
Faulkner & Gray, 800 535-8403
http://www.faulknergray.com

Includes the following:

- Keeping Up with Patients On-line

- The Latest in Cyberspace

- Health Care Benefits Move Onto Computer Screens

- Quality of Information on the Internet

- The Web as a Disease Management Tool

- Is the Web Safe Enough?

- Joining the Worldwide Health Care Dialogue

- Web Pages by Providers and Patients

- Preventive Medicine on the Web

- Directory of Online Health Resources

Peaceful Dying: The Step-by-Step Guide to Preserving Your Dignity, Your Choice, and Your Inner Peace at the End of Life

Daniel R. Tobin
New York: Perseus Books, 1999

Presents a 26-step program to guide people through the final stages of life, from "recognizing individuality of disease, individuality of choice" to "dying with tranquility." Uses a conversational, story-telling style in providing specific tips for taking care of physical, emotional, and spiritual needs in order to live fully and well through the very end of life. Describes techniques for preventing pain and isolation.

Radical Healing: Integrating the World's Great Therapeutic Traditions to Create a New Transformative Medicine

Rudolph Ballentine
Harmony Books, 1999
201 E 50th St
New York, NY 10022

Radical Healing blends the primary holistic schools of healing, allowing readers to understand their common elements. Drawing on 30 years of medical study and practice, Dr. Ballentine integrates the wisdom of the great traditional healing systems (especially Ayurveda, homeopathy, traditional Chinese medicine, and European and Native American herbology) with nutrition, psychotherapy, and bodywork. *Radical Healing* covers the spectrum from plants, natural substances, diet, exercise, and cleansing to principles of spiritual and psychological interventions. Includes case studies and examples.

The Rights of the Dying: A Companion for Life's Final Moments

David Kessler
New York: HarperCollins, 1997

Uses 17 "rights of the dying" principles as a framework for guiding people dealing with life-challenging diseases and their supporters in communicating with one another and with physicians and hospital staff. Stresses the importance of allowing dying people to participate in all decisions and express their feelings and emotions.

Self-Help Groups: Empowerment Through Policy and Partnerships

Hannah Hedrick, Daryl Isenberg, Carlos Martini
In: *Self-Help Concepts and Applications*
Alfred Katz, Hannah Hedrick, Daryl Isenberg, eds.
Charles Press, 1992

Focuses on policy and partnership activities related to the growth of autonomous grassroots self-help groups for persons affected by life-threatening conditions. Describes the empowerment provided by peer action orientation and the characteristics and benefits of such groups. Includes 115 references, many to AMA and other health professional publications.

Strategies for Designing Culturally Relevant Client Education Materials

JL Murphy, NJ Giger, R Davidhizar
Journal of Healthcare Education and Training, 1994; 8(3):8-12

Presents strategies for designing and implementing a culturally significant and appropriate client education tool for use with non-English-speaking clients or for any client in a culture different from the mainstream. These strategies include:

- Understanding the relationship between culture and behavior

- Developing a strategic plan

- Gathering demographic data about the setting

- Evaluating the characteristics of the learner

- Developing culturally specific, unique learning materials

Will Online Support Groups Revolutionize Medicine?

Medicine on the Net, May 1999
PO Box 40959
Santa Barbara, CA 93140-0959
http://www.mednet-i.com

Medicine on the Net frequently includes articles and editorials on the relationship of self-help groups to consumer health and on the continuing growth of online groups. The May 1999 issue contained two articles of particular benefit to physicians:

- **Getting Up To Speed on Consumer Health Resources**: Describes ten steps that will help health care professionals familiarize themselves with consumer health information resources on the Internet from self-help pioneer Tom Ferguson.

- **The Scoop on Self-Help Medicine—Some of the Leading Sites**: Lists major sites where patients are banding together in online support groups to share medical information, tips for daily living, and emotional support. These patients are calling for a dialogue with their physicians.

Women's Concise Guide to Emotional Wellbeing

Karen Carlson, Stephanie Eisenstate, Terra Ziporyn
Harvard University Press, 1997

Describes psychological disturbances and disorders unique to women.

Women's Concise Guide to a Healthier Heart

Karen Carlson, Stephanie Eisenstate, Terra Ziporyn
Harvard University Press, 1997

Considers questions of cholesterol and diabetes, stress and depression, and diet and smoking as well as diagnostic procedures and surgeries.

C. Web Sites

General Web Sites

For a complete listing of Web sites, refer to Section IX: Virtual Resources.

AMA Health Insight

http://www.ama-assn.org/consumer.htm

American Academy of Family Physicians

http://www.aafp.org/family/patient.html

Offers consumer health information for 250 topics.

Better Health

http://www.betterhealth.com/healthwise

Includes topics researched for accuracy and comprehension by a national medical review board. Enables users to explore health topics and problems and consider options for staying healthy, providing home self-care, determining when medical attention is necessary, and preparing for an appointment with a physician.

Central Illinois

http://www.prairienet.org/selfhelp

Family Services/Self-Help Center of Champaign County maintains support group lists for Central Illinois.

DocTom's Online Self-Care Journal

http://www.healthy.net/othersites/
doctom/index.html

drkoop.com

http://www.drkoop.com

Hosts about 100 self-help groups.

General Drug Information

http://www.rxlist.com

Provides general drug information on more than 4,000 US drug products to supplement advice provided by physicians.

Go Ask Alice

http://www.goaskalice.columbia.edu

This Columbia University site accepts e-mail questions and searches its database for answers.

Healthfinder

http://www.healthfinder.gov

A gateway Web site linking consumers and professionals to health and human services information from the federal government and its many partners on more than 1,000 topics.

Health Risk Assessment

http://www.youfirst.com

Users fill out a short questionnaire and are then provided with a free, personalized, confidential health assessment report, including healthy lifestyle recommendations.

JAMA Information Centers

http://www.ama-assn.org/special/

Easy-to-use, peer-reviewed collections of resources on specific conditions, including HIV/AIDS, asthma, migraine and women's health.

Medicine on the Net

http://www.mednet-i.com

National Health Information Center

http://nhic-nt.health.org

Clearinghouse providing a central health information referral for consumers and professionals.

National Library of Medicine

http://www.nlm.nih.gov

888 FIND-NLM
301 402-1384 Fax
E-mail: custserv@nlm.nih.gov

The National Library of Medicine's MEDLINEplus, the database used by librarians and health professionals for nearly 30 years, is available at no cost, 24 hours a day, 7 days a week. Two Web-based interfaces for searching MEDLINE are available: PubMed and Internet Grateful Med.

Reuters Medical News

http://www.reutershealth.com

Publishes 20 full-text online news items every day on recent events from the medical world.

thriveonline.com

http://www.thriveonline.com

Provides information to consumers on healthy lifestyles, with diet, sports, medicine, and fitness subsections.

WebMD

http://my.webmd.com/index.html

Specific Web Sites

Adolescent Health On-Line

http://www.ama-assn.org/adolhlth/adolhlth.htm

Adolescent Health On-Line, the Web site for the AMA's Child and Adolescent Health Program, is designed to provide information to physicians, health care providers, researchers, parents, and teenagers on important adolescent health issues.

Alliance of Genetic Support Groups

http://www.geneticalliance.org

American Self-Help Clearinghouse

http://www.cmhc.com/selfhelp

Cancer Care

http://www.cancercare.org

Offers 1-hour conference calls that provide the latest information from experts in oncology, social work, public policy, and other fields. Teleconference programs feature coping strategies and updates on specific cancers. Register for programs online or by phone at 800 813-HOPE. Also provides information about clinical trials, referrals to related Web sites, and online support groups for patients, partners, and bereavement groups.

Easter Seals

http://www.seals.com

Offers rehabilitation and support services for people with disabilities.

Ethics: EPEC Resource Guide

http://www.ama-assn.org/ethic/epec/rgbuffer.htm

Hepatitis C

http://www.ama-assn.org/med-sci/98oct13b.htm

Illinois Self-Help Coalition

http://www.selfhelp-illinois.org

Inter-Institutional Collaborative Network on End-of-Life Care

http://growthhouse.net/~lastacts

Last Acts—Care and Caring at the End of Life

http://www.rwjf.org

Mental Health Net

http://www.cmhc.com

Provides mental health links.

National Mental Health Consumer's Self-Help Clearinghouse

http://www.mhselfhelp.org

National Osteoporosis Foundation Osteoporosis Patient Information Center (OPIC)

http://www.nof.org

National Women's Health Information Center

http://www.4woman.org

NIH Osteoporosis and Related Bone Diseases—National Resource Center

http://www.osteo.org

Parent's Handbooks

http://www.parentshandbooks.org

Psych Central

http://www.psychcentral.com

Part of John Grohol's extensive mental health site, offering a one-stop index for psychology, support, and mental health issues, resources, and people.

Recovery Network

http://www.recoverynetwork.com

Recovery Network is committed to serving the 100 million Americans affected by alcoholism, drug abuse, eating disorders, child abuse, depression, or gambling problems. In delivering programming for these populations, this site encourages the partnership of public radio, cable television, and other media. On its Internet site, Recovery Network links hundreds of self-help organizations, 12-step groups, national hotlines, and resources.

Self-Help & Psychology Magazine

http://www.shpm.com

Articles on a wide range of self-help topics.

Section VIII

Representative Cultural Competence Publications

Most of the publications referenced in the *Cultural Competence Compendium* have been distributed to sections directly related to their content. This section contains a representative mix of general and population-specific references to give readers a sense of the wide variety of print media through which the call for improved cultural competence is being issued, as well as the variety of organizations and individuals committed to this effort

Most of the book, monograph, report, journal, and newsletter and bulletin titles are followed by brief descriptions. Some books, such as the most relevant AMA publications and Alan Harwood's seminal *Ethnicity and Medical Care*, are described in more detail in earlier sections. Journal articles are summarized only in preceding sections with the organizations that produced them or to which they are thematically related.

Section Contents

A. Books, Monographs, Directories, and Reports

B. Journals, Journal Articles, and Newsletters/Bulletins

A. Books, Monographs, Directories, and Reports

The Americans with Disabilities Act: A Practice of Accommodation
American Medical Association, 1998

This guide, produced by the AMA and the American Academy of Physical and Medical Rehabilitation, is aimed at health care professionals and facilities with the goal of eliminating barriers that may prevent those in the disability community from obtaining and accessing quality health care and employment free from discrimination based on disability.

Caring Across Cultures: The Provider's Guide to Cross-Cultural Health Care
Center for Cross-Cultural Health
410 Church St SE, Ste W-227
Minneapolis, MN 55455
612 624-4668
http://www.umn.edu/ccch

Resource guide designed for use by clinicians, and public health, human services, and health care professionals. Includes quizzes, surveys, and checklists for cultural competence and resources to assist progress toward cultural competence. Includes a listing of community-based organizations addressing health issues in Minnesota.

Caring for Cambodian Americans: A Multidisciplinary Resource for the Helping Professions
SK Ratliff
Garland Publishing Co, 1997
212 751-7447

Deals comprehensively with health care for Cambodians and is designed as a practical resource for health care and social service providers, hospitals, and health care agencies.

Celebrating Diversity: Approaching Families Through Their Food
National Center for Education in Maternal and Child Health, 1994

This monograph provides information on how specific foods mean different things in different cultures. Health promotion can be greatly enhanced when health care professionals are aware of the significance of food and the way it is prepared by their patients. Many cultural groups use foods as medicine or to promote health, and included in this monograph is a chart with examples of medicinal uses of food by various ethnic groups.

Clinical Practice Guidelines Directory
American Medical Association, 1999

Communicating for Cultural Competence
JW Leigh
Allyn & Bacon, 1998

Teaches health professions students to become effective listeners and communicators, while learning to respect and understand other cultural perspectives. Students learn how to gather and use culturally relevant information in order to enhance communication across cultures.

Communication and Culture: A Guide for Practice
C Gallois, V Callan
John Wiley & Sons, 1997

Informs professionals about what research in cross-cultural psychology has revealed about communication across and between cultures.

Communication and Disenfranchisement: Social Health Issues & Implications
EB Ray, ed.
Lawrence Erbaum Association, 1996

Includes chapter titled "Victims of the Franchise: A Culturally Sensitive Model of Teaching Patient-Doctor Communication in the Inner City," by BF Sharf and J Kahler.

Complementary & Alternative Medicine: Legal Boundaries and Regulatory Perspectives
MH Cohen
Johns Hopkins University Press, 1998

Concise summation of the current status of complementary and alternative medicine. Covers areas of regulation, scope of practice, informed consent and malpractice, and describes some of the alternative providers and treatments.

Counseling the Culturally Different: Theory and Practice, 2nd edition
DW Sue, D Sue
John Wiley & Sons Inc, 1990

Explores issues relevant to the culturally different in the United States and cuts across all ethnic/racial minorities. Specific minority groups are given individual treatment to contrast similarities and differences.

Cultural Competence for Evaluators. A Guide for Alcohol and Other Drug Abuse Prevention Practitioners Working with Ethnic/Racial Communities
M Orlandi, ed.
Office for Substance Abuse Prevention
US Department of Health and Human Services, 1992

Cultural Context of Health, Illness, and Medicine
MO Martloustaunau, EJ Sobo
Bergen & Garvey, 1998

Introductory book that describes the role of culture and society in perceptions of illness and health and of the propriety of different approaches to healing. Includes a chapter on different typologies used by medical anthropologists to classify various healing systems.

Cultural Diversity and Geriatric Care: Challenges to the Health Professions
D Wieland, D Benton, BJ Kramer, eds.
Haworth Press, 1994

Has a comprehensive chapter written by M. Kagawa-Singer on diverse cultural beliefs and practices about death and dying in the elderly.

Cultural Diversity in Health and Illness: Guide to Heritage Assessment and Health Traditions, 4th edition
R Spector
Appleton & Lange, 1996

Part of a package that includes a free guide to heritage assessment.

Culturally Competent Health Care for Adolescents: A Guide for Primary Care Providers
American Medical Association, 1994

Introduces health care providers to the complex issues involved in working with diverse populations of adolescents and outlines practical strategies for incorporating cultural issues into health care.

Culture and the Clinical Encounter: An Intercultural Sensitizer for the Health Professions
RC Gropper
Intercultural Press, 1996

Presents some 45 real-life incidents of cross-cultural conflict or difficulty in a clinical context to alert the reader to the intercultural misperceptions and their outcomes. The reader must choose the best of four possible explanations, then read the proposed solutions to gain additional knowledge about the 23 represented cultures.

Culture and Nursing Care: A Pocket Guide
JG Lipson, SL Dibble, PA Minarik, eds.
UCSF Nursing Press, 1996

Box 0608
School of Nursing
University of California, San Francisco
521 Parnassus Ave
San Francisco, CA 94143-0608
415 476-4992
http://nurseweb.ucsf.edu/www/book4.htm

Offers practicing nurses and other health care professionals a snapshot of human diversity; it includes a set of guidelines to assist in the recognition of similarities as well as differences between and within the 24 highlighted groups. Each chapter outlines issues related to health and illness, symptom expression, self-care, birth, death, religion, and family participation in care.

Culture, Health and Illness
C Hellman
Newton, MA: Butterworth & Heinemann, 1995

Developing Intercultural Communication Skills
V Ricard
Krieger Publishing Company, 1993

Aims to identify human responses to commonality and diversity, identify and develop intercultural communication and interaction skills in valuing, observing, listening, thinking, speaking, and gesturing, recognize the influence of human values on the interaction process, and to use a practical, flexible framework for ongoing learning and personal development in the area of intercultural communication and interaction.

Directing Health Messages Towards African Americans: Attitudes Toward Health Care and the Mass Media
JL Sylvester
Garland Publishing, 1998

Explores diversity and similarities between white and African American populations with specific information on how health messages can be effectively communicated to African Americans. Includes chapters on communication theories and crafting an effective health campaign.

Directory of National Helplines: A Guide to Toll-Free Helplines, FaxLines, Web Sites, and Other Public Service Numbers, 1998
Consumers Index
Box 1808
Ann Arbor, MI 48106
800 678-2435
http://www.pierianpress.com

Many organizations and agencies sponsor toll-free public service helplines in order to provide assistance to persons in need of support and advice. This specialized directory contains nearly 300 social, economic, health, and environmental helplines.

Educating Doctors: Crisis in Medical Education, Research and Practice
S Wolf
Transaction Publishers, 1997

Critique of current status of medical education with specific emphasis on lack of doctor-patient discussions and proper medical history taking. Has extensive bibliography.

Ethnic Variations in Dying, Death and Grief
DP Irish, KF Lundquist, VJ Nelsen, eds.
Taylor & Francis, 1993

Includes a chapter written by PC Rosenblatt that examines the cross-cultural variation in the experience, expression, and understanding of grief.

Ethnicity and Medical Care
Alan Harwood, ed.
Harvard University Press, 1981

Includes guidelines for culturally appropriate health care and chapters on various ethnic cultures. Harwood writes, "A personal commitment by health-care personnel to improve face-to-face interactions in health-care situations can make a significant contribution toward greater patient satisfaction and more effective medical care." To deliver culturally competent care, clinicians must learn to deal with class and professional barriers to the realization of ethnically appropriate health care; elicit the patient's model of the problem in treating the illness; make medical treatment more comfortable with the patient's life-style; and improve the articulation between mainstream and non-mainstream sources of health care.

The author warns against using cultural specific information to obscure the individual patient, which "can occur if the health-care provider treats the information stereotypically and acts as if all members of an ethnic category must behave and believe in the same fashion."

Facing Death: Where Culture, Religion, and Medicine Meet
HM Spiro et al, eds.
Yale University Press, 1996

Covers many of the controversial issues surrounding death, such as issues of death in the gay world, euthanasia, hospice care, dignity of dying, and death as a medical proprietorship.

Handbook of Multicultural Counseling
JG Ponterotto
Sage Publications, 1995

Presents recent advances in theory, research, practice, and training in the field of multicultural counseling and examines the latest developments in racial/ethnic identity and acculturation theory.

Healing Traditions: Alternative Medicine and the Health Professions
BB O'Connor
University of Pennsylvania Press, 1995

Health Care for the Homeless Directory, 1998
Health Care for the Homeless Information
Resource Center
Policy Research Associates
262 Delaware Ave
Delmar, NY 12054
888 439-3300
http://www.prainc.com/hch

Provides information on government and private agencies that serve homeless people.

An Introduction to Cultural Competence Principles and Elements: An Annotated Bibliography
JL Mason, K Braker, TL Williams-Murphy
Portland State University, 1995

Research and Training Center on Family Support
and Children's Mental Health
Regional Research Institute for Human Services
Box 751
Portland, OR 97207-0751
503 725-4040

About 115 abstracted listings exemplify aspects of the Child and Adolescent Service System Program's cultural competence model. Emphasis on care of children and youth with serious emotional disabilities. Citations are categorized under the headings Cultural Self Assessment, Dynamics of Difference, Valuing Diversity, Adaptation to Diversity, and Incorporation of Cultural Knowledge.

An Introduction to Spanish for Health Care Workers
RO Chase, CB Medina De Chase
Yale University Press, 1998

Focuses on vocabulary and grammar, including colloquial terms and slang used by Spanish-speaking patients. Provides informative cultural notes on Hispanic values and customs.

Latino Health in the US: A Growing Challenge
C Molina, M Aguirre-Molina, eds.
American Public Health Association, 1994

Comprehensive volume reflecting the research, knowledge, and expertise of nationally recognized Latino researchers, scholars, educators, and activists. Includes profiles of Latinos in the health care system; life cycle and family health; patterns of chronic disease; occupational health; and alcohol, drug, and mental health issues.

The Medical Interview: A Three Function Approach
SA Cohen-Cole
Mosby-Year Book, 1991

Medical Management of the Home Care Patient: Guidelines for Physicians, 2nd edition
American Medical Association, 1998

Includes guidelines to help clarify the physician's role and responsibilities in the organizational framework of home care. Recommendations for designing a curriculum in home care for education and training of physicians at all levels are outlined. Resource listings include state departments on aging, national organizations/programs, and a 61-item bibliography on home care.

Medicine and Ethnology: Selected Essays
E Ackerknecht
Johns Hopkins Press, 1971

Medicine and the Family: A Feminist Perspective
L Candib
Basic Books Inc, 1995

Mosby's Guide to Physical Examination,
3rd edition
St Louis: Mosby, 1995

One chapter, by HM Sediel, JW Ball, JE Danis, and GW Benedict, is devoted to cultural awareness.

Patient Resources on the Internet: A Provider to Patient Resource for On-line Disease Management and Personal Health Information, 1998-1999
Faulkner & Gray
800 535-8403

Patients and Healers in the Context of Culture
Arthur M Kleinman
Berkeley, CA: University of California Press, 1980

The Physician's Guide to Better Communication
BF Sharf
Scott, Foresman and Company, 1984

Practical guide for the improvement of communication skills to enhance the physician-patient relationship as well as the relationship with other health care professionals.

A Pocket Guide to Cultural Assessment
Elaine Geissler
Mosby-Year Book, 1994

Used by health care providers as an introduction to patients from over 150 nations. The guide provides information on the geographic location of the country, the major languages, the health and illness practices of the dominant groups of people, the diverse ethnic groups, and various rites, such as birth and death.

Racial and Ethnic Disparities in Health Care
American Medical Association, 1995

Report prepared for the 1995 Interim Meeting of the House of Delegates. The report recommendations were adopted and are AMA policy. The AMA maintains a position of zero tolerance toward racially or culturally based disparities in care, individuals are encouraged to report physicians to local medical societies where racial or ethnic discrimination is suspected, and the AMA continues to support physician cultural awareness initiatives and related consumer education activities.

Report of the AAP Task Force on Minority Children's Access to Pediatric Care
American Academy of Pediatrics, 1994

The Task Force addresses impediments to the physical well-being of all children, especially those that affect minority group children. The report deals with and makes recommendations in five major areas: Health Status, Access Barriers (among those addressed is cultural insensitivity/racism/classism), Workforce (includes a section on the cultural competence of pediatric care providers), Organizational Response, and the Academy's Role. 131-item bibliography.

Societal Forces Reshaping American Medicine: Implications for Internal Medicine and the Board
American Board of Internal Medicine, 1997

Selected presentations from the 1997 American Board of Internal Medicine Summer Conference address issues on cultural competence, including complementary care and a multicultural society. Has a 77-item bibliography centered on the significance of disparities in care to nonmajority populations.

The Spirit Catches You and You Fall Down: A Hmong Child, Her American Doctors, and the Collision of Two Cultures
A Fadiman
Farrar, Straus & Giroux, 1997

Tells the story of Hmong refugees who spoke little English when they brought their 3-month-old daughter with seizures to a county hospital in California. The book is about cross-cultural communication and miscommunication.

State-of-the-Art Conference on Adolescent Health Promotion Proceedings
American Medical Association, 1993

Participants in the conference, including health professionals from the fields of medicine, school health, and community public health, developed a set of principles to help guide policymakers and administrators to initiate, improve, and integrate adolescent health promotion and preventive strategies provided in medical, school, and community settings.

Strategies for Working with Culturally Diverse Communities and Clients
E Randall-Davis
Association for the Care of Children's Health, 1989

Through the Eyes of Others: Intercultural Resource Directory for Health Care Professionals
Hennepin County Medical Society, 1995

Towards a Culturally Competent System of Care
TL Cross, KW Dennis, MR Isaacs, BJ Bazron, 1989

This monograph provides information on cultural competence in serving children and adolescents with mental health problems. It was written under the auspices of the National Technical Assistance Center for Children's Mental Health at Georgetown University and funded by the National Institute of Mental Health.

Towards a Culturally Competent System of Care: Programs Which Utilize Culturally Competent Principles
MR Isaacs, MP Benjamin
1991

This second monograph identifies and describes several programs that exemplify various aspects of the cultural competence model.

Through the Patient's Eyes: Understanding and Promoting Patient-Centered Care
Margaret Gerteis et al, eds.
San Francisco: Jossey-Bass Publishers, 1993

Transcultural Health Care
G Henderson, M Primeaux, eds
Addison-Wesley Publishing Co, 1981

Transcultural Nursing: Assessment and Intervention
JN Giger, RE Davidhizar
Mosby-Year Book, 1995

Offers a comprehensive conceptual framework and appropriate assessment and intervention guidelines for holistic care of clients who are from diverse cultural backgrounds. The first seven chapters discuss the importance of providing culturally appropriate care and present a model for cultural assessment.

The Ultimate Multi-Ethnic Resource for Chicago
C Linton, ed.
Illinois Ethnic Council

This guide includes information on 450 ethnic organizations, 120 ethnic media outlets and area scholars, and translation services for the Chicago area. The council also published *Ethnic Handbook: A Guide to the Cultures and Traditions of Chicago's Diverse Communities.*

Understanding Cultural Identity in Intervention and Assessment
RH Dana
Portland State University, 1998

Presents a model for effective culture-specific services that emphasizes the description and understanding of cultural/racial identity and the use of this information to develop cultural formulations to increase the accuracy of diagnoses with four chapters devoted to discussions of mental health services.

B. Journals, Journal Articles, and Newsletters/Bulletins

Journals and Newsletters/Bulletins

AHEC at a Glance
Milwaukee Area Health Education Center
2220 E North Ave
Milwaukee, WI 53202
414 226-2432
http://www.biostat.wisc.edu/ahec/mahec.html

The mission of the Milwaukee AHEC is to improve access to health care in Milwaukee's underserved communities, through the development of community-based, client oriented, culturally relevant, collaborative health professions education programs.

Alternative & Complementary Therapies
Mary Ann Liebert Inc
2 Madison Ave
Larchmont, NY 10538
914 834-3100
800 M-LIEBERT
http://www.liebertpub.com

Bimonthly publication for health care practitioners. Includes a "WebWatch" section that lists electronic resources on alternative and complementary therapies on a specific topic each issue, eg, Alternative Cancer Care in August 1998.

Alternative Therapies in Health and Medicine
InnoVision Communications
American Association of Critical-Care Nurses
101 Columbia
Aliso Viejo, CA 92656
714 362-2000
http://www.healthonline.com/altther.htm

A bimonthly peer-reviewed journal that serves as a forum for the development and sharing of information on the practical use of alternative therapies in preventing and treating disease, healing illness, and promoting health. Includes articles on cultural competence issues.

American Journal of Health Promotion
PO Box 1897
810 E 10th St
Lawrence, KS 66044-8897
800 627-0629

Published bimonthly in conjunction with the National Wellness Association. Addresses wellness issues related to nonmajority populations.

American Journal of Public Health
1015 15th St NW
Washington, DC 20005
202 789-5600

Published monthly by the American Public Health Association, the journal aims to promote and protect personal and environmental health by exercising leadership in the development and dissemination of health policy. The majority of articles, editorials, and features related to nonmajority populations.

Closing the Gap

Office of Minority Health Resources Center
800 444-6472

The Office of Minority Health of the Department of Human Services devotes each issue of its monthly newsletter to a specific health topic of concern to minority communities. The September 1997 issue was devoted to mental health and minorities with a cultural competence focus.

Cross Currents

Resources for Cross Cultural Health Care
8915 Sudbury Rd
Silver Spring, MD 20901
301 588-6051
http://www.diversityRx.org

Resources for Cross Cultural Health Care produces this quarterly newsletter, enabling individuals and organizations serving linguistically and culturally diverse populations to stay informed about state-of-the-art practices, training and curriculum reviews, emerging methods and techniques, and government and market forces that have an impact on ethnic communities and health care systems.

Cross Winds

Center for Cross-Cultural Health
410 Church St SE, Ste W-227
Minneapolis, MN 55455
612 624-4668
http://www.umn.edu/ccch

Quarterly newsletter of the Center for Cross-Cultural Health. Provides information and research on the Center's activities, including its participation in developing interpreter standards and in training sessions for an Asian women's health organization and profiles on the Hmong community in Minnesota.

Ethnicity and Disease

The International Society on Hypertension in Blacks
2045 Manchester St, NE
Atlanta, GA 30324
404 875-6263
404 875-6344 Fax
E-mail: ishib@aol.com

A peer-reviewed journal that focuses on the issues of ethnic background and physical conditions.

Ethnicity and Health

Carfax Publishing Co
Customer Services Department
47 Runway Rd, Ste G
Levittown, PA 19057-4700
215 269-0400

Published quarterly, this international academic peer-reviewed journal is designed to meet the fast-growing interest in the health of ethnic groups worldwide; topics include culture, religion, life-style, and race and ethnicity issues.

Focal Point

Regional Research Institute for Human Services
Box 751
Portland, OR 97207-0751
503 725-4040

This bulletin of the Research and Training Center on Family Support and Children's Mental Health of Portland State University reports on culturally competent organizations and projects.

The Forum Newsletter

Association for Death Education and Counseling
638 Prospect Ave
Hartford, CT 06105-4250
860 586-7503
http://www.ADEC.org

Published six times per year. An editorial section of the newsletter, *Culture Corner*, is devoted to multicultural issues in contemporary society, providing information of interest about death-related issues from various cultures and ethnic groups.

The HCMS Bulletin

Hennepin County Medical Society
3433 Broadway St NE, Ste 325
Minneapolis, MN 55413-1761
612 623-2881

In 1994, the Intercultural Awareness Task Force of the Hennepin County Medical Society and United Way of Minneapolis created a special issue of *The HCMS Bulletin* that explores cultural diversity and what it means to health care professionals. The issue, "Through the Eyes of Others: Is Health Care Culturally Competent?" includes community profiles of seven cultures as well as presentations on cultural competence and how it affects patient outcomes.

Health Issues: For Children & Youth and their Families

Institute for Health & Disability
Department of Pediatrics
University of Minnesota
Box 721, 420 Delaware St SE
Minneapolis, MN 55455-0392

Newsletter addresses issues pertinent to improving the health and functioning of children and youths up to 24 years of age within their families and communities, with emphasis on cultural diversity.

Illness, Crisis, & Loss

Sage Publications
PO Box 5084
Thousand Oaks, CA 91359
805 499-9774

Quarterly interdisciplinary journal dealing with the psychosocial and ethical issues of life-threatening illness, grief, and crisis.

The Integrative Medicine Consult: The Essential Guide to Integrating Conventional and Complementary Medicine

43 Bowdoin St
Boston, MA 02114
617 720-4080
http://www.onemedicine.com

Integrative Medicine: Integrating Conventional & Alternative Medicine

Elsevier Science
PO Box 945
New York, NY 10159-0945
888 437-4636
http://www.elsevier.com/locate/intmed

Peer-reviewed quarterly journal integrates the best concepts and techniques of a wide variety of health care practices.

Intercultural Press

PO Box 700
Yarmouth, ME 04096
800 370-2665
207 846-5168
http://www.interculturalpress.com

Publishes country-specific guides from countries ranging from the former Soviet bloc to Thailand.

Journal of Aging and Ethnicity

Springer Publishing Co
536 Broadway
New York, NY 10012-3955

Multidisciplinary peer-reviewed journal for social scientists, health professionals, educators, and practitioners interested in the relationship between aging and ethnicity. Published three times per year.

Journal of Transcultural Nursing

Editorial Office
360 Maclane St
Palo Alto, CA 94306
877 843-0508

This peer-reviewed, semi-annual publication provides substantive content that focuses on transcultural nursing theory, research, and practice.

Last Acts—Care and Caring at the End of Life
http://www.rwjf.org

A quarterly newsletter, published by the Robert Wood Johnson Foundation, that reports on such issues as the challenge of patient diversity and how cultural difference is relevant to clinical decision making at the end of life.

Many Voices, Many Choices
1445 Market St, #350
Denver, CO 80202
303 820-5635

A periodic newsletter, published by the Colorado Collaboration on End-of-Life Care, that features articles on cultural and spiritual issues.

Medicine & Culture Update: International Differences, Outcomes and Values
Lynn Payer
720 W 181 St, #54
New York, NY 10033-9957

Bimonthly reports on international developments in medicine.

NurseWeek/HealthWeek
NurseWeek Publishing Inc
1156 Aster Ave, Ste C
Sunnyvale, CA 94086
408 249-5877
http://www.nurseweek.com/compinfo/comp.html

Magazines reaching more than 100,000 health professionals every other week, with reports on local, regional, and national issues, including topics on multicultural sensitivity and resources.

Pacesetter
PACER Center
4826 Chicago Ave S
Minneapolis, MN 55417-1098
612 827-2966
http://www.pacer.org

Published by the Parent Advocacy Coalition for Educational Rights, this newsletter by and for parents of children and young adults with disabilities frequently addresses racial/ethnic diversity issues.

Park Ridge Center Bulletin
Park Ridge Center for the Study of Health, Faith, and Ethics
211 E Ontario, Ste 800
Chicago, IL 60611-3215
312 266-2222

Publication of the Park Ridge Center for the Study of Health, Faith, and Ethics, with articles on health, faith, and ethics issues for professionals, clergy, policymakers, ethics committee members, scholars, and the public.

Stroke Matters
The Brain Matters Stroke Initiative
c/o Barksdale Ballard & Co.
8027 Leesburg Pike, Ste 200
Vienna, VA 22182

The official newsletter of The Brain Matters Stroke Initiative. The Initiative has five task forces, including one on diversity. The goal of the Diversity Task Force is to educate culturally diverse audiences about stroke symptoms, treatments, and prevention.

WICHE WestLink
WICHE Mental Health Program
Box 9752
Boulder, CO 80301-9752
303 541-0250

Published three times a year by the Mental Health Program of the Western Interstate Commission for Higher Education (WICHE), *Westlink* includes updates on the WICHE Cultural Competence Project.

Women's Health: Alternative Medicine Report
Mary Ann Liebert, Inc.
2 Madison Ave
Larchmont, NY 10538

Journal Articles

Alternative Medicine and the Conventional Practitioner
W Jonas
JAMA, 1998;279:708-709

American Cancer Society Sets Blueprint for Action Against Prostate Cancer in African Americans
C Marwick
JAMA, 1998;279:418-419

As I Was Dying: An Examination of Classic Literature and Dying
RC Bone
Annals of Internal Medicine, 1996;124:1091-1093

Black-White Disparities in Health Care
Council on Ethical and Judicial Affairs, American Medical Association
JAMA, 1990;263(17):2344-2346

Calibrating the Physician: Personal Awareness and Effective Patient Care
DH Novack, AL Suchman, W Clark, et al
JAMA, 1997;278:502-509

A Clinimetric Approach to the Components of the Patient-Physician Relationship
WH Sledge, AR Feinstein
JAMA, 1997;278:2043-2048

Communicating With Patients Who Have Limited Literacy Skills
National Work Group on Literacy and Health
Journal of Family Practice, Feb 1998;46:168-176

Complementary Medicine in the Surgical Wards
MC Oz, GC Whitworth, EH Liu
JAMA, 1998;279:710-711

A Controlled Trial to Improve Care for Seriously Ill Hospitalized Patients: The Study to Understand Prognoses and Preferences for Outcomes and Risks of Treatment (SUPPORT)
SUPPORT Principal Investigators
JAMA, 1995;274:1591-1598

Courses Involving Complementary and Alternative Medicine at US Medical Schools
MS Wetzel, DM Eisenberg, TJ Kaptchuk
JAMA, 1998;280(9):784-787

Creating a Spirituality Curriculum for Family Practice Residents
HD Silverman
Alternative Therapies in Health and Medicine, 1997;3:54-61

Cultural Components in Response to Pain
M Zborowski
J Soc Issues, 1952;816-30

Cultural Considerations in Promoting Wellness
Collen S Keller, Kathleen R Stevens
Journal of Cardiovascular Nursing, 1997; 11:3

Cultural Context of Medical Practice
MM Clark
Western Journal of Medicine, 1983 (special issue);139:806-810

Cultural Diversity, Folk Medicine, and Alternative Medicine
DJ Hufford
Alternative Therapies in Health and Medicine, 1997;3:78-80

Cultural Diversity—Changing the Context of Medical Practice
JC Barker
Western Journal of Medicine, 1992;157(special issue):248-254

Cultural Influences in Community Participation in Health
L Stone
Social Science and Medicine, 1992;35:409-417

Cultural Influences in "Noncompliant" Behavior and Decision Making
CV Charonko
Holistic Nursing Practice, 1992;6:73-78

The Cultural Meanings and Social Uses of Illnesses
AL Kleinman
J Fam Prac, 1983;16:539-545

Cultural Perspectives on Mental Health
M Kohl
Alternative & Complementary Therapies, 1998:4(4):236-240

Cultural-Sensitivity Training in US Medical Schools
CK Lum, SG Korenman
Academic Medicine, 1994;69:239-241

Culture and Clinical Care: Folk Illness Beliefs and Behaviors and Their Implications for Health Care Delivery
LM Pachter
JAMA, 1994;271(9):690-694

Culture and Illness and Care: Clinical Lessons From Anthropologic Cross Cultural Research
AL Kleinman, L Eisenberg, B Good
Annals of Internal Medicine, 1978;88:251-258

Culture, Family Medicine and Society
RP Steiner
American Family Physician, 1992;46:1398-1400

Cross-Cultural Medicine Decoded: Learning About "Us" in the Act of Learning About "Them"
L Marcus, A Marcus
Family Medicine, 1988;20:449-457

A Curriculum for Multicultural Education in Family Medicine
KA Cullhane-Pera, C Reif, NJ Baker, R Kassekert
Educational Research and Methods, 1997;29:771-775

Defining and Evaluating Physician Competence in End-of-Life Patient Care: A Matter of Awareness and Emphasis
LL Blank
Western Journal of Medicine, 1995;163 (special issue):297-301

A Developmental Model of Ethnosensitivity in Family Practice
JM Borkan, JO Neher
Family Medicine, 1991;23:212-217.

Diagnostic Treatment Differences Among Five Ethnic Groups
JH Flaskerud
Psychological Report, 1986;58:219-235

(Dis)respect and Black Mortality
BP Kennedy et al
Ethnicity and Disease, 1997;7:207-214

Effect of Ethnicity on Physician Estimates of Pain Severity in Patients With Isolated Extremity Trauma
KH Todd, T Lee, JR Hoffman
JAMA, 1994; 271:925-928

The Effectiveness of Intensive Training for Residents in Interviewing: A Randomized, Controlled Study
RC Smith, JS Lyles, et al
Annals of Internal Medicine, 1998;128:118-126

Ethical Issues in Managed Care
Council on Ethical and Judicial Affairs, American Medical Association
JAMA, 1995;273:330-335

Ethnic and Racial Differences in Response to Medicines: Preserving Individualized Therapy in Managed Pharmaceutical Programs
RA Levy
Pharmaceutical Medicine, 1993;7:139-165

Ethnic Differences in Insulin Resistance and its Consequences in Older Mexican Americans and Non-Hispanic White Women
MA Aguirre et al
Journal of Gerontolology, 1997;52A(1):M56-M60

Ethnic Variation in the Chronic Pain Experience
MS Bates, WT Edwards
Ethnicity Dis, 1992;2:63-83

Ethnicity and Attitudes Toward Patient Autonomy
LJ Blackhall, ST Murphy, et al
JAMA, 1995;274:820-825

Ethnicity as a Risk Factor for Inadequate Emergency Department Analgesia
KH Todd, N Samaroo, JR Hoffman
JAMA, 1993;269:1537-1539

Evaluating the Alternatives
JH Lin
JAMA, 1998;279:706

Evaluating the Impact of Multicultural Counseling Training
M D'Andrea, R Heck
Journal of Counseling and Development, 1991;70:143-150

Folk Medical Beliefs and Their Implications for Care of Patients: A Review Based on Studies Among Black Americans
LF Snow
Annals of Internal Medicine, 1974;81:82-96

Gender in Medicine: The Views of First and Fifth Year Medical Students
D Field, A Lennox
Med Educ, 1996;30:246-252

Health-Related Behaviors of Women Physicians Vs Other Women in the United States
Archives of Internal Medicine, 1998;158:342-348

Homeopathy: Another Tool in the Bag
MA Johnson
JAMA, 1998;279:707

Influence of Ethnicity on Advance Directives and End-of-Life Decisions
LJ Romero et al
JAMA, 1997;277:298

The Influence of Gender on Physician Practice Style
KD Bertakis, LC Helms, EJ Callahan, R Azari, JA Robbins
Med Care, 1995;33:407-416

Influence of Socioeconomic and Cultural Factors on Racial Differences in Late-Stage Presentation of Breast Cancer
DR Lannin, et al
JAMA, 1998;279(22):1801-1807

Informed Consent, Cultural Sensitivity, and Respect for Persons
LO Gostin
JAMA, 1995;274:844-845

Language Barriers in Medicine in the United States
S Woloshin, NA Bickell, et al
JAMA, 1995;273:724-728

Living With Disability: A Proposal for Medical Education
A Conill
JAMA, 1998;279:83

Malpractice, Patient Satisfaction, and Physician-Patient Communication
T Peskin, C Micklitsch, et al
JAMA, 1995;274:22-24

Managing Diversity in Hospitals
RH Schwartz, DB Sullivan
Health Care Management Review,
1993;18(2):51-56

Managing Personal and Professional Boundaries: How to Make the Physician's Own Issue a Resource in Patient Care
SH McDaniel, TL Campbell, B Seaburn
Fam Syst Med, 1989;7:1-12

MD Programs in the United States With Complementary and Alternative Medicine Education: An Ongoing Listing
B Bhattacharya
Journal of Alternative and Complementary Medicine, 1998;4(3):325-335

Medical Disclosure and Refugees: Telling Bad News to Ethiopian Patients
Y Beyene
Western Journal of Medicine, 1992;157:328-332

Medical Interviewing and Interpersonal Skills Teaching In US Medical Schools: Progress, Problems, and Promise
DH Novack, G Volk, DA Drossman, M Lipkin Jr
JAMA, 1993;269:2101-2105

A Model of Empathic Communication in the Medical Interview
AL Suchman, K Markakis, HB Beckman, R Frankel
JAMA, 1997;277:678-682

Native American Medicine: Traditional Healing
C Avery
JAMA, 1991;265:2271-2273

Nursing in Today's Multicultural Society: A Transcultural Perspective
A Lea
Journal of Advanced Nursing, 1994;20:307-313

Patient-Centered Medicine: A Professional Evolution
C Laine, F Davidoff
JAMA, 1996;275:152-156

Patient-Physician Covenant
R Crawshaw, DE Rogers, et al
JAMA, 1995;273:1553

Patient-Physician Negotiation
M Bernarde, E Mayerson
JAMA, 1978;239:1413-1415

The Patient-Physician Relationship: JAMA Focuses on the Center for Medicine
RM Glass
JAMA, 1996;275:147-148

Patients Lack of Literacy May Contribute to Billions of Dollars in Higher Hospital Costs
C Marwick
JAMA, 1997;278:971-972

Physician-Patient Communication: The Relationship with Malpractice Claims Among Primary Care Physicians and Surgeons
W Levinson, DL Roter, et al
JAMA, 1997;277:553-559

Physician's Emotional Reactions to Patients: Recognizing and Managing Countertransference
AA Marshall, RC Smith
American Journal of Gastroenterology, 1995;90:4-8

Preserving the Physician-Patient Relationship in the Era of Managed Care
EJ Emanuel, NN Dubler
JAMA, 1995;273:323-329

Racial and Ethnic Disparities in the Use of Cardiovascular Procedures: Associations With Type of Health Insurance
DM Carlisle, BD Leake, MF Shapiro
American Journal of Public Health, 1997;87(2):263-267

Racial Variation in the Use of Coronary-Revascularization Procedures. Are the Differences Real? Do they Matter?
ED Peterson, LK Shaw, ER DeLong, et al
N Engl J Med, 1997;336(7):480-486

Refocusing on History-Taking Skills During Internal Medicine Training
GP Schechter, L Blank, HA Godwin, et al
American Journal of Medicine, 1996;101:210-216

Religion and Spirituality in Medicine: Research and Education
JS Levin, DB Larson, CM Puchalski
JAMA, 1997;278:792-793

Sex Differences in Patients' and Physicians' Communication During Primary Care Visits
D Roter, M Lipkin Jr, A Korsgaard
Med Care, 1991;29:1083-1093

Sociocultural Factors in the Use of Prenatal Care Among Women of Minneapolis
MA Spring, PJ Ross, NL Etkins, AS Deinard
American Journal of Public Health, 1995;85:1015-1017

A Teaching Framework for Cross-Cultural Health Care
EA Berlin, WC Fowkes
Western Journal of Medicine, 1983;139:934-938

Through the Eyes of Others: Are You Culturally Competent?
Hennepin County Medical Society, Minneapolis, MN
The HCMS Bulletin, July/August 1994;66(4) (special issue)

Understanding Cultural Difference in Caring for Dying Patients
BA Koenig, J Gates-Williams
Western Journal of Medicine, 1995;163(special issue):244-249

Use of Traditional Health Practices by Southeast Asian Refugees in a Primary Care Clinic
D Buchwald, S Panwala, TM Hooton
Western Journal of Medicine, 1992;156:507-511

The Versatile Doctor's Guide to Ethnic Diversity
N Chesanow
Medical Economics, 1998;75(17):135-146

Western Bioethics on the Navajo Reservation: Benefit or Harm?
JA Carrese, LA Rhodes
JAMA, 1995;274:826-829

Women's Health Care: Cross-Cultural Encounters Within the Medical System

LS Lieberman, EP Stoller, MB Burg

Journal of the Florida Medical Association, 1997;6 (special issue):364-373

Women's Health Care for the Coming Millennium

HW Foster

Journal of the Florida Medical Association, 1997;6 (special issue):358-363

Section IX

Virtual Resources

The American Medical Association, the only professional association detailed in this section, has numerous sites related to the topics and populations included in this *Compendium*. For example, the *American Medical News* site contains reprints of items and editorials related to cultural competence and the International Medical Graduates Section site has the subtitle "Promoting Diversity in Medicine." Because virtual resources with specific Web sites with content related to the cultural competence of physicians were difficult to identify, we invite organizations, federal agencies, educational institutions, and others to provide us with brief descriptions of their resources with such content. The general Web sites for organizations appear in Section I and are not reprinted here.

Readers should look at both the "General Sites" and "Specific Population Sites" categories, because the groups are not mutually exclusive. The titles of some of the following Web sites clearly indicate their relationship to cultural competence topics. Sites with titles that do not reflect cultural or diversity topics contain segments related to specific populations or topics included in this *Compendium*.

Section Contents

A. Web Sites

- American Medical Association Sites
- General Sites
- Specific Population Sites

B. Multimedia Resources

A. Web Sites

American Medical Association Sites

Adolescent Health On-Line

http://www.ama-assn.org/adolhlth/adolhlth.htm

Adolescent Health On-Line, the Web site for the AMA's Child and Adolescent Health Program, is designed to provide information to physicians and teenagers.

AMA Health Insight

http://www.ama-assn.org/consumer.htm

Includes a wealth of consumer information on a variety of health issues, from HIV/AIDS to breast cancer, domestic violence, depression, insomnia, back pain, and more. Divided into four main sections: Specific Conditions, General Health, Family Focus, and Interactive Health.

AMA Health Insight: Family Focus—Adolescent Health

http://www.ama-assn.org/insight/h_focus/adl_hlth/teen/teen.htm

AMA KidsHealth

http://www.ama-assn.org/KidsHealth

American Medical News

http://www.ama-assn.orgpublic/journals/amnews/amnews.htm

Ethics: EPEC Resource Guide

http://www.ama-assn.org/ethic/epec/rgbuffer.htm

Hepatitis C

http://www.ama-assn.org/med-sci/98oct13b.htm

International Medical Graduate Section: Promoting Diversity in Medicine

http://www.ama-assn.org/ama/pub/category/0,1120,17,FF.html

Issues/Advocacy (Section on Medical Schools)

http://www.ama-assn.org/mem-data/special/mdschool/issues.htm

JAMA Information Centers

http://www.ama-assn.org/special/

Easy-to-use, peer-reviewed collections of resources on specific conditions, including HIV/AIDS, asthma, migraine, and women's health.

Minority Physicians Services

http://www.ama-assn.orgmem-data/mimed/mihome.htm

Resources on Alcohol and Tobacco

http://www.ama-assn.org/special/aos/

Talking to Patients About Sex: Training Program for Physicians

http://www.ama-assn.org/mem-data/joint/sex001.htm

Women Physicians Services

http://www.ama-assn.org/mem-data/wmmed/wmhome.htm

General Sites

Alliance of Genetic Support Groups

http://www.geneticalliance.org

American Academy of Environmental Medicine

http://www.aaem.com

American Academy of Family Physicians

http:///www.aafp.org/family/patient.html

American Academy of Oral Medicine

http://www.aaom.org

American Academy of Pain Management

http://www.aapainmanage.org

American Public Health Association

http://www.apha.org

American Self-Help Clearinghouse

http://www.cmhc.com/selfhelp

Better Health

http://www.betterhealth.com/healthwise

Center for Cross Cultural Health

http://www.umn.edu/ccch
Part of the Web site is devoted to "favorite" cross-cultural links.

Central Illinois

http://www.prairienet.org/selfhelp

Community Health/Preventive Medicine

http://www.msm.edu/chpmedept.html

Culture/Nursing—UCSF Nursing Press

http://nurseweb.ucsf.edu/www/book4.htm

Curry School Multicultural Pavilion

http://curry.edschool.virginina.edu

The Curry School of Education of the University of Virginia provides online multicultural resources and links.

Discover with Diversity Rx

http://www.diversityrx.org

A clearinghouse of information addressing the language and cultural needs of minorities, immigrants, and refugees seeking health care.

Diversity Database, University of Maryland

http://www.inform.umd.edu/EdRes/Topic/Diversity/

DiversityWeb Leader's Guide: Curriculum Transformation

http://www.inform.umd.edu/DiversityWeb/Leaders guide/CT/ *(See Section III for a description.)*

Division of General Internal Medicine San Francisco General Hospital

http://www.medicine.ucsf.edu/divisions/

DocTom's Online Self-Care Journal

http://www.healthy.net/othersites/doctom/index.html

drkoop.com

http://www.drkoop.com

Electronic Network of Socio-Cultural Competence in Health Care

http://jonah.creighton.edu/aboutsccnet.htm

Family Services/Self-Help Center of Champaign County

http://www.prairienet.org/selfhelp

General Drug Information

http://www.rxlist.com

Provides general drug information on more than 4,000 US drug products to supplement advice provided by physicians.

Go Ask Alice at Columbia University

http://www.goaskalice.columbia.edu

Health and Literacy Compendium

http://hub1.worlded.org/health/comp/index.html

An annotated bibliography of print and Web-based health materials for use with limited-literacy adults.

Healthfinder

http://www.healthfinder.gov

A gateway Web site linking consumers and professionals to health and human services information from the federal government and its many partners on more than 1,000 topics.

Health Risk Assessment

http://www.youfirst.com

Healthwise Handbook

http://www.betterhealth.com/healthwise

Healthy Living Resource

http://www.thriveonline.com

Illinois Self-Help Coalition

http://www.selfhelp-illinois.org

Inter-Institutional Collaborative Network on End-of-Life Care

http://growthhouse.net/~lastacts

Inter-Links

http://alabanza.com/kabacoff/Interlinks/diversity.html

An Internet navigator, resource locator, and tutorial that includes a Resources for Diversity section and a sampling of ethnicity and culture resource links, such as the African Studies Web, Chicano-LatinoNet, and NativeNet.

Last Acts—Care and Caring at the End of Life

http://www.lastacts.org

Loyola University Medical Center

http://www.lumc.edu/educ/index.htm

Mayo Medical School

http://www.mayo.edu/mms/cur-fac.htm

MCP Hahnemann University School of Medicine

http://www.auhs.edu/medschool/eduprog.html

Medicine on the Net

http://www.mednet-i.com

MedWeb (Emory University)

http://www.MedWeb.Emory.Edu/MedWeb

Milwaukee Area Health Education Center

http://www.medsch.wisc.edu/ahec/mahec.html

Multi-cultural Educational Services

http://www.mcedservices.com

Multilingual Glossary of Medical Terms

http://allserv.rug.ac.be/~rvdstich/eugloss/welcom.html

Technical and popular medical terms in several European languages (Danish, Dutch, English, French, German, Italian, Portuguese, and Spanish) are provided in this glossary developed by the Heymans Institute of Pharmacology, University of Ghent, and Mercator College, Belgium.

National Health Information Center

http://nhic-nt.health.org

National Library of Medicine

http://www.nlm.nih.gov

888 FIND-NLM
301 402-1384 Fax
E-mail: custserv@nlm.nih.gov

The National Library of Medicine's MEDLINEplus, the database used by librarians and health professionals for nearly 30 years, is available at no cost, 24 hours a day, 7 days a week. Two Web-based interfaces for searching MEDLINE are available: PubMed and Internet Grateful Med.

National Multicultural Institute

http://www.nmci.org

National Resources Library

http://www.cyfc.umn.edu/NRL/

New Jersey Medical School—Art of Medicine

http://www.umdnj.edu/njmsweb/educ/course/artmed.htm

New Medicine

http://medworld.biomed.hawaii.edu/prog.html

Nurse Week/Health Week

http://www.nurseweek.com/compinfo/comp.html

Office of Minority Health Resource Center

http://www.omhrc.gov

Established by the Office of Minority Health (OMH) to facilitate the exchange of information and strategies to improve the health status of racial and ethnic minorities, including cultural competence.

One Medicine

http://www.onemedicine.com

PubMed

http://www.ncbi.nlm.nih.gov/PubMed/

This search service of the National Library of Medicine's provides access to over nine million citations in MEDLINE, with links to participating online journals and other related databases. Includes many abstracts on cultural barriers to health care, cross-cultural communication, cultural competence education, multicultural approaches to health care, and cross-ethnic health symptoms that have an impact on compliance.

Resource Bibliography in Cross Cultural Nursing

http://weber.u.washington.edu/~ethnomed/resbib.htm

Reuters Health Information

http://www.reutershealth.com

Robert Wood Johnson Foundation

http://www.rwjf.org

RxList—The Internet Drug Index

http://www.rxlist.com

Search CME Medical Conferences

http://searchcme.com

Self-Help Resource Centre of Greater Toronto

http://www3.sympatico.ca/shrc/ethno.html

Supportive Care of the Dying

http://www.careofdying.org

Has related Internet links, back issues *of Supportive Voice* (the newsletter of Supportive Care of the Dying: A Coalition for Compassionate Care), which emphasizes spiritual issues, caregiver support, and tools to measure the quality of end-of-life care.

thriveonline.com

http://www.thriveonline.com

Provides information to consumers on healthy life-styles, with diet, sports, medicine, and fitness subsections.

Transcultural and Multicultural Health Links

http://www.lib.iun.indiana.edu/trannurs.htm

Comprehensive listing of Web sites with resources for general groups and for religious, ethnic, and special populations groups. Includes links to health profiles, surveys, essays, articles, and position statements. Some topic area links include:

- Cambodian Reproductive Health

- Health and the Amish

- An Islamic Ruling on Brain Death and Life Support: An Overview

- Jehovah's Witnesses and Blood

- Minority and Cultural Issues in Alzheimer's Care

- National Survey of Women's Health

- Tibetan Medicine

UNC-Chapel Hill School of Medicine

http://www.med.unc.edu

University of Iowa

http://www.medicine.uiowa.edu/osac/medcurric.htm

University of Maryland Diversity Database

http://www.inform.umd.edu/EdRes/Topic/Diversity/

Comprehensive index of multicultural and cultural diversity resources, including information specific to categories by age, class, disability, gender, national origin, race, ethnicity, religion, and sexual orientation.

University of Michigan Health System

http://www.med.umich.edu

University of Texas Medical Branch Office of Campus Life

http://ocl.utmb.edu/

University of Washington School of Nursing

http://weber.u.washington.edu/~ethnomed/resbib.htm

An extensive cross-cultural bibliography compiled by Melinda Mich and Noel Chrisman of the School of Nursing.

WebMD

http://my.webmd.com/index.html

Whole Living

http://www.wholeliving.com/

Wisconsin Multiculturalism Web Site

http://www.designwise.net/wis-trec/news1.htm
Stephen Kastner
920 839-2795
920 839-9550 Fax
E-mail: sjk@dcwis.com

Specific Population Sites

Adolescent Health Transition Project

http://weber.u.washington.edu/~healthtr

African American Resources

http://www.rain.org/~kmw/aa.html

Alternative Medicine.Com

http://www.alternativemedicine.com/

Alternative Medicine Connection

http://arxc.com/arxchome.htm

Alternative Therapies in Health and Medicine

http://www.alternative-therapies.com/

Alzheimer's Association

http://www.alz.org

American Academy of Pediatrics

http://www.aap.org

American Academy of Child and Adolescent Psychiatry

http://www.aacap.org

American Academy of Naturopathic Physicians

http://www.aanp.com

American Academy of Pediatrics

http://www.aap.org

American Chiropractic Association

http://www.amerchiro.org

American Geriatrics Society

http://www.americangeriatrics.org

American Holistic Nurses' Association

http://www.ahna.org

American Massage Therapy Association

http://www.amtamassage.org

American Oriental Bodywork Therapy Association

http://www.healthy.net/pan/

American Public Health Association: Children's Health and Advocacy

http://www.apha.org/resources/kids.html

Ask Dr. Weil

http://www.drweil.com

Association for Death Education and Counseling

http://www.adec.org

Cancer Care

http://www.cancercare.org

Offers 1-hour conference calls that provide the latest information from experts in oncology, social work, public policy, and other fields. Teleconference programs feature coping strategies and updates on specific cancers. Register for programs online or by phone at 800 813-HOPE. Also provides information about clinical trials, referrals to related web sites, and online support groups for patients, partners, and bereavement groups.

Center for Complementary and Alternative Medicine Research in Women's Health

http://cpmcnet.columbia.edu/dept/rosenthal/Welcome_Women.html

Computerized Qigong Database

http://www.healthy.net/qigonginstitute/
database.html

DiversityWeb

http://www.inform.umd.edu/Diversityweb/

Dying and Death: Islamic View

http://www.vt.edu:10021/org/islam_sa/death.txt

Islamic Student Assembly, Virginia Polytechnic
Institute and State University

Easter Seals

http://www.seals.com

EthnoMed—Ethnic Medicine Guide

http://www.hslib.washington.edu/clinical/ethnomed/
index.html

Sponsored by the Harborview Medical Center of the
University of Washington; contains information
about cultural beliefs, medical issues, and other
related issues pertinent to the health care of recent
immigrants.

Feldenkrais—Somatic Options

http://www.somatic.com

Gay and Lesbian Medical Association

http://www.glma.org

Health Care for the Homeless Information Resource Center

http://www.prainc.com/hch

HHS Initiative to Eliminate Racial and Ethnic Disparities in Health, US Department of Health and Human Services

http://raceandhealth.hhs.gov

Provides information about opportunities to develop
strategies and implement plans in six health areas:

infant mortality, cancer screening and management,
cardiovascular disease, diabetes, HIV/AIDS, and
immunizations.

Health Promotion Council of Southeastern Pennsylvania

http://www.libertynet.org/hpcpa/

Hispanic Health Course

http://chico.rice.edu/projects/HispanicHealth/
excourse.html

Mental Health Net

http://www.cmhc.com

National Action Plan on Breast Cancer

http://www.napbc.org

The National Clearinghouse for Alcohol and Drug Information

http://www.health.org/DBarea/index.htm
http://www.health.org/multicul/index.htm

Comprehensive clearinghouse offering searchable
databases for bibliographic abstracts pertaining to
all aspects of substance abuse, including culturally
specific approaches to treatment.

NIH Osteoporosis and Related Bone Diseases – National Resource Center

http://www.osteo.org

National Mental Health Consumer's Self-Help Clearinghouse

http://www.mhselfhelp.org

National Mental Health Services Knowledge Exchange Network

http://www.mentalhealth.org

National Organization on Disability

http://www.nod.org

National Osteoporosis Foundation Osteoporosis Patient Information Center (OPIC)

http://www.nof.org

National Resource Library

http://www.cyfc.umn.edu/NRL/

The Institute for Health and Disability's database of information about children and adolescents with disabilities.

The National Women's Health Information Center

800 944-WOMAN
http://www.4woman.org

Access to information from Federal health clearinghouses and hundreds of private sector organizations.

National Women's Health Resource Center

http://www.healthywomen.org

Office of Minority Health

http://www.os.dhhs.gov/progorg/ophs/omh/about.htm

Office of Minority Health Resource Center

http://www.omhrc.gov

Palliative Care Patient and Family Counseling Manual

http://www.aspenpublishers.com

Parent Advocacy Coalition for Educational Rights (PACER)

http:www.pacer.org

Parents Handbooks

http://www.parentshandbooks.org

Patient Resources on the Internet: A Provider to Patient Resource for On-line Disease Management and Personal Health Information, 1998-1999

Faulkner & Gray, 800 535-8403
http://www.faulknergray.com

Physicians' Association for Anthroposophical Medicine

http://www.healthy.net/pan/

Polarity Therapy

http://www.polaritytherapy.org

Psych Central

http://www.psychcentral.com

Recovery Network

http://www.recoverynetwork.com

Religious Needs of the Orthodox Jewish Patient

http://www.shemayisrael.co.il/burial/needs.htm

International Jewish Burial Society

Research and Training Center on Family Support and AMP—Children's Mental Health

http://www.rtc.pdx.edu

Resource Directory for Older People

http://www.aoa.dhhs.gov/aoa/dir/intro.html

Rosenthal Center for Complementary and Alternative Medicine—Research in Women's Health

http://cpmcnet.columbia.edu/dept/rosenthal/

Self-Help & Psychology Magazine

http://www.shpm.com

Self-Help Sourcebook Online

http://www.cmhc.com/selfhelp

Wellness Web Women's Health Center

http://www.wellweb.com/women/woman.htm

Women's Health Issues

http://altmedicine.miningco.com/msub9.htm

Women's Health—Natural & Alternative Approaches

http://www.healthy.net/womenshealth/

B. Multimedia Resources

Communicating Across Cultures

Griggs Publications
302 23rd Ave
San Francisco, CA 94121

A 30-minute video, one of seven produced by Griggs Productions in the "Valuing Diversity" series, which dramatically shows how misunderstandings result from different styles of communication. It also addresses the discomfort people feel when dealing with issues of race and gender and suggests ways to communicate more effectively.

Creating a Multicultural Approach and Environment

American Occupational Therapy Association
1383 Piccard Dr
PO Box 1725
Rockville, MD 20849-1725
301 948-9626

Video offers vignettes of different kinds of clinical situations to improve cultural awareness.

Cross-Cultural Communications

4585 48th St
San Diego, CA 92115
800 858-4478 or 619 583-4478
E-mail: STPhd@aol.com

Offers half- and full-day customized training; books and videos available.

Cultural Assessment

30-minute video, 1997
Medcom
http://www.conceptmedia.com

Cultural Diversity in Physical Therapy

American Physical Therapy Association
1111 N Fairfax St
Alexandria, VA 22314
703 684-2782

A 13-minute video that helps health professionals understand multicultural issues. The video's four vignettes encourage discussion of cultural sensitivity.

Health Videotapes in Multiple Languages

320 623-5478

The Minnesota Department of Health has a variety of multilingual videotapes that are available on loan or for purchase in the following broad categories: general health, women's health, infant and child health, nutrition. Sampling of titles include:

- *Hmong Family Planning*

- *A Visit to the Doctor and A Visit to the Hospital (Cambodian, Hmong, Loatian, Vietnamese and Spanish versions)*

- *A Beautiful Future (Vietnamese)*

- *Before It's Too Late, Vaccinate (Spanish)*

- *Choosing Cambodian Food Wisely*

Office of Minority Health Resource Center

PO Box 37337
Washington, DC 20008-2556
800 444-6472
http://www.omhrc.gov

Extensive repository of cross-cultural documents, books, audiovisual aids, organizations, programs, and funding opportunities by the US Department of Health and Human Services. Materials available specific to African Americans, Asians, Hispanics/Latinos, Native Americans, and Native Hawaiian/Pacific Islanders.

Patient Resources on the Internet: A Provider to Patient Resource for On-line Disease Management and Personal Health, 1998-1999

Faulkner & Gray, 800 535-8403
http://www.faulknergray.com

Includes:

- Keeping Up with Patients On-line

- The Latest in Cyberspace

- Health Care Benefits Move Onto Computer Screens

- Quality of Information on the Internet

- The Web as a Disease Management Tool

- Is the Web Safe Enough?

- Joining the Worldwide Health Care Dialogue

- Web Pages by Providers and Patients

- Preventive Medicine on the Web

- Directory of Consumer Health Resources On-line

Racial and Cultural Bias in Medicine

American Academy of Family Physicians
8880 Ward Pkwy
Kansas City, MO 64114-2797

Video program designed for medical students, resident physicians, and practicing physicians, consisting of 27 dramatized situations on a variety of issues, each of which has some relevance to racial or cultural bias.

Shared Understanding: Bridging Racial and Socioeconomic Differences in Doctor-Patient Communication

Health Sciences Consortium
Chapel Hill, NC
919 942-8731

A 40-minute instructional video based on a cross-cultural medical interview and a bound manual.

Through the Eyes of Others: Is Health Care Culturally Competent?

Hennepin Medical Society
3433 Broadway St, NE, Ste 325
Minneapolis, MN 55413-1761
612 623-2881

A cultural competence education series created by the Intercultural Awareness Task Force of the Hennepin Medical Society and United Way of Minneapolis. The core program is video presentations from representatives of ten cultures plus presentations on cultural competence and how it affects patient outcomes and effective communication using interpreters.

Transcultural Perspectives in Nursing

4 videos
http://www.conceptmedia.com

Section X

Selected AMA Reports, *AMNews* Articles, and AMA Policies

This section contains full-text versions of six AMA reports, seven *American Medical News* articles, and 119 American Medical Association (AMA) policies with relevance to cultural competence. Gathered together under one cover for the first time, these documents provide ample evidence of the breadth and depth of the AMA commitment to cultural competence. (*Note:* Some policies related to special issues in Section IV are not included.)

Section Contents

A. Selected AMA Reports

"Diversity in Medical Education" (available on request)

"Enhancing the Cultural Competence of Physicians"

"Health Literacy"

"Medical Education and Training in Women's Health" (available on request)

"Racial and Ethnic Disparities in Health Care"

"AMA Efforts To Identify and Incorporate Health Needs of Culturally Diverse Populations into Broader Public Health and Community Objectives"

Developed as a presentation summarizing AMA activities related to cultural competence and public health; incorporates much of Racial and Ethnic Disparities in Health Care (BOT Report 50-I-95) and Enhancing the Cultural Competence of Physicians (CME Report 5-A-98)

Diversity in Medical Education

Board of Trustees Report A-99

Being considered at the 1999 Annual Meeting

Enhancing the Cultural Competence of Physicians

Council on Medical Education Report 5-A-98

American Medical Association Policy H-295.905 (*AMA Policy Compendium*), "Promoting Culturally Competent Health Care," calls for the AMA to "encourage medical schools to offer electives in culturally competent health care with the goal of increasing awareness and acceptance of cultural differences between patient and provider." The resolution that established this policy, Resolution 306-A-97, also called on the AMA to "investigate the development of a database for the AMA Homepage addressing the issues of cultural competency in health care." The policy and the directive complement each other: information about medical school electives in culturally competent health care could appear in the proposed database and the database could be an essential resource for these courses. The resolution called for a report of the results of the investigation of the database at the 1998 Annual Meeting of the AMA House of Delegates.

AMA Policy H-350.984 (*AMA Policy Compendium*) expresses zero tolerance of the clearly identified racial and ethnic disparities in health care. Policy H-65.984 and Council on Ethical and Judicial Affairs Opinion E-9.035 (*AMA Policy Compendium*) stress that academic and other medical institutions should offer educational programs about gender and cultural issues to staff, physicians in training, and students. These policies reflect the Association's understanding that knowledge and tolerance of cultural diversity is integral to effective health care delivery and that it must encourage physicians and health care organizations to respond to the social, cultural, economic, and political diversity of their communities, including serious consideration of cultural solutions to illness.

AMA activities to implement its policies include establishing the AMA Minority Affairs Consortium (June 1997). Membership in the Consortium is open to all interested physicians and medical

students, and the participation of ethnic medical associations is also encouraged. The Consortium Governing Committee currently includes formal representation from the National Medical Association, National Hispanic Medical Association, and Association of American Indian Physicians. Consortium goals include the following:

1. monitoring the effects on minority patients of Medicaid/welfare reform and continuing efforts to increase access and maintain quality care for the most vulnerable populations;

2. assisting physicians in developing cultural competency skills;

3. continuing to work with the Federation of medicine to increase the number of minority physicians;

4. monitoring the effects of changes in medical school admission policies and graduate medical education to ensure that additional barriers are not created for minorities; and

5. exploring ways to enhance AMA data on demographic and practice characteristics of minority physicians.

This report responds to Policy H-295.905 and Resolution 306-A-97 by

1. defining "culturally competent health care" as a broad spectrum of attributes;

2. identifying the issues that led to the resolution, including cautions about stereotyping;

3. describing AMA, Federation, and other activities and publications addressing cultural competence issues;

4. describing activities to encourage education and training in culturally competent health care;

5. proposing activities and issues for consideration before work proceeds on the database;

6. presenting recommendations for encouraging education in culturally competent health care and for developing a database and other tools to support physician efforts to improve their management of patients and as a resource for educational activities; and

7. providing a *Sampling of Resources with Cultural Competence Content.* *

1. Defining "Culturally Competent Health Care" as a Broad Spectrum of Attributes

"Culture" as used in this report encompasses more than ethnic, racial, national, and gender designations. The terms "cultural competence" and "culturally competent health care" therefore reflect a broad spectrum of attributes, as indicated in the following definitions:

*   "Complex integration of knowledge, attitudes, and skills that enhances cross-cultural communication and appropriate/effective interactions with others. It includes at least three perspectives:

    1. knowledge of the effects of culture on others' beliefs and behavior,

    2. awareness of one's own cultural attributes and biases and their impact on others, and

---

*   The *Sampling of Resources with Cultural Competence Content* that originally appeared at the end of this document has been incorporated in the *Cultural Competence Compendium,* American Medical Association, June 1999.

3. understanding the impact of the sociopolitical, environmental and economic context on the specific situation." (*Promoting Cultural Competence in and through Nursing Education*, American Academy of Nursing, 1995)

*   "The knowledge and interpersonal skills that allow providers to understand, appreciate, and work with individuals from cultures other than their own. It involves an awareness and acceptance of cultural differences; self-awareness; knowledge of the patient's culture; and adaptation of skills." (*Culturally Competent Health Care for Adolescents,* AMA, 1994)

*   "The delivery of care within the context of appropriate physician knowledge, understanding, and appreciation of cultural distinctions. Such understanding must take into account the beliefs, values, actions, customs, and unique health needs of distinct population groups." (AMA Minority Affairs Consortium, 1997)

*   "A set of congruent behaviors, attitudes, and policies that come together in a system, agency, or among professionals and enables that system, agency, or those professionals to work effectively in cross-cultural situations." (*Towards a Culturally Competent System of Care*, Technical Assistance Center, 1989)

*   "Help that is sensitive and responsive to cultural differences. Caregivers are aware of the impact of their own culture and possess skills that help them provide services that are culturally appropriate in responding to people's unique cultural differences, such as race and ethnicity, national origin, religion, age, gender, sexual orientation, or physical disability. They adapt their skills to fit a family's values and customs." (*Cultural Competence in Serving Children and Adolescents with Mental Health Problems*, Internet Fact Sheet)

*   "Care that takes into account issues related to diversity, marginalization, and vulnerability

due to culture, race, gender, and sexual orientation." (American Academy of Nursing)

- "A competency based on the premise of respect for individual and cultural differences, and an implementation of a trust-promoting method of inquiry." (Diversity Rx Web site)

The definitions have a common explicit or implicit component that culturally competent physicians are able to provide patient-centered care by

1. adjusting their attitudes and behaviors to the needs and desires of different patients and

2. accounting for the impact of emotional, cultural, social, and psychological issues on the main biomedical ailment.

As Dennis Novack, MD, et al, indicated in "Calibrating the Physician: Personal Awareness and Effective Patient Care" (*JAMA*, August 13, 1997), each physician needs "insight into how one's life experiences and emotional makeup affect one's interactions with patients, families and other professionals." The four-part proposed curriculum to enhance physician personal awareness helps to define cultural competence and the training to achieve it, especially the materials related to core beliefs, attitudes, and personal philosophy; influences from family of origin, gender, and socioeconomic status; feelings and emotional response in patient care; and physician self-care. "Support groups, Balint groups, and discussions of meaningful experiences" are recommended for personal assessment. Many of the 142 references, especially those on the physician-patient relationship and respectful communication, emphasize the dependence of an effective physician/patient relationship and patient-centered care on cultural competence.

2. Issues That Led to Resolution 306-A-97, Including Cautions About Stereotyping

The above definitions allude to many of the issues that are currently heightening sensitivity to cultural competence and health care.

Demographic Shifts and Empowerment of Communities of Diversity

Much of the attention to cultural competence is being driven by demographic shifts and the empowerment of communities of diversity. Health care workers are more frequently confronted with the lack of trained medical interpreters for non-English speaking patients, and, increasingly, influential "minority" groups expect providers and facility staff to be culturally sensitive, to reflect diversity themselves, and to be aware of health care problems prevalent among specific populations. These changing demographics and the growing disparities in health status between the dominant society and "minority" populations have been projected, identified, and tracked by decade in the "Healthy People" project. For example, African American men have a 47% higher incidence of prostate cancer and a 128% higher morality rate than comparable groups of white men (*JAMA*, Feb 11, 1998). According to the US Census Bureau, minority populations in the United States will have increased more than 15% between 1990 and the year 2000, with the greatest increase in Hispanic and Asian populations.

In his weekly radio address February 21, 1998, President Clinton proposed a $400 million minority health program, listing a number of serious disorders that disproportionately affect "minority Americans" and declaring that "Racial and ethnic disparities in health are unacceptable in a country that values equality and equal opportunity for all." Health and Human Services Secretary Donna Shalala and Surgeon General David Satcher will lead the effort to abolish disparities between white and minority Americans by the year 2010, with 136 philanthropic organizations set to convene a national conference on "minority health" in the spring of 1998.

This program will likely increase the options available to communities of diversity in selecting health care professionals, providers, and plans, many of whom are already choosing professionals and providers with demonstrated expertise in cross-cultural care. Even health maintenance organizations and insurers are promoting the bridging of cultural gaps as a "way to boost membership, save money and avoid costly medical disasters." More than 400 physicians attended a two-hour workshop for which they received 2% to 5% premium discounts from a medical malpractice insurer.

The Cross-Cultural Health Care Program in Seattle doubled the number of workshops it conducts for doctors and nurses this past year; the 23 workshops drew clients such as Kaiser Permanente and Group Health Cooperative of Puget Sound. Some health plans have voluntarily increased their cultural training for doctors treating the millions of low-income patients who have joined Medicaid HMOs in the last five years, and state regulators, taking steps to ensure that patients with limited English or from nondominant cultures are not neglected, sometimes require interpreters. (*The Wall Street Journal,* September 9, 1997)

Continuous Quality Improvement/Clinical Outcomes

The current emphasis on continuous quality improvement makes it inevitable that satisfactory clinical outcomes will necessitate the provision of culturally effective health care. Demographic changes and participation in insurance programs have led to treatment of a more diverse clientele by "mainstream" health care professionals and providers, which has led to increased attention by those who evaluate the quality and efficiency of linguistically and culturally competent health care. But comprehensive measures of linguistic or cultural competence in health care service delivery have not yet been developed at the national level, and no national studies have been published on the impact of services that enhance linguistic and cultural competence on health care outcomes or systems efficiencies.

In "Women's Health Care: Cross-Cultural Encounters within the Medical System" (*Journal of the Florida Medical Association,* August/September 1997), authors Lieberman, Stroller, and Burg emphasize the relationship

between cultural competence and patient outcomes: "The more a physician knows of the patient's beliefs, communication style, and daily patterns of behavior, the more effective and appropriate the physician-patient encounter will be." Attention to this issue began to appear in journals and other publications in the late 1950s, as researchers presented the results of their studies of health and disease in specific ethnic groups.

By 1981, Alan Harwood was able to cite more than a hundred references in the introductory chapter to *Ethnicity and Medical,* 16 of which were cited as "Guidelines for Culturally Appropriate Health Care." Each of the contributed chapters (on urban Black Americans, Chinese Americans, Haitian Americans, Italian Americans, Mexican Americans, Navajos, and Mainland Puerto Ricans) addressed culture-specific health beliefs and behaviors.

Harwood, like most authors who have developed cultural-specific guides of any kind, strongly cautions against using the document in any way that reflects a stereotypical interpretation of any group, that ignores variation within ethnic groups, or that fails to account for individual patient preferences and needs. In "Recognizing Intraethnic Variation in Clinical Care," Harwood identifies those aspects of ethnic subcultures that are most likely to bear heavily on medical care: "concepts of disease and illness, folk and popular traditions of health care, problems of language and translation, dietary practices, interactional norms, and the role of the family in compliance with long-term treatment" (p 505). Harwood's suggested procedures for responding to the various factors that make folk and popular concepts of disease relevant to medical delivery are applicable nearly 20 years later.

Similar cautions against stereotyping were provided in Elaine Geissler's 1994 *Pocket Guide to Cultural Assessment:* "The reader is *strongly cautioned against* assuming that people from one country or geographic area . . . hold the same beliefs as those held by their neighbors." But she also makes the important point that "Not to use a guide such as this for fear of stereotyping impedes movement toward delivery of culturally relevant health care." Geissler's guide contains information, when available, on the location, major languages, ethnic groups, religions, predominant sick care practices, family role in hospital care, health team relationships, pain reactions, ethnic/race specific or endemic diseases, dominance patterns, eye contact practices, touch practices, perception of time, birth and death rites, food practices and intolerances, infant feeding practices, child rearing practices, and national childhood immunizations for 170 countries.

Attention to clinical outcomes is also evidenced by the number of health-related organizations that have charged special task forces with identifying ways to improve outcomes by providing more culturally competent care, including acknowledging that different methods are needed to disseminate information to different cultures. The Brain Matters Stroke Initiative (instituted in March 1996 by the American Academy of Neurology in partnership with the American Association of Neurological Surgeons, American College of Emergency Physicians, American College of Radiology, American Heart Association, American Society of Neuroimaging, National Institute of Neurological Disorders and Stroke, National Stroke Association, and American Association of Neuroscience Nurses) established five task force committees, including a diversity task force to design public awareness campaigns targeted to people of different races, cultures, gender, and age. Members of the Diversity Task Force are focusing on churches, minority organizations, and community-based groups, are translating the Initiative's public service announcement into different languages, and are distributing multilingual stroke education brochures to community groups.

Areas in Which Patients Need or Want Cross-cultural Understanding

In keeping with the broad definitions presented above, the following areas have been identified as highly important to patients with regard to competent care.

The Importance of and Barriers to Respectful Communication/Language

Because accurate communication is essential to basic, quality health care services, the importance of respectful communication permeates all areas of culturally competent health care. But current medical education and care delivery systems present multiple barriers to such care. Perhaps the most obvious barrier is that of time constraints, convincingly described in "Temporary Matters: The Ethical Consequences of Transient Social Relationships in Medical Training" (Dimitri Christakis, MD, and Chris Feudtner, MD; *JAMA* September 3, 1997).

Even the language used in documenting case histories and in interviewing needs to be examined. "The Language of Medical Case Histories" (William Donnelly, MD; December 1, 1997, *Annals of Internal Medicine*) describes "seven language maladies" that are inappropriately shaping as well as reflecting "the thought, the talk, and the actions of trainees and their teachers" in ways that "derogate, obscure, or simply ignore the person of the patient and much of his or her experience of sickness, disability, and medical care." Dr. Donnelley's seven "remedies" provide a useful guide to respectful communication conducive to culturally competent health care.

Similarly, the January 1998 *Annals of Internal Medicine* laments the paucity of residency training in medical interviewing, "the premier skill in medicine," which "produces the data required for diagnosis more than three fourths of the time, and . . . establishes more diagnoses than physician examination and laboratory data combined." Authors Robert Smith, MD, et al, reported that "an intensive one-month [experiential] training rotation in interviewing improved residents' knowledge about, attitudes toward, and skills in interviewing." A randomized, controlled study design permitted the researchers to differentiate between effects attributable to general residency training and effects specific to the intensive training. The 76-item bibliography, including major publications related to human communication for the past 30 years, indicates increasing attention to psychosocial aspects of care, so important in cultural competence.

Fortunately, a number of recent books and guides are available to assist in overcoming cross-cultural communication language barriers. In 1993, Virginia Ricard identified and developed intercultural communication and interaction skills in valuing, observing, listening, thinking, speaking, and gesturing (*Developing Intercultural Communication Skills*). Other examples include "The Language Link: How to Remove the Communication Barrier" (Carol Berg, Minnesota Department of Health, in the *HCMS Bulletin*). "A Teaching Framework for Cross-cultural Health Care: Application in Family Practice" (*The Western Journal of Medicine*, December 1983), by Elois Berlin, PhD, and William Fowkes, Jr., MD, advocated Listening, Explaining, Acknowledging, Recommending, and Negotiating (LEARN) care issues in conversations with patients. The issue of professionals examining their own beliefs is emphasized, because biases that affect the physician-patient relationship can interfere with the provision of culturally competent care.

Complementary Health Care Practices

The above issues related to respectful communication are directly related to patients who use complementary and alternative health care practices, either as a part of their family or national background or because they believe they are less harmful than "mainstream" medical practices. While Congress and the National Institutes of Health continue to use "alternative," favor seems to be shifting to an "integrative" system that does not call for choosing one system or another. Respectful communication about patient preferences and practices is crucial for adherence to biomedical treatment. Harwood emphasizes the importance of physician understanding of preferences with regard to seemingly minor issues such as injection over oral administration of medication and tablets over capsules, which may be related to cultural experiences.

From the 1970s to the present, researchers have documented the ways in which the biomedical approach to health care precludes or at least inhibits addressing the personal and social concerns confronting patients and their families, some of which are reflected in the use of health care practices that are not respected by mainstream medicine. Since David Eisenberg's frequently

quoted study reported in the *New England Journal of Medicine* in 1993, use of complementary and alternative practices, along with books, journals, and web sites explaining and promoting them, has notably increased. The real issue, as Dr. Walker pointed out in "Delivering Culturally Competent Care in a Multicultural Society," is that physicians must do more than simply know what complementary and alternative practices are being used; they must also acknowledge that health care belief systems "are critical to the patient's healing process."

In the February 1, 1998, issue of the *Annals of Internal Medicine*, Alan Berkenwald, MD, emphasized the importance of attitudes and words that do not alienate the "other." The term "scientific medicine" is rejected because it "lays exclusive claim to a 'scientific' foundation on a body of knowledge . . . chronicled in peer-reviewed journals." But as Berkenwald points out, "alternative practitioners, short on laboratory science but long on case reports, can also point to a historic collection of observations and data," and current support for rigorous clinical studies "may establish a stronger scientific foundations for their work." The term "allopathic" medicine is considered inappropriate because it was established as a contrast to homeopathic medicine, because it has been used with derogatory implications, and because it has "lost its applicability in a world that uses agents created by bioengineers and genetic manipulation."

Spirituality

Frequently included under the category of complementary and alternative practices, the topic of spiritual beliefs and preferences has received recent attention in connection with "comfort care" and decision making at the end of life. Spiritual and religious practices are now being recognized as important in relation to improved outcomes in nonterminal situations. "The Healing Power of Spirituality," Katie Colon's feature story in the December 1996 issue of *Minnesota Medicine*, reports the claim of David Larson, MD, president of the National Institute for Healthcare Research, that although there is mounting evidence "that a positive link exists between a patient's spirituality and that person's recovery and ability to cope with illness,

. . . nearly 90% of physicians do not address their patients' spiritual needs." But centers for spiritual care and healing and lunchtime lectures on spirituality are springing up in places such as Children's Health Care, St. Paul, and the University of Minnesota's Center for Spiritual Care and Healing. Children's Health Care permits shamans for Hmong families, tribal elders for Native Americans, and food and rituals important to Hasidic Jewish families. Classes on religion and medicine are being incorporated into the curricula of medical schools across the country; in 1997, the National Institute for Healthcare Research and the John Templeton Foundation announced $25,000 grants to eight medical schools (*AMNews*, September 15, 1997).

The Catholic Health Association of Wisconsin has developed a six-hour program, including a training manual used by more than a dozen major health care systems across the country. Many of these threads were pulled together at the Third Annual Alternative Therapies Symposium and Exposition, "Integrating Alternative and Spiritual Approaches in Healthcare," with continuing medical education credits designated by the Annenberg Center for Health Sciences. "Spirituality, Cross-Cultural Issues and End of Life Care: Curricular Development," sponsored by the National Institute for Healthcare Research and the Association of American Medical Colleges in March 1998, emphasized the clinical relevance of patient's belief systems and cultural background to treatment and care and the importance of integrating these patient factors in medical school curricula.

End-of–Life Care

"Many Voices, Many Choices," the title of the newsletter of the Colorado Collaboration on End-of-Life Care, indicates the primacy of cultural competence in end-of-life care. In reporting a May 1997 statewide effort to collaboratively address the issues surrounding end-of-life care, the July 1997 newsletter presented the goals identified in the workshop on "Cultural and Spiritual Dimensions of Suffering":

1. develop a resource directory listing individuals and organizations available to help with cultural dimensions of and

provide training related to end-of-life care (including an "interpreter program");

2. teach professionals and groups how to share and pool resources;

3. start a hotline to answer culturally-sensitive questions about advance directives, DNR, etc; and

4. develop programs for use via the Internet.

Although end-of-life care is among the areas in which respect for diversity is receiving the most attention, "Patient Diversity Creates Major Challenges," by Alexandra Mazard, MD (Robert Wood Johnson Foundation quarterly report on its project titled "Last Acts: Care and Caring at the End of Life," August 1997), describes the notable differences between biomedical ethics and practices and the American populace in the areas of "conceptualization of life, personhood, health, illness and death." "Actions that are discordant with the prescripts of western biomedical practices" can result in "coercion masquerading as choice, cultural insensitivity, mistrust and lack of meaningful choice."

Dr. Mazard recommends that "medical professionals familiarize themselves with the literature on cross-cultural issues where religion, gender, age, socioeconomic status, ethnicity, sexual orientation, and acculturation status have been identified as features impacting end-of-life care decisions." Mazard indicates that it is imperative to go beyond identifying group tendencies to individual behavior. The Last Acts Resource Committee on Diversity is charged with helping to integrate the issue of diversity in areas such as culture, ethnicity, disability, and gender as they relate to end-of-life issues.

As did Harwood, medical anthropologist Barbara Koenig, PhD, cautions against using cultural beliefs as "simple predictive variables that can be easily ascertained and inserted into a decision-making algorithm." Since 1992, Dr. Koenig has studied "how cultural difference is relevant to clinical decision making at the end of life." This topic was sensitively depicted by Leslie Blackhall et al in "Ethnicity and Attitudes Toward Patient Autonomy" (*JAMA*, September 13, 1995 – Vol

274, No 10), which illustrates important tenets of a clinical practice sensitive to cultural difference: careful, respectful listening in all situations and, in many situations, an openness to learn from a family, consensus-based approach to decision making.

Literacy/translator service

The importance of having access to accurate translator services was highlighted at the June 3, 1997, national conference on Health Literacy, sponsored by the Center for Health Care Strategies (Princeton NJ) and Pfizer Inc. and attended by 150 representatives from government, insurance, managed care, medical associations, literary groups, foundations, and think tanks (summarized in Medical News & Perspectives, *JAMA*, September 24, 1997). Issues addressed included a description of the impact of functional health illiteracy to the effective flow of information between health care providers and patients and how it complicates the treatment of disease, adversely affecting outcomes (Proceedings, *Health Literacy: A National Conference*).

The National Health Council has two literacy-related programs to help patients navigate successfully within the health care system: "Putting Patients First: Patients' Rights and Responsibilities Program" (involving more than 100 participating organizations) and "Medicine and the Media in the Information Age," (assessing how people receive information and how that information affects subsequent health behaviors). The two Pfizer programs could be considered for the AMA database in the areas of health care literacy, implications for public policy and health plans, and assessment of national readiness.

3. AMA, Federation, and Other Activities and Publications Addressing Cultural Competence Issues

During December 1997, an electronic communication was sent to all employees to solicit information about activities and publications addressing cultural competence issues. Separate solicitations were sent to all AMA staff presumed

to have an interest in this area: women's health and women physicians, minority physicians, international medical graduates, adolescent health, HIV, geriatric health, end-of-life care, physician distribution and practice characteristics, science and medical education staff dealing with alternative and complementary health care practices, and staff responsible for collecting and reporting data. Respondents to the all-employee communication and the separate invitations attended a meeting on December 17, 1997, to explore the individual's or unit's interest in encouraging medical schools to offer electives in culturally competent health care and investigating the development of a database for the AMA home page.

Meeting participants raised the issue of finding a better descriptive term than "cultural competence," such as "culturally effective health care." Because literature searches (print and online) have indicated widespread use and acceptance of "cultural competence" over time, it was decided to retain the term in this report and to allow the House of Delegates to determine its preferred term. It appears that the AMA does not currently have an online database to which information related to enhancing the cultural competence of physicians could be appended. While the AMA has a web site related to women's health, and Minority Services maintains a web site on minority health under "Minority Physicians Services," the AMA does not collect specific information designed to improve cultural competence with those groups or in general. It was agreed that a number of units, such as the Medical Student Section, International Medical Graduate Section, AMA Consortium on Minority Physicians, and American Academy of Pediatrics (with which the AMA has had an ongoing program related to cultural competence), should be integrally involved with enhancing cultural competence.

Invited consultant Daryl Pendleton, PhD, Executive Director, Milwaukee Area Health Education Center (MAHEC), reported on a five-year MAHEC project to assist academic institutions in educating physicians in how to serve increasingly varied and underserved patient populations through development and implementation of cultural competence programs and activities for medical students, family practice residents, and family medicine faculty.

AMA Reports

During late 1997 and early 1998, information was collected by the AMA via the Internet, meetings, telephone, and mail. The results are presented in the *Sampling of Resources with Cultural Competence Content*. Among the most significant AMA activities are "Racial and Ethnic Disparities in Health Care" (Policy H-350-984, *AMA Policy Compendium*, originally Board of Trustees Report 50-I-95) and related ethical opinions. The AMA report condemns in the strongest language the lack of access to services that has deprived segments of our nation of the benefits of advances in medicine and health enjoyed by the dominant population. The report also describes the September 1995 report issued by the Joint Center for Political and Economic Studies, which cites some positive findings, such as evidence that legal actions and government aid have moderately improved the access of minority groups to the health care system.

But negative findings reported in "In the Nation's Interest: Equity in Access to Health Care" demonstrate deplorable disparities. The report cites 25 AMA policies identifying the need to address problems associated with meeting the health care needs of vulnerable racial, social, and ethnic groups and notes that articles with information related to health care disparities in *JAMA* and the *New England Journal of Medicine* for the 10-year period from 1984-1994 cover 66 single-spaced pages.

A related AMA policy, "Racial Disparities in Health Care" (E-9.121, *AMA Policy Compendium*), declares that "Disparities in medical care based on immutable characteristics such as race . . . are unjustifiable and must be eliminated. Physicians should examine their own practices to ensure that racial prejudice does not affect clinical judgment in medical care." The 1995 report on "Racial and Ethnic Disparities in Health Care" summarizes AMA and Federation actions and outreach, including the Advisory Committee on Minority Physicians (now the Consortium on Minority Affairs); the Adolescent Health Initiative; and REACH OUT: Physicians' Initiative to Expand Care to Underserved Americans (of 22 initial

grants, 10 went to local medical societies; of 37 second-phase grants, 14 went to local medical societies). A 1995 AMA survey of more than 2,000 Organized Medical Staff Section members on the subject of racial and ethnic disparities in health care revealed that while only a small percentage of hospitals and other organizations have monitoring mechanisms in place, more than half would consider mechanisms to monitor for variation in the care and delivery and utilization of medical services to patients of specific race or ethnic groups. The 11 recommendations in Board of Trustees Report 50-I-95 were adopted, but most of those that required actions (as opposed to policy statements) have not yet been implemented.

The most visible AMA activities have been in the area of adolescent health, as evidenced by *Culturally Competent Health Care for Adolescents: A Guide for Primary Care Providers* (AMA 1994) and "Developing Culturally Competent Strategies for Adolescents of Color" (in *AMA State-of-the-Art Conference on Adolescent Health Promotion,* (National Center for Education in Maternal and Child Health, 1993). Of the dozens of articles related to health care disparities and cultural competence, "A Clinimetric Approach to the Components of the Patient-Physician Relationship" (*JAMA*, December 17, 1997) and pediatrician Lee Pachter's "Culture and Clinical Care" (*JAMA,* March 2, 1994) are particularly relevant, with comprehensive references.

The AMA also has some existing activities that could be supportive of a cultural competence database. The AMA Minority Affairs Consortium (312 464-4392; see above) has a specific mission "to assist physicians in developing cultural competence skills." The Office of Women and Minority Services maintains a minority web site, "For Physician's Special Interest Groups." The office is in the process of redesigning that site and positioning it as a resource on minority health issues. The Office of Women and Minority Services also staffs a committee that began several years ago to explore with the American Academy of Pediatrics the development of a physician education project on cultural competence. A task force established with representatives of both groups did some preliminary work, including a survey for state medical societies and AAP chapters and a definition for "Culturally Effective

Health Care Delivery." The minority web site would be strengthened by any efforts made to identify resources to enhance the cultural competence of physicians. The Members-Only Web site and the redesigned AMA Web site (*http://www.ama-assn.org*) also present opportunities for incorporating cultural competence content. These include the "Issue of the Month" section, the "What's New" section, profiles of AMA member physicians, the "ethics section," and the modules on Women's Health, Kids' Health, and HIV/AIDS.

Reports and Publications from Other Sources

During the first half of 1998, efforts to identify existing specialty/state society resources addressing cultural competence produced many of the resources cited in the *Sampling of Resources with Cultural Competence Content*. In the late 1970s the *Western Journal of Medicine* began to publish reports in a regular section on "Cross-cultural Medicine," and has since presented the multiple factors related to cultural competence in special theme issues.

In 1983, the *Journal* devoted an entire issue to cross-cultural medicine, with medical anthropologist Margaret Clark, PhD, as special guest editor. Even two decades ago, most major ethnic groups were heavily overrepresented in the Western states. The issues identified as a result of disparities between the cultural backgrounds of patients and practitioners have not changed significantly, and the admonition against lumping rather than individualizing was just as strong as it is in materials appearing today. Language and nonverbal communication patterns is the first category of cultural barriers to clinical care, followed by medical roles and responsibilities, explanatory models of disease, contextual factors, and emotional impact and stigma.

While the issues have remained basically the same, there is currently more attention to the general use of a wider variety of complementary and alternative practices and to issues surrounding end-of-life care than there was even a decade ago. By September 1995, the topic of cultural competence had assumed such importance that in the special end-of-life care issue of the *Western Journal of Medicine*, it was the focus of the first four articles

("Frustrated Mastery—The Cultural Context of Death in America," "Religious Dimensions of Dying and Death," "Patients' Perspective on Dying and on the Care of Dying Patients," and "Understanding Cultural Difference in Caring for Dying Patients") and a part of several others.

The Hennepin County (MN) Medical Society is placing a similar emphasis on this topic. In July/August 1994, the *Special Edition of the HCMS Bulletin* explored "cultural diversity and what it means to health care professionals." Brief, simple community profiles of what is called the Minnesota "tossed salad" are offered for African American, Cambodian, Hmong, Latino, Native American, Russian, and Somali communities (including family structure and roles, interpersonal relationships, communication, religion, health and hygiene, food, holidays and celebrations, dress and personal appearance, history and traditions, and education and cultural values). Diversity is an important issue in Minnesota, where the "minority" population grew 72% between 1980 and 1990, the fourth highest rate of increase in the country. The lead article, by Marvin Brooks, MD, chair of the HCMS Cultural Diversity Task Force, praises his diverse patient mix for bringing "unique cultural gifts as well as different perspectives and news way of healing which . . . can be incorporated into our Western medical mode, much as acupuncture has been over the past several years."

To assist physicians in delivering culturally competent care in a multicultural society, Minnesota has developed a body of literature, community resources, and competent providers that have resulted in gradual improvement in health outcomes for Southeast Asians. Minnesota has developed an "International Clinic," for which Patricia Walker, MD, is the lead physician.

Another excellent example of medical society efforts to improve cultural competence appears in *The Journal of the Florida Medical Association* (August/September 1997). This special issue, devoted to "Women's Health Care for the Coming Millenium," contains "Cross-Cultural Encounters Within the Medical System," with a chart on "Important Features of Physician-Patient Interethnic Communication." If the recom-mendations to develop a database and promote related activities are adopted, our AMA could use federation communication vehicles to identify relevant resources or the extent of interest in a database.

Medical textbooks have also begun to include content related to cultural competence. The 1995 edition of *Mosby's Guide to Physical Examination* includes a full chapter on "Cultural Awareness" (H. M. Sediel, et al). Health and diet practices, ranging from the use of herbs and dietary manipulations to acupuncture and acupressure and spiritual practices involving supernatural intervention, are arranged in chart form for 10 ethnic groups. Information on these kinds of units could be included in the proposed database.

4. Encouraging Education and Training in Culturally Competent Health Care

The ability of academic institutions to prepare medical students and resident physicians to serve an increasingly varied patient population depends on the extent to which faculty and administrators will modify curricula and clinical education to correspond with social change and will help a reasonable portion of students who are not from the dominant culture. While numerous training programs exist in cultural sensitivity (32 are described in "Training in Cultural Sensitivity" in *Cultural Diversity in Nursing: Issues, Strategies, and Outcomes,*" American Academy of Nursing, 1997) and skills development (36 are described in "Models of Organizational Structures and Processes to Improve Organizational Multicultural Competence Training" in *Cultural Diversity in Nursing),* most of them feature a fairly narrow area or a specific nonphysician health care segment. A recent survey revealed that only 30% of urban hospitals have instituted programs to manage workforce diversity ("Managing Diversity: A Senior Management Perspective," P. E. Wallace et al; *Hospital and Health Service Administration 41,* no. 1, 1996). No comprehensive program targeted to enhancing the cultural competence of physicians was identified.

Medical schools and academic health centers throughout the country are offering a wide range of programs to promote enhancing patient outcomes through improved cross-cultural understanding.

Recent offerings include a one-day continuing medical education simulation program sponsored by the University of Oklahoma Health Sciences Center to provide participants with the basic experiential background and motivation to broaden their understanding of various cultures. Much of the current cultural competence training in health care institutions is restricted to one to eight hours of awareness-based training to encourage participants to value diversity by learning about themselves in relation to others who are different in a wide variety of ways, usually with a focus on the broader categories of race/ethnicity, class or occupational levels (providers and support staff), and gender.

The objective of this type of training is to improve cross-cultural communication skills and avoid confrontation. The one-shot, one-hour lecture approach is preferred by busy clinicians because it "leaves their biomedical paradigm intact, and their personal opinions unaltered" (Noel Chrisman, PhD, MPH, "Transforming Health Care through Cultural Competence Training," *Cultural Diversity in Nursing).*

The success of these interventions depends on the extent to which an institutional approach requires universal attendance; otherwise, the message is conveyed that the most privileged groups are not required to change behavior. A second approach to cultural competence training, which can span three days, moves beyond learning about and respecting differences to strengthening the ability of managers to build on the outcomes of the awareness-based sessions. "Managing a Culturally Diverse Workforce" (P. M. Husting; *Nursing Management* 26, no. 8, 1995) includes a four-phase framework for measuring organizational progress in culturally congruent management.

Multicultural education is also beginning to be evaluated. The results of the evaluation of a three-year curriculum implemented by the Minnesota Department of Family and Community Medicine, Regions Hospital, St. Paul Ramsey Family Practice Residency, were positively reported in the November-December 1997 issue of *Family Medicine* in "A Curriculum for Multicultural Education in Family Medicine." Cultural competence curricular objectives were arranged in five levels, and content was integrated through didactic sessions, clinical settings, and community medicine projects.

At least one state—North Carolina—has launched a statewide diversity initiative in the area of public health, after concluding that services or programs geared to African Americans (22% of the state population), Hispanics/Latinos (100,000—growing at three times the rate of other groups), and Native Americans (80,000 reported in the 1990 census) were insufficient. With a consultant from Training Research Development, a private North Carolina group, the North Carolina Office of Minority Health conducted the Organizational Climate Assessment and then developed a guide for cultural diversity training specific to public health, used for pilot training in 1995 and 1996. Train-the-trainer sessions, started in February 1996, are supported by copyrighted guides for facilitators and participants. Because interpreter services were also found to be inadequate, a document titled *Interpreter Services for Hispanic/Latino Clients: Report and Recommendations* was subsequently developed. Ohio, South Carolina, and Pennsylvania have instituted similar programs in the area of families with children needing access to mental health services.

There is less evidence that sponsors of continuing medical education activities are displaying initiative in programs promoting cultural competence or that practicing physicians are convinced that the evolution of health care in our society requires them to individualize continuing medical education activities to improve their ability to provide culturally effective health care.

Nursing and Other Nonphysician Health Professions Organizations

As indicated above, nursing has clearly devoted more attention to cultural competence than organized medicine. Several other health care professional organizations have also developed multicultural resources specifically related to issues special or unique to the profession. For example, the American Speech-Language Hearing Association (ASHA) has a multicultural resource center that remains alert to issues such as the choice of foods for use during swallowing training because they might conflict with a patient's dietary customs and therefore adversely affect clinical

outcomes. Speech therapists unfamiliar with common dialects might embarrass and frustrate clients by insisting on a particular pronunciation in connection with therapy following a stroke. The ASHA web site includes reading lists, a multicultural history and demographic profile of the US regional and social dialects, cultural differences in communication and learning styles, and bibliographies on specific ethnic groups. The ASHA multicultural affairs department lends many of the cited documents; its five cultural caucuses also have information and materials. Although specific information is provided, ASHA emphasizes that it is advocating recognizing and showing respect for differences, not memorization of characteristics.

The American Occupational Therapy Association offers ongoing workshops and continuing education, *Multicultural Education and Resource Guide for Occupational Therapy Educators and Practitioners*, and a video on "Creating a Multicultural Approach and Environment."

Materials developed by the American Physical Therapy Association (APTA) emphasize that understanding a person's cultural background should be part of any clinical interaction, even when that background may appear similar to that of the clinician. The APTA Department of Minority and International Affairs provides a bibliography of minority and cross-cultural materials and distributes a 13-minute video, "Cultural Diversity in Physical Therapy."

The National Association of Social Workers has several books available on cultural diversity, including *Multicultural Issues in Social Work*, and is developing guidelines for cultural competency in social work.

Some organizations, such as Hennepin County (MN) Medical Center, have assigned staff to assist with spoken language interpreter services; state departments of health also have helpful resources, such as the Community Interpreter Services in Minnesota. While interpreter services and translations are mandated in Title VI of the Civil Rights Act of 1964 (42USC 2000d), many physicians depend solely on children, close friends, or relatives of the patient, which may not be appropriate.

5. Proposed Activities and Issues for Consideration Before Work Proceeds on the Database

In response to the first part of Amended Resolution 306-A-97, a number of activities have been continued or initiated to encourage education in culturally competent health care. Resolution 306 reported that only 13 of 98 medical school respondents offered cultural-sensitivity courses to their students. In light of recent attention to this issue, this number has probably increased since that survey was conducted. Medical education staff have provided medical schools and residency program directors with information about the resolution and the recommended activities through items in the *Graduate Medical Education Bulletin* and the *Section on Medical Schools Report.*

If the recommendation to develop the database is adopted, the 1998 survey cycle of medical schools, residency programs, and accredited CME sponsors could ask for general information about education related to cultural competence. Interested parties could contact an AMA location to provide detailed information to be considered for inclusion in a cultural competence database.

Surveys across the continuum of medical education could inquire about instruction that emphasizes the following:

- Important features of physician-patient cross-cultural communication,

- Ethnomedical beliefs and practices that show between-group variation,

- Sociodemographic factors that show within-group variation,

- Personal features that show within-group variation,

- Issues of education, patient recall, adherence, and compliance related to ethnomedical beliefs, sociodemographic factors, and personal features,

- Implications of divergent representations of disease and of chronic vs acute conditions,

- Impact of home remedies and complementary and alternative practices,

- Efficacy of cultural-specific self-care, and

- Role of religious beliefs and spiritual practices.

Medical practitioners and educators face many challenges in becoming prepared to administer humanistic, respectful, and technically competent care to each patient. AMA staff are continuing to explore the practical use of existing resources to promote the cultural competence of physicians and to present these resources through existing databases to serve as tools to be accessed by physicians to improve their ability to care for patients and by educators. Review of the literature (including online resources) will continue to identify resources. But a number of issues should be explored to ensure the most useful presentation of materials.

1. Which would be of most benefit to physicians—a database based on a generic approach, using different cultures to exemplify particular attributes, or on a specific approach, focusing on selected groups and providing a detailed description?

2. How inclusive should the definition of "culture" be that guides the review and selection of materials for the database? Should extra attention be paid to competencies required to provide care to "vulnerable" groups?

3. How much emphasis should be placed on the cultural self-awareness of health providers, without which it would be difficult to achieve the goal of respecting, affirming, and even celebrating differences?

4. How could the database and related educational materials maintain awareness of the need to respond to cultural commonalities and still acknowledge patients as individuals who uniquely interpret and reflect influences of the various cultures that might impact on their health care?

5. What teaching/learning strategies should be
    reflected to accommodate diverse learning
    types and to stimulate creative approaches?
    Specifically, how can interactive modalities
    (perhaps the best way to increase cultural
    competence in practice) be used to provide
    simulated experiential learning?

6. What problem-based case studies, simulations,
    and peer group work should be identified in
    the database or used in related programs?

7. Should the database contain information on
    available clinical experiences in diverse
    community and home settings?

8. Would forming a cultural competence journal
    club be useful to practicing physicians?

9. How can AMA and Federation electronic
    communication be used to promote cultural
    competence in education and practice? Should
    we develop an Internet listserv, Culture-and-
    Physicians (similar to Culture-and-Nursing,
    with more than 200 subscribers worldwide)? A
    "cultural competence" hotline? An ongoing
    feature in *AMNews*?

10. Should the database contain a section on
    encouraging diversity in medical education?
    (The AMA has participated in initiatives with
    the Association for American Medical
    Colleges and conferences sponsored by the
    American Council on Education designed to
    continue the thrust toward diversity that has
    been deflected by recent decisions and
    legislation).

Systematic Approaches To Evaluate a Physician's Competence To Work Cross-culturally

Information about systematic approaches to
evaluate a physician's competence to work cross-
culturally should be considered as part of the
content of the database. Information collection
efforts to date have revealed that the Hennepin
County (MN) Medical Society is among the
organizations that have developed cultural
competence assessment tools. Evelyn Lee, PhD,
identified the knowledge, skills/abilities, and

attitudes that are the "hallmarks of the Culturally
Competent Clinician":

> *Knowledge of*: history and culture of country
> of origin; pertinent psychosocial stresses,
> family life and intergenerational issues;
> culturally acceptable behaviors vs psycho-
> pathology; role of religion; cultural beliefs
> about causes and treatments of disease; and
> differences in disease prevalence and response
> to medicine and other treatments.

> *Skills/Abilities*: interview and assess patients in
> the target language (or via translator);
> communicate with sensitivity to cross-cultural
> issues; avoid under/over diagnosing disease
> states; understand the patient's perspective;
> formulate culturally sensitive treatment plans;
> effectively utilize community resources; and
> act as a role model and advocate for
> bilingual/bicultural staff and patients.

> *Attitudes*: as evidence of understanding,
> acknowledge the degree of differentness
> between patient and physician; to demonstrate
> empathy, recall the patient's history of
> suffering; have patience in shifting away from
> the Western view of time and immediacy;
> respect the importance of culture as a
> determinant of health, the existence of other
> world views regarding health and illness, the
> adaptability and survival skills of patients, the
> influence of religious beliefs on health, and the
> role of bilingual/bicultural staff; and
> demonstrate humor by having the ability to
> laugh with oneself and others.

A comprehensive questionnaire has been
developed by Portland (OR) State University's
Research and Training Center on Family Support
and Children's Mental Health, based on the Child
and Adolescent Service System Program Cultural
Competence Model (Cross, Bazron, Dennis, and
Isaacs, 1989), which describes competency in
terms of attitude, practice, policy, and structure.
The Cultural Competence Self-Assessment
Questionnaire, while used primarily by human
service disciplines, has produced results allowing
organizations to identify their training needs in
improving service delivery, to identify cross-
cultural strengths, and to determine training topics
for service providers.

To support the database, it is proposed that the AMA consider a larger program of Cultural Competence Aids for Physicians to include developing and updating the following:

- Bibliography of electronic databases, books, journals, audio and video tapes, and other print and media products

- National listing of speakers and on-site training courses

- Listing of culture-specific diseases and conditions, values, beliefs, and behaviors

- Samples of listening and interviewing skills for different cultures

- Presentations of the varieties of nonverbal communication, with examples

- Materials related to cultural competence in specific areas of interest to the AMA, such as end-of-life care, religious/spiritual practices, and complementary and alternative health care practices

- Calendar of events

- Searchable Web Links to organization and reference materials

- Statistical information (incidence and mortality; minority populations by state)

- Language references in key languages provided in text and in audio formats that actually pronounce words and phrases

For maximum impact, the database could include training programs to fill in identified gaps and to support physician efforts to assume responsibility for improving their ability to achieve satisfactory clinical outcomes. Issues to be resolved include

1. the location of the web site,

2. identifying expanded potential audiences,

3. establishing the goals of the site,

4. planning the activities needed to accomplish the goals (with costs and timelines), and

5. developing recognition mechanisms, such as continuing medical education credit, a special Physician's Recognition Award acknowledgement, or a credential that could be included in AMA Physician Select.

Recommendations

In view of the complexity of developing a database and ensuring that it is effectively utilized, the Council on Medical Education recommends that the following recommendations be adopted and the remainder of the report be filed:

1. That the American Medical Association (AMA) continue to inform medical schools and residency program directors about activities and resources related to assisting physicians in providing culturally competent health care to patients throughout their life span and encourage them to include the topic of culturally effective health care in their curricula;

2. That the AMA continue research into the need for and effectiveness of training in cultural competence, using existing mechanisms such as the annual medical education surveys and focus groups at regularly scheduled meetings;

3. That an expert national advisory panel be formed (including representation from the AMA Minority Affairs Consortium) to consult on all areas related to enhancing the cultural competence of physicians, including developing a list of resources on cultural competencies for physicians and maintaining it and related resources in an electronic database;

4. That the AMA assist physicians in obtaining information about and/or training in culturally effective health care through development of an annotated resource database on the AMA home page, with information also available through postal distribution on diskette and/or CD-ROM.

That external funding be sought to develop a five-year program for promoting cultural competence in and through the education of physicians, including a critical review and comprehensive plan for action, in collaboration with the AMA Consortium on Minority Affairs and the medical associations that participate in the consortium (National Medical Association, National Hispanic Medical Association, and Association of American Indian Physicians,) the American Medical Women's Association, the American Public Health Association, the American Academy of Pediatrics, and other appropriate groups. The goal of the program would be to restructure the continuum of medical education and staff and faculty development programs to deliberately emphasize cultural competence as part of professional practice.

Health Literacy

Council on Scientific Affairs 1-A-98

Members of the Ad Hoc Committee on Health Literacy, selected by a key informant process, examined the scope and consequences of poor health literacy in the United States, characterized its implications for patients and physicians, and identified policy and research issues.

The literature review included searching the MEDLINE database for January 1966 through October 1, 1996, using the text words health or literacy in the title, abstract, or medical subject heading. The search also included articles published between 1993 and October 1, 1997. Authors of relevant published abstracts were asked to provide manuscripts. Experts in health services research, health education, and medical law identified proprietary and other unpublished references.

Consensus among committee members was reached through review of written materials and telephone and Internet conferencing. All committee members approved the final report.

Members of the Ad Hoc Committee concluded that patients with inadequate health literacy have a complex array of communication difficulties, which may interact to influence health outcome. These patients report worse health status and have less understanding about their medical conditions and treatment. Preliminary studies indicate that inadequate literacy may increase the risk of hospitalization. The Committee concluded that professional and public awareness of the health literacy issue must be increased, beginning with the education of medical students and physicians, including improved patient-physician communication skills. Future research should evaluate optimal methods of screening patients to identify those with poor health literacy, effective health education techniques, outcomes and costs associated with poor health literacy, and understanding the causal pathway of how poor health literacy influences health.

Policy Statements

The following statements, recommended by the Council on Scientific Affairs, were adopted at the 1998 AMA Annual Meeting.

- The AMA recognizes that limited patient literacy is a barrier to effective medical diagnosis and treatment.

- The AMA will work with members of the Federation and other relevant organizations to make the health care community aware that approximately one fourth of the adult population has limited literacy and difficulty understanding both oral and written health care information.

- The AMA encourages the development of undergraduate, graduate, and continuing medical education programs that train physicians to communicate with patients who have limited literacy skills.

- The AMA encourages Medicare and other third-party payers to reimburse for formal patient education programs directed at individuals with limited reading ability.

- The AMA encourages the US Department of Education to include questions regarding health status, health behaviors, and difficulties communicating with health care professionals in the National Adult Literacy Survey of 2002.

- The AMA encourages the allocation of federal and private funds for research on health literacy.

Note: The full text of this report was published in *JAMA,* February 10, 1999; 281:552-557.

Medical Education and Training in Women's Health

CME and CSA Report - A-99

Being considered at the 1999 Annual Meeting

Racial and Ethnic Disparities in Health Care

Board of Trustees Report 50-I-95

Almost thirty years ago and over one hundred years after the end of the Civil War, our nation was confronting head-on the racial hatred that is all too evident in our history. The civil rights movement was in full blossom, blatant segregation was disappearing and many people were smug in the assumption that "we shall overcome." However, while our society did not appear to be agitated on the surface, the reality of persistent racial tension springing from our history of inequality was roiling to the point where actions were about to be taken that would demonstrate the intensity of the need for empowerment in the minority communities.

The summer of 1967 witnessed horrendous examples of racially based disorders in American cities, most notably in Detroit and Newark, and prompted President Johnson to appoint a special commission under the leadership of then Illinois Governor Otto Kerner. The Commission's 1968 report, *Report of the National Advisory Commission on Civil Disorder*, examined the root causes of what *The New York Times* characterized as the "violent racial crisis in America today."

The disparity in meeting the health care needs of the nonwhite population was cited by the Commission as one factor underlying this racial crisis. According to the report:

> The residents of the racial ghetto are significantly less healthy than most other Americans. They suffer from higher mortality rates, higher incidence of major diseases, and lower availability and utilization of medical services.

In calling for action to reverse what the Commission described as the "deepening racial division," the Commission stated: "This is our basic conclusion.

Our nation is moving toward two societies, one black, one white; separate and unequal."

As we approach the end of the millennium, twenty-seven years after this stern harbinger of the future, it is lamentable to note the continued persistence of racial hatred and the fact that in too many aspects of our society the movement toward two societies continues. Even though this period has been marked by advances in medicine and health care that most would have classified as belonging in the realm of science fiction, and where this has resulted in a society that generally is healthier, with people living far longer and being more productive than our counterparts from thirty years ago, racial problems are chronic. As physicians, we are particularly saddened by the fact that one of the most conspicuous of these problems exists under our very noses. One only has to look at the key manifestation that the health system reform debate of last year was trying to address, the lack of access to health care, to see that this symptom is felt far worse in our nation's minority communities.

The Existence of Racial and Ethnic Disparities

A March 20, 1995, Commonwealth Fund study (based on a Louis Harris and Associates survey of 3,789 adults: 1,114 whites, 1,048 African-Americans, 1,001 Hispanics and 632 Asian-Americans, conducted between May 13 and July 28, 1994, with a margin of error of +/- 2%) presented the following findings:

- 31% of minority adults, ages 18-64, do not have insurance, compared with 14% of white adults in the same age group;

- 29% of minorities said they have little or no choice about where to get health care, compared with 16% of whites;

- 56% of minorities receive health insurance coverage from their employers, compared with 66% of whites;

- Lapses in health insurance coverage were more common for minority adults, 20%, than for white adults, 15%, during the past two years;

- Minority adults report more problems with receiving care. 40% say they have "a major problem with having to pay too much for care," compared with 26% of whites;

- 18% of minorities said they have difficulty obtaining specialty care, compared with 8% of whites;

- 21% of minority adults have problems with language differences in receiving care, with about one quarter of those who do not speak English as a first language needing an interpreter when seeking health care services;

- 60% of whites said they are satisfied with their health care, compared with 46% of minorities;

- 15% of adults in all minority groups believe their medical care would have been better if they were of a different race; and

- When asked about quality of life, 36% of minorities report "high" stress levels, compared with 26% of whites.

This information was buttressed by a September 18, 1995, report issued by the Joint Center for Political and Economic Studies (JCPES), titled, "In The Nation's Interest: Equity in Access to Health Care." The study, which was by the Johns Hopkins University School of Hygiene and Public Health with financial support from The Commonwealth Fund,

updated the nation's progress in "reducing . . . barriers" experienced by minority groups in obtaining equitable access to health care. The study's key negative findings include:

- 42% of the 41 million uninsured Americans in 1993 were members of a racial or ethnic minority group;

- A large number of low-income Americans (persons with incomes below 200% of poverty) do not get routine care during the year, with Hispanics and African Americans the "least likely to get such care." In addition, low-income persons, regardless of race, spend more out-of-pocket income (7-11%) on medical expenses than higher income Americans (1-2%);

- "Disparities in health coverage are both geographic- and race-specific." Hispanics in the southern United States are nearly three times as likely to be uninsured as their northeastern counterparts (55% versus 19%), and African Americans in the South are 1.5 times as likely to be uninsured as their counterparts in the northeast (37% versus 25%); and

- Obstacles to care also stem from cultural differences, such as language barriers experienced by Hispanics who speak only Spanish.

The JCPES study does cite some recent progress in the area of minority access to health care. The study's positive findings include:

- Neighborhood clinics and hospital outpatient departments are offering care to minority groups that is "comparable" to services provided by private physicians, and minority groups receiving regular care from such facilities reported access similar to patients with private physicians;

- "Providers who are members of racial/ethnic minority groups appear to be filling a critical void for minority patients"; and

- There is evidence that legal actions and government aid have helped minority groups to "gain a 'foot' in the door of the health care system."

The JCPES study declares that the door has not been "sufficiently" opened, and one of the actions called for in the report is for physicians and other health care providers to "become more sensitive and responsive" to the cultural differences in their patients and that more resources be directed toward strengthening health services such as primary care.

Council on Ethical and Judicial Affairs Report 6-I-95, pending before this meeting of the House of Delegates, highlights the problem of minority population access to cutting-edge care. Similar to the documented under-representation of women in past research protocols, the report cites a lack of minority involvement in such studies. This has immediate ramifications in terms of early access to the care being studied and long-term ramifications regarding the efficacy of the study and future application of the study results. There also appears to be a lag in minority patient access to investigational therapies.

An analysis of infant mortality data, a common measure often cited as evidence of problems in the American health care system, also presents evidence of disparities in care. According to data released last July by the National Center for Health Statistics:

- The infant mortality rate in the last forty years has declined faster for whites than for blacks, with the longstanding disparity actually increasing from 1.6 times the rate for whites in 1950 to 2.2 times the rate in 1991;

- Of the 34,628 infant deaths in 1992, 33%, or 11,427, were black children;

- Japanese, Chinese, Cuban, Central and South American, and Mexican infants in the United States had a significantly lower infant mortality rate than white infants; and

- Puerto Rican, Hawaiian, and American Indian infants had a higher mortality rate than white infants, but a lower rate than black infants.

This is consistent with findings released in a November 1990 informational report from the AMA Council on Scientific Affairs, Infant Mortality and Access to Care. One of the problems directly associated with a higher than necessary infant mortality rate is limited utilization of prenatal care. In citing the fact that the percentage of births to women receiving no prenatal care has increased since 1980, the report makes these points on minority mothers:

- Black women are twice as likely as white women to obtain late or no prenatal care;

- Hispanic women are three times as likely to obtain inadequate or no prenatal care than non-Hispanic white women; and

- American Indian women are more likely than either white or black women to obtain late or no prenatal care at all.

Even though the most frequently cited barrier to prenatal care was financial limitations, all of the evidence shows disparities in care continue to exist even where the financial barriers are eliminated to the greatest extent possible. This is seen through an analysis of the Medicare population and its access to care.

According to a Physician Payment Review Commission's (PPRC) 1992 report, Monitoring Access of Medicare Beneficiaries, "the impact of race on the elderly's access to care is a longstanding concern. An analysis of 1969 HHS data found that the black elderly received substantially less care than average." The PPRC found that this situation continued even under the new physician and hospital payment systems provided under the umbrella of Medicare insurance coverage. This 1992 report states:

Black beneficiaries were approximately 9% less likely to ever see a physician during the year and used about 8% less medical care on average. This included lower use of almost all services, but a substantially higher use of hospital emergency and outpatient departments. In terms of outcomes, black beneficiaries were only slightly more likely to be hospitalized, but were substantially more likely to be admitted on an emergency basis, to be an outlier case, and to die in the hospital. In addition, the overall mortality rate for black beneficiaries was almost 16% higher than for other beneficiaries.

Two years later, in its 1994 report, Monitoring Access of Medicare Beneficiaries, the PPRC found that African American beneficiaries continue to experience access problems. The report also said: "Vulnerable populations also use emergency rooms more than other beneficiaries, suggesting that they may lack a usual source of care." The key point from the PPRC analysis (of the Medicare covered population) is that the disparity in the receipt of care continues even when the primary barrier to care, financial limitations, is addressed. This information is buttressed by a just-released Health Care Financing Administration (HCFA) study, as reported in the November 20, 1995, issue of *AMNews*. While this study also identified access problems for low-income white people, it points out that race is an exacerbating factor. As reported in *AMNews*: "The study notes that for blacks, race and not income appears to be the determining factor on access to care. Like poorer whites and blacks, higher income blacks are less likely to visit the doctors and more likely to use emergency departments than are higher income whites."

While there has been little research into the matter of disparities in care based on health insurance coverage mechanism, there is some preliminary information that disparities continue to exist within the managed care environment. According to a leading researcher writing for the Leonard Davis Institute for Health

Policy, race may be a factor when managed care patients are denied emergency department (ED) care. As published in the October 1995 *LDI Issue Brief*:

"Preliminary studies have found that African Americans are more likely to be denied authorization by their primary care physician, even after adjusting for severity of symptoms. The cause of this association is unclear, but raises substantial concerns about the equity with which gatekeeping is practiced.

- The findings could represent a difference in severity of illness that was inadequately measured by a triage score.

- The race differential could be due to racism on the part of the ED providers or primary care physicians.

- Alternatively, the findings could represent unmeasured racial differences in communication patterns, relationships to doctors, or the quality of doctors."

AMA Policy Addressing Disparities in Care

Racially based disparities in access to care persist even though medicine has made substantial efforts to identify and address the problems associated with meeting the health care needs of those in minority communities. In recent years, there have been substantial policy directives on this issue from organized medicine, and the AMA has a plenitude of policy addressing these issues. Some of the relevant policy, from the *AMA Policy Compendium*:

20.974, AIDS Prevention Through Educational Materials Directed at Minority Populations;

65.990, Civil Rights Restoration;

65.999, Equal Opportunity;

160.959, Health Care Access for the
Inner-City Poor;

200.972, Primary Care Physicians in the Inner
City;

245.986, Infant Mortality in the United States;

350.985, Physicians' Role in Preparing
Minority and Disadvantaged Youth for Careers
in Medicine and the Health Professions;

350.986, Project 3000 by 2000; Medical
Education for Under-Represented Minority
students;

350.987, Hispanic Health in the United States;

350.988, AMA Initiatives Regarding
Minorities;

350.989, Continued AMA Support
for Minority Health Improvement;

350.990, Black-White Disparities in Health
Care;

350.991, Minorities in the Health Professions;

350.992, Indian Health Service Contract Care
Program;

350.993, Minority Physician Manpower;

350.994, Funding for Affirmative Action Programs

350.995, Minority and Economically Disadvantaged
Representation in the Medical Profession;

350.996, Health Care of the American Indian;

350.997, Amalgamation of AMA and NMA;

350.999, Sickle Cell Anemia;

410.995, Participation in the Development of
Practice Guidelines by Individuals Experienced in
the Care of Minority and Indigent Patients;

420.972, Prenatal Services to Prevent Low
Birthweight Infants;

420.995, Medical Care for Indigent and Culturally
Displaced Obstetrical Patients and Their Newborns;

500.992, Tobacco Advertising Directed
to Children, Minorities and Women;

515.979, Violence as a Public Health Issue; and

555.982, Participation of Minorities
in Organized Medicine.

Peer-Reviewed Articles on Disparities in Medical Care Delivery

In addition to the extensive policy of just the AMA
on this issue, there have been volumes written on the
topic of access and disparities in minority medical
care delivery. For the ten-year period of 1984 to
1994, the bibliography of articles published in just
the *Journal of the American Medical Association
(JAMA)* and the *New England Journal of Medicine
(NEJM)* stretches on for sixty-six, single-spaced
pages. Noteworthy studies include:

- Analysis of Quality of Care for Patients Who
  Are Black or Poor in Rural and Urban
  Settings, Kahn KL, Pearson ML, Harrison
  ER, Rogers WH, Brook RH, Desmond K,
  Keller EB, *RAND* (1993).

- Black-White Disparities in Health Care,
  AMA Council on Ethical and Judicial
  Affairs, *JAMA* (1990;2344).

- Differences by Race in the Rates of
  Procedures Performed in Hospitals for
  Medicare Beneficiaries, McBean AM,
  Gornick M, *Health Care Financing Review*
  (Summer 1994;77).

- Implications of Race/Ethnicity for Health
  and Health Care Use: Racial/Ethnic
  Differences in Health Care Utilization of
  Cardiovascular Procedures: A Review of
  the Evidence, Ford ES, Cooper RS, *Health
  Services Research* 30:1 (April 1995, Part II,
  237).

- Income, Race, and Surgery in Maryland,
  Gittelsohn AM, Halpern J, Sanchez RL,

American Journal of Public Health (1991;1435).

- National Comparative Survey of Minority Health Care, *The Commonwealth Fund* (1995).

- Physician Race and Care of Minority and Medically Indigent Patients, Moy E, Bartman BA, *JAMA* (1995;1515).

- Racial Differences in the Elderly's Use of Medical Procedures and Diagnostic Tests, Escarce JL, Epstein KR, Colby DC, Schwartz JS, *American Journal of Public Health* (1993;948).

- Racial Differences in the Use of Drug Therapy for HIV Diseases in an Urban Community, Moore RD, Stanton D, Gopalan R, Chaisson RE, *NEJM* (1994;763).

- Racial Differences in the Use of Invasive Cardiovascular Procedures in the Department of Veterans Affairs Medical System, Whittle J, Conigliaro J, Good CB, Lofgren RP, *NEJM* (1993;621).

- Racial Variation in Cardiac Procedure Use and Survival Following Acute Myocardial Infarction in the Department of Veterans Affairs, Peterson ED, Wright SM, Daily J, Thibault GE, *JAMA* (1994;1175).

- Relationship Between Patient Race and the Intensity of Hospital Service, Yergan J, Flood AB, LoGerfo JP, Diehr P, *Medical Care* (1987;592).

- The Roles of Race and Socioeconomic Factors in Health Service Research, Schulman KA, Rubenstein LE, Chesley FD, Eisenberg JM, *Health Services Research* (1995).

More specifically, the literature clearly identifies four conditions in which the patient's race represented a significant characteristic in determining the type and amount of care provided:

1. Pneumonia. In 1987, Yergen et al documented that, once hospitalized and after adjusting for length of stay and quality of care, nonwhite patients suffering from pneumonia received fewer services, fewer consultations and less intensive care.

2. Cardiovascular Procedures. Whittle et al in 1993, found race related inequities in the Veterans Administration system when studying the use of invasive cardiovascular procedures. White patients were more likely than blacks to undergo invasive cardiac procedures, including cardiac catheterization, PTCA and CABG. Similar findings were present in the Ford and Cooper study of the private sector published in 1995.

3. HIV. Black patients were significantly less likely than whites to receive anti-retroviral therapy or PCP prophylaxis when first referred to an HIV clinic in Moore's study for the *NEJM*, 1994.

4. Kidney Disease. The AMA Council on Ethical and Judicial Affairs in 1990 chronicled other studies indicating black-white disparities in care among patients with kidney disease, including long-term hemodialysis or kidney transplants. This report also included evidence of racial disparities in general internal medicine and obstetrical care.

Ethical Opinion on Disparities in Care

Even if disparities in care are subtle differences that are difficult to identify in a small mix of patients, such as a single medical practice or even a hospital may see, the reality of the problem is too large to ignore. The existence of ethnic and racial disparities needs to be acknowledged, and this acknowledgment carries the responsibility of action to work for the elimination of disparities. Physicians operate under an ethical edict that in very clear terms sets out how they must respond to this problem. The AMA Council on Ethical and Judicial Affairs Opinion 9.121, Racial Disparities in Health Care, reads as follows:

Disparities in medical care based on immutable characteristics such as race must be avoided. Whether such disparities in health care are caused by treatment decisions, differences in income and education, sociocultural factors, or failures by the medical profession, they are unjustifiable and must be eliminated. Physicians should examine their own practices to ensure that racial prejudice does not affect clinical judgment in medical care.

The problem of meeting the health care needs of our minority populations is undeniable. For all of the policy pronouncements and actions to date, the impact unfortunately has been minimal. While it is far easier today to point to examples of success, those examples still turn out to be isolated instances that seem to only address the portion of the iceberg, this collective national shame of neglect, that is visible above the waterline. More needs to be done and the time to begin action is yesterday, now, and in the future. The key is action. We can no longer afford to wait until we get another wake-up call like the one that instituted the Kerner Commission.

AMA Actions

The AMA has taken actions in the past that range from steps to provide care for minority populations to setting the stage for more action in the future. Some of these actions include

- Project USA: This initiative, founded in 1973 under a government contract, has allowed the AMA to place approximately 7,750 physicians in short-duration positions at sites throughout the country primarily serving minority populations. Most of the postings have been to positions in the Indian Health Service.

- Advisory Committee on Minority Physicians: The goal of this committee, founded in 1992, is to formally embody the AMA's organization-wide commitment to take a leading role in improving minority health, increase the number of practicing minority physicians, and expand the role and influence of minorities in organized medicine.

- Adolescent Health Initiative: Recognizing the unique health care needs of the adolescent population, the AMA formed the Department of Adolescent Health in 1988. As part of its activities, the Department reaches out to practitioners to help them in meeting the care needs of this population. In 1994, the Department published a guide for primary care practitioners, *Culturally Competent Health Care for Adolescents*, designed to "facilitate delivery of health care that is individualized to take into account cultural, socioeconomic and other differences between patient and provider."

The key to these directions is that they all seek to influence the delivery of care at the local level. While the AMA will continue to take the lead, the solutions will have to be local. The fact that disparities in meeting minority health care needs continues under the umbrella of essentially universal health care coverage for the Medicare population speaks to why the answers must be found locally. According to our Committee on Minority Physicians:

> Ultimately, however, much of the responsibility for finding and implementing solutions rests with every individual physician. The opportunities are many: from personal efforts, such as encouraging minority students to enter medicine and developing a greater degree of sensitivity to the cultural distinctions among minorities, to broader initiatives, such as improving access to and quality of health care for minorities and identifying and eliminating institutionalized racism and discrimination in the health care system.

Federation Outreach

Robert Wood Johnson Initiative: The AMA and organized medicine are involved with the Robert Wood Johnson Foundation initiative "REACH OUT: Physicians' Initiative to Expand Care to Underserved Americans." REACH OUT is a major national effort to mobilize private physicians to improve care for the underserved at the local level. Of the twenty-two initial grants made under this program, it is noted with pride that ten of the grants went to local medical societies. (Medical society recipients of grants include Sacramento-El Dorado County, California; Colorado Chapter of the American Academy of Pediatrics; Capital Medical Society, Florida; Jefferson County Medical Society, Kentucky; Kalamazoo Academy of Medicine, Michigan; Lancaster County Medical Society, Nebraska; Buncombe County Medical Society, North Carolina; Montgomery County Medical Society, Ohio; Academy of Medicine of Toledo, Ohio; and Lane County Medical Society, Oregon.)

On August 7, 1995, the Robert Wood Johnson Foundation announced the awarding of thirty-seven grants for the second phase of the REACH OUT program. Again, local medical societies continue to exert a prominent role, with 14 of the grants going to local medical societies. (Medical society recipients of grants include Sacramento-El Dorado County, California; Colorado Chapter of the American Academy of Pediatrics; Capital Medical Society, Florida; Jefferson County Medical Society, Kentucky; Kalamazoo Academy of Medicine, Michigan; Lancaster County Medical Society, Nebraska; Buncombe County Medical Society, North Carolina; Reach Out of Montgomery County (successor to Montgomery County Medical Society), Ohio; Academy of Medicine of Toledo and Lucas County, Ohio; Lane County Medical Society, Oregon; C. V. Roman Medical Society [Dallas], Texas; Arizona Chapter of the American Academy of Pediatrics; Worcester District Medical Society, Massachusetts; and Rock County Medical Society, Wisconsin.)

Leadership: Another reason the AMA expects to have a significant impact on this imposing issue is the historic presence of AMA President Lonnie R. Bristow, MD, the first African-American to assume Medicine's leadership position. When Dr. Bristow began his term as AMA President last June, he

identified a series of "problems left to solve," and cited "addressing the specific health needs of minority Americans."

Organized Medical Staff Section Survey: Since Dr. Bristow became president, the AMA has surveyed over 2,000 Organized Medical Staff Section members with a survey headed Survey of Racial and Ethnic Disparities in Health Care. In addition to sensitizing physicians and others on this issue, the primary goal of the initial survey was to ascertain the extent of processes to identify and act on disparities in care, and the willingness to establish such monitoring and action mechanisms. While this survey found only a small percentage of hospitals and other organizations have monitoring mechanisms in place, it also found that over half of the organizations would consider developing mechanisms to monitor for variations in the care delivery and utilization of medical services to patients of different race or ethnicity. The survey also identified clear roles for the AMA and the state and local medical societies in working to address and eliminate care disparities.

Conclusion

In conclusion, the task is before our AMA and every physician to help address the terrible problem of racial and ethnic disparities in health care. Both short- and long-term approaches to this problem will be required. Short-term goals that already are being addressed include sensitizing physicians and others to this problem; trying to determine the extent of the problem on a national and organizational basis; encouraging the establishment of monitoring mechanisms to identify and eliminate the problem to the extent possible; identifying successful model programs already in place to address the problems; and educating and motivating others to adopt appropriate models in their communities and practice settings. The ultimate long-term goal is to eliminate racial and ethnic disparities in care. This will require an ongoing effort that will include the development of measuring tools, recommendations for local action, and continual reporting to prevent this nightmare within our health care system from being overlooked.

While the AMA and organized medicine can provide the push, the solution must come from local action. The time to move away from societal divergence is past due, and it is time for us to make sure that Medicine's house, meeting the health care needs of the American people, all of the people, is in order. It is time to stake out a position of zero tolerance toward disparities in care.

Recommendations

The Board of Trustees recommends that the following recommendations be adopted:

1. That the AMA maintain a position of zero tolerance toward racially or culturally based disparities in care;

2. That the AMA complete a Policy Consolidation of AMA Policy relating to meeting the health care needs of minority patients and communities for consideration at the 1996 Interim Meeting;

3. That the AMA continue to support physician cultural awareness initiatives and related consumer education activities, such as the publication Culturally Competent Health Care for Adolescents, and that the AMA develop a series of publications on culturally competent health care;

4. That, where relevant, the AMA consider and comment on the impact on minority populations in testifying before Congress and in commenting on regulatory proposals;

5. That the AMA develop assessment tools to enable individual physicians and groups of physicians to identify and act on care disparities;

6. That the AMA encourage individuals to report physicians to local medical societies where racial or ethnic discrimination is suspected and that the AMA develop a process to be used by local medical societies in instances where they are told of physicians operating in violation of Ethical Opinion 9.12;

7. That the AMA continue to strengthen relationships with organizations representing minority physicians, including the National Medical Association;

8. That the AMA communicate its policies relating to meeting the health care needs of minority populations to the Office of Minority Health, Department of Health and Human Services, and initiate and maintain a two-way line of communications with this Office;

9. That the AMA develop, possibly with data pooled from hospitals and other sources, and regularly use a survey instrument to identify the degree of racial and ethnic disparities in health care;

10. That the AMA regularly monitor and report on progress being made to address racial and ethnic disparities in care; and

11. That the AMA disseminate this report throughout the Federation with a request that it be distributed to local physicians and serve as the basis for organized discussions.

AMA Efforts to Identify and Incorporate Health Needs of Culturally Diverse Populations into Broader Public Health and Community Objective

Hannah L. Hedrick, PhD, Medical Education Products
Bruce Blehart, Health Law
Michael J. Scotti, Jr., MD, Vice President for Medical Education
September 1998

Note: This report integrates much of Board of Trustees Report 50-I-95 and Council on Medical Education Report 5-A-98

The 1968 *Report of the National Advisory Commission on Civil Disorder* established beyond doubt that disparity in meeting the health care needs of nonwhite, nonmajority populations was a major factor underlying the disorders: "The residents of the racial ghetto are significantly less healthy than most other Americans. They suffer from higher mortality rates, higher incidence of major diseases, and lower availability and utilization of medical services."

That these disparities persist in multiple individual and community health markers is all the more lamentable, given the remarkable advances in medicine and technology that are enabling many people in the United States to live longer, healthier, and more productive lives.

In recent years, the American Medical Association (AMA) has intensified its efforts to research and combat the unmet health needs of culturally diverse populations, with the following outcomes:

I.   AMA reports to educate members about the unmet health needs of culturally diverse populations, especially in the areas of prenatal care, high infant mortality rates, and inadequate access to elder care;

II.   Ethical opinions, policies, and activities to identify and address unmet needs; and

III. An association-wide effort to enhance the cultural competence of physicians, including developing an annotated online and print resource list.

AMA Reports Educate Members About Unmet Health Needs

1990: Disparities in Prenatal Care and Higher Infant Mortality Rates

Important findings were released in a November 1990 informational report from the AMA Council on Scientific Affairs (CSA), "Infant Mortality and Access to Care." One of the problems directly associated with a higher than necessary infant mortality rate was limited utilization of prenatal care in general and alarming disparities among particular groups. The CSA reported that black women were twice as likely as white women to obtain late or no prenatal care; Hispanic women were three times as likely as non-Hispanic white women to obtain inadequate or no prenatal care; and American Indian women were more likely than either white or black women to obtain late or no prenatal care at all.

A 1993 analysis of 1991 infant mortality data released by the National Center for Health Statistics indicated that the long-standing disparity in infant mortality actually increased from 1.6 times the rate for whites in 1950 to 2.2 times the rate in 1991. Of the 34,628 infant deaths in 1992, 33%, or 11,427, were black children. Puerto Rican, Hawaiian, and American Indian infants had a higher mortality rate than white infants, but a lower rate than black infants. Even though the most frequently cited barrier to prenatal care was financial limitations, all of the evidence shows disparities in care continue to exist even when the financial barriers are eliminated to the greatest extent possible.

1995: Inadequate Access to Health Care Continues

In 1995, the AMA repeatedly pointed out that lack of access to health care was far more serious in our nation's minority communities than in the country in general. The AMA Board of Trustees informed its House of Delegates of the disturbing findings from a March 20, 1995, report by the Commonwealth Fund (based on a 1994 Louis Harris and Associates survey of 3,789 adults: 1,114 whites, 1,048 African-Americans, 1,001 Hispanics and 632 Asian-Americans). A September report issued by the Joint Center for Political and Economic Studies, "In the Nation's Interest: Equity in Access to Health Care," presented similarly negative findings:

- Of the 41 million uninsured Americans in 1993, 42% were members of a racial or ethnic minority group.

- A large number of persons with incomes below 200% of the poverty level did not get routine care during the year, with Hispanics and African Americans the "least likely to get such care." Low-income persons, regardless of race, spent more out-of-pocket income (7-11%) on medical expenses than higher income Americans (1-2%).

- Disparities in health coverage are both geographic- and race-specific. Hispanics in the South were nearly three times as likely to be uninsured as their Northeastern counterparts (55% versus 19%), and African Americans in the South were 1.5 times as likely to be uninsured as their counterparts in the Northeast (37% vs 25%).

- Language barriers, such as those experienced by Hispanics who speak only Spanish, also formed obstacles to care.

The Joint Center for Political and Economic Studies did cite some progress. Neighborhood clinics and hospital outpatient departments were offering care to minority groups that was "comparable" to services provided by private physicians, and minority groups receiving regular care from such facilities reported access similar to patients with private physicians. The AMA has paid particular attention to the finding that "Providers who are members of racial/ethnic minority groups appear to be filling a critical void for minority patients."

The AMA has responded to the call of the Joint Center for physicians and other health care providers to "become more sensitive and responsive" to the cultural differences in their patients and for more resources to be directed toward strengthening health services such as primary care. At the December 1995 AMA Interim Meeting, the Council on Ethical and Judicial Affairs (CEJA) highlighted the problem of access by minority populations to cutting-edge care. The CEJA report cited a lack of minority involvement in research protocols and access to investigational therapies. This underinvolvement has ramifications in terms of early access to care and of the efficacy and future application of study results.

Inadequate Access to Care by the Elderly Continues Under New Payment Systems

According to a Physician Payment Review Commission (PPRC) 1992 report, "Monitoring Access of Medicare Beneficiaries," data in 1969 indicated that black elderly people received substantially less care than average, and this situation continued even under the new physician and hospital payment systems provided under the umbrella of Medicare insurance coverage. While use of almost all services was less, there was a substantially higher use of hospital emergency and outpatient departments, and black Medicare beneficiaries were substantially more likely to die in the hospital. In addition, the overall mortality rate for black beneficiaries was almost 16% higher than for other beneficiaries.

Distressingly, the disparity in the receipt of care continued in 1994, even when the primary barrier to care, financial limitations, was addressed. A study by the Health Care Financing Administration (HCFA), as reported in the November 20, 1995, issue of *AMNews*, pointed out that "for blacks, race and not income appears to be the determining factor on access to care. Like poorer whites and blacks, higher income blacks are less likely to visit the doctors and more likely to use emergency departments than are higher income whites."

Disparities continue to exist within the managed care environment. In 1995, preliminary evidence presented by the Leonard Davis Institute for Health Policy suggested that race may be a factor when managed care patients are denied emergency department (ED) care (October 1995 *LDI Issue Brief*). These findings raised substantial concerns about the equity of managed care gatekeeping practices.

II. AMA Ethical Opinions, Policies, and Activities Address Unmet Needs

Physicians operate under an ethical edict, AMA Council on Ethical and Judicial Affairs Opinion 9.121, Racial Disparities in Health Care, which requires very clear actions:

> *Disparities in medical care based on immutable characteristics such as race must be avoided. Whether such disparities in health care are caused by treatment decisions, differences in income and education, sociocultural factors, or failures by the medical profession, they are unjustifiable and must be eliminated. Physicians should examine their own practices to ensure that racial prejudice does not affect clinical judgment in medical care.*

The AMA continues to prepare reports and develop policy to inform members and guide activities related to the health needs of diverse populations.

Directives to Enhance the Cultural Competence of Physicians

AMA policies are used to guide practice, educational, legislative, and advocacy activities. For example, during the 1998 AMA Annual Meeting, recommendations were adopted from a major report, "Enhancing the Cultural Competence

of Physicians," which direct the AMA to accomplish the following activities:

- Provide medical schools and residency program directors with information related to assisting physicians in providing culturally competent health care to patients throughout their lives and encourage them to include the topic of culturally effective health care in their curricula;

- Continue research into the need for and effectiveness of training in cultural competence;

- Form an expert national advisory panel, including representation from the AMA Minority Affairs Consortium, to consult on all areas related to the topic, including developing a list of resources and maintaining it in an electronic database;

- Assist physicians in obtaining information about and/or training in culturally effective health care through development of an annotated resource database on the AMA home page; and

- Seek external funding to develop a 5-year program for promoting cultural competence in and through the education of physicians, with the goal of restructuring the continuum of medical education and staff and faculty development programs to deliberately emphasize cultural competence as part of professional practice.

Other reports at the AMA 1998 Annual Meeting also contained recommendations related to cultural competence:

- An informational report from the AMA Minority Affairs Consortium included support for Performance Measurement Criteria to monitor and motivate implementation of existing minority policies and "the successful development of an electronic communication mechanism or forum."

- The AMA supports (1) health benefit plan coverage for interpreters for the hearing impaired and the use of culturally and linguistically appropriate patient education programs for managing asthma and (2) federal guidelines for standardization of race/ethnicity codings.

- The AMA recognizes the importance of correctly identified racial and ethnic influences on disease or disease susceptibility and for external funding to develop a conference on race, ethnicity, and medical research.

- The AMA encourages allocation of financial resources for research to document the scope of limited patient literacy and the implications for effective medical diagnosis and treatment; for dissemination of practical interventions that solve health literacy problems; and for development of medical education programs that train physicians to communicate with patients who have limited literacy skills.

Sample Educational Activities and Publications Addressing Culturally Effective Care

The most visible AMA activities in the mid-1990s activities were in the area of adolescent health, as evidenced by *Culturally Competent Health Care for Adolescents: A Guide for Primary Care Providers* (AMA, 1994) and "Developing Culturally Competent Strategies for Adolescents of Color" (in *AMA State-of-the-Art Conference on Adolescent Health Promotion* (National Center for Education in Maternal and Child Health, 1993).

In the late 1970s *The Western Journal of Medicine* brought many cultural issues to the forefront when it began to publish reports in a regular section on "Cross-cultural Medicine." The journal since dedicated entire issues to the multiple factors related to cultural competence, including an issue on cross-cultural medicine in 1983. In the September 1995 issue on end-of-life care, cultural competence was the focus of the first four articles ("Frustrated Mastery—The Cultural Context of Death in America," "Religious Dimensions of Dying and Death," "Patients' Perspective on Dying and on the Care of Dying Patients," and "Understanding Cultural Difference in Caring for Dying Patients") and a part of several others.

The Hennepin County (MN) Medical Society exemplifies the emphasis local medical societies are placing on this topic. In July/August 1994, the *Special Edition of the HCMS Bulletin* explored "cultural diversity and what it means to health care professionals." Brief, simple community profiles of what is called the Minnesota "tossed salad" are offered for African American, Cambodian, Hmong, Latino, Native American, Russian, and Somali communities (including family structure and roles, interpersonal relationships, communication, religion, health and hygiene, food, holidays and celebrations, dress and personal appearance, history and traditions, and education and cultural values). Diversity is an important issue in Minnesota, where the "minority" population grew 72% between 1980 and 1990, the fourth highest rate of increase in the country.

Another excellent example of medical society efforts to improve cultural competence appears in *The Journal of the Florida Medical Association* (August/September 1997) in "Cross-Cultural Encounters Within the Medical System," with a chart on "Important Features of Physician-Patient Interethnic Communication."

Encouraging Education and Training in Culturally Competent Health Care

The ability of academic institutions to prepare medical students and resident physicians to serve an increasingly varied patient population depends on the extent to which faculty and administrators will modify curricula and clinical education to correspond with social change and will help a reasonable portion of student who are not from the dominant culture. Medical schools and academic health centers throughout the country are offering programs to promote enhancing patient outcomes through improved cross-cultural understanding. A recent survey revealed that only 30% of urban hospitals have instituted programs to manage work force diversity ("Managing Diversity: A Senior Management Perspective," P. E. Wallace et al; *Hospital and Health Service Administration 41*, no. 1, 1996).

Much of the current cultural competence training in health care institutions is restricted to one to eight hours of awareness-based training to encourage participants to value diversity, usually with a focus on the broader categories of race/ethnicity, class or occupational levels (providers and support staff), and gender. The success of these interventions depends on the extent to which an institutional approach requires universal attendance; otherwise, the message is conveyed that the most privileged groups are not required to change behavior. The one-shot, one-hour lecture approach does very little to change the biomedical paradigm of clinicians or alter their personal opinions.

Efforts to evaluate multicultural education began to be reported in the mid-1990s. The results of the evaluation of a three-year curriculum implemented by the Minnesota Department of Family and Community Medicine, Regions Hospital, St. Paul Ramsey Family Practice Residency, were positively reported in the November-December 1997 issue of *Family Medicine* in "A Curriculum for Multicultural Education in Family Medicine." At least one state—North Carolina—has launched a statewide diversity initiative in the area of public health, after concluding that services or programs geared to African Americans (22% of the state population), Hispanics/Latinos (100,000—growing at three times the rate of other groups), and Native Americans (80,000 in 1990) were insufficient. The North Carolina Office of Minority Health conducted an Organizational Climate Assessment and then developed a guide for cultural diversity training specific to public health, used for pilot training in 1995 and 1996. Train-the-trainer sessions, started in February 1996, are supported by copyrighted guides for facilitators and participants. Because interpreter services were also found to be inadequate, a document titled *Interpreter Services for Hispanic/Latino Clients: Report and Recommendations* was subsequently developed. Ohio, South Carolina, and Pennsylvania have instituted similar programs in the area of families with children needing access to mental health services.

Nursing and Other Nonphysician Health Professions Organizations

Nursing has clearly devoted more attention to cultural competence than organized medicine. Several other health care professional organizations have also developed multicultural resources specifically related to issues special or unique to the profession. The American Association for

Respiratory Care has an association-wide program to enhance the cultural competence of practitioners nationwide. The American Occupational Therapy Association (AOTA) offers ongoing workshops and continuing education, a *Multicultural Education and Resource Guide for Occupational Therapy Educators and Practitioners*, and a video on "Creating a Multicultural Approach and Environment."

Materials developed by the American Physical Therapy Association (APTA) emphasize that understanding a person's cultural background should be part of any clinical interaction. The APTA Department of Minority and International Affairs provides a bibliography of minority and cross-cultural materials and distributes a 13-minute video, "Cultural Diversity in Physical Therapy." The American Speech-Language Hearing Association maintains a multicultural resource center that remains alert to issues such as patient dietary customs to determine the choice of appropriate foods for use during swallowing and maintains a web site with reading lists, a multicultural history and demographic profile of the US, regional, and social dialects, cultural differences in communication and learning styles, and bibliographies on specific ethnic groups. The National Association of Social Workers has several books available on cultural diversity, including *Multicultural Issues in Social Work*, and is developing guidelines for cultural competence in social work.

Physician Education Through Peer-Reviewed Articles on Unmet Needs

In addition to the information about AMA policy and initiatives, physicians have access to extensive medical literature on the topic of disparities in non-majority medical care delivery. A list of articles published in *the Journal of the American Medical Association (JAMA)* and the *New England Journal of Medicine (NEJM)* since 1984 covers more than 60 single-spaced pages. Studies published in these and other journals indicate the continuing severity of the problem.

Many of these studies identify specific conditions such as pneumonia, cardiovascular procedures, HIV/AIDS, and kidney disease, in which the patient's race represented a significant characteristic in determining the type and amount of care provided.

AMA Activities To Influence the Delivery of Care at the Local Level

The AMA is committed to continue its long-standing efforts to present compelling data on disparities in health care due to race and ethnicity, to operationalize recommendations and policy, and to enforce ethical opinions. In 1995 the AMA House of Delegates established policy and directives to influence the delivery of care at the local level:

- maintain a position of zero tolerance toward racially or culturally based disparities in care;

- consolidate AMA policy on meeting the health care needs of minority patients and communities;

- continue to support physician cultural awareness initiatives and related consumer education activities;

- develop publications on culturally competent health care;

- testify before Congress and comment on regulatory proposals;

- develop assessment tools to enable individual physicians and groups of physicians to identify and act on care disparities;

- encourage individuals to report suspected racial or ethnic discrimination by physicians to local medical societies and develop a process to be used by local medical societies when physicians are reported to be in violation of Ethical Opinion 9.121;

- continue to strengthen relationships with organizations representing minority physicians;

- establish two-way communication with the DHHS Office of Minority Health about meeting the health care needs of minority populations; and

- develop and regularly use a survey instrument to identify the degree of racial and ethnic disparities in health care and report on progress being made to address these disparities.

III. Project to Enhance the Cultural Competence of Physicians

After the June 1998 Annual Meeting, the AMA examined policies and directives adopted through the years. The examination included "Promoting Culturally Competent Health Care" (Policy H-295.905 *AMA Policy Compendium*) which called for the AMA to "encourage medical schools to offer electives in culturally competent health care with the goal of increasing awareness and acceptance of cultural differences between patient and provider" and "investigate the development of a database for the AMA Homepage addressing the issues of cultural competence in health care." The first iteration of an online and published annotated resource list is scheduled for June 1999.

As indicated in Council on Medical Education Report 5-A-98, Enhancing the Cultural Competence of Physicians, the following issues have increased the need to identify and incorporate health needs of culturally diverse populations into broader public health and community objectives.

Demographic Shifts

Demographic shifts and empowerment of diverse non-majority communities have driven much of the attention to cultural competence. Health care workers are more frequently confronted with the lack of trained medical interpreters for non-English speaking patients, and increasingly influential "minority" groups expect providers and facility staff to be culturally sensitive, to reflect diversity themselves, and to be aware of health care problems prevalent among specific populations. These changing demographics and the growing disparities in health status between the dominant society and non-dominant populations have been projected, identified, and tracked by decade in the "Healthy People" project, in which the AMA participates.

Continuous Quality Improvement/Clinical Outcomes

Demographic changes and participation in insurance programs requiring health care professionals and providers to treat a more diverse clientele have led to evaluation of the quality and efficiency of linguistically and culturally appropriate health care. Attention has been given to measuring linguistic or cultural competence in health care service delivery since the late 1950s, when researchers presented the results of their studies of health and disease in specific ethnic and racial groups. Recently, more organizations and health care and educational institutions are identifying ways to improve outcomes. These groups acknowledge that different methods are needed to disseminate information to and care for people from diverse cultures.

Barriers to Respectful Communication

Because accurate communication is essential to basic, quality health care services, the importance of respectful communication permeates all areas of culturally effective health care. But current medical education and care delivery systems present multiple barriers to such care. Perhaps the most obvious barrier is that of time constraints, convincingly described in "Temporary Matters: The Ethical Consequences of Transient Social Relationships in Medical Training" (Dimitri Christakis, MD, and Chris Feudtner, MD; *JAMA,* September 3, 1997). The language currently used in documenting case histories and in interviewing is another barrier ("The Language of Medical Case Histories," William Donnelly, MD; December 1, 1997, *Annals of Internal Medicine*).

Although time constraints are increasing, resources are available to address some of the other communication barriers. Since "A Teaching Framework for Cross-cultural Health Care: Application in Family Practice," by Elois Berlin, PhD, and William Fowkes, Jr, MD, appeared in the December 1983 issue of *The Western Journal of Medicine*, hundreds of articles books, videos, CD-ROMs, tutorials, courses, etc, have presented strategies for improving cross-cultural communication.

Complementary and Alternative Health Care Practices

Respectful communication is imperative when treating patients who use complementary and alternative health care practices, either as a part of their family or national background or because they believe such practices are less harmful than "mainstream" medical practices. Harwood emphasizes the importance of physician understanding of preferences with regard to seemingly minor issues such as injection over oral administration of medication and tablets over capsules, which may be related to cultural experiences. The real issue, as Dr. Walker pointed out in "Delivering Culturally Competent Care in a Multicultural Society," is that physicians must acknowledge that health care belief systems "are critical to the patient's healing process."

Spirituality

Spiritual beliefs and preferences have received detailed attention in connection with "comfort care" and decision making at the end of life. They are now being recognized as essential to improved outcomes in nonterminal situations. "The Healing Power of Spirituality" (*Minnesota Medicine,* December 1996) quotes the claim of David Larson, MD, president of the National Institute for Healthcare Research, that in spite of mounting evidence of "a positive link between a patient's spirituality and that person's recovery and ability to cope with illness,. . . nearly 90% of physicians do not address their patients' spiritual needs." National arenas in which spirituality has been addressed include annual presentations on "Integrating Alternative and Spiritual Approaches in Healthcare," with continuing medical education credits designated by the Annenberg Center for Health Sciences, and "Spirituality, Cross-Cultural Issues and End of Life Care: Curricular Development," sponsored by the National Institute for Healthcare Research and the Association of American Medical Colleges in March 1998. Both emphasized the clinical relevance of patients' belief systems and cultural background to treatment and care and the importance of integrating these patient factors into medical school curricula.

End-of-Life Care

Many Voices, Many Choices, the title of the newsletter of the Colorado Collaboration on End-of-Life Care, indicates the primacy of cultural competence in the final stages of life and the widespread national attention being focused on meeting the end-of-life care needs of culturally diverse populations. However, the preferences and practices of the American populace in the areas of "conceptualization of life, personhood, health, illness, and death" are very different from those recommended by some biomedical ethicists ("Patient Diversity Creates Major Challenges," by Alexandra Mazard, MD, in the Robert Wood Johnson Foundation quarterly report on its project entitled "Last Acts: Care and Caring at the End of Life," (August 1997). "Actions that are discordant with the prescripts of Western biomedical practices" can result in "coercion masquerading as choice, cultural insensitivity, mistrust and lack of meaningful choice."

Dr. Mazard recommends that "medical professionals familiarize themselves with the literature on cross-cultural issues where religion, gender, age, socioeconomic status, ethnicity, sexual orientation, and acculturation status have been identified as features impacting end-of-life care decisions." The Last Acts Resource Committee on Diversity is charged with helping to integrate the issue of diversity in areas such as culture, ethnicity, disability, and gender as they relate to end-of-life issues.

Literacy/Translator Service

While interpreter services and translations are mandated in Title VI of the Civil Rights Act of 1964, many physicians depend solely on children, close friends, or relatives of the patient, which may not be appropriate. The importance of having access to accurate translator services was highlighted at the June 3, 1997, national conference on Health Literacy, sponsored by the Center for Health Care Strategies and Pfizer Inc. and attended by 150 representatives from government, insurance, managed care, medical associations, literary groups, foundations, and think tanks (summarized in Medical News & Perspectives, *JAMA*, September 24, 1997).

Issues addressed included a description of the impact of functional health illiteracy to the effective flow of information between health care providers and patients and how it complicates the treatment of disease, adversely affecting outcomes (Proceedings, *Health Literacy: A National Conference*). The National Health Council has two literacy-related programs to help patients navigate successfully within the health care system.

The AMA is planning to develop a Health Literacy Initiative and will include health literacy as a topic in its web-based and print-annotated resource list. Some organizations, such as Hennepin County (MN) Medical Center, have assigned staff to assist with spoken language interpreter services; state departments of health also have helpful resources, such as the Community Interpreter Services in Minnesota.

Systematic Approaches To Evaluate Competence To Work Cross-culturally

Information about systematic approaches to evaluate a physician's competence to work cross-culturally will be included in the AMA annotated resource list. Evelyn Lee, PhD, has identified the following knowledge, skills/abilities, and attitudes as the "hallmarks of the Culturally Competent Clinician":

Knowledge of: history and culture of country of origin; pertinent psychosocial stresses, family life and intergenerational issues; culturally acceptable behaviors vs psycho-pathology; role of religion; cultural beliefs about causes and treatments of disease; and differences in disease prevalence and response to medicine and other treatments.

Skills/Abilities: interview and assess patients in the target language (or via translator); communicate with sensitivity to cross-cultural issues; avoid under/over diagnosing disease states; understand the patient's perspective; formulate culturally sensitive treatment plans; effectively utilize community resources; and act as a role model and advocate for bilingual/bicultural staff and patients.

Attitudes: as evidence of understanding, acknowledge the degree of differentness between patient and physician; to demonstrate empathy, recall the patient's history of suffering; have patience in shifting away from the Western view of time and immediacy; respect the importance of culture as a determinant of health, the existence of other world views regarding health and illness, the adaptability and survival skills of patients, the influence of religious beliefs on health, and the role of bilingual/bicultural staff; and demonstrate humor by having the ability to laugh with oneself and others.

Next Steps to Enhance the Cultural Competence of Physicians

The print and online compilations will assist physicians and other health care providers in responding to the social, cultural, economic, and political diversity of their communities, including the impact of cultural solutions to illness. The AMA Cultural Competence Initiative is also considering the following components:

1. A listing of national speakers, electronic and on-site educational programs, and calendar of events;

2. Samples of listening and interviewing skills for different cultures, presentations of the varieties of nonverbal communication (with examples), and references in key languages

provided in text and in audio formats that actually pronounce words and phrases;

3. Training programs through multiple modalities: web-based, DirectTV, interactive self-instructional learning packages, and face-to-face programs;

4. Developing modules of materials related to cultural issue in specific areas such as end-of-life care, religious/spiritual practices, literacy, organization, genetics, and complementary and alternative health care practices;

5. Providing searchable web links to organization and reference materials;

6. Developing mechanisms, such as continuing physician professional development education credit and appropriate designation of competence at a site such as AMA Physician Select, or via the American Medical Accreditation Program; and

7. Emphasizing cultural competence in medical education data collection surveys across the continuum of medical education. including

The outcomes of these efforts to identify and respond to the health needs of culturally diverse populations will be described in future reports.

B. Selected *American Medical News* Articles

AMNews also features cultural competence publications on its Web site at
http://www.ama-assn.org/public/journals/amnews/amnews.htm

"Culturally Effective Communication"

"Different Doctors Make Decisions in Different Ways"

"Cancer Studies Fail Minorities"

"Managing Diversity"

"Pew: Encourage Minority Physicians"

"Crossing the Cultural Divide"

"Mistaking Medicine"

Culturally Effective Communication

AMNews, Editorial, February 22, 1999

The common thread running through a number of recent articles published in AMNews has been the growing interest in cultural awareness in medicine.

Our recent reports have covered such topics as culturally sensitive end-of-life care, how cancer studies fail minorities, special treatment concerns for gays and lesbians, and the likeliness of Medicaid and managed care plans to introduce standards for cultural competency in patient care. On the other side of the patient-doctor interaction, we've touched on how a physician's own background can affect treatment decisions.

The current groundswell of exploration into cultural awareness is a logical extension of long-standing concerns about the role of communication in the doctor-patient relationship. There is a well-known disconnect between the demonstrated high intellect required to become a physician and the ability of many physicians to communicate effectively with patients.

Physicians in every specialty and practice setting can expect to encounter patients—and, often just as important, their families—who have traditions, cultural values and language needs that affect how care should be given and how treatment options should be explained. Adding to both the tension and the need to be prepared is that these interactions may be in the context of the considerable stress of a crisis or serious medical problem.

How well the message about cultural awareness takes among doctors is still an open question. To some physicians, no doubt, this must all seem too politically correct. To others, it may appear divisive, condescending or simply the road to more bureaucratic meddling in medicine. Physicians may well have concerns about treading what may be a fine line between being culturally sensitive and stereotyping patients on the basis of race or ethnicity.

Yet the medical profession has long, and properly, held onto the idea that it is not only science that defines medicine but also such things as patient choice and informed consent. Medicine rightfully rails against managed care gag clauses. But that begs the question: Is the net result so very different when a doctor can't, or won't, communicate with patients in an effective way?

Late last year, an AMA Council on Medical Education report examined issues in cultural competency and found the need for medicine to do more. The AMA House of Delegates approved the report's recommendations, including raising awareness of teaching materials (especially in medical school and residency), the creation of an expert advisory panel, and continued research into the issue. A compendium of practical information is now being developed.

Getting out good information about cultural effectiveness is important. It has got us thinking about a communication problem that we have as a newspaper. The life of a newspaper article tends to be brief, and gathering a number of articles from different issues is more trouble than most readers want to go through. Now, using the World Wide Web, we have put our articles on cultural awareness together in one spot, on our Web edition. And there they can remain available for a long time, which happens to be how long we expect cultural awareness to remain an issue for medicine.

Different Doctors Make Decisions in Different Ways

Mark Moran, *AMNews*, February 8, 1999

Medical decisions by physicians are often strongly influenced by a host of nonmedical factors, a finding that challenges efforts to standardize care.

A doctor is a doctor is a doctor—right?

It is a cardinal assumption behind the movement toward evidence-based medicine: Reduce idiosyncrasies in medical decision-making and you improve efficiency, raise quality and lower costs. And if one doctor is little different than another, then standardizing medical care is largely a matter of agreeing on guidelines and protocols.

But what if any one physician is not like another? And what if a host of individual physician characteristics confound "rational" decision-making?

That's what recent research suggests, showing significant variation in the way different physicians diagnose and manage common critical conditions.

Physicians' age, race and specialty all appear to play a role in the way they diagnose and treat their patients, according to a study conducted by the New England Research Institutes, in Watertown, Mass., and Boston University School of Medicine.

Younger physicians appear to approach the diagnosis and management of certain conditions commonly seen in primary care differently than older physicians. And in the diagnosis of at least one condition, younger family physicians and black family physicians appear more likely to order more tests than their older, white counterparts.

One of the most striking findings in the study is one showing that different primary care physicians manage the same condition in a different manner.

John McKinlay, PhD, senior vice president and director of NERI, said the findings add to a body of

work suggesting that clinically extraneous physician and patient factors can affect decision-making. But the NERI study uses a rare design allowing researchers to highlight factors influencing decision-making, while controlling for confounding effects.

For instance, variation in the way physicians manage patients could not be attributed to differences in knowledge about the two conditions, which were demonstrated to be similar.

Dr. McKinlay said the findings contradict "decision theorists" who view medical care less as a relationship between doctor and patient and increasingly as an industrial transaction.

Clinicians involved in the research said the findings highlight the difficulty of using evidence-based medicine and clinical guidelines in the real world. They also said physicians need to be aware of extraneous factors that may influence decision-making.

"From a purely rational perspective, you would expect that a physician is a physician is a physician," said Mark Moskowitz, MD, vice chair of the department of medicine at Boston University School of Medicine, and one of the investigators in the study. "But to think that physicians function in a purely scientific model is somewhat naive. For good or for bad, we do things that are based on nonclinically relevant factors. Physicians are not computers or robots."

Primary care differences

In the study, 128 primary care physicians—equally divided between internists and family physicians—viewed one of 16 different videotapes depicting a patient presenting with either polymyalgia rheumatica or depression. The different videotapes showed patients with a unique combination of four characteristics—67 or 79 years of age; male or female; black or white; and blue- or white-collar occupation.

Physicians then answered questions regarding differential diagnosis, management and treatment.

Analysis of the results showed the different patient characteristics, epidemiologically relevant to both conditions, had no significant effect on how physicians treated them. But nonclinically relevant characteristics of the physician—especially age, race and specialty—did have an effect.

Internists in the study were better at diagnosing PMR and depression, a finding that upended researchers' hypothesis that family physicians would be better at recognizing psychosocial conditions. And internists diagnosing PMR were significantly more likely to order the test for erythrocyte sedimentation, a relatively inexpensive assay that is all but definitively diagnostic for the condition.

"Primary care physicians are not a homogenous group," said Dr. Moskowitz. "This has policy relevance because the mix of physicians in a managed care plan may impact on the ability to manage common clinical conditions, on resource utilization, and on patients' overall health."

But he cautioned that since only two conditions were studied, it cannot be inferred that internists serve as more efficient gatekeepers in a managed care plan. And he noted that family physicians who made the diagnosis of depression were more likely to start patients on anti-depressant therapy—in keeping with recommendations from the Agency for Health Care Policy and Research—than were internists.

Other factors also appeared to affect decision-making. Younger physicians were more likely to diagnose depression in younger patients and in males, while older physicians were more likely to diagnosis depression in older patients and in females. And in diagnosing and managing patients with polymyalgia rheumatica, both younger family physicians and black family physicians tended to order significantly more tests than did older, white internists.

Cancer Studies Fail Minorities

Stephanie Stapleton, *AMNews,* February 8, 1999

An Institute of Medicine panel concludes that researchers should increase resources and infrastructure dedicated to studying patterns of cancer among minority and medically underserved populations.

Washington—For the first time in decades, scientific inroads into cancer control, prevention, detection and treatment have led the United States to experience an overall, sustained decline in cancer mortality rates.

But behind the good news is another reality—statistical snapshots that leave the unsettling impression that not everyone is sharing equally in medicine's advances.

Black men, for instance, are still 15% more likely to develop cancer than their white counterparts. Although black women are less likely to be diagnosed with breast cancer, they are more likely than white women to die from it. Stomach and liver cancer strike Asian-Americans at rates much higher than others. And Alaska natives are more likely to suffer from colon and rectal cancer.

Growing awareness of these persistent patterns triggered a committee of the Institute of Medicine to issue a congressionally requested report Jan. 20 outlining ways in which the National Institutes of Health should expand its efforts to understand better why cancer has become a burden borne unequally across ethnic and socioeconomic boundaries.

"With the population becoming increasingly diverse, it is critical that we learn why some ethnic minorities and the medically underserved are more prone to cancer and less likely to survive it," said committee chair M. Alfred Haynes, MD, former president and dean of Drew Postgraduate Medical School.

The IOM committee concluded that although the NIH's National Cancer Institute is making extraordinary progress in the "war on cancer," it still has a long way to go—both in terms of the money it allocates to targeted cancer research regarding minorities and the overall systems in place to coordinate that research across the NIH.

The IOM panel "reinforced what many of us have known for years—that the culture, structure and programs of the NCI and NIH as a whole serve the white population well, but fall short in addressing the needs of ethnic minorities," said former Health and Human Services Secretary Louis Sullivan, MD.

Dr. Sullivan, now president of Morehouse School of Medicine and principal investigator for the National Black Leadership Initiative on Cancer, spoke at a Senate hearing reviewing the IOM's findings a day after its release.

"These are not simple problems, and there are no simple solutions," agreed NCI Director Richard Klausner, MD, in his testimony before the Senate Appropriations Subcommittee. "Many of the issues go well beyond the scope of a single institute at NIH, and in some cases they have at their core some of the major social and public health challenges that face our entire nation," he added.

The question of improving data collection and surveillance efforts marked one of the strongest areas of agreement between the IOM report and ongoing efforts at NCI.

By law, NCI's disease data are classified according to one of four basic racial categories—American Indian or Alaska Native; Asian or Pacific Islander; black or African-American; or white—and as either Hispanic or non-Hispanic.

The IOM, though, found these categories to be of "limited utility for purposes of health research."

Instead, the committee recommended classifying information on a more ethnic-specific basis to highlight how differences in cancer incidence and mortality rates may be linked to a range of cultural factors, behaviors, health attitudes and lifestyle conditions.

Dr. Klausner agreed that these current categories were "not scientifically sound" and failed "to reflect the variables important to the cancer burden." As a result, NCI has already "gone well beyond" the basic data gathering required by statute to reflect cancer incidence rates among specific ethnic groups and to link its databases with other information sources such as Medicare and the census to evaluate socioeconomic status and other factors of ethnicity.

Differences on how funds are spent

One of the elements with which Dr. Klausner expressed the strongest disagreement, however, had to do with its recommendation that NCI change the way it accounts for the amount of minority-related research included in the overall portfolio.

NCI estimates that it spent about $124 million in 1997 on such targeted projects. This amount is based on a "% relevancy" formula that credits a fraction of costs of large or multifaceted studies toward the minority research total—based on participation. But the IOM committee argued that this method does not provide a true reflection of expenditures because the research in question is not linked to very specific, relevant research questions. Based on the IOM's more stringent approach, the panel estimated that NIH actually allocated only slightly more than $24 million or 1% of its total budget to these questions.

"The committee finds these resources are insufficient relative to the burden of disease among ethnic minority and medically underserved communities, the changing U.S. demographics and the scientific opportunities inherent in the study of diverse populations," according to the report.

But Dr. Klausner said taking the IOM's view would lead to the creation of a parallel structure, segregated from the researchers, projects, programs and infrastructures that NCI supports for all cancer research.

"This is impractical and inefficient and will fail to answer many of the questions posed by the IOM report," he said. Weaving research regarding ethnic minorities into the "full fabric of our research" offers the best course for success, Dr. Klausner added.

Meanwhile, the panel also concluded that concerted steps must continue to enhance clinical and prevention participation, or else ethnic minorities and medically underserved communities will be at risk of missing science's potential opportunities.

When the drug tamoxifen, for example, was recently found to be effective in preventing breast cancer in thousands of high-risk women, only about 2% of the study participants were black and even fewer represented other ethnic groups. Dr. Haynes cited these tests as an example of what the outcome can be. "The absence of minorities . . . raises questions about how applicable the results are to minority populations."

The panel also called on NCI to improve its methods of providing information about cancer to patients, clinicians and others in ethnic minority and underserved populations. Cancer survivors in ethnic minority groups should be tapped as important resources for educating others in the community about cancer.

"The report is correct. . . . We need to focus more attention on documenting, understanding and disseminating [the] knowledge gained," Dr. Klausner said.

An Institute of Medicine panel concluded that the National Cancer Institute should expand its efforts to understand why some ethnic minorities are more likely to suffer from certain types of cancer.

Among the recommendations, NCI should:

- Expand its cancer data collection and classifications to better measure the influence of ethnicity on incidence and mortality rates.

- More accurately assess and increase the NCI research resources dedicated to studies targeted to minority and medically underserved groups.

- Establish a formal system to report to Congress about the amount of minority-targeted research that is included in the overall cancer research portfolio.

- Improve minority participation in clinical trials by addressing barriers created by current informed consent processes.

- Tap cancer survivors in minority groups as a resource for educating others in the community about their risks.

Managing Diversity

Howard Kim, *AMNews,* January 25, 1999

New managed care rules propose cultural competency guidelines. Health plans hope for better outcomes and more satisfied patients.

Family physician Edmund Shaheen, MD, attracts large numbers of Middle Eastern patients to his Kaiser Permanente medical office in Woodland Hills, Calif.

Yet Dr. Shaheen isn't Middle Eastern. Although his heritage is partially Lebanese, the American-born Dr. Shaheen looks more like he hails from Boston than Beirut.

The confusion doesn't bother the 53-year-old physician, nor does it bother his managed care organization. Indeed, Kaiser Permanente, like many managed care groups nationwide, wants doctors and patients to speak the same language when it comes to medical care, whatever language that may be.

For doctors, the goal is cultural competence, which Dr. Shaheen says he's acquired through in-service training and hundreds of patient encounters.

More and more, physicians are finding that their patients have diverse ethnic backgrounds, and health plans and provider networks are urging them to become better at cultural sensitivity.

Even in once-homogeneous rural areas, it isn't unusual to see patients from Mexico, Vietnam and Africa.

Ethnic sensitivity isn't a condition for keeping a provider contract yet, but trends seem to be pointing that way, some health officials say. "Cultural competence has become a watchword in medicine," says Elena Rios, MD, president of the 6,000-member National Hispanic Medical Assn. in Washington, D.C.

Health plans are asking physicians to get closer to their patients in hopes of improving outcomes and boosting patient satisfaction, even if it means thinking ethnically, Dr. Rios says. Employers who pay the bills seek the same goals.

Physicians and hospitals have followed suit because cultural sensitivity happens at the point of patient contact. Providers have been judged the best qualified to determine what works best with patients, says Herbert Nickens, MD, vice president of community and minority programs at the Assn. of American Medical Colleges in Washington, D.C.

The association has been tracking the issue because of low minority enrollment in medical schools.

The American Medical Association's Minority Affairs Consortium last year recognized the need to boost minority enrollments. The association has also supported cultural competence and plans to launch an online bibliography to initiate cultural competence learning.

Now Medicaid is getting into the act. As part of a major revision of Medicaid managed care rules, the Health Care Financing Administration in September proposed new regulations mandating that states establish cultural competence guidelines for Medicaid contracted health plans.

HCFA painted the proposed directives in broad strokes, leaving it to the states to define cultural competence. But the agency did set minimum standards for states to follow.

Health plans have seen the trend coming, says Barbara Stern, vice president of diversity at Harvard Pilgrim Health Care, an HMO based in Brookline, Mass. Demonstrated cultural competency is likely to evolve from a guideline into a requirement in Medicaid contracting, she says.

Once HCFA adopts the regulations, physicians are expecting an explosion of interest in ethnicity training and staff development. The more culturally diverse a medical practice can be, the better it will comply with future contracting demands, Dr. Rios predicts.

An HMO original

Health plans opened the door. Less than a decade ago, HMOs, primarily in California, vigorously sought out black, Latino and Asian physicians.

The health plans' goal was to contract with the physicians as part of a marketing strategy aimed at boosting minority enrollments.

The marketing continues in almost every major city. Minority enrollments are up, but the marketing effort has been stymied by a severe shortage of minority physicians.

"After trumpeting ethnic diversity, plans discovered they couldn't build the infrastructure. We don't have enough representative minority physicians in the community," says East Los Angeles surgeon Robert Beltran, MD.

Some HMOs dropped out or scaled back their efforts. Even HMOs that market exclusively to groups such as Latinos or blacks have struggled to maintain market share.

In the early 1990s, Blue Shield of California, based in San Francisco, and CareAmerica, an HMO based in Woodland Hills, Calif., pushed into minority marketing.

They publicized ethnically sensitive services and sought out contracts with minority physicians from Asian, Latino and African-American communities.

Today, despite a statewide presence, Blue Shield contracts with one African-American and two primarily Latino medical groups, says District Manager Jim Arriola.

It also promotes a Spanish-language prenatal care program.

The company does not get into physician sensitivity training but does contract with minority physicians when possible. It also operates a Spanish-language 800-number where members can get general information. CareAmerica folded its ethnic marketing efforts when Blue Shield acquired it in 1998.

Besides a minority physician shortage, HMOs have been stymied by a lack of useful clinical information across ethnic communities, says Gary Dennis, MD, president of the National Medical Assn. in Washington, D.C. The group represents the nation's 22,000 African-American physicians.

Searching for a definition

Cultural competence requires that doctors work effectively with patients from different ethnic backgrounds. It goes well beyond language barriers, says Dr. Dennis, who argues that a lot of lip service has been paid to the effort.

Most health plans have focused on business strategies to boost membership. "No one is investigating the hard facts between ethnicity and good medical care," Dr. Dennis contends.

In light of these issues, some HMOs have begun to take a different tack: formal sensitivity training for nonminority physicians. Plans such as Kaiser Permanente and Harvard Pilgrim have been among the few to roll out training programs aimed at coaching doctors on everything from cultural stereotypes to the importance of physical gestures, folk medicines and ethnic foods in medicine.

Yet only a handful of health plans offer such programs, and they vary widely. And physicians, after being coached, aren't sure they will be any more effective in treating patients.

Kaiser Permanente integrates cultural sensitivity into a variety of continuing medical education courses on communicating with patients.

In the summer, the HMO videotaped a staged enactment of several physician-patient encounters using doctors and professional actors. The goal was to teach physicians to narrow the culture gap with patients, says M. Jean Gilbert, PhD, a medical anthropologist hired by Kaiser to help lead its diversity training.

Harvard Pilgrim's three-day diversity training sessions cover the gamut, from staged role-playing to community visits.

An independent Seattle-based group, Cross-Cultural Health Care Program, also conducts patient-centered ethnicity workshops. And Baltimore's Medical Education Group, which is headed by a physician, provides cultural diversity training.

Physicians generally support diversity training but aren't sure whether cultural competence works.

"We know a lot about diabetes among Latinos and heart disease among blacks," but similar studies don't exist on the effectiveness of cultural competence, says Dr. Gilbert. "The whole issue is so new, we're merely scratching the surface."

However, physicians intuitively recognize that ethnic sensitivity means good medicine. "It boils down to communication," says J. Mario Molina, MD, president of Molina Medical Centers in Long Beach, Calif. The HMO serves large Latino, black, Cambodian and Vietnamese communities and contracts with Caucasian and minority physicians.

The challenge lies in balancing a respect for culture with the skill to get patients to comply with good medical care and knowing the nuances, Dr. Molina says.

Some things can't be taught. For example, making direct eye contact when speaking to African-American or Latino patients implies strength and inspires confidence.

But eye contact is considered rude in Asian cultures. Getting approval from elders on medical decisions and validating traditional foods and herbal remedies to treat diseases can lead to trust in Asian and South American families.

Some physicians better address these subtle issues than others, Dr. Molina says.

And some physicians scoff. "Multiculturalism is a gigantic mistake," says Robert McElmurry, MD, a solo-practice physician in Lansing, Mich.

Patients don't want to be treated differently; they want the same quality of medical care as everyone else, Dr. McElmurry says. "Tailoring medicine to a patient's cultural differences is divisive, racist, and can only lead to anxiety in patients."

Most providers disagree. In fact, the link between cultural norms and Western medicine has important clinical implications, says Dr. Dennis of the NMA. It can help explain why patients fail to comply with medication orders or distrust the medical establishment.

It can also offer important clues about ethnicity and disease states.

"If we knew more about lifestyle factors in the black community, for example, the effects of diet on health or cultural attitudes on certain treatments, we could amass enough study data to actually influence outcomes and lower mortality and morbidity rates," Dr. Dennis says. "Unfortunately, nobody is tracking this data across ethnic lines."

Getting more minorities through medical school will help, he says.

Recognizing culture's effect on medicine is a start, says Kaiser Permanente's Dr. Gilbert. "The train is already moving."

Recommendations for cultural competency

To meet proposed federal Medicaid managed care guidelines, provider networks should:

- Identify potential Medicaid patients in the community whose cultural norms and practices may affect their access to health care.

- Improve access for at-risk ethnic groups through advertising, community outreach and hiring culturally compatible physicians and office personnel.

- Acknowledge the patients' racial and ethnic concerns at the initial office visit and continue to do so throughout the care process.

- Provide translation services to patients if language poses a barrier.

- Include enough physicians who are aware of the values, beliefs, traditions, customs and parenting styles of the community.

- Account for factors such as nonverbal communication, folk medications, foreign dietary customs and healing rituals used by patients.

- Learn about the medical risks associated with the patient population's racial, ethnic and socioeconomic conditions.

Pew: Encourage Minority Physicians

Jay Greene, *AMNews,* December 28, 1998

More needs to be done to help minority students go to medical school, according to a Pew Commission report.

Charles Peters grew up in a small upstate New York town with few African-Americans and fewer opportunities to learn about his chosen profession of medicine. He found guidance in a minority program as an undergraduate student at Duke University.

Bradley Carthon took advantage of a minority program for high school students in his hometown of Fort Valley, Ga. He spent a summer working at the Medical College of Georgia, where he made his decision to pursue medicine.

Peters and Carthon are two medical students at the University of Pennsylvania and Harvard, respectively, who agree with a recent report from the Pew Health Professions Commission that more needs to be done to encourage minorities to seek careers in medicine.

In its 185-page report, the commission said because minority physicians are more likely to serve the poor and uninsured, increasing minority physicians in the work force is the most direct way to improve the health care needs of the underprivileged.

Peters, who is president of the Student National Medical Assn., said the 5,000 minority medical students who are part of the SNMA provide a wide range of free community services. They also provide guidance to college students seeking careers in medicine.

"Performing free community service is nothing new for minorities," said Peters, 29, who is in his eighth year in a dual medical and doctorate program at the University of Pennsylvania. "Members in our organization pledge to do that, and many schools encourage it. At Penn, time to do community service is built into the curriculum, but it is not required."

One of the Pew Commission's recommendations is a requirement that medical students provide free community services as a condition of graduation. Peters said he sees no problem in that requirement because he believes nonminorities could enrich their education by performing free services. However, Herbert Nickens, director of community and minority programs with the Assn. of American Medical Colleges, said medical schools should probably just encourage students to donate their time, not require it.

Echoing several other groups, including the AMA, the Pew report also called for an end to an estimated $500 million annual government subsidy to train 8,000 international medical graduates each year. In addition, the report recommended increasing subsidies to train physicians in ambulatory settings so that residents can hone their team skills with allied health professionals. The report also calls for insurance companies, HMOs and self-funded plans—an all-payer pool—to help pay for graduate medical education.

"We have made some progress in diversifying the physician work force over the last 20 years," said Edward O'Neil, Pew's executive director. "What remains is an enormous policy machinery that keeps us from moving forward. We need to get education and the workplace better connected for the next century. A whole lot more work needs to be done."

O'Neil said many top medical schools have minority recruitment programs that not only seek to attract and support minorities, but also include working with high schools to help counsel bright students who are considering medicine.

"We are now up against an anti-affirmative action backlash that is reversing gains in some states," Nickens said. Affirmative action has been outlawed in California, Texas, Louisiana, Mississippi and the state of Washington.

"It is chilling in many ways and affects more than just admissions. It also chills the launching of [kindergarten through 12th-grade education] and faculty development programs," Nickens said. Since 1991, the AAMC has been working with its medical school members to offer a wide range of programs to increase minority applications to medical schools.

The Pew report also recommends that schools do a better job of looking beyond test scores and consider more heavily such factors as ethnicity, socio-cultural status and commitment to community service.

Nickens and O'Neil agreed that some medical schools are backing away from considering other factors besides test scores. "People are leery because they don't want to get sued [by a nonminority who was denied admission]," Nickens said. "There is a hostility in the public mind to such [affirmative action] programs."

As a result, underrepresented minority enrollment declined for the second straight year to 11.6% after peaking at 12.3% in 1995, AAMC said. In those states that have eliminated affirmative action, applications to medical schools for minorities have dropped more than 20%. Underrepresented minorities are African-Americans, American Indians, Mexican-Americans and mainland Puerto Ricans.

Peters and Carthon said affirmative action opened the doors for them at Penn and Harvard. For others, however, the doors may be closing, according to the report.

"We minorities face obstacles. Simple things like exposure to medical opportunities through relatives or parents or encouragement from teachers. We don't have that," said Carthon, 24, who is president-elect of the SNMA. "We encounter cultural insensitivities. It is absolutely important for minorities to get as much encouragement and guidance in high school and college and then support in medical school."

Carthon knew that when he chose Hampton College, a predominantly black college in Virginia, he would be at a disadvantage when the time came to apply for medical school.

"Harvard looked at more than my college and my test scores," said Carthon, who is in his second year. "They took into account my background and career goals. Not all schools have such a balanced approach, and that is a disadvantage to many black professionals who choose small schools."

Crossing the Cultural Divide

Rachel Kreier, *AMNews,* January 25, 1999

A physician's need to be sensitive to a patient's cultural concerns is amplified when the illness is terminal and end-of-life care issues are at stake.

To Arthur Kleinman, MD, the Harvard psychiatrist and anthropologist who is one of the seminal thinkers in the field of cross-cultural health care, every encounter between a physician and a patient is cross-cultural, because the "illness experience" of the patient is different from the "disease process" that is the natural province of the physician.

"The disease process of diabetes has to do with levels of insulin and their relationship to receptors," Dr. Kleinman said. "That's not what diabetes the illness is—the illness is about the fear of becoming comatose, of going blind, of kidney failure or of amputation."

That primordial cultural divide is intensified, he said, when "you deal with real cultural difference, with ethnic groups, religious differences—even differences in age cohorts." Those distinctions are further intensified, he added, when the condition is a terminal illness and the physician is providing end-of-life care.

"End of life is a culture by itself. In the end of life, people are in a mood of separating, in a reflective mode, searching for meanings. That is very different from what a busy young clinician is doing."

"It is very important that doctors be aware of both cultures," Dr. Kleinman said. "It is essential that they be competent in technical management. This is what they can do to help. But they also must respect the patient's and family's experience at the end of life."

As physicians struggle to provide the best end-of-life care possible for patients from diverse backgrounds, there are some easy issues and some difficult ones for doctors to address, said Barbara A. Koenig, PhD, of the Center for Biomedical Ethics at Stanford University.

"It is easy to teach that people vary tremendously in their ability to talk about pain or that different religions specify certain ways in which the body must be handled after death," she said.

"The hard issues are those that violate the culture of biomedicine or of the recently instituted bioethics, like when a family doesn't want to reveal the diagnosis or prognosis to the patient."

And of course, even Dr. Koenig's "easy issues" can fail to be addressed in practice. Bookda Gheisar, executive director of the Cross-Cultural Health Program in Seattle, described a recent case in which the 9-year-old daughter of an Arab family died in a Seattle hospital. "The father called the relatives, who arrived within a couple of hours. They go to the nursing station saying, "We're here to take the body." Well, the body was no longer in the hospital. They had already moved it to the morgue."

The family, Gheisar said, was appalled. "The room seemed absolutely untouched by the life and death of this child."

The issue of "truth-telling"—of telling a patient that the physician expects him or her to die—and the related issue of asking a patient to make decisions about do-not-resuscitate orders or advance directives arise over and over in the literature and in conversations about cross-cultural end-of-life care. These issues arise repeatedly in clinical practice as well.

"So many family members say, "If the test result is bad, we want you to tell us first and let us decide whether to tell our father or our mother." But the providers say, "I have responsibilities here—and liabilities. I have to tell, " said Gheisar, whose work in multicultural Seattle puts her in contact with families from the Asian Pacific Islands, Southeast Asia, East Africa, and recently, Bosnia and Iraq, among many other locales.

The reasons families may wish to prevent discussion of death with the patient vary.

"Some cultural groups feel that talking about what might happen makes it happen and that focusing on negative things can kill people. You see that sort of attitude in all groups, but maybe it is more common in recent immigrants," said Diane E. Meier, MD, the director of the palliative care program at Mount Sinai School of Medicine in New York City.

What Dr. Meier called "the protective impulse toward dishonesty" can also arise from the simple desire to shield a frail family member from emotional pain. She described with admiration her recent experience caring for an elderly Filipina woman with metastatic lung cancer.

"She had nine totally loving children," Meier said. "I watched this, almost like a minuet, a sort of gentle attentiveness to her space. Not forcing it on her, although the necessary discussions did take place, the decisions did get made. There was a recognition that she was not purely an autonomous person, that she was a frail elderly woman highly enmeshed in her family."

Making it clear when care is futile

Questions about when and how to end treatment must also be viewed through a culturally sensitive prism.

"The whole issue of limiting treatment is quite foreign to many people," Dr. Koenig said. "We have this sort of Love Story image, that at some point the doctor will have a discussion with you, you'll decide to stop treatment and you'll die. That is not a narrative everybody understands. You'll have a very well-meaning doctor, maybe through an interpreter, talk to a patient about stopping treatment, and the patient will misinterpret these efforts to withhold treatment as meaning that they're better."

Barbara Sharf, PhD, a professor of health communication at Texas A&M in College Station, described the case of a Syrian man in his 30s hospitalized for cancer.

"The medical staff wanted to talk to him, or someone, about treatment protocols. One they felt might have extended his life but was more brutal than chemo. The issue was complicated because he had a young wife who was pregnant. The wife wasn't part of the decision-making in this culture," she said. "The question was, did he want to extend his life to see the new child? The medical staff felt this should be his decision, but the elder brother had laid down as a ground rule that there should be no discussion of cancer or death with the patient."

"There's an irony here," Dr. Sharf added, "because until recently, doctors were still into being paternalistic and shielding patients from the truth. Now we've re-geared them to be candid and talk with patients, but in some cultures, that may not be a good thing to do."

Dr. Sharf suggested that "we broaden our notions of informed consent, that the patient decide what he wants to be informed about and when he wants to delegate responsibility."

"Anybody who says there's some cut-and-dried rule there, in cases that are cross-cultural or otherwise, is lying," said Anne Fadiman, author of *The Spirit Catches You and You Fall Down* (Farrar Straus & Giroux, 1997), a chronicle of the tragedy of errors that resulted from the collision of cultures between two Hmong parents and their doctors over the care of their epileptic daughter.

Can cultural competence be taught?

Some argue that efforts to become culturally competent entail their own pitfalls.

Dr. Koenig, in fact, objected to the very phrase "cultural competence."

"It's become a growth industry, with people who go out and do trainings," she said. "They treat culture as though it's just another one of many diagnostic variables. . . . You can talk about these kinds of trends in populations, but you can never assume that for any individual, because of skin color or ethnic heritage, you know what they will want."

In a recent paper, Dr. Koenig and her co-authors described two patients, both working-class Chinese women in their 40s who had immigrated to the United States within the past decade and who were dying of cancer. The first woman had shielded herself, or had been shielded by her family, from understanding that she was dying. To the distaste of her physician, who described the family as "abnormal," she had ceded to her older brother the responsibility of making decisions about her care. In contrast, the second woman, who had been the economic mainstay of her family, was very much in control of the decision-making about treatment.

"We have two women from 'the same' culture, yet their ways of being in the world are radically different," the authors wrote.

Fadiman expressed a more positive view of training programs and efforts to integrate cross-cultural care into medical school curricula.

While acknowledging that, "Yes, they can reinforce stereotypes," Fadiman argued that training programs can also give efforts to be alive to cultural differences "a sort of official imprimatur" that will improve care.

"Anybody who thinks that one three-day course is going to be a panacea is arrogant as well as wrong," she said. "However, the solution is not to have no training."

Dr. Koenig acknowledged that familiarity with specific cultures can be of value. "I think if you're working in Fresno, it's malpractice if you know nothing about the Hmong," she said.

"In my experience in New York City, the heterogeneity of individuals swamps the cultural differences," said Mount Sinai's Dr. Meier. "It is very important not to generalize."

She cited the "received wisdom that people from nondominant cultures, from lower socioeconomic groups, have the least trust in the medical system." But while she has found that true in some instances, others "didn't fit the paradigm."

She described the case of a Latina woman with breast cancer who delegated decisions about her care to one of her sons "because of her desire to keep peace in the family." The son was distrustful of the medical establishment, accusing the doctors of wanting "to experiment on my mother," and blocked surgery, with the result that "her whole chest wall was gone because of him."

On the other hand, she described her recent experience with an African-American man hospitalized after a heart attack that left him with substantial brain damage. "This guy's wishes were well known to everybody. Over and over he had said he didn't want to be kept alive in that sort of state. This family was very, very clear that they wanted everything stopped, and they were very grateful to the high tech medicine at Mount Sinai that had kept him alive so long."

Her conclusion: "You can't substitute anything for sitting down and talking with them."

Harvard's Dr. Kleinman expressed uneasiness about whether there is time in modern medicine for such conversations.

"It is much less likely the doctor is going to do that now because of the compression of space and time and funding, vis-à-vis managed care," he said. "You can't see an elderly diabetic patient in 15 minutes in an outpatient setting and deal with these issues. Doctors, morally, they know that engaging the patient is critical for their care; but in terms of practical life, they just can't do it."

Mistaking Medicine

Deborah L. Shelton, *AMNews,* September 21, 1998

At a time when patients are expected to understand—even manage—more of their own health care, illiteracy is growing. Physicians can help.

Not everyone can carry out doctor's orders.

Take the woman who was asked how she'd administer the antibiotics prescribed to treat her child's ear infection. She measured the amoxicillin in a large serving spoon and then asked whether to pour it in the baby's ear or mouth.

Then there's the elderly man who landed in an emergency department with congestive heart failure. He had stopped taking his ACE inhibitor while his daughter was on vacation because he couldn't read the pill bottle.

In another case, a woman with diabetes who had been taught self-injection using oranges, routinely injected her insulin into an orange and then ate it.

Health illiteracy, the inability of patients to read, comprehend and/or act appropriately on medical instructions, is a widespread problem, but one that many doctors are unaware of.

Physicians might wrongly assume patients are being willfully noncompliant when they don't show up for medical appointments or fail to take medications as prescribed. In fact, the patients might not know how to read a thermometer, the label on a medicine bottle or an appointment slip.

Communication involves "a lot of back and forth between people, and that's not what [physicians] were trained to do," said Karen Hein, MD, former executive director of the Institute of Medicine, a private agency that advises Congress on public health issues. "We were trained to tell people things, not to listen."

Illiteracy is an invisible but extensive problem.

About 21% of adults, or 40 million to 44 million people, are functionally illiterate, reading at or below a fifth grade level, according to the U.S. Dept. of Education's 1993 National Adult Literacy Survey. An additional 25% of adults, another 50 million people, are only marginally literate, meaning they cannot understand, interpret and apply written material to accomplish daily tasks.

Yet, patients are being asked to monitor and provide more of their own care, which requires strong reading and comprehension skills. Consider that 25 years ago, the instruction to patients newly diagnosed with asthma was simply to take theophylline as prescribed, noted a recent AMA Council on Scientific Affairs report.

"Today [asthma] patients are asked to objectively monitor their disease with a peak flow meter, select and correctly use the appropriate inhalers, sometimes augment therapy with tapering doses of oral steroids, and identify and avoid triggers that exacerbate their asthma," the report said.

The AMA addressed the issue in June when delegates to its Annual Meeting called for increased awareness of health illiteracy and third-party reimbursement for physicians offering patient education programs for individuals with limited reading, writing and comprehension skills.

Health illiteracy "should be in our minds every time we make a decision," said William J. Terry, MD, an Alabama delegate who said the report was the most important document before that House of Delegates. "These statistics are overwhelming. How can you communicate with patients if they can't understand you?"

Colliding trends

The Robert Wood Johnson Foundation funded the largest study ever to examine the prevalence of health illiteracy. The findings, published in the *Journal of the American Medical Association* in 1995, were eye-opening.

About 42% of 2,659 mostly indigent and minority patients at two urban hospitals didn't know what it meant to take medication on an empty stomach. More than 59% didn't understand a standard consent form, and 26% couldn't figure out when their next appointment was.

Among those older than 60, the prevalence of inadequate or marginal functional health literacy was 81%, which points out that "this is clearly an issue for the elderly," said study co-author Mark V. Williams, MD, associate professor at Emory University School of Medicine and director of the Center for Clinical Effectiveness.

In another study, Dr. Williams and colleagues, using a 50-item test, rated the literacy skills of 402 patients with hypertension and 114 with diabetes at the two hospitals. Most of the patients with inadequate or marginal health literacy—63% of those with hypertension and 55% of the diabetics—didn't know that canned vegetables contain a lot of salt or that feeling shaky is an indication of a low glucose level.

"Clearly, it's in our best interests to try and develop a response—short of teaching people how to read—to improve treatment outcomes," said Stephen A. Somers, PhD, president of the Center for Health Care Strategies, a nonprofit policy and resource center affiliated with the Woodrow Wilson School of Public and International Affairs at Princeton University.

Illiteracy could become an even bigger problem in medicine as a result of demographic and health industry trends.

The elderly have higher rates of illiteracy, and their numbers have been growing rapidly. The elderly are also more likely to have multiple health care providers and take more than one medication.

But as health care shifts more to self-care, said Joanne Schwartzberg, MD, director of the AMA's department of geriatric health, "we're setting patients up for failure."

Technology and health care delivery systems, services and products are also becoming more complex, making it "even harder for those with poor navigational skills," said Dr. Somers.

For example, drugs that once were accessible only by prescription are now widely available over the counter. Their safe use requires, among other things, an understanding of proper dosages and possible interactions with other prescription and nonprescription medications.

Communication in both directions

It's not always easy to identify who has poor literacy skills. The greatest number of low-literate Americans are native-born whites, but the elderly, nonwhites, immigrants and the poor are disproportionately low-skilled.

"The biggest problem is that some patients don't even recognize that they have diminished literacy skills," Dr. Williams said.

And shame can prevent some individuals from acknowledging that they can't read or understand instructions.

Even though time constraints are forcing many physicians to spend less time with patients, "doctors need to sit down and not just tell them what to do, but make sure they understand," he said.

One solution is the "show-me" approach, which involves asking patients to demonstrate how they would take their medications or perform a certain procedure.

"See if they can read the label on the medicine bottle," suggests Dr. Schwartzberg. "Ask them to read it and find out if they understand it."

But don't be surprised if they say they can't read because they left their glasses at home, a common ploy used by someone who's illiterate. Physicians can follow up by asking if anyone assists them with their medicine or if they ever have trouble reading or remembering how to take it, Dr. Schwartzberg said.

Tools also exist to help physicians and other health professionals assess a patient's literacy skills.

The Rapid Estimate of Adult Literacy in Medicine is a three-minute assessment of a patient's recognition of commonly used medical terms and provides an approximate grade level of their reading ability.

The Test of Functional Health Literacy in Adults is a more sophisticated tool that uses written forms, such as medication labels or those explaining Medicaid rights and responsibilities, to measure individuals' reading and numeric literacy skills and their ability to interpret and act on forms, medication directions and other forms of communication that are typical in health care settings.

While some experts say nurses, educators or other health professionals can do such assessments, Dr. Schwartzberg says it's critical for doctors to do it. Evaluating patients' skills first-hand gives the physician the opportunity to make prescriptions simpler if it's too difficult for them to understand, she said.

There are other strategies. People at all literacy levels prefer simple, attractive educational materials, such as pictures, diagrams or symbols to replace words, and videotapes that use common words instead of medical terminology, Dr. Somers said. Color-coding medicines and tailoring medication schedules to fit a patient's daily routine can also improve compliance, he said.

"This smacks of patient education, and many physicians think that's up to somebody else: a nurse or educator," added Dr. Hein. "But if [physicians] don't do this or do it poorly, it's a big opportunity missed. What good does it do our patients if we have all the latest knowledge about diseases and treatments but can't communicate it?"

The serious health consequences of low literacy

- More than 40% of chronically ill Americans are functionally illiterate.

- More than 66% of people older than 60 have inadequate or marginal literacy skills.

- Of 58 low-literate patients surveyed, 67% had never told their spouse about their reading difficulties; 19% had never told anyone.

- Low-literate patients are 52% more likely to be hospitalized than those with adequate literacy skills.

- Only 50% of low-literate diabetic patients know the symptoms of low blood sugar; more than 90% of literate diabetic patients know.

Source: Center for Health Care Strategies Inc.

How to test your patients

For more information about testing patients' literacy skills, see:

Davis et al: "Rapid estimate of adult literacy in medicine: a shortened screening instrument," *Family Medicine,* 1993;25:391-395.

Parker et al: "The test of functional health literacy in adults: a new instrument for measuring patients' literacy skills," *Journal of General Internal Medicine,* 1995;10:537-541.

C. Selected AMA Policies

H-160.991   Health Care Needs of the
              Homosexual Population

H-165.877   Universal Coverage for Prenatal
              Care, Children and Adolescents

H-170.974   Update on AMA Policies on Human
              Sexuality and Family Life Education

H-200.972   Primary Care Physicians in the
              Inner City

H-210.980   Physicians and Family Caregivers:
              Shared Responsibility

H-210.981   On-Site Physician Home Health
              Care

H-210.986   Physicians and Family
              Caregivers—A Model for
              Partnership

H-210.991   The Education of Physicians in
              Home Health Care

H-210.992   Tax Deduction for Individuals
              Rendering Home Care to Family
              Members with a Long-Term Illness

H-215.985   Child Care in Hospitals

H-245.986   Infant Mortality in the United States

H-295.897   Enhancing the Cultural Competence
              of Physicians

H-295.902   Alternative Medicine

H-295.905   Promoting Culturally Competent
              Health Care

H-295.912   Education of Medical Students and
              Residents About Domestic Violence
              Screening

H-295.932   End of Life Care

H-295.950   Patient Physician Communication

H-295.975   Educating Competent and Caring
              Health Professionals

H-295.981   Geriatric Medicine

H-295.999   Medical Student Support Groups

H-320.996   Confidentiality

H-350.971   AMA Initiatives Regarding Minorities

H-350.972   Improving the Healthcare of Black and
              Minority Populations in the United
              States

H-350.973   Sickle Cell Anemia

H-350.974   Racial and Ethnic Disparities in Health
              Care

H-350.975   Improving the Healthcare of Hispanic
              Populations in the United States

H-350.976   Improving the Healthcare of American
              Indians

H-350.977   Indian Health Service

H-350.978   Minorities in the Health Professions

H-350.979   Increase the Representation of Minority
              and Economically Disadvantaged
              Populations in the Medical Profession

H-350.980   AMA's Role in Preparing Minority and
              Disadvantaged Youth for Careers in
              Medicine and the Health Professions

H-350.981   AMA Support of American Indian Health
              Career Opportunities

H-350.982   Project 3000 by 2000—Medical
              Education for Under-Represented
              Minority Students

H-350.983   Federal Guidelines for Standardization
              of Race/Ethnicity

H-370.974   Working Toward an Increased Number
              of Minorities Registered as Potential
              Bone Marrow Donors

H-370.975   Ethical Issues in the Procurement of
              Organs Following Cardiac Death

B-1.50 Discrimination

Membership in any category of the American Medical Association or in any of its constituent associations shall not be denied or abridged because of sex, color, creed, race, religion, disability, ethnic origin, national origin, sexual orientation, age, or for any other reason unrelated to character or competence. Nor shall membership in any category of the AMA or in any of its constituent associations be denied to any person who meets the requirements for membership as set forth in these Bylaws and in the bylaws of the applicant's respective constituent association. In considering applicants for membership, information as to the character, ethics, professional status, and professional activities of the individual may be considered.

E-8.18 Informing Families of a Patient's Death

Disclosing the death of a patient to the patient's family is a duty that goes to the very heart of the physician-patient relationship and should not be readily delegated to others by the attending physician. The emotional needs of the family and the integrity of the physician-patient relationship must at all times be given foremost consideration.

Physicians in residency training may be asked to participate in the communication of information about a patient's death, if that request is commensurate with the physician's prior training or experience and previous close personal relationship with the family.

It would not be appropriate for the attending physician or resident to request that a medical student notify family members of a patient's death. Medical students should be trained in issues of death and dying, and should be encouraged to accompany attending physicians when news of a patient's death is conveyed to the family members.

(Issued March 1992 based on the report "Informing Families of a Patient's Death: Guidelines for the Involvement of Medical Students," issued December 1989; updated June 1994)

E-9.035 Gender Discrimination in the Medical Profession

Physician leaders in medical schools and other medical institutions should take immediate steps to increase the number of women in leadership positions as such positions become open. There is already a large enough pool of female physicians to provide strong candidates for such positions. Also, adjustments should be made to ensure that all physicians are equitably compensated for their work. Women and men in the same specialty with the same experience and doing the same work should be paid the same compensation.

Physicians in the workplace should actively develop the following:

(a) Retraining or other programs that facilitate the reentry of physicians who take time away from their careers to have a family;

(b) On-site child care services for dependent children;

(c) Policies providing job security for physicians who are temporarily not in practice due to pregnancy or family obligations.

Physicians in the academic medical setting should strive to promote the following:

(a) Extension of tenure decisions through 'stop the clock' programs, relaxation of the seven-year rule, or part-time appointments that would give faculty members longer to achieve standards for promotion and tenure;

(b) More reasonable guidelines regarding the appropriate quantity and timing of published material needed for promotion or tenure that would emphasize quality over quantity and that would encourage the pursuit of careers based on individual talent rather than tenure standards that undervalue teaching ability and overvalue research;

(c) Fair distribution of teaching, clinical, research, administrative responsibilities, and access to tenure tracks between men and women. Also, physicians in academic institutions should consider formally structuring the mentoring process, possibly matching students or faculty with advisors through a fair and visible system.

Where such policies do not exist or have not been followed, all medical workplaces and institutions should create strict policies to deal with sexual harassment. Grievance committees should have broad representation of both sexes and other groups. Such committees should have the power to enforce harassment policies and be accessible to those persons they are meant to serve.

Grantors of research funds and editors of scientific or medical journals should consider blind peer review of grant proposals and articles for publication to help prevent bias. However, grantors and editors will be able to consider the author's identity and give it appropriate weight. (Issued June 1994 based on the report "Gender Discrimination in the Medical Profession," issued June 1993 [See H-65.904])

E-9.065 Caring for the Poor

Each physician has an obligation to share in providing care to the indigent. The measure of what constitutes an appropriate contribution may vary with circumstances such as community characteristics, geographic location, the nature of the physician's practice and specialty, and other conditions. All physicians should work to ensure that the needs of the poor in their communities are met. Caring for the poor should be a regular part of the physician's practice schedule.

In the poorest communities, it may not be possible to meet the needs of the indigent for physicians' services by relying solely on local physicians. The local physicians should be able to turn for assistance to their colleagues in prosperous communities, particularly those in close proximity.

Physicians are meeting their obligation, and are encouraged to continue to do so, in a number of ways such as seeing indigent patients in their offices at no cost or at reduced cost, serving at freestanding or hospital clinics that treat the poor, and participating in government programs that provide health care to the poor. Physicians can also volunteer their services at weekend clinics for the poor and at shelters for battered women or the homeless.

In addition to meeting their obligation to care for the indigent, physicians can devote their energy, knowledge, and prestige to designing and lobbying at all levels for better programs to provide care for the poor. (Issued June 1994 based on the report "Caring for the Poor," issued December 1992)

E-9.12 Physician-Patient Relationship: Respect for Law and Human Rights

The creation of the physician-patient relationship is contractual in nature. Generally, both the physician and the patient are free to enter into or decline the relationship. A physician may decline to undertake the care of a patient whose medical condition is not within the physician's current competence. However, physicians who offer their services to the public may not decline to accept patients because of sex, color, creed, race, religion, disability, ethnic origin, national origin, sexual orientation, age, or any other basis that would constitute invidious discrimination. Furthermore, physicians who are obligated under preexisting contractual arrangements may not decline to accept patients as provided by those arrangements. (Issued July 1986; updated June 1994)

E-9.121 Racial Disparities in Health Care

Disparities in medical care based on immutable characteristics such as race must be avoided. Whether such disparities in health care are caused by treatment decisions, differences in income and education, sociocultural factors, or failures by the medical profession, they are unjustifiable and must be eliminated. Physicians should examine their own practices to ensure that racial prejudice does not affect clinical judgment in medical care. (Issued March 1992 based on the report "Black-White Disparities in Health Care," issued December 1989; updated June 1994)

E-9.122 Gender Disparities in Health Care

A patient's gender plays an appropriate role in medical decision making when biological differences between the sexes are considered. However, some data suggest that gender bias may be playing a role in medical decision making. Social attitudes, including stereotypes, prejudices, and other evaluations based on gender role expectations, may play themselves out in a variety of subtle ways. Physicians must ensure that gender is not used inappropriately as a consideration in clinical decision making. Physicians should examine their practices and attitudes for influence of social or cultural biases that could be inadvertently affecting the delivery of medical care.

Research on health problems that affect both genders should include male and female subjects, and results of medical research done solely on males should not be generalized to females without evidence that results apply to both sexes. Medicine and society in general should ensure that resources for medical research should be distributed in a manner that promotes the health of both sexes to the greatest extent possible. (Issued March 1992 based on the report "Gender Disparities in Clinical Decision Making," issued December 1990; updated June 1994)

E-9.131 HIV-Infected Patients and Physicians

A physician may not ethically refuse to treat a patient whose condition is within the physician's current realm of competence solely because the patient is seropositive for HIV. Persons who are seropositive should not be subjected to discrimination based on fear or prejudice.

When physicians are unable to provide the services required by an HIV-infected patient, they should make appropriate referrals to those physicians or facilities equipped to provide such services.

A physician who knows that he or she is seropositive should not engage in any activity that creates an identified risk of transmission of the disease to others. A physician who has HIV disease or who is seropositive should consult colleagues as to which activities the physician can pursue without creating a risk to patients. (Issued March 1992 based on the report "Ethical Issues in the Growing AIDS Crisis," issued December 1987; updated June 1996)

H-5.989 Freedom of Communication Between Physicians and Patients

It is the policy of the AMA:

(1) to strongly condemn any interference by the government or other third parties that causes a physician to compromise his or her medical judgment as to what information or treatment is in the best interest of the patient;

(2) working with other organizations as appropriate, to vigorously pursue legislative relief from regulations or statutes that prevent physicians from freely discussing with or providing information to patients about medical care and procedures or which interfere with the physician-patient relationship;

(3) to communicate to HHS its continued opposition to any regulation that proposes restrictions on physician-patient communications; and

(4) to inform the American public as to the dangers inherent in regulations or statutes restricting communication between physicians and their patients.

(Sub. Res. 213, A-91; Reaffirmed: Sub. Res. 232, I-91; Reaffirmed by Rules & Credentials Cmt., A-96; Reaffirmed by Sub. Res. 133 and BOT Rep. 26, A-97; Reaffirmed by Sub. Res. 203 and 707, A-98)

H-20.966 AMA HIV Policy Update

(Note: Only relevant portions of this policy are cited.)

Media (2b): [The AMA] continues to encourage public service announcements on abstinence, condom usage, and safer sex and encourages specifically targeted messages. Among the audiences that should receive focused messages in an appropriate language and style are intravenous drug users and their sexual partners and minority groups such as blacks and Hispanics;

Encouraging School HIV Education (14b): [The AMA] endorses and supports the education of elementary, secondary and college students regarding the modes of HIV transmission and prevention.
(BOT rep. X, I-89; reaffirmed: BOT Rep. I-93-34)

H-20.974 AIDS Prevention Through Educational Materials Directed at Minority Populations

The AMA supports attention to language and cultural appropriateness in HIV educational materials and encourages the development of additional materials designed to inform minorities of risk behaviors associated with HIV infection.
(Res. 121, I-88)

H-20.977 Reducing Transmission of Human Immunodeficiency Virus (HIV)

(Note: Only relevant portions of this policy are cited.)

In view of the urgent need to curtail the transmission of HIV infection in every segment of the population, including intravenous drug abusers, their sex partners, and offspring, the AMA:

(4) Continues to work with and encourage appropriate organizations to foster the development and/or enhancement of programs to provide comprehensive training of primary care physicians and other front-line health workers, specifically including those in drug treatment and community health centers and correctional facilities, focusing on basic knowledge of HIV infection, modes of transmission, and recommended risk reduction strategies.

(7) Urges development of educational, medical, and social support programs for pregnant IVDAs and those who may become pregnant to address the current and future health care needs of both mothers and newborns.

Further, the AMA advocates development of optimal care programs for HIV-positive and AIDS-symptomatic infants and their families. Such programs should include support systems to help parents care for these infants and simplified foster care arrangements for children whose parents are unable to provide such care.

(8) Advocates design of special education and service delivery programs to reduce the risk of HIV infection in, and provide appropriate treatment to, adolescent substance abusers, especially homeless, runaway, and detained adolescent who are seropositive or AIDS symptomatic and those whose lifestyles place them at risk for contracting HIV infection.

(10) Continues its efforts to bring to the profession and the public credible, up-to-date information on HIV infection and substance abuse through its publications, conferences, and participation in appropriate fora and demonstration projects.
(CSA Rep. C, A-88; amended: BOT Rep. I-93-34; reaffirmed I-96)

H-20.979 Alternatives to Inpatient Care for Persons with AIDS or ARC

The AMA supports increased funding for reimbursement and other incentives to encourage expanded availability of alternatives to inpatient care of persons with AIDS and ARC, including intermediate care facilities, skilled nursing facilities, home care, residential hospice, home hospice, and other support systems.
(Res. 54, A-88)

H-25.993 Senior Care

The AMA supports accelerating its ongoing efforts to work responsibly with Congress, senior citizen groups, and other interested parties to address the health care needs of seniors. These efforts should address but not be limited to:

(1) multiple hospital admissions in a single calendar year;

(2) long-term care;

(3) hospice and home health care; and

(4) pharmaceutical costs.
(Sub. Res. 181, I-89)

H-25.999 Health Care for Older Patients

The AMA

(1) endorses and encourages further experimentation and application of home-centered programs of care for older patients and recommends further application of other new experiments in providing better health care, such as rehabilitation education services in nursing homes, chronic illness referral centers, and progressive patient care in hospitals;

(2) recommends that there be increased emphasis at all levels of medical education on the new challenges being presented to physicians in health care of the older person, on the growing opportunities for effective use of health maintenance programs and restorative services with this age group, and on the importance of a total view of health, embracing social, psychological, economic, and vocational aspects, and

(3) encourages continued leadership and participation by the medical profession in community programs for seniors.
(Committee on Aging Report, I-60; reaffirmed: CLRPD Rep. C, A-88)

H-55.984 Screening and Treatment for Breast and Cervical Cancer

The AMA

(1) supports increased funding for comprehensive programs to screen low income women for breast and cervical cancer and to assure access to definitive treatment; and

(2) encourages state and local medical societies to monitor local public health screening programs to assure that they are linked to treatment resources in the public or private sector.
(Res. 411, A-92)

H-55.999 Symptomatic and Supportive Care for Patients with Cancer

The AMA recognizes the need to ensure the highest standards of symptomatic, rehabilitative, and supportive care for patients with both cured and advanced cancer. The Association supports clinical research in evaluation of rehabilitative and palliative care procedures for the cancer patient, this to include such areas as pain control, relief of nausea and vomiting, management of complications of surgery, radiation and chemotherapy, appropriate hemotherapy, nutritional support, emotional support, rehabilitation, and the hospice concept. The AMA actively encourages the implementation of continuing education of the practicing American physician regarding the most effective methodology for meeting the symptomatic, rehabilitative, supportive, and other human needs of the cancer patient. It is also recognized that the substantial cost of cancer management must be a continuing concern of the practicing physician caring for the cancer patient.
(CSA Rep. H, I-78; reaffirmed: CLRPD Rep. C, A-89)

H-60.974 Children and Youth With Disabilities

It is the policy of the AMA

(1) to inform physicians of the special health care needs of children and youth with disabilities;

(2) to encourage physicians to pay special attention during the preschool physical examination to identify physical, emotional, or developmental disabilities that have not been previously noted;

(3) to encourage physicians to provide services to children and youth with disabilities that are family-centered, community-based, and coordinated among the various individual providers and programs serving the child;

(4) to encourage physicians to provide schools with medical information to ensure that children and youth with disabilities receive appropriate school health services;

(5) to encourage physicians to establish formal transition programs or activities that help adolescents with disabilities and their families to

plan and make the transition to the adult medical care system;

(6) to inform physicians of available educational resources, such as the National Center for Youth with Disabilities and the National Center for Networking Community Based Services and other local resources, as well as various manuals that would help prepare them to provide family-centered health care; and

(7) to encourage physicians to make their offices accessible to patients with disabilities, especially when doing office construction and renovations.
(CSA Rep. J, I-91)

H-65.990 Civil Rights Restoration

The AMA reaffirms its long-standing policy that there is no basis for the denial to any human being of equal rights, privileges and responsibilities commensurate with his or her individual capabilities and ethical character because of an individual's sex, sexual orientation, race, religion, disability, ethnic origin, national origin, or age.
(BOT Rep. LL, I-86; amended by Sunset Report, I-96)

H-65.999 Equal Opportunity

The AMA endorses the principle of equal opportunity of employment and practice in the medical field.
(Sub. Res. 61, part 1, A-76; reaffirmed: CLRPD Rep. C, A-89)

H-85.966 Hospice Coverage and Underutilization

The policy of the AMA is that:

(1) The use of hospice care be actively utilized to provide the patient and family with appropriate physical and emotional support, but not preclude or prevent the use of appropriate palliative therapies to continue to treat the underlying malignant disease if the

patient is showing response to such palliative therapy;

(2) The goal of terminal care is to relieve patient suffering and not necessarily to cure incurable disease;

(3) Appropriate active palliation should be a covered hospital benefit; and

(4) The initiation of hospice care may be done at the discretion of the attending physician without stopping whatever medical care is being rendered if the physician believes the patient is in the last six months of life.
(Res. 515, A-94)

H-85.967 Good Care of the Dying Patient

The AMA

(1) encourages research into the needs of dying patients and how the care system could better serve them;

(2) encourages education programs for all appropriate health care professionals, and the public as well, in care of the dying patient; and

(3) supports improved reimbursement for health care practices that are important in good care of the dying patient, such as the coordination and continuity of care, "maintenance" level services, counseling for patient and family, use of multidisciplinary teams, and effective palliation of symptoms.
(CSA Rep. 2-A-94)

H-85.968 Patient Self Determination Act

The AMA will:

(1) lend its administrative, legislative, and public relations support to assuring that the specific wishes of the individual patient as specified in his or her advance directive be strictly honored in or out of the hospital setting;

(2) encourage all physicians and their patients to execute an advance directive prior to the time of severe acute or terminal illness; and

(3) promote efforts to develop a national system to assist emergency medical personnel to rapidly ascertain a person's wishes with regard to resuscitation, regardless of his or her state of location.
(Res. 228, I-93)

H-85.971 Resource on Death and Dying

The AMA will collect and make available in one publication or packet existing AMA reports and policy statements on death and dying to include:

(1) a definition of death;

(2) guidelines for withholding treatment; and

(3) information on living wills, durable powers of attorney, patient autonomy, medical-legal aspects of end-of-life care, and related matters.
(Sub. Res. 1, A-92)

H-85.972 Compassionate Care of the Terminally III

The AMA will work with appropriate entities to promote the awareness of modern high-quality hospice-type care to all those who prefer such care and urges physicians to advise patients about this option, which can be exercised directly, when competent, or via advance directive when incompetent.
(Res. 705, A-92)

H-85.979 Informing Families of a Patient's Death: Guidelines for the Involvement of Medical Students

Specific training and experience provide invaluable assistance to physicians who must communicate information about a patient's death to members of the patient's family. Medical students therefore should be provided with appropriate training in issues related to death and dying. As one component of such training, students should be encouraged to accompany attending physicians when news of a patient's death is conveyed to family members. Students then should be afforded the opportunity to

openly discuss the experience with the attending physician, as well as with others who provide emotional support to the family. However, it would not be appropriate for the attending physician to request that a medical student notify family members of a patient's death. The communication of such information goes to the very heart of the physician-patient relationship and, as such, is a solemn duty that ought not to be readily delegated by the attending physician. As part of their clinical training, however, house staff may be asked to participate in the communication of information about a patient's death. Such participation must be commensurate with the physician's prior training and experience and, as with other components of clinical training, must be appropriately supervised until the physician has demonstrated his or her ability to perform the task independently. Even house staff who are appropriately trained may not be asked, as a mere convenience to a senior physician, to notify family members of a patient's death. The emotional needs of the family and the integrity of the physician-patient relationship must at all times be given foremost consideration.
(CEJA Rep. B, I-89)

H-140.953 Patient Responsibilities

The AMA has adopted the following principles of patient responsibility:

(1) Good communication is essential to a successful physician-patient relationship. To the extent possible, patients have a responsibility to express their concerns clearly to their physicians and be honest.

(2) Patients have a responsibility to provide a complete medical history, to the extent possible, including information about past illnesses, medications, hospitalizations, family history of illness, and other matters relating to present health.

(3) In addition to explaining known medical background to their physician, patients have a responsibility to request information or clarification about their health status or treatment when they do not fully understand what has been described.

(4) Once patients and physicians agree upon the goals of therapy, patients have a responsibility to cooperate with the treatment plan. Compliance with physician instructions is often essential to public and individual safety. Patients also have a responsibility to disclose whether previously agreed upon treatments are being followed and to indicate when they would like to reconsider the treatment plan.

(5) Patients generally have a responsibility to meet their financial obligations with regard to medical care or to discuss financial hardships with their physicians. Patients should be cognizant of the costs associated with using a limited resource like health care and should try to use medical resources judiciously.

(6) Patients should discuss end-of-life decisions with their physicians and make their wishes known. Such a discussion might also include writing an advance directive.

(7) Patients should be committed to health maintenance through health-enhancing behavior. Illness can often be prevented by a healthy lifestyle, and patients must take personal responsibility when they are able to avert the development of disease.

(8) Patients should also have an active interest in the effects of their conduct on others and refrain from behavior that unreasonably places the health of others at risk. Patients should inquire as to the means and likelihood of infectious disease transmission and act upon that information which can best prevent further transmission.

(9) Patients should discuss organ donation with their physicians and make applicable provisions. Patients who are part of an organ allocation system and await needed treatment or transplant should not try to go outside or manipulate the system. A fair system of allocation should be answered with public trust and an awareness of limited resources.

(10) Patients should not initiate or participate in fraudulent health care and should report illegal or unethical behavior to the appropriate law enforcement authorities, licensing boards, or medical societies.
(CEJA Rep. A, A-93)

H-140.966 Decisions Near the End of Life

The AMA believes that:

(1) The principle of patient autonomy requires that physicians must respect the decision to forgo life-sustaining treatment of a patient who possesses decision-making capacity. Life-sustaining treatment is any medical treatment that serves to prolong life without reversing the underlying medical condition. Life-sustaining treatment includes, but is not limited to, mechanical ventilation, renal dialysis, chemotherapy, antibiotics, and artificial nutrition and hydration.

(2) There is no ethical distinction between withdrawing and withholding life-sustaining treatment.

(3) Physicians have an obligation to relieve pain and suffering and to promote the dignity and autonomy of dying patients in their care. This includes providing effective palliative treatment even though it may foreseeably hasten death. More research must be pursued, examining the degree to which palliative care reduces the requests for euthanasia or assisted suicide.

(4) Physicians must not perform euthanasia or participate in assisted suicide. A more careful examination of the issue is necessary. Support, comfort, respect for patient autonomy, good communication, and adequate pain control may decrease dramatically the public demand for euthanasia and assisted suicide. In certain carefully defined circumstances, it would be humane to recognize that death is certain and suffering is great. However, the societal risks of involving physicians in medical interventions to cause patients' deaths is too great to condone euthanasia or physician-assisted suicide at this time.

(CEJA Rep. B, A-91; reaffirmed by BOT Rep. 59, A-96; reaffirmation, A-97)

H-140.970 Decisions to Forgo Life-Sustaining Treatment for Incompetent Patients

The AMA believes that

(1) Advance directives (living wills and durable powers of attorney for health care) are the best insurance for individuals that their interests will be promoted in the event that they become incompetent. Generally, it is most effective if the individual designates a proxy decision maker and discusses with the proxy his or her values regarding decisions about life support.

(2) Without an advance directive that designates a proxy, the patient's family should become the surrogate decision maker. Family includes persons with whom the patient is closely associated. In the case when there is no person closely associated with the patient, but there are persons who both care about the patient and have some relevant knowledge of the patient, such relations should be involved in the decision-making process, and may be appropriate surrogates.

(3) It is the responsibility of physicians to provide all relevant medical information and to explain to surrogate decision makers that decisions should be based on substituted judgment (what the patient would have decided) when there is evidence of patients' preferences and values. If there is not adequate evidence of preferences and values, the decision should be based on the best interests of the patient (what outcome would most likely promote the patient's well-being).

(4) Institutional ethics committees should be established for the purpose of facilitating sound decision making. These ethics committees should be structured so that a diversity of perspectives, including those from outside medicine, are represented.

(5) The surrogate's decision should almost always be accepted by the physician. However, there are four situations that may require either institutional or judicial review and/or intervention in the decision-making process. These situations are when

(a) there is no available family willing to be the patient's surrogate decision maker;

(b) there is a dispute among family members and there is no decision maker designated in an advance directive;

(c) a health care provider believes that the family's decision is clearly not what the patient would have decided if competent; and

(d) a health care provider believes that the decision is not a decision that could reasonably be judged to be in the patient's best interests. Decisions based on a conflict of interest generally would not be in the patient's best interest. In these four cases, the guidelines outlined in the report should be followed. In particular, when there are disputes among family members or between family and health care providers, the use of ethics committees specifically designed to facilitate sound decision making is recommended before resorting to the courts.

(6) Judicial review for decisions about life-sustaining treatment should be a last resort. It is strongly encouraged that when judicial review is necessary, in nonemergency situations, the courts should determine who is to make treatment decisions, including appointing a guardian, rather than making treatment decisions.

(7) When a permanently unconscious patient was never competent or had not left any evidence of previous preferences or values, since there is no objective way to ascertain what would be in the best interests of the patient, the surrogate's decision should not be challenged as long as the decision is based on the decision maker's true concern for what would be best for the patient.

(8) In the case of seriously ill or handicapped newborns, present and future interests of the infant must be considered. Due to the

complexities involved in deciding about life support for seriously ill newborns, physicians should specifically discuss with parents the risks and uncertainties involved. When possible, parents should be given time to adjust to the shock of the situation and absorb the medical information presented to them before making decisions about life-sustaining treatment. In addition, counseling services and an opportunity to talk with couples who have had to make similar decisions should be available to the parents.

(9) Due to the complexity of decisions for permanently unconscious patients and newborns, an ethics committee should be available, whenever possible, to facilitate the surrogate's decision making.

(10) Hospitals and other health care facilities should establish protocols regarding assessment of decision-making capacity, informing patients about advance directives, identifying surrogate decision makers, the use of advance directives, substituted judgment and best interests in decision making, and the procedures for challenging the decision of a surrogate. These protocols should be in accordance with the preceding CEJA guidelines.
(CEJA Rep. D, A-91)

H-140.975 Fundamental Elements of the Patient-Physician Relationship

From ancient times, physicians have recognized that the health and well-being of patients depends upon a collaborative effort between physician and patient. Patients share with physicians the responsibility for their own health care. The patient-physician relationship is of the greatest benefit to patients when they bring medical problems to the attention of their physicians in a timely fashion, provide information about their medical condition to the best of their ability, and work with their physicians in a mutually respectful alliance. Physicians can best contribute to this alliance by serving as their patients' advocate and by fostering these rights:

(1) The patient has the right to receive information from physicians and to discuss the benefits, risks, and costs of appropriate treatment alternatives. Patients should receive guidance from their physicians as to the optimal course of action. Patients are also entitled to obtain copies or summaries of their medical records, to have their questions answered, to be advised of potential conflicts of interest that their physicians might have, and to receive independent professional opinions.

(2) The patient has the right to make decisions regarding the health care that is recommended by his or her physician. Accordingly, patients may accept or refuse any recommended medical treatment.

(3) The patient has the right to courtesy, respect, dignity, responsiveness, and timely attention to his or her needs.

(4) The patient has the right to confidentiality. The physician should not reveal confidential communications or information without the consent of the patient, unless provided for by law or by the need to protect the welfare of the individual or the public interest.

(5) The patient has the right to continuity of health care. The physician has an obligation to cooperate in the coordination of medically indicated care with other health care providers treating the patient. The physician may not discontinue treatment of a patient, as long as further treatment is medically indicated, without giving the patient sufficient opportunity to make alternative arrangements for care.

(6) The patient has a basic right to have available adequate health care. Physicians, along with the rest of society, should continue to work toward this goal. Fulfillment of this right is dependent on society providing resources so that no patient is deprived of necessary care because of an inability to pay for the care. Physicians should continue their traditional assumption of a part of the responsibility for the medical care of those who cannot afford essential health care.
(CEJA Rep. A, A-90; reaffirmed: BOT Rep. I-93-25; reaffirmed by BOT Rep. 1 - I-94)

H-140.977 Residency Training in Medical-Legal Aspects of End-of-Life Care

The AMA encourages residency training programs, regardless of or in addition to current specialty- specific ACGME requirements, to promote and develop a high level of knowledge of and ethical standards for the use of such documents as living wills, durable powers of attorney for health care, and ordering DNR status, which should include medical, legal, and ethical principles guiding such physician decisions. This knowledge should include aspects of medical case management in which decisions are made to limit the duration and intensity of treatment.
(Res. 66, A-90)

H-140.990 Ethical Considerations in Health Care

1) When making treatment decisions that involve ethical choices, health care professionals and patients (or their authorized representatives) should strive for a high level of mutual understanding and shared decision-making.

2) The establishment of ethics committees at health care facilities to provide ethical guidance to protect patients' rights and responsibilities should be encouraged.

3) The inclusion of ethics in the curricula of health professions education programs and emphasis on ethical concerns in the traditional peer review process should be encouraged.
(BOT Rep. NN, A-87; reaffirmed: Sunset Report, I-97)

H-150.993 Medical Education in Nutrition

The AMA recommends that instruction on nutrition be included in the curriculum of medical schools in the United States.
(Sub. Res. 82, I-80; reaffirmed: CLRPD Rep. B, I-90; reaffirmed: CME Rep. 3, I-97)

H-160.931 Health Literacy

Our AMA:

(1) recognizes that limited patient literacy is a barrier to effective medical diagnosis and treatment;

(2) will work with members of the Federation and other relevant medical and nonmedical organizations to make the health care community aware that approximately one fourth of the adult population has limited literacy and difficulty understanding both oral and written health care information;

(3) encourages the development of undergraduate, graduate, and continuing medical education programs that train physicians to communicate with patients who have limited literacy skills;

(4) encourages all third-party payers to compensate physicians for formal patient education programs directed at individuals with limited literacy skills;

(5) encourages the US Department of Education to include questions regarding health status, health behaviors, and difficulties communicating with health care professionals in the National Adult Literacy Survey of 2002; and

(6) encourages the allocation of federal and private funds for research on health literacy.
(CSA Rep. 1, A-98)

H-160.959 Health Care Access for the Inner-City Poor

(1) The AMA reaffirms the following statement from Policy 140.975: Physicians should continue their traditional assumption of a part of the responsibility for the medical care of those who cannot afford essential health care.

(2) The AMA will pursue the following initiatives to improve access to health care in the inner city:

(a) Encourage the development of a congressional inner-city coalition, modeled after the Rural Health Care Coalition, to move an inner-city legislative health care agenda through Congress.

(b) Urge Congress to consider appropriate AMA-supported provisions from the rural health legislative agenda for application to health care services in the inner city as well; specifically those related to:

    i.   extension of Medicare and Medicaid bonuses to physicians practicing in medical service areas in the inner city where the poverty rate exceeds a certain threshold;

    ii. expanded private and federal funding of state-of-the-art medical equipment;

    iii. limited exemption for inner-city physicians from federal or state antitrust or other limitations prohibiting physicians from more effectively pooling their resources and otherwise working together;

    iv. tax credits for physicians practicing in underserved inner city areas to help make up practice-related income differentials for choosing to practice in those areas; and

    v.   loan forgiveness for practice in underserved areas

(c) Consider the development or support of additional legislation to implement such incentives for practice in the inner city as:

    i.   financial assistance with start-up costs; and

    ii. assistance with property and casualty insurance costs.

(d) To supplement overall efforts at tort reform, continue to pursue innovative approaches for relief of professional liability costs for inner-city physicians such as:

    i.   payment of malpractice damages by a state or local government agency; and

    ii. assistance in reducing physician costs for professional liability insurance

through payment of premiums or discounts on such premiums by a government agency.

(e) Encourage appropriate funding from public and private sources for inner-city hospitals.

(f) Encourage additional funding of community health resources through federal and private grants.

(3) The AMA urges medical schools to identify, expand, and publicize the roles they play in educating students to serve the inner-city poor. These include but are not limited to:

    (a) Recruiting more students likely to practice in the inner city;

    (b) Developing incentives for medical students to choose to practice in the inner city;

    (c) Providing exposure during undergraduate and graduate medical education to inner-city practice and practice role models; and

    (d) Working cooperatively with community groups to develop model health care training sites in the inner city.

(4) The AMA will encourage and where appropriate assist physicians and their local medical societies to work with teaching institutions, local health department, and community organizations in developing innovative service and financing mechanisms for delivering care in the inner city.

(5) The AMA supports the further development of innovative, multidisciplinary approaches to delivering health care in the inner city, including use of a wide variety of health professionals under proper physician (ie, MD/DO) supervision on a part-time or consultant basis and expanded use of physician assistants, nurse practitioners, nurse midwives, nutritionists, social workers, community outreach personnel, and lay workers.

(6) The AMA will work to reduce the professional and personal isolation of physicians working in the inner city by encouraging:

(a) Increased outreach activities and supportive interaction with such physicians by area medical schools;

(b) Increased availability and use of telecommunications and on-site consultant visits from such teaching centers;

(c) Practitioner linkages with the surrounding community through local customs and language training for health professionals where appropriate and the use of lay advisory committees for community clinics; and

(d) Local government measures to enhance personal safety.

(7) The AMA will stimulate more effective ways in which health education and preventive health services can be more effectively provided to and utilized by the inner-city underserved. Such services may include:

(a) Immunizations;

(b) Nutritional guidance;

(c) Family planning;

(d) Programs for prevention of sexually transmitted diseases;

(e) Substance abuse programs;

(f) Programs on domestic violence;

(g) Education in healthy lifestyles; and

(h) Parenting assistance and education.

(8) The AMA encourages efforts to address the transportation problems that interfere with access to health care for underserved populations.

(9) The AMA will study innovative approaches to assure patient access to prescription drugs.

(10) The AMA will identify and publicize models of successful health care delivery for underserved populations as examples for other medical schools, physicians, and community groups.

(11) The AMA will sponsor a national conference on access to health care for the inner-city poor.

(12) The AMA will study and develop a plan for provision and retention of generalist physicians for service to the inner-city poor.
(CMS/CME Rep., I-92)

H-160.978 The Mentally Ill Homeless

(1) The AMA believes that public policy initiatives directed to the homeless, including the homeless mentally ill population, should include the following components:

(a) access to care (eg, integrated, comprehensive services that permit flexible, individualized treatment; more humane commitment laws that ensure active inpatient treatment; and revisions in government funding laws to ensure eligibility for homeless persons);

(b) clinical concerns (eg, promoting diagnostic and treatment programs that address common health problems of the homeless population and promoting care that is sensitive to the overriding needs of this population for food, clothing, and residential facilities);

(c) program development (eg, advocating emergency shelters for the homeless; supporting a full range of supervised residential placements; developing specific programs for multiproblem patients, women, children, and adolescents; supporting the development of a clearinghouse; and promoting coalition development);

(d) educational needs;

(e) housing needs; and

(f) research needs.

(2) The AMA encourages medical schools and residency training programs to develop model curricula and to incorporate in teaching programs

content on health problems of the homeless population, including experiential community-based learning experiences.

(3) The AMA urges specialty societies to design interdisciplinary continuing medical education training programs that include the special treatment needs of the homeless population.
(BOT Rep. LL, A-86; reaffirmed: Sunset Report, I-96)

H-160.991 Health Care Needs of the Homosexual Population

(1) The AMA believes that the physician's nonjudgmental recognition of sexual orientation and behavior enhances the ability to render optimal patient care in health as well as in illness. In the case of the homosexual patient this is especially true, since unrecognized homosexuality by the physician or the patient's reluctance to report his or her sexual orientation and behavior can lead to failure to screen, diagnose, or treat important medical problems. With the help of the gay and lesbian community and through a cooperative effort between physician and the homosexual patient, effective progress can be made in treating the medical needs of this particular segment of the population.

(2) The AMA is committed to taking a leadership role in:

(a) educating physicians on the current state of research in and knowledge of homosexuality and the need to take an adequate sexual history; these efforts should start in medical school, but must also be a part of continuing medical education;

(b) educating physicians to recognize the physical and psychological needs of their homosexual patients;

(c) encouraging the development of educational programs for homosexuals to acquaint them with the diseases for which they are at risk; and

(d) encouraging physicians to seek out local or national experts in the health care needs of gay men and lesbians so that all physicians will achieve a better understanding of the medical needs of this population; and

(e) working with the gay and lesbian community to offer physicians the opportunity to better understand the medical needs of homosexual and bisexual patients.
(CSA Rep. C, I-81; reaffirmed: CLRPD Rep. F, I-91; CSA Rep. 8 - I-94)

H-165.877 Universal Coverage for Prenatal Care, Children, and Adolescents

The AMA supports appropriate legislation that will provide health coverage for the greatest number of children, adolescents, and pregnant women.
(Sub. Res. 208, A-97)

H-170.974 Update on AMA Policies on Human Sexuality and Family Life Education

(1) The AMA will work with educational and public health organizations to encourage development of systems for monitoring the implementation and evaluation of sexuality and HIV/AIDS education programs and establishing criteria to ensure that programs are comprehensive, developmentally appropriate, and effective.

(2) The AMA will indicate its willingness to assist the Centers for Disease Control and Prevention in updating the Guidelines for Effective School Health Education to Prevent the Spread of AIDS.

(3)

(a) Essential elements of effective sexuality education programs include the development of interpersonal skills and health-promoting attitudes, as well as factual information about sexual health.

(b) Coordination of developmentally age-appropriate school-based sexuality education programs with school- or community-based health services is an important part of comprehensive school health programs.

(c) School-based approaches to educating youth about condoms should be developed as part of comprehensive health education programs. Programs emphasizing condom negotiation skills, age-appropriate instructions on condom use, and availability of condoms in schools should be developed with participation of school administrators, parents, students and community health professionals. (Reaffirmed by CSA Rep. 3, A-95)

(d) The AMA supports efforts by secondary schools to provide training for teachers and staff on the educational and health needs of gay and lesbian youth and to discourage negative treatment of youth in school settings. (CSA Rep. D, A-93)

H-200.972 Primary Care Physicians in the Inner City

The AMA should pursue the following plan to improve the recruitment and retention of physicians in the inner city:

(a) Encourage the creation and pilot-testing of school-based, church-based, and community-based urban "family" health clinics, with an emphasis on health education, prevention, primary care, and prenatal care.

(b) Encourage the affiliation of these family health clinics with urban medical schools and teaching hospitals.

(c) Promote medical student rotations through the various inner-city neighborhood family health clinics, with financial assistance to the clinics to compensate their teaching efforts.

(d) Encourage medical schools and teaching hospitals to integrate third- and fourth-year

undergraduate medical education and residency training into these teams.

(e) Urge Congress to supplement federal funding for medical education to enhance incentives for entering primary care specialties.

(f) Urge the federal government to allow students who receive federal funds the option of participating in a "national urban service program," whereby federal and/or state loans would be repaid by service given to medically underserved urban areas. This might be done by urging the federal government to revitalize the National Health Service Corps or some other federal service program.

(g) Advocate the implementation of AMA policy that supports extension of the rural health clinic concept to urban areas with appropriate federal agencies.

(h) Study the concept of having medical schools with active outreach programs in the inner city offer additional training to physicians from nonprimary care specialties who are interested in achieving specific primary care competencies.

(i) Consider expanding opportunities for practicing physicians in other specialties to gain specific primary care competencies through short-term preceptorships or postgraduate fellowships offered by departments of family practice, internal medicine, pediatrics, etc. These may be developed so that they are part-time, thereby allowing physicians enrolling in these programs to practice concurrently.

(j) Encourage the AMA Senior Physicians Services Group to consider the use in underserved urban settings of retired physicians, with appropriate mechanisms to ensure their competence.

(k) Urge urban hospitals and medical societies to develop opportunities for physicians to work part-time to staff urban health clinics.

(l) Encourage the AMA and state medical associations to incorporate into state and federal health system reform legislative relief or immunity from professional liability for senior, part-time, or other physicians who serve the inner-city poor.

(m) Urge medical schools to seek out those students whose profiles indicate a likelihood of practicing in underserved urban areas, while establishing strict guidelines to preclude discrimination.

(n) Encourage medical school outreach activities into secondary schools, colleges, and universities to stimulate students with these profiles to apply to medical school.

(o) Encourage medical schools to continue to change their curriculum to put more emphasis on primary care.

(p) Urge state medical associations to support the development of methods to improve physician compensation for serving this population, such as Medicaid case management programs in their respective states.

(q) Urge urban hospitals and medical centers to seek out the use of available military health care resources and personnel, which can be used to fill gaps in urban care.

(r) Urge HCFA to explore the use of video and computer capabilities to improve access to and support for urban primary care practices in underserved settings.

(s) Urge urban hospitals, medical centers, state medical associations, and specialty societies to consider the expanded use of mobile health care capabilities.

(t) Continue to urge measures to enhance payment for primary care in the inner city.
(CMS Rep. I-93-2)

H-210.981 On-Site Physician Home Health Care

The AMA:

(1) recognizes that timely access to physician care for the frail, chronically ill, or disabled patient is a goal that can only be met by an increase in physician house calls to this vulnerable, underserved population;

(2) strongly supports the role of interdisciplinary teams in providing direct care in the patient's own home, but recognizes that physician oversight of that care from a distance must sometimes be supplemented by on-site physician care through house calls;

(3) advocates that the physician who collaborates in a patient's plan of care for home health services should see that patient on a periodic basis;

(4) recognizes the value of the house call in establishing and enhancing the physician-patient and physician-family relationship and rapport, in assessing the effects of the social, functional and physical environment on the patient's illness, and in incorporating the knowledge gained into subsequent health care decisions;

(5) believes that physician on-site care through house calls is important when there is a change in condition that cannot be diagnosed over the telephone with the assistance of allied health personnel in the home and assisted transportation to the physician's office is costly, difficult to arrange, or excessively tiring and painful for the patient;

(6) recognizes the importance of improving communication systems to integrate the activities of the disparate health professionals delivering home care to the same patient. Frequent and comprehensive communication between all team members is crucial to quality care, must be part of every care plan, and can occur via telephone, fax, e-mail, videotelemedicine. and in person;

(7) recognizes the importance of removing economic, institutional, and regulatory barriers to physician house calls;

(8) supports the requirement for a medical director for all home health agencies, comparable to the statutory requirements for medical directors for nursing homes and hospice;

(9) recommends that all specialty societies address the effect of dehospitalization on the patients that they care for and examine how their specialty is preparing its residents-in-training to provide quality care in the home;

(10) encourages appropriate specialty societies to continue to develop educational programs for practicing physicians interested in expanding their involvement in home care;

(11) urges HCFA to clarify and make more accessible to physicians information on standards for utilization of home health services, such as functional status and severity of illness;

(12) urges HCFA, in its efforts to redefine homebound, to consider the adoption of criteria and methods that will strengthen the physician's role in authorizing home health services, as well as how such criteria and methods can be implemented to reduce the paperwork burden on physicians.
(CSA Rep. 9, I-96; reaffirmed and appended: CMS Rep. 4, I-97)

H-210.986 Physicians and Family Caregivers—A Model for Partnership

The AMA

(1) encourages residency review committees and residency program directors to consider physician needs for training in evaluation of caregivers. Emphasis at both the undergraduate and graduate level is needed on the development of the physician's interpersonal skills to better facilitate assessment and management of caregiver stress and burden;

(2) supports health policies that facilitate and encourage home health care. Current regulatory and financing mechanisms favor institutionalization, often penalizing families attempting to provide lower cost, higher quality-of-life care;

(3) reaffirms support for reimbursement for physician time spent in education and counseling of caregivers and/or home care personnel involved in patient care; and

(4) supports research that identifies the types of education and support services that most effectively enhance the activities and reduce

the burdens of caregivers. Further research is also needed on the role of physicians and others in supporting the family caregiver.
(CSA Rep. I, I-91)

H-210.991 Education of Physicians in Home Health Care

It is the policy of the AMA that:

(1) faculties of the schools of medicine be encouraged to teach the science and art of home health care as part of the regular undergraduate curriculum;

(2) graduate programs in the fields of family practice, general internal medicine, pediatrics, obstetrics, general surgery, orthopedics, physiatry, and psychiatry be encouraged to incorporate training in home health care practice;

(3) the concept of home health care as part of the continuity of patient care, rather than as an alternative care mode, be promoted to physicians and other health care professionals;

(4) assessment for home health care be incorporated in all hospital discharge planning;

(5) the AMA develop programs to increase physician awareness of and skill in the practice of home health care;

(6) the AMA foster physician participation (and itself be represented) at all present and future home health care organizational planning initiatives (eg, Joint Commission on Accreditation of Healthcare Organizations, American Society for Testing and Materials, Food and Drug Administration, etc);

(7) the AMA encourage a leadership role for physicians as active team participants in home health care issues such as quality standards, public policy, utilization, and reimbursement issues, etc; and

(8) the AMA recognize the responsibility of the physician who is involved in home health care and recommend appropriate reimbursement for those health care services.
(Joint CSA/CME Rep. A-90)

H-210.992 Tax Deduction for Individuals Rendering Home Care to Family Members With a Long-term Illness

The AMA supports legislation to provide a federal tax deduction and/or additional appropriate incentives for individuals rendering home care to family members with a long-term illness.
(Res. 28, A-88)

H-215.985 Child Care in Hospitals

(1) The AMA strongly encourages hospitals to establish and support child care facilities.

(2) The AMA encourages that priority be given to children of those in training and that services be structured to take their needs into consideration.

(3) The AMA supports informing the American Hospital Association, hospital medical staffs, and residency program directors of these policies.

(4) The AMA supports studying the elements of quality child care and availability of child care on a 24-hour basis.
(BOT Rep. J, I-90)

H-245.986 Infant Mortality in the United States

It is the policy of the AMA:

(1) to work with the World Health Organization toward the development of standardized international methodology for collecting infant mortality data, which will include collecting information regarding racial/ethnic background in order to document the needs of infants, children, and adolescents of subpopulations of society, and which will improve the basis on international comparisons are made;

(2) to continue to work to increase public awareness of the flaws in comparisons of infant mortality data between countries, as

well as of the problems that contribute to infant mortality in the United States;

(3) to continue to address the problems that contribute to infant mortality within its ongoing Health of the Public activities. In particular, the special needs of adolescents and the problem of teen pregnancy should continue to be addressed by the Adolescent Health Initiative; and

(4) to be particularly aware of the special health access needs of pregnant women and infants, especially racial and ethnic minority group populations, in its advocacy on behalf of its patients.
(BOT Rep. U, I-91; modified by BOT Rep. 8, A-97)

H-295.897 Enhancing the Cultural Competence of Physicians

The AMA will:

(1) continue to inform medical schools and residency program directors about activities and resources related to assisting physicians in providing culturally competent care to patients throughout their life span and encourage them to include the topic of culturally effective health care in their curricula;

(2) continue research into the need for and effectiveness of training in cultural competence, using existing mechanisms such as the annual medical education surveys and focus groups at regularly scheduled meetings;

(3) form an expert national advisory panel (including representation from the AMA Minority Affairs Consortium and International Medical Graduate Section) to consult on all areas related to enhancing the cultural competence of physicians, including developing a list of resources on cultural competencies for physicians and maintaining it and related resources in an electronic database;

(4) assist physicians in obtaining information about and/or training in culturally effective health care through development of an annotated resource database on the AMA home page, with

information also available through postal distribution on diskette and/or CD-ROM; and

(5) seek external funding to develop a five-year program for promoting cultural competence in and through the education of physicians, including a critical review and comprehensive plan for action, in collaboration with the AMA Consortium on Minority Affairs and the medical associations that participate in the consortium (National Medical Association, National Hispanic Medical Association, and Association of American Indian Physicians,) the American Medical Women's Association, the American Public Health Association, the American Academy of Pediatrics, and other appropriate groups. The goal of the program would be to restructure the continuum of medical education and staff and faculty development programs to deliberately emphasize cultural competence as part of professional practice. (CME Rep. 5, A-98)

H-295.902 Alternative Medicine

AMA policy states that courses offered by medical schools on alternative medicine should present the scientific view of unconventional theories, treatments, and practice as well as the potential therapeutic utility, safety, and efficacy of these modalities.

Our AMA will work with members of the Federation to convey physicians' and patients' concerns and questions about alternative care to the NIH Office of Alternative Medicine and work with them and other appropriate bodies to address those concerns and questions. (CSA Rep. 12, A-97; amended by Res. 525, A-98)

H-295.905 Promoting Culturally Competent Health Care

The AMA encourages medical schools to offer electives in culturally competent health care with the goal of increasing awareness and acceptance of cultural differences between patient and provider. (Res. 306, A-97)

H-295.912 Education of Medical Students and Residents About Domestic Violence Screening

The AMA will continue its support for the education of medical students and residents on domestic violence by advocating that medical schools and graduate medical education programs educate students and resident physicians to sensitively inquire about family abuse with all patients, when appropriate and as part of a comprehensive history and physical examination, and provide information about the available community resources for the management of the patient. (Res. 303, I-96)

H-295.932 End-of-Life Care

The AMA will continue to work with others on developing a curriculum on end-of-life care for medical schools and residency programs. (Res. 305, A-93)

H-295.950 Patient Physician Communication

The AMA promotes the teaching of communication skills to resident physicians and medical students and encourages the implementation of such teaching during residency and medical school training. (Res. 51, A-91)

H-295.975 Educating Competent and Caring Health Professionals

(1) Programs of health professions education should foster educational strategies that encourage students to be independent learners and problem solvers. Faculty of programs of education for the health professions should ensure that the mission statements of the institutions in which they teach include as an objective the education of practitioners who are both competent and compassionate.

(2) Admission to a program of health professions education should be based on more than grade point average and performance on admissions tests. Interviews, applicant essays, and references should continue to be part of the application process in spite of difficulties inherent in evaluating them. Admissions

committees should review applicants' extra-curricular activities and employment records for indications of suitability for health professions education. Admissions committees should be carefully prepared for their responsibilities, and efforts should be made to standardize interview procedures and to evaluate the information gathered during interviews. Research should continue to focus on improving admissions procedures. Particular attention should be paid to improving evaluations of subjective personal qualities.

(3) Faculty of programs of education for the health professions must continue to place more emphasis than they have in the past on educating practitioners who are skilled in communications and interviewing and listening techniques and who are compassionate and technically competent. Faculty of health professions education should be attentive to the environment in which education is provided; students should learn in a setting where respect and concern are demonstrated. The faculty and administration of programs of health professions education must ensure that students are provided with appropriate role models; whether a faculty member serves as an appropriate role model should be considered when review for promotion or tenure occurs. Efforts should be made by the faculty to evaluate the attitudes of students toward patients. Where these attitudes are found lacking, students should be counseled. Provisions for dismissing students who clearly indicate personality characteristics inappropriate to practice should be enforced.

(4) In spite of the high degree of specialization in health care, faculty of programs of education for the health professions must prepare students to provide integrated patient care; programs of education should promote an interdisciplinary experience for their students.
(BOT Rep. NN, A-87; modified by Sunset Report, I-97)

H-295.981 Geriatric Medicine

The AMA reaffirms its support for the incorporation of geriatric medicine into the curricula of medical school departments and its encouragement for further education and research on the problems of aging and health care of the aged at the medical school, graduate, and continuing medical education levels.
(Res. 137, A-85; reaffirmed by CLRPD Rep. 2, I-95)

H-295.999 Medical Student Support Groups

(1) The AMA encourages the development of alternative methods for dealing with the problems of student-physician mental health among medical schools, such as:

(a) introduction to the concepts of physician impairment at orientation;

(b) ongoing support groups, consisting of students and house staff in various stages of their education;

(c) journal clubs;

(d) fraternities;

(e) support of the concepts of physical and mental well-being by heads of departments, as well as other faculty members; and/or

(f) the opportunity for interested students and house staff to work with students who are having difficulty.

(2) The AMA supports making these alternatives available to students at the earliest possible point in their medical education.
(Res. 164, A-79; reaffirmed by CLRPD Rep. B, I-89)

H-320.996 Confidentiality

The AMA continues to encourage state legislatures to amend their current privileged communication statutes pertaining to physician-patient relationships so as to assure appropriate protection for communications between patients and all health care providers.

(CMS Rep. J, A-80; reaffirmed by CLRPD Rep. B, I-90)

H-350.971 AMA Initiatives Regarding Minorities

The House of Delegates commends the leaders of our AMA and the National Medical Association for having established a successful, mutually rewarding liaison and urges that this relationship be expanded in all areas of mutual interest and concern. Our AMA will develop publications, assessment tools, and a survey instrument to assist physicians and the federation with minority issues. The AMA will continue to strengthen relationships with minority physician organizations, will communicate its policies on the health care needs of minorities, and will monitor and report on progress being made to address racial and ethnic disparities in care. It is the policy of our AMA to establish a mechanism to facilitate the development and implementation of a comprehensive, long-range, coordinated strategy to address issues and concerns affecting minorities, including minority health, minority medical education, and minority membership in the AMA. Such an effort should include the following components:

(a) Development, coordination, and strengthening of AMA resources devoted to minority health issues and recruitment of minorities into medicine;

(b) Increased awareness and representation of minority physician perspectives in the Association's policy development, advocacy, and scientific activities;

(c) Collection, dissemination, and analysis of data on minority physicians and medical students, including AMA membership status, and on the health status of minorities;

(d) Response to inquiries and concerns of minority physicians and medical students; and

(e) Outreach to minority physicians and minority medical students on issues involving minority

health status, medical education, and participation in organized medicine.
(Dec. 1998; incorporates components of previous policies H-350.984, H-350.988, and H-350.997)

H-350.972 Improving the Health of Black and Minority Populations

Our AMA supports:

(1) A greater emphasis on minority access to health care and increased health promotion and disease prevention activities designed to reduce the occurrence of illnesses that are highly prevalent among disadvantaged minorities.

(2) Authorization for the Office of Minority Health to coordinate federal efforts to better understand and reduce the incidence of illness among minority Americans as recommended in the 1985 Report to the Secretary's Task Force on Black and Minority Health.

(3) Continuing efforts for improving the health status of minority Americans through the Pepper Commission.

(4) Continued encouragement at the federal and state levels to expand Medicaid coverage to include all those below the federal poverty level.

(5) The speedy implementation of JCAHO's policy that hospitals provide for effective communication with predominant population groups served by each hospital.

(6) Encouraging employers to offer health insurance for employees working in companies of 25 persons or more.

(7) Advising our AMA representatives to the Liaison Committee on Medical Education to request data collection on medical school curricula concerning the health needs of minorities.

(8) The promotion of health education through schools and community organizations aimed at teaching skills of health care system access,

health promotion, disease prevention, and early diagnosis.
(Dec. 1998; incorporates components of previous policies H-350.987 and H-350.989)

H-350.973 Sickle Cell Anemia

Our AMA supports:

(1) Research and educational efforts directed to the profession and the public for the prevention of sickle cell anemia and the development of treatment forms.

(2) Efforts to evaluate the effectiveness of screening and counseling programs and involvement with issues in genetic counseling.

(3) Ongoing research programs, and recommends that all sickle cell programs have input in the planning stage from the local African American community and all other sectors that would be involved and affected by sickle cell disease.
(Dec. 1998; incorporates components of previous policies H-350.998 and H-350.999)

H-350.974 Racial and Ethnic Disparities in Health Care

The AMA maintains a position of zero tolerance toward racially or culturally based disparities in care; encourages individuals to report physicians to local medical societies where racial or ethnic discrimination is suspected; and will continue to support physician cultural awareness initiatives and related consumer education activities. The AMA emphasizes three approaches that it believes should be given high priority:

(1) Greater access—the need for ensuring that black Americans without adequate health care insurance are given the means for access to necessary health care. In particular, it is urgent that Congress address the need for Medicaid reform.

(2) Greater awareness—racial disparities may be occurring despite the lack of any intent or purposeful efforts to treat patients

differently on the basis of race. Encourages physicians to examine their own practices to ensure that inappropriate considerations do not affect their clinical judgment. In addition, the profession should help increase the awareness of its members of racial disparities in medical treatment decisions by engaging in open and broad discussions about the issue. Such discussions should take place in medical school curriculum, in medical journals, at professional conferences, and as part of professional peer review activities.

(3) Recognizes that racial disparities in access to treatment indicate that inappropriate considerations may enter the decision-making process. The efforts of the specialty societies, with the coordination and assistance of our AMA, to develop practice parameters should include criteria that would preclude or diminish racial disparities.
(Dec. 1998; incorporates components of previous policies H-350.984 and H-350.990)

H-350.975 Improving Health Care of Hispanic Populations in the United States

It is the policy of our AMA to:

(1) Encourage health promotion and disease prevention through educational efforts and health publications specifically tailored to the Hispanic community.

(2) Promote the development of substance abuse treatment centers and HIV/AIDS education and prevention programs that reach out to the Hispanic community.

(3) Encourage the standardized collection of consistent vital statistics on Hispanics by appropriate state and federal agencies.

(4) Urge federal and local governments, as well as private institutions, to consider including Hispanic representation on their health policy development organization.

(5) Support organizations concerned with Hispanic health through research and public

acknowledgment of the importance of national efforts to decrease the disproportionately high rates of mortality and morbidity among Hispanics.

(6) Promote research into effectiveness of Hispanic health education methods.

(7) Continue to study the health issues unique to Hispanics, including the health problems associated with the United States/Mexican border.
(Dec. 1998; incorporates components of previous policy H-350.987)

H-350.976 Improving Health Care of American Indians

Our AMA recommends that:

(1) All individuals, special interest groups, and levels of government recognize the American Indian people as full citizens of the United States, entitled to the same equal rights and privileges as other U.S. citizens.

(2) The federal government provide sufficient funds to support needed health services for American Indians.

(3) State and local governments give special attention to the health and health-related needs of nonreservation American Indians in an effort to improve their quality of life.

(4) American Indian religions and cultural beliefs be recognized and respected by those responsible for planning and providing services in Indian health programs.

(5) The AMA recognize the "medicine man" as an integral and culturally necessary individual in delivering health care to American Indians.

(6) Strong emphasis be given to mental health programs for American Indians in an effort to reduce the high incidence of alcoholism, homicide, suicide, and accidents.

(7) A team approach drawing from traditional health providers supplemented by psychiatric social workers, health aides, visiting nurses, and health educators be utilized in solving these problems.

(8) Our AMA continue its liaison with the Indian Health Service and the National Indian Health Board and establish a liaison with the Association of American Indian Physicians.

(9) State and county medical associations establish liaisons with intertribal health councils in those states where American Indians reside.

(10) Our AMA support and encourage further development and use of innovative delivery systems and staffing configurations to meet American Indian health needs but oppose overemphasis on research for the sake of research, particularly if needed federal funds are diverted from direct services for American Indians.

(11) AMA strongly support those bills before Congressional committees that aim to improve the health of and health-related services provided to American Indians, and further recommends that members of appropriate AMA councils and committees provide testimony in favor of effective legislation and proposed regulations.
(Dec. 1998; incorporates components of previous policy H-350.996)

H-350.977 Indian Health Service

The policy of the AMA is to support efforts in Congress to enable the Indian Health Service to meet its obligation to bring American Indian health up to the general population level. The AMA specifically recommends:

(1) Indian Population:

(a) In current education programs, and in the expansion of educational activities suggested below that special consideration be given to involving the American Indian and Alaska native population in training for the various health professions, in the expectation that such professionals, if provided with adequate professional resources, facilities, and income, will be more likely to serve the tribal areas permanently;

(b) Exploration with American Indian leaders of the possibility of increased numbers of nonfederal American Indian health centers, under tribal sponsorship, expand the role of American Indians into its own health care;

(c) Increased involvement of private practitioners and facilities in American Indian care, through such mechanisms as agreements with tribal leaders or Indian Health Service contracts, as well as normal private practice relationships; and

(d) Improvement in transportation to make access to existing private care easier for the American Indian population.

(2) Federal Facilities: Based on the distribution of the eligible population, transportation facilities and roads, and the availability of alternative non federal resources, that those Indian Health Service facilities currently necessary for American Indian care be identified and that an immediate construction and modernization program be initiated to bring these facilities up to current standards of practice and accreditation.

(3) Manpower:

(a) Compensation for Indian Health Service physicians be increased to a level competitive with other Federal agencies and nongovernmental service;

(b) Consideration should be given to increased compensation for service in remote areas;

(c) In conjunction with improvement of service facilities, efforts should be made to establish closer ties with teaching centers, thus increasing both the available manpower and the level of professional expertise available for consultation;

(d) Allied health professional staffing of service facilities should be maintained at

a level appropriate to the special needs of the population served;

(e) Continuing education opportunities and increased peer contact should be provided for those health professionals serving these communities, and especially those in remote areas, both to maintain the quality of care and to avert professional isolation; and

(f) Consideration should be given to a federal statement of policy supporting continuation of the Public Health Service to reduce the great uncertainty now felt by many career officers of the corps.

(4) Medical Societies: In those states where Indian Health Service facilities are located, and in counties containing or adjacent to Service facilities, the appropriate medical societies should explore the possibility of increased formal liaison with local Indian Health Service physicians. Increased support from organized medicine for improvement of health care provided under their direction, including professional consultation and involvement in society activities, should be pursued.

(5) Our AMA also supports the removal of any requirement for competitive bidding in the Indian Health Service that compromises proper care for the American Indian population.
(Dec. 1998; incorporates components of previous policies H-350.992 and H-350.996)

H-350.978 Minorities in the Health Professions

The policy of our AMA is that:

(1) Each educational institution should accept responsibility for increasing its enrollment of members of underrepresented groups.

(2) Programs of education for health professions should devise means of improving retention rates for students from underrepresented groups.

(3) Health profession organizations should support the entry of disabled persons to programs of education for the health professions, and

programs of health profession education should have established standards concerning the entry of disabled persons.

(4) Financial support and advisory services and other support services should be provided to disabled persons in health profession education programs. Assistance to the disabled during the educational process should be provided through special programs funded from public and private sources.

(5) Programs of health profession education should join in outreach programs directed at providing information to prospective students and enriching educational programs in secondary and undergraduate schools.

(6) Health profession organizations, especially the organizations of professional schools, should establish regular communication with counselors at both the high school and college level as a means of providing accurate and timely information to students about health profession education.

(7) The AMA reaffirms its support of:

(a) efforts to increase the number of black Americans and other minority Americans entering and graduating from U.S. medical schools; and

(b) increased financial aid from public and private sources for students from low income, minority, and socioeconomically disadvantaged backgrounds.

(8) The AMA supports counseling and intervention designed to increase enrollment, retention, and graduation of minority medical students and supports legislation for increased funding for the HHS Health Careers Opportunities Program.
(Dec. 1998; incorporates components of previous policies H-350.991, H-350.993, and H-350.994)

H-350.979 Increase the Representation of Minority and Economically Disadvantaged Populations in the Medical Profession

Our AMA supports increasing the representation of minorities in the physician population by:

(1) Supporting efforts to increase the applicant pool of qualified minority students by:

(a) Encouraging state and local governments to make quality elementary and secondary education opportunities available to all;

(b) Urging medical schools to strengthen or initiate programs that offer special premedical and precollegiate experiences to underrepresented minority students;

(c) Urging medical schools and other health training institutions to develop new and innovative measures to recruit underrepresented minority students; and

(d) Supporting legislation that provides targeted financial aid to financially disadvantaged students at both the collegiate and medical school levels.

(2) Encouraging all medical schools to reaffirm the goal of increasing representation of underrepresented minorities and women in their student bodies and faculties.

(3) Urging medical school admission committees to consider minority representation as one factor in reaching their decisions.

(4) Increasing the supply of minority health professionals.

(5) Continuing its efforts to increase the proportion of minorities and women in medical schools and medical school faculty.

(6) Facilitating communication between medical school admission committees and premedical counselors concerning the relative importance of requirements, including grade point average and Medical College Aptitude Test scores.

(7) Continuing to urge state legislation that will provide funds for medical education both directly to medical schools and indirectly through financial support to students.

(8) Continuing to provide strong support for federal legislation that provides financial assistance for able students whose financial need is such that otherwise they would be unable to attend medical school.

(Dec. 1998; incorporates components of previous policies H-350.995, H-350.987 and H-350.989)

H-350.980 AMA's Role in Preparing Minority and Disadvantaged Youth for Careers in Medicine and the Health Professions

The policy of our AMA is to:

(1) Initiate the development of a multi-organizational commission on minority health and education designed to coordinate programs and initiatives to address issues relating to the improvement of minority health and the enrollment and retention of minorities in medical school.

(2) Pursue this commission in conjunction with other appropriate national organizations, including the National Medical Association.

(3) Encourage, sponsor, and promote, as appropriate, the development of innovative elementary, secondary, and undergraduate school programs designed to better prepare minority students and socioeconomically disadvantaged students for careers in medicine and the other health professions.

(4) Strongly encourage state, county, medical specialty societies, medical schools, and individual physicians to make an ongoing commitment to participate in these or other programs designed to better prepare minority students for careers in medicine and the other health professions.

(5) Encourage individual physicians to make a personal, ongoing commitment to participate in elementary, secondary, and undergraduate school programs designed to better prepare minority students and students from socioeconomically disadvantaged background for careers in medicine and the other health professions.

(Dec. 1998; incorporates components of previous policies H-350.985 and H-350.988)

H-350.981 AMA Support of American Indian Health Career Opportunities

AMA policy on American Indian health career opportunities is as follows:

(1) Our AMA and other national, state, specialty, and county medical societies recommend special programs for the recruitment and training of American Indians in health careers at all levels and urge that these be expanded.

(2) Our AMA supports the inclusion of American Indians in established medical training programs in numbers adequate to meet their needs. Such training programs for American Indians should be operated for a sufficient period of time to ensure a continuous supply of physicians and other health professionals.

(3) Our AMA will utilize our resources to create a better awareness among physicians and other health providers of the special problems and needs of American Indians and that particular emphasis be placed on the need for additional health professionals to work among the American Indian population.

(4) Our AMA will continue to support the concept of American Indian self-determination as imperative to the success of American Indian programs and recognize that enduring acceptable solutions to American Indian health problems can only result from program and project beneficiaries having initial and continued contributions in planning and program operations.

(Dec. 1998; incorporates components of previous policy H-350.996)

H-350.982 Project 3000 by 2000— Medical Education for Underrepresented Minority Students

The AMA supports the concept of the Association of American Medical Colleges' project "3000 by 2000," which has as its objective achieving 3000 under-represented minority students entering medical schools annually by the year 2000.
(Dec. 1998; incorporates components of previous policy H-350.986)

H-350.983 Federal Guidelines for Standardization of Race/Ethnicity Codings

It is AMA policy that the military system of race and ethnicity coding should be adopted for use as the US Census race/ethnicity coding method.

H-370.974 Working Toward an Increased Number of Minorities Registered as Potential Bone Marrow Donors

The AMA supports efforts to increase the number of all potential bone marrow donors registered in national bone marrow registries, especially minority donors, to improve the odds of successful HLA matching and bone marrow transplantation.
(Res. 501, I-94)

H-370.975 Ethical Issues in the Procurement of Organs Following Cardiac Death

The following guidelines, based on the Pittsburgh Protocol have been adopted:

The Pittsburgh protocol, in which organs are removed for transplantation from patients who have had life-sustaining treatment withdrawn, may be ethically acceptable and should be pursued as a pilot project. The pilot project should (1) determine the protocol's acceptability to the public and (2) identify the number and usability of organs that may be procured through this approach.

The protocol currently has provisions for limiting conflicts of interest and ensuring voluntary consent. It is critical that the health care team's conflict of interest in caring for potential donors at the end of life be minimized, as the protocol currently provides, through maintaining the separation of providers caring for the patient at the end of life and providers responsible for organ transplantation. In addition to the provisions currently contained in the protocol, the following additional safeguards are recommended:

(a) To protect against undue conflicts of interest, the protocol should explicitly warn members of the health care team to be sensitive to the possibility that organ donation decisions may influence life-sustaining treatment decisions when the decisions are made by surrogates. Further, if there is some reason to suspect undue influence, then the health care team members should be required, not merely encouraged, to obtain a full ethics consultation.

(b) The recipients of organs procured under the Pittsburgh protocol should be informed of the source of the organs as well as any potential defects in the quality of the organs, so that they may decide with their physicians whether to accept the organs or wait for more suitable ones.

(c) Clear clinical criteria should be developed to ensure that only appropriate candidates, whose organs are reasonably likely to be suitable for transplantation, are considered eligible to donate organs under the Pittsburgh protocol.
(CEJA Rep. 4-I-94)

H-370.977 The Inclusion of Advance Directives Concerning Organ Donation in Living Wills

The AMA will develop model legislation that would create provisions for organ donation within living will forms and other health care advance directives, including but not limited to durable power of attorney forms and encourage physicians to discuss advance directives and organ donation as a part of the ongoing doctor-patient relationship.
(Res. 218, I-93)

H-370.978 The Use of Minors as Organ and Tissue Sources

The AMA has adopted the following guidelines on the use of minors as organ and tissue sources:

(1) Society is charged with the responsibility of protecting minor children from harm, including intrusion of bodily integrity as a consequence of participation as sources in organ transplantation. Minors need not be prohibited from acting as sources of organs, but their participation should be limited.

(2) Different procedures pose different degrees of risk and do not all require the same restrictions. In general, minors should not be permitted to serve as a source when there is a very serious risk of complications (eg, partial liver or lung donation, which involve a substantial risk of serious immediate or long-term morbidity). If the safeguards in the remainder of the items are followed, minors may be permitted to serve as a source when the risks are low (eg, blood or skin donation, in which the donated tissue can regenerate and spinal or general anesthesia is not required), moderate (eg, bone marrow donation, in which the donated tissue can regenerate but brief general or spinal anesthesia is required), or serious (eg, kidney donation, which involves more extensive anesthesia and major invasive surgery).

(3) If a child is capable of making his or her own medical treatment decisions, he or she should be considered capable of deciding whether to be an organ or tissue donor. However, physicians should not perform organ retrievals of serious risk without first obtaining court authorization. Courts should confirm that the mature minor is acting voluntarily and without coercion.

(4) If a child is not capable of making his or her own medical decisions, all transplantations should have parental approval, and those which pose a serious risk should receive court authorization. In the court authorization process, the evaluation of a child psychiatrist or psychologist must be sought and a guardian ad litem should be assigned to the potential minor donor in order to fully represent the minor's interests.

(5) When deciding on behalf of immature children, parents and courts should ensure that a transplantation presents a "clear benefit" to the minor source, which entails meeting the following requirements:

(a) Ideally the minor should be the only possible source. All other available sources of organs, both donor pools and competent adult family members, must be medically inappropriate or significantly inferior. An unwilling potential donor does not qualify him/her as medically inappropriate.

(b) For transplantations of moderate or serious risk, the transplantation must be necessary with some degree of medical certainty to provide a substantial benefit; that is, it both prevents an extremely poor quality of life and ensures a good quality of life for the recipient. A transplant should not be allowed if it merely increases the comfort of the recipient. If a transplant is not presently considered to provide a substantial benefit but is expected to do so within a period of time, the transplant need not be delayed until it meets this criterion, especially if the delay would significantly decrease the benefits derived from the transplant by the recipient.

(c) The organ or tissue transplant must have a reasonable probability of success in order for transplantation to be allowed. What constitutes a reasonable chance of success should be based on medical judgments about the physical condition of the recipient and the likelihood that the transplant will not be rejected or futile or produce benefits that are very transient. Children should not be used for transplants that are considered experimental or non-standard.

(d) Generally, minors should be allowed to serve as a source only to close family members.

(e) Psychological or emotional benefits to the potential source may be considered, although evidence of future benefit to the minor source should be clear and convincing. Possible benefits to a child include: continued emotional bonds between the minor and the recipient; increased self-esteem; prevention of adverse reaction to death of a sibling. Whether a child will capture these benefits depends upon the child's specific circumstances. A minor's assent or dissent to a procedure is an important piece of evidence that demonstrates whether the transplant will offer psychological benefits to the source. Dissent from incompetent minors should be powerful evidence that the donation will not provide a clear benefit, but may not present an absolute bar. Every effort should be made to identify and address the child's concerns in this case.

(f) It is essential to ensure that the potential source does not have any underlying conditions that create an undue individual risk.

(CEJA Rep. I-93-3)

H-370.979 Financial Incentives for Organ Procurement

Ethical Aspects of Future Contracts for Cadaveric Donors: The AMA has adopted the following guidelines for a pilot program of financial incentives for future contracts regarding organ donations:

(1) There is enough evidence in favor of employing some form of financial incentive to justify the implementation of a pilot program. This program, as with any policy involving financial incentives to encourage organ donation, should have adequate regulatory safeguards to ensure that the health of donors and recipients is in no way jeopardized and that the quality of the organ supply is not degraded. This pilot program should operate for a limited time, in a limited geographical region, and have the following safeguards.

(2) Incentives should be limited to future contracts offered to prospective donors. By entering into a future contract, an adult would agree while still competent to donate his or her organs after death. In return, the appropriate state agency would agree to give some financial remuneration to the donor's family or estate after the organs have been retrieved and judged medically suitable for transplantation. Under a system of future contracts, several other conditions would apply:

(a) No incentives should be allowed for organs procured from living donors.

(b) It would be inappropriate to offer financial incentives for organ donation to anyone other than the person who would actually serve as the source of the organs. Only the potential donor, and not the potential donor's family or other third party, may be given the option of accepting financial incentives for the donation of his or her own organs. In addition, the potential donor must be a competent adult when the decision to donate is made, and the donor must not have committed suicide.

(c) Any incentive should be of moderate value and should be the lowest amount that can reasonably be expected to encourage organ donation. By designating a state agency to administer the incentive, full control over the level of incentive can be maintained.

(d) Payment of any incentive should occur only after the harvested organs have been judged medically suitable for transplantation. Suitability should continue to be determined in accordance with the procedures of the Organ Procurement and Transplantation Network.

(e) Incentives should play no part in the allocation of donated organs among potential transplant recipients. The distribution of organs for transplantation should continue to be governed only by ethically appropriate criteria relating to medical need.

(CEJA Rep. I-93-6)

H-370.980 Strategies for Cadaveric Organ Procurement: Mandated Choice and Presumed Consent

The AMA recommends that:

(1) A system of mandated choice for organ donation, in which individuals are required to express their preferences regarding organ donation, is an ethically appropriate strategy for encouraging people to become organ donors and should be pursued. The AMA should work with state medical societies to draft model legislation for implementing a policy of mandated choice and should encourage its adoption by state legislatures. To be effective, information on the importance of organ donation and the success of organ transplantation must be provided when the donation decision is made.

(2) A system of presumed consent for organ donation, in which individuals are assumed to consent to be organ donors after death unless they indicate their refusal to consent, raises serious ethical concerns. For presumed consent to be ethically acceptable, effective mechanisms for documenting and honoring refusals to donate must be in place. In addition, when there is no documented refusal by the individual, families of decedents would have to be routinely contacted to verify that they do not know of any objections to donation by the decedent while living.
(CEJA Rep. I-93-2)

H-370.982 Ethical Considerations in the Allocation of Organs and Other Scarce Medical Resources Among Patients

The AMA has adopted the following guidelines as policy:

(1) Decisions regarding the allocation of scarce medical resources among patients should consider only ethically appropriate criteria relating to medical need.

(a) These criteria include likelihood of benefit, urgency of need, change in quality of life, duration of benefit, and, in some cases, the amount of resources required for successful treatment. In general, only very substantial differences among patients are ethically relevant; the greater the disparities, the more justified the use of these criteria becomes. In making quality of life judgments, patients should first be prioritized so that death or extremely poor outcomes are avoided; then, patients should be prioritized according to change in quality of life, but only when there are very substantial differences among patients.

(b) Research should be pursued to increase knowledge of outcomes and thereby improve the accuracy of these criteria.

(c) Nonmedical criteria, such as ability to pay, social worth, perceived obstacles to treatment, patient contribution to illness, or past use of resources should not be considered.

(2) Allocation decisions should respect the individuality of patients and the particulars of individual cases as much as possible.

(a) All candidates for treatment must be fully considered according to ethically appropriate criteria relating to medical need, as defined in Guideline 1.

(b) When very substantial differences do not exist among potential recipients of treatment on the basis of these criteria, a "first-come-first-served" approach or some other equal opportunity mechanism should be employed to make final allocation decisions.

(c) Although there are several ethically acceptable strategies for implementing these criteria, no single strategy is ethically mandated. Acceptable approaches include a three-tiered system, a minimal threshold approach, and a weighted formula.

(3) Decision-making mechanisms should be objective, flexible, and consistent to ensure that all patients are treated equally. The nature of the physician-patient relationship entails that physicians of patients competing for a scarce resource must remain advocates for their patients, and therefore should not make the actual allocation decisions.

(4) Patients must be informed by their physicians of allocation criteria and procedures, as well as their chances of receiving access to scarce resources. This information should be in addition to all the customary information regarding the risks, benefits, and alternatives to any medical procedure. Patients denied access to resources have the right to be informed of the reasoning behind the decision.

(5) The allocation procedures of institutions controlling scarce resources should be disclosed to the public as well as subject to regular peer review from the medical profession.

(6) Physicians should continue to look for innovative ways to increase the availability of and access to scarce medical resources so that, as much as possible, beneficial treatments can be provided to all who need them.
(CEJA Rep. K, A-93)

H-370.983 Tissue and Organ Donation

The AMA will assist the United Network for Organ Sharing in the implementation of its recommendations through broad-based physician and patient education.
(Res. 533, A-92)

H-370.984 Organ Donation Education

The AMA encourages local organ procurement organizations to provide educational materials to driver education and safety classes.
(Res. 504, I-91)

H-370.986 Donor Tissues and Organs for Transplantation

The AMA strongly urges physicians or their designees to routinely contact their hospital's designated tissue or organ procurement agency (as appropriate), at or near the time of each patient's death, to determine the feasibility of tissue and/or organ donation.
(Res. 103, I-90)

H-370.987 Transplant Centers

It is the policy of the AMA to continue to work with the United Network for Organ Sharing, the national organ procurement and transplantation network, to evaluate the correlation of delivery system factors that impact graft survival and patient survival in transplantation.
(Sub. Res. 69, I-90)

H-370.994 Sale of Donor Organs for Transplant

The AMA opposes the sale of nonrenewable, transplantable organs for the purpose of profit.
(Sub. Res. 16, I-83; reaffirmed by CLRPD Rep I-93-1)

H-370.995 Organ Donor Recruitment

The AMA supports development of "state of the art" educational materials for the medical community and the public at large, demonstrating at least the following: (1) the need for organ donors; (2) the success rate for organ transplantation; (3) the medicolegal aspects of organ transplantation; (4) the integration of organ recruitment, preservation, and transplantation; (5) cost/reimbursement mechanisms for organ transplantation; and (6) the ethical considerations of organ donor recruitment.
(Res. 32, A-82; reaffirmed by CLRPD Rep. A, I-92)

H-370.996 Organ Donor Recruitment

Our AMA:

(1) continues to urge Americans to sign donor cards;

(2) supports continued efforts to teach physicians through continuing medical education courses and the lay public through health education programs about transplantation issues in general and the importance of organ donation in particular;

(3) encourages state governments to attempt pilot studies on promotional efforts that stimulate each adult to respond "yes" or "no" to the option of signing a donor card; and

(4) in collaboration with all other interested parties, supports the exploration of methods to greatly increase organ donation, such as the "presumed consent" modality of organ donation.

(CSA Rep. D, A-81; reaffirmed by CLRPD Rep. F, I-91; amended: Res. 509, I-98)

H-370.999 Computerized Donor Registry

The AMA approves of the concept of computerized donor registration systems to identify available organs for transplantation. (Res. 11, A-78; reaffirmed by CLRPD Rep. C, A-89)

H-385.963 Physician Review of Accounts Sent for Collection

(1) The AMA encourages all physicians and employers of physicians who treat patients to review their accounting/collection policies to ensure that no patient's account is sent to collection without the physician's knowledge

(2) The AMA urges physicians to use compassion and discretion in sending accounts of their patients to collection, especially accounts of patients who are terminally ill, homeless, disabled, impoverished, or have marginal access to medical care.
(Res. 127, I-92)

H-410.995 Participation in the Development of Practice Guidelines by Individuals Experienced in the Care of Minority and Indigent Patients

The AMA encourages those experienced in the care of poor and minority patients (eg, minority and public hospital providers and organizations) to participate actively in the development of clinical guidelines, practice parameters, patient management guidelines, medical practice guidelines, etc.
(Res. 87, A-90)

H-420.962 Perinatal Addiction—Issues in Care and Prevention

The AMA:

(1) adopts the following statement: Transplacental drug transfer should not be subject to criminal sanctions or civil liability;

(2) encourages the federal government to expand the proportion of funds allocated to drug treatment, prevention, and education within the context of its "War on Drugs." In particular, support is crucial for establishing and making broadly available specialized treatment programs for drug-addicted pregnant women wherever possible;

(3) urges the federal government to fund additional research to further knowledge about and effective treatment programs for drug-addicted pregnant women, encourages also the support of research that provides long-term follow-up data on the developmental consequences of perinatal drug exposure and identifies appropriate methodologies for early intervention with perinatally exposed children;

(4) reaffirms the following statement: Pregnant substance abusers should be provided with rehabilitative treatment appropriate to their specific physiological and psychological needs;

(5) through its communication vehicles, encourages all physicians to increase their knowledge

regarding the effects of drug and alcohol abuse during pregnancy and to routinely inquire about alcohol and drug use in the course of providing prenatal care; and

(6) will address the special needs of pregnant drug abusers within the context of its ongoing Health Access America programs.
(CSA Rep. G, A-92)

H-420.972 Prenatal Services to Prevent Low Birthweight Infants

The AMA encourages all state medical associations and specialty societies to become involved in the promotion of public and private programs that provide education, outreach services, and funding directed at prenatal services for pregnant women, particularly women at risk for delivering low birthweight infants.
(Res. 231, A-90)

H-420.978 Access to Prenatal Care

(1) The AMA supports development of legislation or other appropriate means to provide for access to prenatal care for all women, with alternative methods of funding, including private payment, third party coverage, and/or governmental funding, depending on the individual's economic circumstances.

(2) In developing such legislation, the AMA urges that the effect of medical liability in restricting access to prenatal and natal care be taken into account.
(Res. 33, I-88)

H-420.995 Medical Care for Indigent and Culturally Displaced Obstetrical Patients and Their Newborns

The AMA:

(1) reaffirms its long-standing position regarding the major importance of high-quality obstetrical and newborn care by qualified obstetricians, family physicians, and pediatricians and the need to make such care available to all women and newborns in the

United States;

(2) favors educating the public to the long-term benefit of antepartum care and hospital birth, as well as the hazards of inadequate care; and

(3) favors continuing discussion of means for improving maternal and child health services for the medically indigent and the culturally displaced.
(CSA Rep. C, A-80; reaffirmed by CLRPD Rep. B, I-90)

H-430.990 Bonding Programs for Women Prisoners and Their Newborn Children

Because there are insufficient data at this time to draw conclusions about the long-term effects of prison nursery programs on mothers and their children, the AMA supports and encourages further research on the impact of infant bonding programs on incarcerated women and their children. The AMA recognizes the prevalence of mental health and substance abuse problems among incarcerated women and continues to support access to appropriate services for women in prisons. The AMA recognizes that a large majority of female inmates who may not have developed appropriate parenting skills are mothers of children under the age of 18. The AMA encourages correctional facilities to provide parenting skills training to all female inmates in preparation for their release from prison and return to their children. The AMA supports and encourages further investigation into the long-term effects of prison nurseries on mothers and their children.
(CSA Rep. 3, I-97)

H-480.964 Alternative Medicine

Policy of the AMA on alternative medicine:

(1) There is little evidence to confirm the safety or efficacy of most alternative therapies. Much of the information currently known about these therapies makes it clear that many have not been shown to be efficacious. Well-designed, stringently controlled research should be done to evaluate the efficacy of alternative therapies.

(2) Physicians should routinely inquire about the use of alternative or unconventional therapy by their

patients and educate themselves and their patients about the state of scientific knowledge with regard to alternative therapy that may be used or contemplated.

(3) Patients who choose alternative therapies should be educated as to the hazards that might result from postponing or stopping conventional medical treatment.
(CSA Rep. 12, A-97)

H-480.967 Alternative Therapies for the Symptoms of Menopause

Although many patients use alternative therapies to treat the symptoms of menopause, there is very little scientific evidence about the safety or efficacy of most of these therapies. In some cases, use of alternative therapies by patients may delay use of conventional therapies proven to have benefit for disease prevention in addition to relief of symptoms. The Council on Scientific Affairs of the AMA cannot recommend the use of unproven alternative therapies for the treatment of the symptoms of menopause.

Physicians should routinely learn about and ask patients about their use of alternative therapies and educate them about the level of scientific information available about the therapy they are using, as well as conventional alternatives. Physicians should inquire about the presence of unpleasant or uncomfortable symptoms among patients in the perimenopausal stage of development. In this way, the physician can assist the patient in gaining relief while providing an opportunity to discuss the importance of preventing menopause-related disease processes.
(CSA Rep. 4, I-96)

H-480.973 Unconventional Medical Care in the United States

The AMA encourages the Office of Alternative Medicine of the National Institutes of Health to determine by objective scientific evaluation the efficacy and safety of practices and procedures of unconventional medicine and encourages its members to become better informed regarding

the practices and techniques of alternative or unconventional medicine.
(BOT Rep. 15-A-94; reaffirmed and modified by Sub. Res. 514, I-95)

H-500.992 Tobacco Advertising Directed to Children, Minorities, and Women

The AMA:

(1) recognizes and condemns the targeting of advertisements for cigarettes and other tobacco products toward children, minorities, and women as representing a serious health hazard and calls for the curtailment of such marketing tactics; and

(2) supports joining the efforts of established coalitions promoting awareness of tobacco-related health risks to children, minorities, and women in a national forum as an extension of the stated AMA goal to achieve a smoke-free America.
(Res. 254, A-89; reaffirmed A-97)

H-515.969 Domestic Violence Intervention

Valid arguments can be made on both sides of the mandatory reporting issue, and various laws have been adopted among the states. These laws differ widely, with variations in who is required to report, what is reported, how reports must be made, to whom the reports are made, and the use of identifiers. In the absence of formal evaluations, however, the benefits and costs of the laws are open to question and interpretation. More important, it is impossible to make informed judgments on their value. In addition, such laws are at odds with the AMA's ethical opinions on the rights of adult patients and the responsibilities of physicians.

(1) The AMA opposes the adoption of mandatory reporting laws for physicians treating competent adult victims of domestic violence if the required reports identify victims. Such laws violate basic tenets of medical ethics and are of unproved value.

(2) If and where mandatory reporting statutes are adopted, the AMA believes the laws must incorporate provisions that

  (a) do not require the inclusion of victims' identities;

  (b) allow competent adult victims to opt out of the reporting system if identifiers are required;

  (c) provide that reports be made to public health agencies for surveillance purposes only;

  (d) contain a sunset mechanism; and

  (e) evaluate the efficacy of those laws.

(3) The AMA encourages states with mandatory reporting laws to undertake careful evaluations of the effectiveness and value of their laws, with particular attention to effects on victim safety, and to repeal or amend those laws should they be found to be ineffective.

(4) The AMA encourages state governments to adopt an anonymous public health reporting system for surveillance of all violence and abuse to identify risk factors, target interventions, and develop intervention strategies.
(BOT Rep. 11, A-97)

H-515.970 Campaign Against Family Violence: Annual Update

The AMA:

(1) restates its belief that family violence is a major threat to the public health and urges the profession, both individually and collectively, to work with other interested parties to address the needs of its victims. To this end, our AMA will continue to commit resources to the Campaign Against Family Violence for the foreseeable future;

(2) will continue to call attention to the impact of violence in this country through its media

efforts, including the annual report card on violence and awards for public-spirited efforts like that presented to Washington's professional basketball team for changing its name;

(3) remains open to working with all interested parties to address violence in U.S. society and will work with those parties to develop programs designed to lessen the prevalence, scope, and severity of violence. In particular, our AMA will pursue, in cooperation with the American Bar Association, additional regional conferences on family violence, which are designed to support the efforts of local, coordinated programs dealing with violence;

(4) will expand anti-violence efforts to deal with such concerns as the impact of media violence and the interplay of substance abuse and family violence as appropriate and as resources permit; and

(5) will continue to encourage all physicians to participate in the Physicians Coalition Against Family Violence in order to receive additional protocols and information to improve diagnostic and treatment abilities.
(BOT Rep. 19, A-96)

H-515.971 Public Health Policy Approach for Preventing Violence in America

The AMA supports the ongoing efforts of the CDC to develop appropriate and useful surveillance methodologies for tracking violence-related injuries and encourages the CDC to develop tracking strategies that can be efficiently implemented by physicians, with careful evaluations of pilot programs and demonstration projects prior to their implementation, and will report back on these CDC efforts.
(BOT Rep. 34, A-95; reaffirmed by BOT Rep. 16, A-96)

H-515.972 Violence Toward Men: Fact or Fiction?

The AMA:

(1) recognizes that men also are among the victims of intimate violence and encourages other

organizations to recognize this fact. Information collected and presented on male victims of intimate violence should include data on the rate of victimization compared with women, information on the rate of injury-producing violence, the sequence of violence, and the context of the violence. This type of information should be included in AMA-sponsored publications, training programs, and curricula.

(2) will develop a protocol for physicians to use to identify men who are victimized in intimate relationships. Such a protocol should aim at distinguishing those men who are victims of physical violence and who have not physically or emotionally assaulted their partners from men who are hit and assaulted in self-defense. Moreover, the AMA believes physicians should be alert to men presenting with injuries suffered as a result of intimate violence because these men may require intervention as either victims or abusers themselves.

(3) urges hospitals, community mental health agencies, and other helping professions to develop appropriate interventions for all victims of intimate violence. Such interventions might include individual and group counseling efforts, support groups, and shelters.

(4) believes it is critically important that programs be available for victims and perpetrators of intimate violence and that these programs include training on nonviolent methods to control anger and respond to threats of physical or emotional violence.
(CSA Rep. 9 - I-94)

H-515.975 Alcohol, Drugs, and Family Violence

(1) Given the association between alcohol and family violence, physicians should be alert to look for the presence of one behavior given a diagnosis of the other. Thus, a physician with patients with alcohol problems should screen for family violence, while physicians with patients presenting with problems of physical or sexual abuse should screen for alcohol use.

(2) Physicians should avoid the assumption that if they treat the problem of alcohol or substance use and abuse they also will be treating and possibly preventing family violence.

(3) Physicians should be alert to the association, especially among female patients, between current alcohol or drug problems and a history of physical, emotional, or sexual abuse. The association is strong enough to warrant complete screening for past or present physical, emotional, or sexual abuse among patients who present with alcohol or drug problems.

(4) Physicians should be informed about the possible pharmacological link between amphetamine use and human violent behavior. The suggestive evidence about barbiturates and amphetamines and violence should be followed up with more research on the possible causal connection between these drugs and violent behavior.

(5) The notion that alcohol and controlled drugs cause violent behavior is pervasive among physicians and other health care providers. Training programs for physicians should be developed that are based on empirical data and sound theoretical formulations about the relationships among alcohol, drug use, and violence.
(CSA Rep. A, A-93; reaffirmed: BOT Rep. I-93-8)

H-515.976 Mental Health Consequences of Interpersonal and Family Violence: Implications for the Practitioner

The AMA encourages physicians to:

(1) routinely inquire about the family violence histories of their patients as this knowledge is essential for effective diagnosis and care;

(2) make appropriate referrals to address intervention and safety needs as a matter of course upon identifying patients currently experiencing abuse or threats from intimates;

(3) screen patients for psychiatric sequelae of violence and make appropriate referrals for these conditions upon identifying a history of family or other interpersonal violence; and

(4) become aware of local resources and referral sources that have expertise in dealing with trauma from victimization.
(CSA Rep. B, A-93)

H-515.979 Violence as a Public Health Issue

The AMA:

(1) reaffirms and expands current policy by

    (a) declaring violence in America to be a major public health crisis;

    (b) supporting research into the causes of violent behavior and appropriate interventions that may result in its prevention or cure; and

    (c) supporting an educational program designed to increase public knowledge of the causes, manifestations, and harmful effects of interpersonal violence; and

(2) will direct its programs, policies, and other resources as appropriate toward achieving a violence-free society.
(Sub. Res. 408, I-92)

H-515.980 Update on the AMA's National Campaign Against Family Violence

Ongoing efforts on family violence will continue to be an action item at each annual meeting of the AMA, and the impact of drugs and alcohol on family violence will be studied and included in future updates.
(BOT Rep. FF, A-92)

H-515.981 Family Violence— Adolescents as Victims and Perpetrators

The AMA:

(1) will use its communications mechanisms to

    (a) encourage physicians to screen adolescents about a current or prior history of maltreatment. Special attention should be paid to screening adolescents with a history of alcohol and drug misuse, irresponsible sexual behavior, eating disorders, running away, suicidal behaviors, conduct disorders, or psychiatric disorders for prior occurrences of maltreatment; and

    (b) urge physicians to consider issues unique to adolescents when screening youths for abuse or neglect.

(2) encourages state medical society violence prevention committees to work with child protective service agencies to develop specialized services for maltreated adolescents, including better access to health services, improved foster care, expanded shelter and independent living facilities, and treatment programs.

(3) will investigate research and resources on effective parenting of adolescents to identify ways in which physicians can promote parenting styles that reduce stress and promote optimal development.

(4) will alert the national school organizations to the increasing incidence of adolescent maltreatment and the need for training of school staff to identify and refer victims of maltreatment.

(5) urges youth correctional facilities to screen incarcerated youth for a current or prior history of abuse or neglect and to refer maltreated youth to appropriate medical or mental health treatment programs.

(6) encourages the National Institutes of Health and other organizations to expand continued research on adolescent initiation of violence and abuse to promote understanding of how to prevent future maltreatment and family violence.
(CSA Rep. I, A-92)

H-515.983 Physicians and Family Violence

Ethical Considerations:

(1) Because of its prevalence and medical consequences, abuse must be considered by physicians in the differential diagnosis for a number of medical complaints, particularly when treating women, children, and elderly persons.

(2) Physicians who are likely to have the opportunity to detect abuse in the course of their work have an obligation to familiarize themselves with

  (a) protocols for diagnosing and treating family violence,

  (b) their state reporting requirements and protective services, and

  (c) community resources for victims of abuse.

(3) Physicians also have a duty to be aware of societal misconceptions about family violence and to prevent these from affecting the diagnosis and management of abuse. Such misconceptions include the belief that abuse is a rare occurrence; that "normal" individuals are not abusive; that family violence is a private problem best resolved without outside interference; and that victims are responsible for abuse.

(4) The medical profession must demonstrate a greater commitment to ending family violence and helping its victims. Physicians must play an active role in advocating increased services for victims and abusers. Protective services for abused children and elders need to be better funded and staffed, and follow-up services should be expanded. Shelters and safe homes for battered women and their children must be expanded and better funded. Mechanisms to coordinate the range of services, such as legal aid, employment services, welfare assistance, day care, and counseling, should be established in every community. Mandatory arrest of abusers and greater enforcement of protection orders are important law enforcement reforms that should be expanded to more communities. There should be more research into the effectiveness of rehabilitation and prevention programs for abusers.

(5) Informed consent for interventions should be obtained from competent victims of abuse. For minors who are not deemed mature enough to give informed consent, consent for emergency interventions need not be obtained from their parents. Physicians can obtain authorization for further interventions from a court order or a court-appointed guardian.

(6) Physicians should inform parents of a child-abuse diagnosis and they should inform an elderly patient's representative when the patient clearly does not possess the capacity to make health care decisions. The safety of the child or elderly person must be ensured prior to disclosing the diagnosis when the parents or caretakers are potentially responsible for the abuse. For competent adult victims physicians must not disclose an abuse diagnosis to caregivers, spouses, or any other third party without the consent of the patient.
(CEJA Rep. B, I-91)

H-515.984 Violence Against Women

It is the policy of the AMA:

(1) working with members of the Federation and other relevant organizations, to undertake a campaign to alert the health care community to the widespread prevalence of violence against women—that the effects of such violence are likely seen on a regular basis—and to sensitize them to the needs of victims of violence;

(2) to encourage physicians to routinely incorporate screening leading to identification of female patients who are or have been victims of violence;

(3) to encourage physicians to give due validation to the experience of victimization and of observed symptomatology as possible sequelae;

(4) to encourage physicians to record a patient's victimization history, observed traumata potentially linked to the victimization, and referrals made;

(5) to encourage physicians, after diagnosing a violence-related problem, to refer patients to appropriate medical or health care professionals and/or community-based trauma-specific resources as soon as possible;

(6) to encourage the incorporation of training on interviewing techniques, risk assessment, safety planning, and procedures for linking to resources into undergraduate, graduate, and continuing medical education programs;

(7) to collect and disseminate protocols on identifying and treating victims of violence and to develop, in conjunction with other relevant organizations, guidelines for treatment where protocols are absent; and

(8) to include appropriate information detailing the important role of substance abuse in the etiology, treatment, and prevention of violence against women in its efforts.
(CSA Rep. B, I-91; reaffirmed I-96)

H-515.985 Identifying Victims of Adult Domestic Violence

It is the policy of the AMA:

(1) to work with social services and law enforcement agencies to develop guidelines for use in hospital and office settings in order to better identify victims of adult domestic violence and to better serve all of the victim's needs, including medical, legal and social aspects; and

(2) to ask appropriate organizations to support the inclusion of curricula that address adult domestic violence.
(Res. 419, I-91; reaffirmed I-96)

H-515.986 Proposed AMA National Campaign Against Family Violence

It is the policy of the AMA to:

(1) develop a media campaign that announces and elaborates the AMA's efforts to address family violence;

(2) establish a national coalition of Physicians Against Violence;

(3) establish an AMA resource center/ clearinghouse to collect, evaluate, and disseminate information concerning family violence and abuse based on reports in the scientific literature and from local initiatives;

(4) host a national conference to address family violence in conjunction with other relevant organizations;

(5) include appropriate information detailing the important role of substance abuse in the etiology, treatment, and prevention of family violence in its current efforts; and

(6) issue an expanded report that addresses important epidemiologic issues, including, but not limited to, substance abuse and handguns.
(BOT Rep. G, I-91)

H-515.991 Elder Abuse and Neglect

The AMA supports

(1) the establishment of a multidisciplinary task force to develop approaches to intervention and prevention of elder abuse and to coordinate mutually supportive activities of various constituencies;

(2) development of diagnostic and treatment guidelines concerning elder abuse and neglect; and

(3) programmatic efforts through state medical societies to address the national concern of elder abuse.
(CSA Rep. J, A-86; reaffirmed: Sunset Report, I-96)

H-515.992 Abuse of Elderly Persons

The AMA urges state societies to support legislation mandating physician reporting of elderly abuse in states where such legislation does not currently exist.
(Res. 112, I-85; reaffirmed: CLRPD Rep. 2, I-95)

H-515.993 Child Sexual Abuse

The AMA has a continuing commitment to the area of child abuse and neglect and recognizes the need to assert medical leadership in that segment of the problem represented by sexual abuse.
(BOT Rep. U, I-85; reaffirmed: CLRPD Rep. 2, I-95)

H-515.994 Child Abuse and Neglect

The AMA urges all US medical schools to provide instruction for students and residents in the diagnosis, treatment, and reporting of child abuse and neglect.
(Sub. Res. 136, A-85; reaffirmed: CLRPD Rep. 2, I-95)

H-515.997 AMA Diagnostic and Treatment Guidelines Concerning Child Abuse and Neglect

The AMA supports diagnostic and treatment guidelines for cases involving child abuse and neglect; advocates physician education on the problem of child sexual abuse; and encourages physicians to take an expanded role in identifying, preventing and treating the problem.
(CSA Rep. I, I-84; reaffirmed by CLRPD Rep. 3, I-94)

H-515.998 Violence Against Women

The AMA:

(1) opposes the use of images depicting sexual subjugation of, or violence against, any individual in the promotion of products; and

(2) supports publicizing this position to all appropriate organizations and agencies; and

(3) will correspond, in particular, with major record companies who have utilized images of violence against women and all children in the promotion of products, stating opposition to the use of those images in the promotion of their product, and requesting review of corporate policy in this matter.
(Sub. Res. 164, A-78; reaffirmed by CLRPD Rep. C, A-89)

H-525.988 Gender Differences in Medical Research

The AMA:

(1) reaffirms that gender exclusion in broad medical studies questions the validity of the studies' impact on the health care of society at large;

(2) affirms the need to include both genders in studies that involve the health of society at large and publicize its policies; and

(3) supports increased funding into areas of women's health research.
(Res. 80, A-91)

(1) H-525.990 Gender Disparities in Clinical Decision-Making

(1) **Attitudes and practices**. Physicians should examine their practices and attitudes for influence of social or cultural biases that could be inadvertently affecting delivery of medical care. Further research and education should be conducted to increase awareness of the possible influences that social perceptions of gender roles may have on health care.

(2) **Research**. More medical research on women's health and women's health problems should be pursued. Results of medical testing done solely on males should not be generalized to females without evidence that results apply equally to both genders. Research on health problems that affect both genders should include male and female subjects. Sound medical and scientific reasons should be required for excluding females from medical tests and studies, such as that the proposed research does not or would not

affect the health of females. An example would be research on prostatic cancer.

(3) **Removing gender bias**. Physicians must ensure that gender is not used inappropriately as a consideration in clinical decision making. The development and implementation of procedures and techniques that preclude or minimize the possibility of gender bias should be developed. For instance, a gender-neutral determination for kidney transplant eligibility should be used.

(4) **Medical staff assessment**. Medical staffs should develop programs to determine whether treatment decisions are influenced by gender bias and whether either gender is being disadvantaged by treatment decisions generally.

(5) **Remedial action**. Instances in which a physician's treatment decision appears to turn inappropriately on the patient's gender deserve further scrutiny. If evidence of systematic gender bias in clinical decision making is found, then appropriate review or corrective proceedings should be undertaken.

(6) **Increasing numbers of female physicians in leadership positions**. Awareness of and responsiveness to sociocultural factors that could lead to gender disparities may be enhanced by increasing the number of female physicians in leadership roles and other positions of authority in teaching, research, and the practice of medicine. The AMA should continue its efforts to ensure access of higher-level positions in medicine for female physicians.

(7) **Further study to determine causes of disparities**. Further research into the possible causes of gender disparities should be conducted. It is important to ascertain to what extent gender disparities in medical care are a result of biological differences between the genders and to what extent utilization practices and physician/patient interactions are influenced by cultural and social conceptions of gender.

(CEJA Rep. B, I-90; see also Current Opinions, Section 9.122)

H-525.991 Inclusion of Women in Clinical Trials

The AMA encourages the inclusion of women in all research on human subjects, except in those cases for which it would be scientifically irrational, in numbers sufficient to ensure that results of such research will benefit both men and women alike. (Res. 183, I-90)

H-555.982 Participation of Minorities in Organized Medicine

The AMA:

(1) supports active recruitment of minority physicians into membership through all reasonable means and encourages their participation in leadership positions within the AMA; and

(2) encourages the efforts of the Federation to continue to involve minority physicians in both membership and leadership positions at all levels.
(Res. 259, A-89)